The Western Philosophers

Also by E. W. F. Tomlin

The Oriental Philosophers: an introduction

The Western Philosophers

an introduction

by

E. W. F. Tomlin

Perennial Library ·

Harper & Row, Publishers, New York

Contents

Introduction

'The curse of ignorance,' Socrates is made to say in Plato's dialogue called the *Symposium,* 'is that a man without being good or wise is nevertheless satisfied with himself: he has no desire for that of which he feels no want.'

By ignorance Socrates did not mean to imply simply lack of information. He meant lack of wisdom. And the wisdom in which he found his fellow-men to be most deficient was that concerning their own hearts and minds. How, he asked, can you be satisfied with yourself if you do not know who you are and what, being here in this world, you are meant to do with your lives? The satisfaction of a man who is ignorant in this sense is poor satisfaction indeed. The road to happiness, like the road to virtue, is the road not of self-satisfaction but of self-knowledge.

Few of us are really satisfied with ourselves in the way that Plato described. Even those who appear to display excessive self-conceit are forced by their very over-assertiveness to betray an inner disquiet. Almost everybody at some period of his life is prompted to ask himself such questions as: What am I? and why am I here? And this curiosity sometimes gives rise to the reflection that as these questions have never been satisfactorily met, the human mind is perhaps incapable of answering them. Before we confess our complete mental bankruptcy, however, we must attempt to discover what are the limits, if any, of our knowledge. And this in turn may lead us on to enquire what knowledge is and wherein it differs from, say, imagination and belief.

Such inner questionings—which, if the individual stifles them in one form, will reappear in another—are the beginnings of philosophy. And, having made a beginning, we must choose whether to allow our minds simply to drift, to accept our conclusions at secondhand, or to think things out to some sort of conclusion, even if the conclusion be that we must go on thinking.

Our covert respect for philosophy is revealed in everyday speech. Of a person who resolutely endures misfortune, we say that he has 'taken it philosophically'. By this we mean that he has faced with courage the situation in which he finds himself, that he has made the best of a bad job, and that he has refrained from giving vent to rancour either against his fellows or against the providence of which he is temporarily the victim. When the Roman consul Boethius (470-526) was condemned to imprisonment and death on an unjust and indeed imaginary charge, he wrote a book of sublime and noble thoughts to which he gave the title of *The Consolation of Philosophy*. Such, then, are the rewards of the philosophical attitude: courage and consolation, in a world that never ceases to call for the first and so often fails to provide material for the second.

The Great Philosophers are merely those for whom the impulse to enquire into the nature of things has become a passion. Thought is the profession from which they never retire. Almost all such men have been distinguished by the nobility of their lives, and particularly by that form of courage which is needed to plough a lonely furrow, to voyage through 'strange seas of thought alone'. For philosophy is essentially the flower of solitude; it is the unstill and unstillable small voice in each of us which we can ignore at our peril. It is conscience resurgent, exchanging the rôle of plaintiff for that of judge.

That the frank, open and essentially humble attitude of the greatest philosophers should so often have been exchanged for its opposite—namely, an attitude of clever, showy logic-chopping, designed to bewilder and to befuddle the laity—is perhaps no more than evidence of a profound philosophical truth, namely, that the corruption of the best is the worst. Certainly it is one of the curses of philosophy that so many books should have been written making difficult problems more difficult still: or, worst of all, obscuring the comparatively simple problems with which philosophy begins by a parade of conundrums, paradoxes, pseudo-problems calculated to put the innocent reader into a state of alarm and despondency. One of the reasons why the term 'academic' is so often associated with arid pedantry is that the commentaries and exposés of those of purely academic training seem often to lack appreciation of what the problems they claim to be treating actually are. The subject, as we say, is of 'purely academic interest', which is as much as to imply that it is of no real interest at all—at least to those ordinary folk who have a job to do and a living to earn.

For this reason, if for no other, there is something to be said for an approach to philosophy through the lives of the great philosophers: lives that so often remain unknown even to those who can discourse at length upon the problem of universals, cause and effect, the '*a priori* synthesis', and so on. For we are too ready to assume that thought is something produced in a vacuum, a process that can operate independently of any particular mind, and consequently something that can be ignored by people who have to employ their thoughts upon more practical matters. We do not realize, in fact, that a great philosopher makes his own age the subject of his thoughts and, in so doing, becomes a kind of keeper of the public conscience; that the great philosopher, like the great historian (who, as we are seeing today, must be a kind of philosopher), is a man who reveals to humanity its own state of mind and thus makes not merely progress but equilibrium possible; and that, in short, all the science and art, the inherited skill and technique, which we assume to be our inalienable possession, and without which our whole civilized life would disintegrate in a short time, are upheld by the kind of knowledge of which the philosopher in all of us, and above all the great philosophers among us, are the chief sustainers. To know more about these unacknowledged leaders of men is not merely entertaining but instructive.

This book, as the table of contents shows, is more than a series of separate lives. It is also one continuous life— the life of philosophical thought in the Western world. A work purporting to deal with the lives of philosophers which confined itself to a string of anecdotes—and it must be admitted that the lives of certain philosophers, notably Kant, lend themselves to anecdotes—would be like a book of musical biography which confined itself to stories about Beethoven and his cook and Schubert and his unmended socks. Sufficient play has been made, as it is, of Kant's sartorial eccentricities. In the chapters that follow, we have adopted no hard and fast rule as to how the 'life' and 'thought' should be related, the tendency being for later chapters (and such earlier ones as that on Abelard) to combine biography and philosophy in the way best calculated to illumine both. For while we have assumed no initial knowledge of philosophy on the reader's part, save such general notions as have prompted him to embark upon the reading of this book, we have assumed that he will be able to take his philosophy in stronger doses as the book proceeds. For the same reason, we have scrupulously avoided introducing a false simplicity into the exposition of the various systems of thought; for we believe—and the belief is based upon experience—that those who are genuinely interested in philosophy are not likely to tolerate being 'written down' to. The difficulty in 'writing down' is that of knowing just how far down, and such over-simplification usually lands us in a trough of puerility where nothing worth while can be said at all.

We are writing, then, of adults for adults. And if we have succeeded in representing these remarkable men as credible human beings, facing real problems and engaged upon matters of real moment, then this book will have justified its purpose.

The Western Philosophers

Socrates

'True philosophers are always occupied in the practice of dying.'

—Phædo

1

Philosophy did not begin with Socrates. With Socrates, however, it not merely entered upon a new road but took the direction which, in spite of numerous setbacks, it has since followed. This remarkable man wrote nothing.[1] He had few possessions. For the greater part of his life he did not work for his living. Yet his influence upon a few contemporaries, some of them gifted statesmen and writers, was such that we know a fair amount about his character, his habits, and the events of his life. Above all we know something of the way he thought and the way he believed men should be trained to think. And we are aware that his ideas inspired not merely two other great philosophers in the next generations, but all those who have since endeavoured to think in a philosophical or orderly manner. Possibly no other man, with the exception of the founders of the great religions, practised what he preached so thoroughly and consistently as this intrepid, somewhat uncouth figure of fifth-century Athens.

From what sources do we learn about Socrates? We owe most of what we know about him to two men, Plato (427-347 B.C.) and Xenophon (430-357 B.C.). But, even so, our knowledge is limited. Both of these men were junior to Socrates by about forty-five years. Save

[1] Epictetus, the Stoic philosopher of the first century, alone maintains that Socrates occasionally wrote down his thoughts (*Discourses*, Book II, Chapter I, 5); but his poetic compositions in prison may have been purely extempore effusions.

for the last decade of his life, therefore, the authorities are few and of doubtful value. The great comedian, Aristophanes (*b.* 488), introduces Socrates into one of his plays, *The Clouds,* with the object of poking fun at him. But the Socrates who is ridiculed by Aristophanes and his contemporary, Ameipsias, is already a man in his middle forties. Of Socrates as a youth we have no authentic picture. We have to go upon what he tells us, or rather upon the account put into his mouth by the two friends of his old age.

Socrates was born near Athens in the year 469 B.C., ten years after the battle of Salamis, in which the Athenians, aided by the Spartans, crushed the sea-power of Xerxes, the Persian King. Socrates' father, Sophroniscus, is reputed to have been a sculptor, but on this point there is some uncertainty. (Our only authority for the statement is a third-century writer, Timon of Phlius.) That he was a friend of Aristeides, Commander of the Athenians at the battle of Platæa (479) and nicknamed 'The Just', we know for certain. His mother, Phænarete, was by occupation a midwife, or at least she was accustomed to act as one; and it is interesting to remember that, according to Plato, Socrates used to describe his method of extracting knowledge as a kind of intellectual midwifery. From later writers we deduce that, if in fact his father's calling was that of a sculptor, the son not merely followed the same trade but excelled in it. A sculptured group representing the Three Graces and preserved in the Acropolis was supposed to have been the work of the young Socrates, and was exhibited as such up to the time of Pausanias, the geographer (late second century A.D.).[1] So far as we know, Socrates followed no other profession except that for which he later became renowned. But the circumstances which induced him to become a 'free-lance' philosopher—perhaps the last of that category and without doubt the greatest—will be described in due course.

If we possess scant information about the events of the life of Socrates, we do not lack impressive evidence as to his outstanding character. In the first place he seems

[1] Diogenes Laërtius of the third century A.D., author of *Lives of the Philosophers,* records the tradition. Archæologists now suggest an earlier sculptor.

to have been one of the toughest physical specimens of his time. Winter and summer, year in and year out, he apparently wore the same light garment, with neither shirt nor shoes. Accustomed to an outdoor existence, he was always to be seen either in the streets, in the market-place, or in the gymnasium, hobnobbing with young and old. Neither heat nor cold appeared to worry him. Even his bitterest enemies testify to his great physical courage. He served as a hoplite, or foot-soldier, in several military campaigns. He was at Samos, between 441 and 440, at the battle of Potidæa (432-430), at Delium (424) and probably at Amphipolis (442? or 437-436?). At Potidæa he saved the life of Alcibiades, the headstrong young Athenian politician, who repaid the compliment at Delium, and whose tribute to the philosopher's bravery is recorded in Plato's *Symposium*:

'I was wounded,' recounts Alcibiades, 'and he would not leave me, but he rescued me and my arms; and he ought to have received the prize for courage which the generals wanted to confer upon me on account of my rank, and I told them so, but he was more eager than the generals that I and not he should have the prize. There was another occasion on which his behaviour was very remarkable—in the flight of the army after the battle of Delium. He and Lactes were retreating, for the troops were in flight, and I met them and told them not to be discouraged, and promised to remain with them; and there you might see him, just as he is in the streets of Athens, stalking like a pelican, and rolling his eyes, calmly contemplating enemies as well as friends, and making very intelligible to anybody, even from a distance, that whoever attacked him would be likely to meet with a stout resistance.'

Alcibiades also records how, one morning during the expedition to Potidæa, Socrates was pondering a problem which he could not resolve. 'He would not give it up, but continued thinking from early dawn until noon—there he stood fixed in thought; and at noon he was noticed, and the rumour ran through the wondering crowd that Socrates had been standing and thinking about something ever since the break of day. At last, in the evening after supper, some Ionians out of curiosity brought out their mats and slept in the open air in order to watch him and see whether he would stand all night. There he stood until the following morning; and with the return of light he offered up a prayer to the sun and went his way.'

Not merely did Socrates live in a condition of which many a slave would have been ashamed; he was for most of his life desperately poor. Indeed, his extreme poverty was the principal source of the mockery of contemporary comedians. Aristophanes goes so far as to represent him, most unfairly, as a mad, impoverished star-gazer who was prepared to give instruction for money in a bogus kind of philosophy. As to star-gazing, both Xenophon and Plato witness to the great interest he displayed in astronomy and geometry, but, unlike the Sophists or professional teachers of philosophy; Socrates never taught for gain. On this subject he spoke feelingly to his accusers at the end of his trial: 'If I had gained anything, or if I had been paid for my preaching, there would have been some sense in my doing so; but now you see not even the imprudence of my accusers dares to say that I have ever taken or asked for pay from anyone; of that they have no witness. And I have sufficient witness to the truth of what I say—my poverty.'

In spite of his straitened circumstances, which the abandonment of a regular profession increased, Socrates was married rather late in life to a woman called Xanthippe. Of the character of this woman, who bore him three sons, we know little, though Xenophon declares that she was a hot-tempered creature.[1] A remark in Aristotle's book on Rhetoric suggests that the boys grew up to be nondescript men, without a spark of their father's genius. The last occasion on which we hear of Xanthippe is when she paid a brief visit to her husband in prison, bringing the youngest of her children with her. Although Socrates' attitude to his wife might suggest that his was a cold and reserved temperament, we learn from other sources, particularly Plato and Æschines, that the reverse was true. Even if we admit that he exercised considerable self-control, it is a mistake to regard him as a self-denying, ascetic kill-joy. He was by temperament ardent, prone to gaiety, with an irrepressible sense of humour (manifested not least in his final speech to his friends).

[1] He says that she was 'the most insupportable woman that is, has been, or ever will be' (*The Banquet*).

He also had a healthy contempt for those who, like Antisthenes and certain disciples of Pythagoras, identified wisdom and sanctity with dirt, vermin and squalor.

But to return to the circumstances of his life. Between the first performance of Aristophanes' play *The Clouds* (423 B.C.) and the trial of Socrates (399), great changes had occurred in Athens. There had been a political revolution in consequence of which the Democratic party had returned to power. Although a firm supporter of democracy (he could hardly be otherwise), Socrates had a number of friends, like Critias and Alcibiades, who were associated with the old order. And so the gentle and not too bitter burlesque of Socrates in Aristophanes' play (which, being a failure on its first production, the author rewrote in somewhat stronger terms) was taken more seriously a quarter of a century later. Nor was Socrates under any illusion as to the harm done to him, albeit inadvertently, by Aristophanes; he deliberately referred to the play in his last speech, chiding his judges for repeating as literally true that which had been originally intended as jest.

Two questions concerning the relation between Aristophanes and Socrates are still a source of perplexity to us. The first is at what point their friendship, or at any rate their respect one for the other, began to cool; and the second is what Aristophanes, still a comparatively young man, was doing at the time of the trial of Socrates. We know that Aristophanes and Plato remained on terms of friendship long after Socrates' death—and this is surely incompatible with their holding opposite views about the man whom Plato, for one, regarded as 'the most righteous of the whole age'. It is possible that at the time of the trial Aristophanes was absent on military service. There is no record that he intervened or showed any particular interest in the shameful proceedings taking place in the court at Athens.

Although the motives for the final arrest of Socrates were probably semi-political, Socrates himself had throughout life taken little part in politics. As he pointed out to his judges, the holding of political office was directly contrary to his principles. A man so much in the public eye, however, could not avoid becoming involved indirectly in political controversies. For one complete year, 406-405, he was a member of the Council of 500, where his influence was all for moderation. When the victors of the battle of Arginusæ were being tried, he alone opposed the condemnation of the generals. Under the Reign of Terror of the Thirty Tyrants in 404, his stubborn refusal to agree to the arrest of Leon, who had incurred public displeasure at the time, nearly cost him his life. Had it not been for the counter-revolution of the Democrats, he would have been indicted for disobedience. And that is another reason why it cannot be maintained that he was a whole-hearted sympathizer with the old order.

Nevertheless, although the Democrats proclaimed a general amnesty soon after their return to power, and although Socrates was known to have had nothing to do with the outrages and tyrannies of the old régime, he was summarily charged with impiety in the year 399 on two main counts: first, that he had been responsible for 'corrupting' the youth of Athens; and secondly, that he had neglected the traditional gods by introducing in their place a variety of religious novelties. What exactly lay behind these allegations? To answer this question, we must go back to the time of his youth.

At what age Socrates first became conscious of the promptings of a divine or supernatural voice, rather like the traditional voice of conscience only much more authoritative, we do not know. Although he frequently referred to this mysterious power, he could never make up his mind when first he became accustomed to obey its injunctions. As in most cases of this kind, the experience probably began much earlier than he realized, growing more insistent with the dawn of adolescence, when the sense of right and wrong is sharpened. What distinguished the 'voice' or 'demon' of Socrates from other 'inner' oracles is that it afforded him warnings of a particular kind. It gave him negative information, never positive. It told him not to do things; it never told him what he should do. It was a check, not a prompter.

Thus, early in life, Socrates, otherwise the most humble of men and without riches or power save the friendship of certain distinguished contemporaries, became convinced that he was entrusted with a divine mission. Whatever his critics and later accusers might say, his belief in God and spiritual values, and even his reverence for the traditional deities of his country, were never for a moment in doubt. He was by disposition a religious man. Unlike the common people of his day, however, he refused to credit with literal truth the mythology and legend so deeply interwoven with the traditions of Greek society. Such tales of gods and goddesses he ascribed to poetic invention; but he saw no harm in their being handed down from generation to generation, just as he saw no harm in the poetic fancies they had inspired. And, sceptic though he was, he refused to ignore the testimony of supernatural signs and portents, oracles and seers, for was he not himself given to mystical transports, being to that extent a disciple of the cults of the Pythagoreans and of the Orphic mysteries?

Indeed, it was to the deliverances of an Oracle that he owed what he believed to be a striking confirmation of his missionary status. One day, he tells us, a friend of his, Chærephon by name, visited the famous Oracle at Delphi for the express purpose of asking whether any man was wiser than Socrates. Without hesitation, the Oracle replied that no one was wiser. Now the Oracle at Delphi was famous for a command that it issued to all those who came to seek its aid. This command was the single motto 'Know Thyself'. In what sense, then, did the Oracle intend its statement about Socrates to be interpreted? Why was Socrates to be judged wiser than any man living (and perhaps dead)? The answer was not that Socrates knew everything, but that on the contrary he knew little or nothing. But the difference between Socrates and other people was that whereas they were ignorant but thought themselves wise, Socrates was ignorant and knew himself to be so. In other words, Socrates 'knew himself' in the true sense.

The Oracle's revelation caused Socrates to ponder deeply. If the statement were true, it must be acted upon; for the words of an Oracle represented a command, a summons to action. And so, after due reflection, Socrates made up his mind that his true vocation in life, the work to which he must henceforth devote himself, was to examine, analyse, and if necessary expose, the wisdom of those whom the world called wise.

And that was how the trouble began. His fellow-citizens did not welcome this relentless inquisition into what they believed or supposed themselves to believe. To them Socrates was the worst sort of busybody—a man who asked intricate questions with no other motive than that of satisfying an insatiable curiosity. It was this very 'disinterestedness' of Socrates that upset them most of all. What was the object of it? The man did no work. He had nothing to offer. His one object was to disturb people's preconceived opinions. And no one was proof against him.

As for Socrates himself, he realized early in his new career that he was likely to provoke much enmity. But this did not deter him. According to the account in Plato's *Apology*, he tried his first experiment upon a politician who was 'thought wise by many and still wiser by himself'; but he soon took his leave. 'Although I do not suppose that either of us has any knowledge of goodness and beauty,' he said to himself, 'I am better off than he is, for he knows nothing, and thinks that he knows: I neither know nor think that I know. In this latter point I seem to have slightly the advantage of him.' But, as a result of this difficult interview, the politician came to hate him bitterly, and so did many others who were in the audience at the time. Thoroughly baffled, he then went elsewhere to one 'who had still higher pretensions to wisdom', but fared no better and made another enemy in consequence. And so he passed on from one man to another, from the poets to the artisans and to those practising intermediate trades, probing and drawing out of them admission after admission as to the shallowness of their wisdom, exposing their downright ignorance, and on each occasion asking himself on behalf of the Oracle whether he would prefer to be as he was, 'neither having their knowledge nor their ignorance', or to be like them in both, and always answering that he was better off as he was.

However much they feared and hated him, the contemporaries of Socrates were finally obliged to admit that he was a very shrewd man. Yet this was not the impression he necessarily wanted to create. It was a constant source of embarrassment to him to find that his hearers always considered him to be possessed of the wisdom which he found wanting in others. In this they laboured under a misapprehension. 'The truth is,' he explained, 'that God only is wise; and by His answer' (*i.e.* through the medium of the Oracle) 'He intends to show that the wisdom of men is worth little or nothing; He is not speaking of Socrates, He is only using my name by way of illustration, as if He said, he is the wisest who, like Socrates, knows that his wisdom is in truth worth nothing.' And recalling the accusation that he was no better than the Sophists, he added: 'My occupation quite absorbs me, and I have no time to give either to any public matter of interest or to any concern of my own, but I am in utter poverty through my service to the god.'

The legal prosecutor of Socrates was a man named Meletus, a writer of inferior tragedies and a thoroughly worthless fellow, probably bribed to participate in this outrage, but the enemy behind the scenes was Anytus, a wealthy Athenian who had played a leading part in the overthrow of the Thirty Tyrants by the Democrats. Lycon, an orator by profession and a friend of Anytus, was another of Socrates' accusers. As for his judges— men with little public experience but with a number of private scores to settle—they had themselves not long returned from banishment. Nevertheless, it must not be supposed that Socrates' prosecution was simply the consequence of a political reversal of fortune. Under the rule of the Thirty Tyrants, he had fared little better. In fact, Critias, the leader, had gone so far as to issue a proclamation stipulating that Socrates, and indeed the Sophists in general, were to desist from the work of teaching; and we have already referred to those earlier occasions on which he acted contrary to the wishes and orders of the authorities. In the turmoil of political reaction, however, a man's precise status and reputation under the former régime are rarely assessed with impartiality.

To the credit of the Tribunal, the initial vote cast against Socrates after his 'trial' was very far from unanimous. Two hundred and eighty votes were cast against him, and two hundred and twenty in his favour.[1] The accusers thereupon asked for a sentence of death to be pronounced. In all cases of this kind, however, it was the

[1] The jury consisted of five hundred members, and Plato affirms that Socrates was condemned by a majority of sixty.

custom in Athenian law for the accused to be allowed to make a counter-proposal, following which the judges might be induced to modify their sentence. Socrates took full advantage of this privilege, but in his own fashion. He suggested that, instead of being punished, he should first be proclaimed a public benefactor, and thereafter maintained, as was the custom with celebrities, at the public expense. As a 'token' fine, however, he suggested that he should pay 1 *mina*.

Couched in typically ironic terms, no statement was better calculated to arouse the wrath of Anytus and his colleagues. The feeling of the court immediately went against Socrates. Nor did the action of his friends in suggesting a fine of 30 *minæ* serve any purpose. The court had been insulted, the accusers made to look foolish, just as Socrates' interlocutors had in the past been held up to ridicule. Socrates was proving himself incorrigible. As a result, a greatly increased majority demanded the imposition of the death sentence.

Socrates entertained no fear of death. But he had made it clear that if by chance the judges should decide to let him go free, he would not merely revert to his previous mode of life but interpret the acquittal as a direct invitation to do so. If, on the other hand, they refused to tolerate his public teaching and interrogating, his probing into questions of justice and virtue, or his mixing freely with the impressionable young men of Athens, then, said Socrates, 'I should reply: Men of Athens, I honour and love you; but I shall obey God rather than you, and while I have life and strength I shall never cease from the practice and teaching of philosophy, exhorting anyone whom I meet and saying to him as my habit is: You, my friend —a citizen of the great and mighty and wise city of Athens—are you not ashamed of trying to get as much money and honour and reputation as possible, while remaining careless and indifferent to wisdom and truth and the greatest perfection of your soul? . . . For I know that this is the commandment of God; and I believe that no greater good has ever happened to Athens than my service to God.'

Whether the moving speech delivered after the passing of the sentence was that actually spoken by Socrates, or whether it was put into his mouth by his disciple Plato, we shall never know. All we know is that the thoughts expressed therein are such as Socrates must certainly have tried to put into words, for they are in harmony with everything he is reported to have said and done in the course of his career. They represent not merely one of the greatest speeches ever uttered, but one of the profoundest statements of that view of life which, perfected in the Christian teaching, still forms the moral basis of our civilization. Socrates had reached the age when he no longer wished to prolong his life, if to do so meant enforced silence and ostracism. Consequently, his final words to his judges dwell upon the theme of death and the fear of death, and form a kind of summing-up of his life's teaching, and of what is sometimes called the 'perennial philosophy'.

'There is great reason to hope,' he said, 'that death is good; for either death is a state of nothingness and utter unconsciousness, or, as men say, there is a change and migration of the soul from this world to another. . . . Now if death is like the former, I say that to die is gain; for eternity is then only a single night. But if death is the journey to another place, and there, as men say, all the dead abide, what good, my friends and judges, can be greater than this? If indeed, when the pilgrim arrives in the world below, he is delivered from the professors of justice in this world, and finds the true judges who are said to give judgment there . . . that pilgrimage will be worth making. What would not a man give if he might talk with Orpheus and Musæus and Hesiod and Homer?

'I myself, too, shall have a wonderful interest in there meeting and talking with Palamedes, and Ajax the son of Telamon, and any other ancient hero who was unjustly sentenced to death; and there will be no small pleasure, I think, in comparing my own suffering with theirs. Above all I shall then be able to continue my search into true and false knowledge, as in this world so also in the next; and I shall find out who is wise, and who pretends to be wise and is not. . . . What infinite delight would there be in talking with them and asking them questions! In another world they do not put a man to death for asking questions; assuredly not. For besides being happier than we are, they will be immortal, if what is said is true. So, my judges, you too should face death confidently and reflect on this one truth, that no evil can happen to a good man, either in life or after death. He and his are not neglected by the gods; nor is my own approaching end a matter of mere chance.

'I see clearly that the time has arrived when it was better for me to die and be released from trouble. And so I am not angry with those who condemned and those who accused me; they have done me no harm, although they did not mean to do me any good; and for this I may gently blame them. But I have a favour to ask them. When my sons are grown up, punish them and trouble them, as I have troubled you, if they seem to care about riches, or anything, more than about virtue; or if they pretend to be something when they are really nothing— then reprove them, as I have reproved you, for not caring about that for which you ought to care, and thinking that they are something when they are really nothing. And if you do this, both I and my sons will have received justice at your hands. The hour of departure has arrived, and we go our ways—I to die, and you to live. Which is better only God knows.'

With these calm and noble words Socrates passed out of public life. But fortunately we have a record, again due to the artistry of Plato, of what happened to Socrates and his small circle of loyal friends in the interval between his trial and his death. In fact we are much better informed about these last days than about the whole seventy-three years that preceded them.

It was the custom in Ancient Greece for a man condemned to death to drink a draught of hemlock within twenty-four hours. Such would have been Socrates' fate but for an interesting circumstance. It so happened that the sacred ship from Delos[1] had not yet returned, and there was no question of an execution taking place before its arrival.

In this way Socrates' life was prolonged by thirty days, during which time he devoted himself, with all his former enthusiasm, to philosophical speculation and also apparently to his first essays in writing poetry. The poetry, it is sad to say, has not survived; but the philosophizing is preserved in two immortal dialogues of Plato, the *Crito*

---

[1] An island sacred to Apollo. The custom was to celebrate the deliverance of the city by Theseus.

and the *Phædo*. Crito was, next after Plato, Socrates' most loyal friend. He it was who had offered to stand surety for his master when the latter, half in earnest, had suggested that his sentence should be commuted to the payment of a fine. In a last passionate display of devotion, Crito now tried to persuade the condemned Socrates to make his escape, and went to great trouble to prepare a stratagem to deceive the jailers. Somewhat to the surprise of his friends, Socrates refused to contemplate any such action. He proceeded to defend his decision by an argument concerning the duty of obedience to the laws of the state which, read out of its context, might strike the modern reader as unnecessarily submissive. He points out, however, that if a man has lived in a particular city, and has accepted its constitution and protection for the greater part of his life, he has no right to try to evade its ordinances when they are invoked, however unjustly, to condemn him to imprisonment or death. If he did not approve of the laws of his country, he could long ago have taken his leave and made his home elsewhere—a practice rather more open to a Greek, provided he had sufficient means, than to a modern national.

Having lived in Athens through so many different régimes and having survived them all, Socrates had no intention of taking flight at the eleventh hour. 'Listen, then, Socrates,' he imagines the Laws as saying, 'to us who have brought you up. Think not of life and children first, and of justice afterwards, but of justice first, that you may be justified before the rulers of the world below. . . . Now you depart in innocence, a sufferer and not a doer of evil; a victim not of the laws but of men. But if you go forth, returning evil for evil, and injury for injury, breaking the covenants and agreements which you have made with us and wronging those whom you ought least of all to wrong . . . we will receive you as an enemy. . . . Listen, then, to us and not to Crito.'

And so, reconciled to his fate and with a profound peace in his soul, Socrates made a habit each day of receiving his friends, in discoursing with them, and answering their questions. In due time, the sacred ship from Delos arrived; and Plato recounts in the *Phædo* how the loyal company assembled early the next morning, only to be kept waiting rather longer than usual. For the prison officials were closeted with their charge, giving him instructions as to his last moments, and taking off his chains. Xanthippe, his wife, had also been summoned to bid him farewell. When Crito and his friends entered (Plato, incidentally, was not able to be present on this last occasion, owing to illness), Xanthippe burst into loud lamentations and had to be led away. Socrates looked up at the visitors with a quizzical expression, slowly rubbing his bruised leg. The removal of his chains had set a train of thought going.

'How singular is the thing called pleasure,' he reflected, 'and how curiously related to pain; for a man never feels both at the same instant, and yet he who pursues either is generally compelled to take the other; their bodies are two but they are joined by a single head.' Warming to the theme, he went on to express his regret that Æsop had not composed a fable on this matter, showing how God, in order to reconcile the strife between pleasure and pain, had decided to fasten their heads together.

Soon the conversation took a more serious turn. The sense of death oppressed the company; Socrates alone, whose end was to come that same day, proclaimed his unshakable conviction that the soul, purged of its sins, was destined for immortality. His discourse on the subject, which is preserved for us in the *Phædo,* culminates in the statement that if a man shall 'cast away the pleasures and ornaments of the body as alien things which do him harm rather than good, and pursue the pleasures of knowledge', he may well be 'confident about his soul'.

By this time the day was wearing on, and Socrates suggested that he should take a bath, in order to save the women the trouble of washing his body after death. Crito, anxious not to waste a moment, begged him first to tell them whether there was anything they could do either for him or for his children. How, for instance, did he wish to be buried?

Socrates' reply was characteristically simple. He told his friends merely to 'take care of themselves', and to remember what he had tried to teach them. As to how he should be buried, he replied: 'In any way you like; but,' he added, with a touch of whimsical humour, 'you must get hold of me, and take care that I do not run away from you.' And, turning from Crito to the others, he remarked: 'I want you to go bail for me now, as at the trial he [Crito] went bail to the judges for me; but let the promise be of another sort; for he was surety for me to the judges that I would stay here, and you must be my surety to him that I shall not stay, but go away and depart.'

Then he got up and went into the next room, followed by Crito. Phædo and his companions stayed where they were, talking of their sorrow; for, as he observed, Socrates 'was like a father whom we were losing, and we were going to be orphans for the rest of our lives'. When Socrates had bathed, he received for the last time his family, commending them to the care of Crito; and finally, just when the sun was sinking, he returned to the others.

After the performance of these last rites, the atmosphere changed. Few words were spoken. Then, as if to break the tension, the jailer entered. He was clearly much affected by the scene, and addressed Socrates in a tone almost of apology. Accustomed to be greeted by an outburst of rage or grief on the part of the prisoner, he hardly knew how to disclose his mission to one whom he described, quite unaffectedly, as 'the noblest and gentlest and best of all who ever came to this place'. 'I am sure,' he added, 'you will not be angry with me; for others, as you are aware, and not I, are to blame. And so good-bye, and try to bear lightly what must needs be —you know my errand.' Then he suddenly burst into tears and hurried out.

Socrates remarked upon his courtesy. And then, turning to Crito again, he requested that the poison should be prepared.

Crito still saw no reason for haste. Most condemned persons, he pointed out, were accustomed to defer the fatal drink as long as possible, employing their last hours with eating and drinking and, in some cases, with other pleasures. Again Socrates shook his head. There was nothing, he insisted, to be gained by waiting. His life was already forfeit. And he had no wish to prolong unnecessarily the sufferings of his companions. He would therefore drink the hemlock without further ado.

Realizing that the old man's mind was quite made up, Crito directed one of the servants to summon the jailer once more. When the latter entered carrying the cup of poison, Socrates, still without turning a hair, said to him: 'You are an expert in these matters, my friend. Tell me what I must do.'

The jailer answered that, having drunk the poison, he must walk about the room until his legs began to grow heavy and then lie down. The poison would then do its work. So saying, he handed Socrates the cup.

Socrates received it quietly; but suddenly, as if in afterthought, he exclaimed: 'What about making a libation out of the cup?' meaning that he considered it appropriate to pour away some of its contents, as was the custom, in honour of the gods. When the jailer replied that he had prepared, according to official instructions, no more than was absolutely necessary, Socrates nodded in understanding, and, calling upon the gods to prosper his journey to the other world, he resolutely drank the poison in one draught.

It was a tragic moment. Those in the room who had hitherto managed to control their feelings could restrain themselves no longer.

Several minutes elapsed before they realized that one of their company had retained his full composure. This was Socrates himself. 'What are you doing, you strange people?' he asked. 'I sent the women away that they might not strike this false note. Be quiet then and have patience.'

These words, criticizing their demonstrativeness, calmed them in an instant. Then, almost incredulously, they beheld Socrates arise from his couch and begin to pace about the room, methodically acting upon the jailer's instructions. And so he continued, in the unbroken silence, until in due time his legs grew heavy, and he was obliged to lie down. Pressing one of his feet, the jailer asked whether he could feel anything. Socrates replied that he could not. The jailer continued to feel his limbs until it was obvious that a general numbness was creeping up his frame. Just before the poison took effect, however, Socrates, uncovering his face for an instant, murmured: 'Crito, I owe a cock to Asclepius; will you remember to pay the debt?' By this he meant that he wished to do honour to the god of health, in gratitude for having at last recovered from that prolonged malady, human life.

'It shall be done,' answered Crito. 'Is there anything else?' To this question there was no reply. When they uncovered Socrates again, the life had ebbed completely.

In recounting the life of Socrates, the concluding words of the *Phædo,* addressed to a common friend, form the most fitting close: 'Such was the end, Echecrates, of our friend; of whom I may truly say, that of all the men of his time whom I have known, he was the wisest and justest and best.'

2

More than any other man of his time, and possibly more than anyone before or since, with the exception of certain great religious leaders, Socrates lived his own philosophy. It was he, indeed, who, in criticizing the Sophists, laid such emphasis upon the necessity of realizing virtue in practice. Mere exhortations to moral virtue, so easy to give and so comfortable to listen to, were not enough. The injunction to 'Know Thyself' imposed upon the devotee of philosophy a discipline more rigorous than anything hitherto either recommended or followed. But it also implied a new theory of human conduct. Virtue, that is to say, was the consequence of self-knowledge; and moral goodness was the greatest value in the universe.

In following this line of thought, Socrates was, in effect, inaugurating a new departure in philosophy. During the centuries before he embarked upon his mission, many thinkers of great originality had appeared on the borders of the Ægean, though our records of their thought are scanty and in most cases garbled. We know enough of their ideas, however, to form a general picture of what it is that they were trying to find out about the world. We know that certain things interested them in particular, that certain problems baffled them, and that by certain aspects of reality they were left apparently unmoved. Above all we know that their attitude to the universe was characterized by an intense desire to discover the ultimate *constituents* of matter and life. They were in fact the first philosophers of Nature, or, as we should call them today, the first natural scientists.

Of Thales of Miletus, who lived about 600 B.C., we know no more than that he was the first investigator of the natural world to work out a coherent, if elementary, science of matter.

His chief claim to fame is his assertion that the immense variety of the natural world ultimately sprang from one element or principle. To us, this way of regarding the world of Nature may not commend itself very strongly; but that is merely because we have been long accustomed to think of the universe, if not as composed of a single material, then at least as a coherent whole. To the early Greeks, this latter was an idea of brilliant originality. Now the element or ἀρχή from which everything else originated was, according to Thales, water. Water is that which envelops the earth. The earth, in fact, may be said to float upon an ocean infinite in extent, and to derive its nourishment, like a huge organism, from this circumambient flood.

A disciple of Thales, Anaximander, while accepting the view that everything in Nature derived from a single principle, differed from his master on the question of what this principle was. Instead of water, Anaximander maintained that the generative element was the boundless atmosphere itself, from which everything was formed by gradual separation and into which everything was finally resolved. Pursuing his speculations into what we should today call the Origin of Species, Anaximander made some suggestions as to the evolution of man which have a surprisingly modern ring; but with this aspect of his work we are not at the moment concerned. Yet a third philosopher, Anaximenes, also from the town of Miletus, modified the principle of Anaximander to the extent of calling the generative principle air or 'breath'. In other words, the philosophers of the so-called Ionian School were serious philosophers of Nature, and their overriding aim was to explain how Nature *came into being*.

The philosophers who followed these pioneer thinkers were concerned, as might be expected, with the problem of evolution itself. Whereas their predecessors had established, or at least postulated, the fact that all things developed from some primal substance or element, men such as Xenophanes (a contemporary of Anaximander), Parmenides, Zeno (fifth century B.C.), and Gorgias(485-380?) concentrated upon the problem of how such development, process, or 'becoming', took place. Thus they set to work to analyse a concept which had been arrived at by the process of *abstraction*. Moreover, in the few fragments that we possess of the work of Parmenides (who expounded his thought in the form of a philosophical poem called *The Way of Truth and the Way of Belief*), we witness the first attempt of a Greek philosopher to engage in a form of thought which, for reasons to be discussed later, may be described as 'metaphysical'.

The conclusion at which Parmenides arrived, however, was the startling one that change was not a fact but an illusion. And he supported his contention by the logical argument that what exists can never either cease to exist or become anything different. For if it changes, it must have changed either from itself or from nothing. If it has changed from itself, however, it can have undergone no fundamental change at all; and as for the notion that it has come from nothing, that is preposterous. Being, therefore, must be eternal, infinite and unchanging. Zeno, who followed Parmenides' line of thought, illustrated the theory by the famous example of an arrow travelling through space. The arrow, he contended, must reach its destination by passing through an infinite number of successive points, each of which it occupies in turn. This can only mean that at every single point in its course the arrow is at rest. The 'movement' of the arrow is therefore something which exists wholly in our imagination. It has no reality in itself.

Zeno's pupil Gorgias carried this argument a stage farther. In fact, he tipped it over into the abyss of absurdity. It is all very well, he argued, to maintain that Being is both infinite and eternal. That which is both infinite and eternal obviously cannot be located anywhere, since to locate it in space would be to render it finite, while to locate it in time would be to render it temporal. If, therefore, Being is both infinite and eternal, it cannot enjoy any existence whatever. Hence Being and Nothing are identical.[1] Clearly this is the *reductio ad absurdum* of Parmenides' theory.

Now if you push an extreme argument far enough, it turns into its opposite. That is what happened with the argument that all change is an illusion. The philosopher Heraclitus, who lived at Ephesus in the fifth century B.C., countered the ideas of Parmenides, Zeno and Gorgias with an argument that has exerted a profound effect on philosophical thought down to our own time.[2] It is perfectly true, he argued, that Being and Not-Being are the same, because changeless Being is itself an illusion. The world that we know is always in a state of change or flux; that is its most obvious characteristic. We can never grasp anything and say 'this is unchanging or stationary', because that which we intend to grasp has already suffered change by the time we are able to set our hands upon it. Reality is a stream into which we cannot plunge twice. Everything flows. We can arrest the flow only in thought. Consequently the idea of permanence is something that we ourselves have invented; but it would be foolish to imagine that reality exhibits any permanence beyond the fact that it is in a permanent state of flux.[3]

To outline the thought of all the pre-Socratic philosophers, of whom there were a great many, would take too long; but it is impossible to understand the work of Socrates, and the great revolution in thought that he effected, without referring to one more distinguished name, a name familiar to all, even schoolchildren: Pythagoras. Born at Samos in the early sixth century B.C., Pythagoras was a man of such influence over his contemporaries that he inspired a school of philosophers who interested themselves in almost every form of speculation—mathematics, music, medicine, religion. This school or Order had flourishing branches at Crotona, Tarentum, and later at Athens and Thebes; and historians are still debating how far Pythagoras himself was responsible for some of the ideas defined by later historians and philosophers as 'Pythagorean'.

What chiefly distinguishes the Pythagorean School

[1] This argument was revived, as we shall see, by the German philosopher Hegel.
[2] See the chapter on Bergson.
[3] Heraclitus also had some interesting things to say about the concept of unity in diversity and *vice versa*.

from that initiated by Thales is its emphasis upon mathematics as the 'key' to the nature of reality. Whereas the Ionian School had been obsessed with the *material* constituents of Nature, the Pythagoreans were more interested in the types of order or *form* to be found in Nature. The basis of geometry, astronomy and music was harmony and proportion; and harmony and proportion were ultimately reducible to Number. Number, in fact, assumed for the Pythagoreans an almost mystical significance.

Both Socrates and Plato were greatly influenced by the doctrines of the Pythagorean School, above all those concerning the nature and destiny of the human soul. With thinkers such as Democritus (460 B.C.), however, Greek thought took a decidedly materialistic direction. Born at Abdera (in Thrace), Democritus was the founder of the school of Atomists; and although most of his writings— and he is said to have written a great deal—have perished, we can learn something about his theories from the great poem of his disciple Lucretius, *On the Nature of Things*. According to Democritus, both matter and mind are composed of atoms; and these constituent atoms, though varying in shape, are by nature indestructible. Even the gods themselves are formed of combinations of atomic particles, their so-called immortality being due to superior and therefore more lasting combinations than those of mortals. Nevertheless, we cannot suppose that such combinations will last indefinitely; for death will one day overtake even the most transcendent of Beings. Only the individual atom, then, is assured of immortality. Although its partnership with other atoms may be dissolved, it will remain free to enter into other partnerships, and so on for ever. About 2405 years after the birth of Democritus, his theory of the hard, indestructible nature of the atom received striking refutation in practice.

The thinkers whose work we have outlined in the foregoing pages were not isolated figures, speculating in the void and exerting little influence upon the ordinary people of their day. Some, like Gorgias, held important public positions. Many were skilled in various sciences, such as medicine or astronomy, and became renowned for their spectacular cures and prognostications. Empedocles of Agrigentum (450 B.C.), poet, orator and seer, was such a one. Others, like Anaxagoras, who began teaching at Athens about 460, were friends and advisers of the great statesmen of the time. In an age when the sources of knowledge were so few, the sage or wise man was a figure of eminence, whether he taught what was popular, or whether, like Anaxagoras and Socrates, he defied current beliefs and incurred the odium of the authorities.[1] The fame of a great teacher would spread so rapidly that young men, anxious to acquire wisdom, would travel great distances to attend his lectures, and sometimes to consult him upon subjects not always strictly philosophical. The Greek world was already famous for the wisdom of its Oracles. These philosophers were living, moving and sometimes equally expensive oracles. For there were not a few charlatans among them. Inevitably, in time, there grew up schools of *professional* wise men, or, as they were known by their contemporaries, Sophists: individuals who went into the business of purveying wisdom for gain, charging high prices for instructing pupils in the art of persuasion and rhetoric. At their best, the Sophists induced people to examine their own consciences, to revise their everyday assumptions, to curb their prejudices, and so to broaden their outlooks, with a view to influencing their conduct of affairs. At their worst, they imparted nothing more than intellectual 'sales talk', casuistry, logic-chopping and quibbling—in short, the art, so cruelly ascribed by Aristophanes to Socrates in *The Clouds* of 'making the worst cause seem the better'.

The first well-known figure in ancient Athens to impart knowledge and instruction for gain was a Sophist called Protagoras (481-411 B.C.), a friend of Democritus, about whom Plato wrote an entertaining and not too friendly dialogue. Plato pictures Protagoras as always surrounded by a group of earnest young men who listened in awe to his least remark, firmly believing that, in return for a moderate sum of money, he would make them wise. For the disciples of the Sophists appeared to

[1] Anaxagoras's works were publicly burned in Athens in 411 B.C.

labour under the delusion that wisdom, at least as possessed by these professional teachers, was a commodity capable of being transferred *en bloc* from one person to another. The teaching of Protagoras possessed all the attractions of being somewhat daring and 'advanced'; hence its fascination for those who, like the smart young men of Athens, wished to emphasize their superiority over the masses. The promoter of scepticism is not necessarily an evil influence in society, for no society can afford to dispense with healthy criticism; what is important is that the critic shall be animated by the right motives. As for the Sophists, their motives were frequently tainted with mischief; for their aim was not so much to enlighten as to bewilder. They wished to inspire awe instead of respect, or to enforce a reluctant respect by a display of intellectual virtuosity.

According to Socrates and Plato, such was the underlying motive that inspired the Sophists Protagoras and his colleague Hippias. The scepticism of Protagoras took the form of casting doubt upon the power of the human intellect to arrive at truth; an entertaining but dangerous doctrine. Every man, Protagoras argued, has nothing but his own senses upon which to rely; but your senses and mine may register different conclusions, and which of us is to claim that he is the more trustworthy in his impressions? The answer must seemingly be that both are right, because each has reached his own truth, so that there are an infinite number of possible 'truths'.

Such a theory, it is obvious, leads us nowhere. All authorities, being equally useful, become equally useless. Truth has been shattered into a myriad particles, each of which neutralizes and dulls the brilliance of the others. The result is not illumination but obscurity. And the student who sets out to find a sure guide to conduct retires in a state of mental befuddlement. In return for his money, he possesses nothing but a store of useless jargon. He has bartered good coinage for the 'snide' of intellectual conceit. Such was the effect of much of the Sophistic teaching.

Of Protagoras and his colleagues at least it may be said that they stumbled upon an important truth without knowing it. In their attack upon the lofty but vague speculations of their predecessors and contemporaries, they laid bare the fact, so rightly insisted upon by Socrates, that 'the proper study of mankind is man'. Where they erred was in their excessive emphasis upon that which distinguished and separated one man from another. When Socrates set out to discover the meaning of the Delphic Oracle's maxim 'Know Thyself', on the other hand, he began by considering human nature in general. His argument was as follows. To lay bare the secrets of the universe, its origin and destiny, must assuredly take centuries of patient investigation; perhaps those secrets will never be fully revealed to man, given faculties of such limitation as those which he possesses. But man can here and now embark upon the road to self-knowledge. He does not need complicated instruments for that. In reflecting upon his own conduct, in examining the discrepancy between what he is and what he ought to be— what he does and what he ought to do—he will find mental occupation sufficient to enlist his energies to the full.

Thus Socrates laid the foundations of a science which his successors, Plato and Aristotle, and their successors in turn up to our own day, have developed and debated, though never fundamentally altered; namely, the science of human conduct or, as the text-books call it, Ethics. To Socrates, the science of conduct was that to which man should devote his most earnest attention, because by no other path could true wisdom be found; and by calling Ethics a science, Socrates meant to imply that it was governed by principles of universal validity, so that what was good for one was good for all, and what was my neighbour's duty was my duty also. Socrates was therefore not merely the founder of the science of ethics; he was the first great opponent of the doctrine most destructive of rational morality, namely, ethical *relativism*.

In seeking to prove the existence of a law for mankind transcending personal differences—a law valid at all times and places, and one which imposed its own rewards and punishments by conferring or withholding happiness —Socrates was in effect contending that, beneath the mass of opinions and prejudices entertained by mankind, something in the nature of a 'universal conscience' existed, and, despite external pressure, never ceased to carry weight and authority. The crucial problem was how to break through the overgrowth of opinion and prejudice and contact the root itself: to shut out the clamour and hear the 'still, small voice'.

Socrates claimed—and he made good his claim in action—that this could best be done by endeavouring to discover, through a technique of questioning, what precisely each man's personal opinions were, and how far he was prepared to go in backing them by argument. And the kind of individual whom he found to respond most satisfactorily to this treatment was he who imagined, at least to begin with, that his views were absolutely proof against argument: in short, the man who, far from wishing to acquire wisdom, was convinced that he already possessed it.

The Socratic method of examining men's everyday opinions (for these were good enough for his purpose) by means of a carefully elaborated system of questioning or, as Plato called it, dialectic, was not instruction in the ordinary sense. Socrates was concerned less with imparting knowledge—indeed, he claimed that he had none to impart—than with exposing and expelling ignorance. His object was to extract admission after admission from his interlocutor, until the latter, deflated in his initial belief that his ideas were sound and consistent, realized that in fact he knew very little.

'My art,' Socrates explained on one occasion, 'is like that of the midwives, but differs from theirs, in that I attend men and not women, and I look after their souls when they are in labour, and not after their bodies; and the triumph of my art is in thoroughly examining whether the thought which the mind of the young man brings forth is a phantom and a lie, or a fruitful and true birth. And, like the midwives, I am barren, and the reproach often made against me, that I ask questions of others and have not the wit to answer them myself, is very just—the reason is, that the god compels me to be a midwife, but does not allow me to have children. . . . Dire are the pangs which my art is able to arouse and to allay in those who consort with me, just like the pangs of women in childbirth; night and day they are full of perplexity and travail, which is even worse than that of women.'

This method of approach entailed a view of education which differed profoundly from that commonly held at the time. Education, in Socrates' view, implied above all the stripping away of prejudice, the probing of superficial opinions, with the object of arriving at that hard *substratum* of knowledge which everyone, if sufficiently well examined, would be found to possess. For the truth is in all of us, only it needs to be brought to birth. Education, in short, can produce nothing that is not already latent in the soul. The 'idea' of justice, goodness, beauty and truth is common to all mankind; and if a man acts always with sufficient self-knowledge, he will inevitably act rightly. Those who have no 'sense' of what is right or wrong are beyond the reach of rational persuasion and must be pronounced abnormal.

In preaching his new gospel, Socrates was endeavouring to fulfil a social purpose, to serve his fellow Athenians. Against the view that philosophy deals with ideas divorced from practical, everyday life, he contended that the aim of philosophy was to purify the social conscience, and thereby to strengthen the 'morale' of the community. It needed strengthening then as now. In concerning himself with the problems affecting each individual man, the true philosopher helped the society in which he lived to become conscious of itself; by shouldering the burdens of his neighbours, he assisted in making their tasks lighter; by sacrificing his life for what he believed to be the truth—albeit the unpalatable truth—he ennobled the very people who were base enough to condemn him. For, as has so often happened, the unanimous indictment of Socrates gave place, within a short time of his decease, to a violent social reaction, in the course of which his prosecutors, once the idols of the mob, became the objects of universal execration, ending their lives by being stoned to death in that same market-place where a humbler leader had taught the principles of the good life.

Plato

'The noblest of all studies is the study of what man is and what he should pursue.'

—Gorgias

1

Socrates was a man of the people, or more accurately of the middle-classes. According to all accounts, he was a person of grotesque, almost repulsive, appearance: short and stout, with a snub nose, large prominent eyes, thick lips, full of wit and irony, ready to take a joke against himself, a good mixer, no respecter of persons. Plato, his disciple, presented a complete contrast. By birth he was an aristocrat, in appearance dignified and handsome, brilliant and polished in speech, a man careful of his associates, a stately visionary and a visionary statesman. Yet, though so different in character from Socrates, Plato confesses that his meeting with this ungainly fellow inspired in him the desire to devote his whole career, which already promised great things, to the search for truth behind appearances, while not abandoning the hope that one day he might find a ruler great enough to unite philosophy and statecraft in a true Republic of justice and peace.

Concerning the date and even the place of Plato's birth there is still a great measure of uncertainty. It is presumed that he was born in either 429 or 428 B.C., most probably at Athens, but possibly in the island of Ægina. As to the circumstances of his birth, there is an abundance of fancy and legend of which little need here be repeated, save perhaps the story that bees settled on the lips of the sleeping child in anticipation of the honeyed words that promised to issue therefrom. He was the son of Ariston and Perictione or Polone, the former

29

of whom claimed descent from Codrus, the last King of
Athens (1068 B.C.?), and the latter from Solon, the famous Athenian law-giver (born 638 B.C.?). One tradition insists that he was originally named after his
grandfather Aristocles, but that the name Plato was substituted because of his gift for fluent speech (others say
it was because of his broad chest). Whatever the value
of these legends, it is clear that he belonged to one of the
best and oldest of Athenian families, and that he was
given a chance in life such as few enjoy and from which
fewer still contrive to take advantage.

As a boy, Plato's interests and pursuits were those of
a typical, though unusually talented, child of well-to-do
parents. He was an athlete of no mean ability; in the
Isthmian games on one occasion he won the wrestling
competition. He indulged in the usual youthful 'scrib-
bling', turning out a stream of epic and lyric poetry, and
also some full-length tragedies, of which nothing but a
few fragments has survived. That he displayed any particular interest in the activity of thinking for thinking's
sake, or philosophy, we have no reason to suppose.
Something had to happen, some powerful influence to be
brought to bear, before his deepest creative instincts and
his desire for knowledge and wisdom were stirred. Nevertheless, he probably became acquainted with the speculations of Heraclitus and Anaxagoras, because there were
few subjects upon which he did not receive regular
instruction from the best available teachers. When he
was in his twentieth year,[1] however, he met Socrates and
joined his little circle. Such a dramatic encounter might
have been expected to call forth a special memoir, and
later writers have commented upon the fact that nothing
of this kind has been preserved. They are mistaken.
Plato has left us a record of this meeting in his entire
published works, for the hero and chief spokesman
throughout is Socrates himself.

The fact that Plato put almost all his ideas into the
mouth of Socrates, mentioning himself by name only a
few times, does not necessarily imply that his thought is
not original. There are several possible explanations for
his unique method of exposition. Most of his works are
in the form of dialogues, and Plato must early have been

[1] Perhaps earlier, but Diogenes Laërtius said twenty.

attracted to the technique of 'question and answer' that
Socrates had brought to such a pitch of perfection. Nor
did Plato wish to conceal the fact that both in form and
in context his ideas were of Socratic origin. Even so, we
have no reason to suppose that the development and
working out of these ideas is not Plato's own: in fact, we
need only compare the temperament and interests of
master and pupil to perceive that the one was concerned
to evolve a *method* while the other was endeavouring to
erect a *system*. Socrates, as we have seen, did not write
a line. Plato, on the other hand, not merely wrote a very
great deal; he left behind him the first systematic body of
philosophical literature that the ancient world had produced. Of the works of philosophers before Plato, we
possess only a few fragments that can be described as
genuine. Of the works of Plato, the genuine books are
almost all known, though there are certain dialogues or
fragments that may well be by other hands.

The meeting with Socrates was not in itself remarkable. No clever and cultivated young man of Athens
at the time could have failed to be attracted within the
Socratic orbit. The significance lay in what Plato made
out of this association, which became closer and closer.
For while it is true that without Socrates we should have
had no Plato, or at least a very different sort of Plato, it
is equally true that without Plato we should have had no
Socrates, or at least only the Socrates portrayed by Xenophon, who is a far less interesting figure. At the
same time, Plato is not a mere Boswell; and he exhibits
an artistry and range of thought which, if Socrates did
not himself possess them, it was his gift to be able
to stimulate in others.

In pursuing his enquiries on the subject of virtue,
Socrates had always before his mind the idea of a happier and better society which he hoped to persuade man
to establish. Plato's interests were equally practical. He
felt, with that half-conscious conviction and self-assurance characteristic of the young, that he was cut out
to be a great statesman, a master of men. Those companions with whom he mixed—the great men of the time
—encouraged him to nourish such ambitions because
they realized his unusual distinction of mind. His future
thus seemed assured. He had been born great. Honours

were plentifully thrust upon him. It required but little effort, or so it appeared, for him to achieve greatness.

And then, at the critical moment of his career, his beloved master was arrested on the charge of worshipping false gods and of corrupting the young. To Socrates himself, now a weary old man, the event must have come as no great surprise; he had expected—almost courted—it. But the effect upon his small band of disciples was devastating. From Socrates, Plato had derived the emotional stimulus that he felt he would need to transform himself from a mere politician, a party manager, into a statesman of lofty ideals. He was to be the first man of his time to demonstrate the workability of a political plan based upon justice instead of self-interest. He was to be the instrument whereby the glory of Athens, now in danger from formidable external enemies, was to be regenerated from within. The democratic régime under which he had grown up seemed to be based upon false— that is to say, materialistic—values; and when in turn that régime was overthrown and a new government of thirty reformers (the 'Thirty') substituted for it, Plato, being personally acquainted with many of the latter, had sincerely believed that the Athenian state would now at last recover its soul.

'I thought,' he later explained in one of the most interesting of his letters, 'that it [the rule of the Thirty] would substitute the reign of justice for the reign of injustice, and so I gave it my closest attention to see what it would do. And I saw these gentlemen within a very short time make the democracy they had destroyed seem like a golden age! I was deeply disgusted and dissociated myself entirely from this deplorable government. Shortly afterwards the Thirty were turned out and their régime destroyed. Once again I was filled with a desire to take an active part in politics. It was not surprising that those revolutionary times resulted in personal reprisals of a violent character; but on the whole the restored democracy exercised considerable moderation. And yet, as ill-luck would have it, certain influential persons brought an action against Socrates. The charge was an outrageous one, of which Socrates was completely innocent. They accused him of irreligion, and on this count the jury condemned him to death.'

Henceforth Plato was to entertain towards politics and the profession of statecraft feelings of unconcealed revulsion. 'The more I considered it,' he wrote, 'and the older I grew, the more difficult appeared to me to be the task of decent government. Traditions of honesty and the actual observance of law alike were degenerating in Athens with surprising rapidity, and when I saw how chaotic the political situation was, I felt completely baffled. . . . Finally I came to the conclusion that every state without exception is badly governed, and that the state of legislation is everywhere so deplorable that no improvement is possible without drastic reconstruction combined with some very good luck. And so I was forced to extol true philosophy and to declare that through it alone can real justice both for the state and for the individual be discovered and enforced.' And he concluded with the following profound observation: 'Mankind will find no cessation from evil until either the real philosophers gain political control or else the politicians become by some miracle real philosophers.'

True philosophy; real philosophers. Not, in other words, the philosophy that amounted simply to juggling with words (rhetoric) or juggling with ideas (casuistry); nor the philosophers who regarded their profession solely as a means to money-making. True philosophy, as Plato was henceforth to conceive it, was practical philosophy; but this practical philosophy was to be very different from that of the Sophists, who wished to press wisdom into the service of material advancement, and to use their tricks to gain control over men and their possessions, making the worse cause the better and the worst of all the best.

In other words, the task to which Plato—moved to the depth of his soul by the prosecution of Socrates—henceforth dedicated himself was that of laying the foundations, at first in theory only, of the ideal City. We are accustomed to Utopias, but for Plato's contemporaries the ideal was quite original, even startling. In Greece at that time the political unit was the City State, a unit much more manageable than our modern nation-states, and more easily reorganized as a result of conquest or revolution. But Plato was concerned with something more than a mere blue-print of a political system to be established in a particular locality. His vision was not provincial but universal. He wanted world revolution, but within the human heart.

He saw, as Socrates had taught him, that the most urgent and difficult of all reforms was that to be undertaken within man himself, a reform that should ultimately extend to all mankind, embracing both Greeks and barbarians, slaves and free men. That a truly just society could be established within measurable time he was too disillusioned to believe. A long period of education must prepare the way for any such millennium. Nevertheless, if his ideals were pronounced too lofty to be realized, he was convinced that no goal less lofty was worth pursuing. Greek civilization could survive, he believed, only through the kind of spiritual renewal that would render impossible a repetition of the scandal of Socrates's persecution. Indeed, the test of a just society was simply whether it would foster and honour its great reformers and teachers, or whether, out of crass ignorance on the part of the masses or from fear of exposure and ridicule on the part of a few tyrants, it would seek to muzzle them.

In order to equip himself for this self-imposed task, Plato decided upon a course of action that has recommended itself to many men similarly resolved. He travelled. Deep and prolonged meditation is not necessarily accomplished best in seclusion. The senses need to refresh themselves with new sights and sounds, the body to engage in unaccustomed exertions, in order that the mind, quietly disengaging itself from stale routine, may go freely about its business of self-examination. How frequently men of action have reported, in later years, that their minds were most at peace at the time when their physical being was subject to greatest agitation! In one sense, Plato's excursion abroad represented a kind of retirement and even exile. He was away from Athens for about eleven years. In the case of one so full of vitality, however, this long period was devoted to much else besides thinking, reading, and writing. As we shall see in due course, he twice became involved in complicated political affairs. Nevertheless, this departure from Athens marks the beginning of his creative period, the renewal of his zest for the pursuit of truth.

At first he withdrew to Megara, a town only twenty-six miles from Athens, and here he probably wrote some of his early dialogues. Possibly he formed one of a small band of disciples of Socrates, another of whom, Euclides (not to be confused with the mathematician of that name), composed similar works of which none have survived. Deciding to venture farther afield, Plato then set out for the town of Cyrene in North Africa (now in the Libyan province of Cyrenaica), perhaps at the invitation of the well-known philosopher Theodosius. The latter had been given the title of Atheist in consequence not so much of his denial of the gods as of his outspoken comments upon the religious beliefs and practices of the time. He was a man for whom, in the circumstances, Plato would have felt a special sympathy.

Later still, Plato visited Egypt and Sicily, and the flourishing Greek cities of Lower Italy, impelled both by an insatiable thirst for knowledge and by the desire, understandable in a young man of his nature, to make personal contact with the famous men of the day. Long after his death, these wanderings were made to assume a romantic colouring which, though no doubt justified in part, was on the whole greatly exaggerated. We have no reason to give credence to the stories—as fantastic as that which made him out to be the son of Apollo—concerning his mysterious journeys to the Hebrews, to the Babylonians, to the Assyrians, and even to the Magi, a religious sect of the Medes and Persians whose representatives made a journey to Bethlehem a few centuries later.

Of the details of his visits to Sicily, however, we have more reliable information. He went there first in 389, when he was forty years of age. Here he soon won the respect and finally the friendship of Dion, brother-in-law of the tyrant of Syracuse, Dionysius. Already a man of upright character, Dion had but to come under the influence of Plato to conceive an immediate distaste for the life of dissipation, luxury, and sloth which he and his fellow-courtiers had been leading. Nevertheless, whereas Dion maintained good relations with Dionysius the Elder, he soon fell out with the latter's son, whose mode of life was characterized by excesses of an even more revolting kind, and to whom the newly-assumed austerity of his uncle Dion was both a reproach and a source of irritation.

Plato, unlike Dion, soon quarrelled with the elder Dionysius and is said by some historians to have been sold into slavery by him. This story is probably without foundation. We do know, however, that Dion, determined to gain influence over his nephew, the younger Dionysius, and believing that no one but Plato could effect his 'conversion', begged the philosopher to make a second journey to Syracuse, which he did shortly after the death of the Elder Dionysius, in 367. On arrival, Plato was accorded a reception such as has rarely greeted a man renowned for wisdom, even in days when personages of this type were honoured to a marked degree. In spite of his strenuous efforts to win the young ruler to the cause of philosophy, however, Plato was obliged to admit failure. For he was faced with two forms of opposition, that resulting from Dionysius's early training, and that from Syracusan party politicians, who regarded such a disinterested mission on the part of a foreigner with undisguised hostility. And so, in the end, not merely was Plato forced to make a hasty retreat, but Dion, his host, was obliged to accompany him back to Athens, where he remained for some time in exile. Thus concluded Plato's second attempt to turn a statesman into a philosopher.

His third and last venture, which occurred in 360 B.C., nearly cost him his life. It was concerned with the same ruler, Dionysius II. Now anxious to reconcile himself with Dion, Dionysius, who seems to have been a man of most changeable temper, invited Plato to act as mediator once more. But the man whose advice had been sought by both parties to the quarrel was again ill-paid for his efforts.

Dionysius, on receiving Plato at his unruly court, took it into his head to resent the very counsel he had so earnestly solicited; and had it not been for the intervention of Archytas, himself a philosopher of repute as well as a general, Plato might have spent the rest of his life in the diabolical quarry-prison of Syracuse, where, it is said, the tyrant had already incarcerated the poet Philoxenus for daring to ridicule some royal attempts at versification. Nevertheless, Plato had not altogether failed in his efforts to educate Dionysius II as the Philosopher-King. The royal disposition underwent another change. For a time all went well: the courtiers abandoned their dissipations and even set about studying geometry, tracing figures on the ground which had been specially strewn with sand for the purpose. Later (357) Dion returned to Syracuse and ousted Dionysius. In 353, however, Dion was himself murdered, and a great ruler was thus probably lost to the world.

After his return from his first visit to Syracuse, Plato had purchased a home and a garden in a suburb of Athens near the river Cephissus. Not far away was a plot of land which had originally belonged to Academus, the Attic hero. This had been later turned into a sanctuary and gymnasium, planted with plane and olive trees, and decorated with groups of statuary. Here, in what came to be known as the Academy, as well as in his own garden at Colonus, Plato began to teach and to lecture. He taught free of charge, and his pupils were at first a small circle of intimate friends. Above the entrance to his house he affixed the inscription: 'Let no one enter who is unacquainted with geometry.'

The disciples of Plato at this time were almost all persons of distinction. There was his nephew Speusippus, a keen student of philosophy who was to accompany him on his third journey to Syracuse. There was Xenocrates of Chalcedon, also a philosopher of some merit who, like Speusippus, later became president of the Academy. There was an extraordinary young man from Stagira called Aristotle, of whom we shall hear more. There was Heraclides Ponticus, mathematician and philosopher, Hestiæus of Perinthus, Phillipus the Arpuntian, and many others. Apart from this inner circle, however, there were men of wisdom and learning from all parts of Greece and sometimes beyond, who, hearing of the great abilities of Plato as a teacher, made journeys to Athens for the purpose of becoming acquainted with him.

Women, too, were among those who attended his courses of instruction. For although in Ancient Greece women played practically no part in public affairs and enjoyed no higher education, Plato, almost alone among the thinkers of antiquity, advocated the equality of the sexes. As he declared in the *Republic*: 'If women are to have the same duties as men, they must have the same upbringing and education.'

Of the forty or so literary works said to have been written by Plato, thirty are today regarded as genuine. But even so his output was enormous. Except during his two eventful journeys to Syracuse after the foundation of the Academy, he was occupied with teaching and writing up to and including the day of his death.[1] This took place at the ripe age of eighty-two in 347 B.C., fifty-three years having elapsed since the death of Socrates.

The removal of the leader, however, did not mean the breaking up of the philosophical conclave, still less of the Academy. In his will, Plato left his properties to the school he had founded, and its members faithfully preserved those hallowed places. In course of time they became a shrine, a centre of pilgrimage, where the anniversaries of the death of Plato and Socrates were celebrated year by year with true devotion. Finally the Academy passed into the hands of the Neo-Platonists, remaining open as a school of philosophical research and debate for more than five centuries into the Christian era. Thus Plato's Academy was in reality the world's first university; and hence the word 'academic' is today inseparably linked with university life, though with slightly derogatory associations for which its originator was in no way responsible. Having been founded in 380 B.C. and closed by order of the Emperor Justinian in A.D. 529, it survived without a break for longer than any other university of which we have record. Meanwhile, the influence of Plato's philosophical ideas had spread to the confines of the civilized world, informing the thought of the Fathers of the Christian Church, penetrating and fertilizing the speculations of the peoples of the East, and inspiring every philosopher worth the name down to our own time. A modern thinker, whose work we shall later discuss,[2] has even gone so far as to describe the course of Western philosophy since the fifth century B.C. as nothing but a series of 'footnotes to Plato'.

What was Plato like as a man? We know almost as little about Plato's private life and character as we know about Shakespeare: which means that of the two supreme

[1] Plato's lectures have not survived.
[2] A. N. Whitehead.

men of genius of the Western world we know practically nothing. The bust that has been preserved, with its tangled beard and penetrating eyes, suggests a man of profound, almost fiery, temperament, presenting a marked contrast to the judicial countenance of Aristotle. There are suggestions, derived from Plato's own works and from those of his contemporaries and successors, that he was a man of ardent disposition. Ardent he must certainly have been; whether he exhibited the frankly erotic tendencies that have been attributed to Socrates is more than doubtful. Both the passionate love of intellectual beauty that animates all his work, and his reputation as a man of supreme wisdom and goodness, are irreconcilable with the notion that he (or Socrates for that matter) was merely another, though vastly more intelligent, Alcibiades. At the same time we have no reason to suppose that he was a prig or a recluse. The Academy was a place of good fellowship; and how striking is the difference between the modern word 'symposium', with its exclusively literary significance, and the original Symposium (literally 'a drinking together'), that greatest of all drinking parties of which Plato has left us such a lively record!

2

If we devote more space to both Plato and Aristotle than to most of the philosophers of whom we shall be speaking, it is because the work of these two thinkers, master and pupil, has exerted such a profound influence upon everything that has since happened in the realm of philosophy. Their achievement represents the rock or foundation upon which subsequent thinkers have constructed their habitations, great or small, weather-proof or gimcrack. They drew up the Constitution, to which their successors have made amendments of varying importance.

Of Plato's use of the dialogue in expounding his ideas, we have already spoken. He was not the only thinker to use it. Zeno did so, and also Xenophon and Æschines (both acquaintances of Socrates), Antisthenes, founder of the school of Cynics, and Euclides. With Plato, however, the dialogue form took on a more significant aspect both as a literary convention and as a method of expounding ideas. From Socrates Plato had grasped what may seem to us a self-evident fact, namely, that the right way to acquire knowledge is to ask questions. Admittedly, in order to proceed in the correct way, we must know what questions to ask. It was Socrates' achievement to have made clear that there is, for those who seek it diligently, a correct order in thought, a natural unfolding of logical argument. Thinking, he said in effect, is not just the 'hit and miss' activity which for most of us it remains throughout life. Or rather, it resembles the shooting at a target only in the sense that each shot is intended as a nearer approximation to the bull's-eye. It is a case of hit-and-near-miss, with the margin of error being steadily whittled down.

In other words, the dialogue form is admirably adapted to the view that truth is attained in a series of definite and recognizable stages. In most modern books concerned with the exposition of ideas, the argument flows on uninterruptedly from beginning to end, as if it were a string unwound from a ball. And this regular 'paying out' of ideas is something upon which the writer is inclined to pride himself. This may perhaps be called the 'horizontal' method of approach. Plato and some of his contemporaries used a different one, which might be called the 'vertical' method of approach. Convinced that the search for truth must be a slow, gradual process, Plato sets out to make clear the exact stage, at any one moment, that he has reached in his argument. This he does by making each conclusion the subject of a kind of bilateral pact between the persons engaged in the dispute. As a result, his dialogues sometimes give the impression of being a series of separate 'bones of contention', without these components ever forming a complete frame or skeleton; but the frame is being built up all the time, even though we do not easily perceive its formation while we are absorbed in the structure of a particular section.

There is a further reason why Plato, seeking for the most effective means of expounding philosophical arguments, decided upon the use of dramatic dialogue. He was intent upon showing, by literary means, that thought is a growing, living, almost organic, process. Why was he so concerned to show this? Because he had been given the unique opportunity of observing it thus developing, thus germinating, in the mind of a living person. He was seeking to put Socrates on paper: to preserve as best as artificial means could afford the creative spontaneity, the personal magnetism, of the master.

For us, living more than two thousand years after, philosophy chiefly implies a book, a treatise, or a paper read before a learned society: a thing written down, a topic of limited interest and application, a subject in an Honour School. We do not live our philosophy, or rather we do not live the philosophy that we read, if we read any at all; we observe a marked distinction between theory and practice, bridging the gulf as a rule by our sense of irony and humour. Such a state of affairs would have seemed odd, even deplorable, to Plato. Plato regarded Socrates as the first of a series of truly practical, because practising, philosophers, whose line should culminate in the messianic figure of the Philosopher King. He was not to know that Socrates, while being the first of his kind, was also in a sense to be the last.

Since he could imagine no philosophy worth the name as being anything but the expression of a personality, the mainspring of conduct in some individual, Plato introduced into his dialogues real historical personages— Alcibiades, Protagoras, Critias, Parmenides. Into their mouths he put words and arguments which, if always 'in character', are not, so far as we know, verbatim records of speeches actually delivered. Like the historian Thucydides, who put long speeches into the mouths of historical characters without claiming that they were necessarily spoken in that form, Plato tried to expound various 'points of view' by the realistic method of assembling a number of typical spokesmen. Not merely had he observed Socrates living and working out his philosophy 'in the open', without recourse to books; he had observed his enlistment of other people, not as passive objects for experimental purposes, but as partners in the business of seeking ultimate truth.

The 'artistry' of Plato, of which so much has been written, is not merely the artistry of a man who, besides being a master-thinker, knows how to write. It is the artistry of a man who recaptures in writing the drama of a philosophy that was in essence a spoken and extempore philosophy. Moreover it had the advantage of being spoken and extemporized by one of the greatest of all talkers. How vast a gulf separates a 'spoken' philosophy such as that of Plato from our modern 'written' philosophies will be observed when we come to discuss the work of another master of philosophizing, Immanuel Kant. While acutely aware that thought and action were inseparable, Kant lacked the literary skill to transcribe his ideas in the language of everyday life, with the result that his writings tend to be as forbidding to the ordinary reader as his lectures and conversation were reported to have been stimulating.

Taking his clue from Socrates that the aim of philosophy is to prescribe the kind of life most likely to promote the happiness of man, Plato realized that such a subject of enquiry depends for its clarification upon the answer to the question: what kind of a being is this creature, man, that he should need to be concerned with his own happiness? What distinguishes him as a living entity from the rest of Creation? In seeking to answer these questions, Plato pursued his speculations to a point where Socrates, content to 'shelve' metaphysical matters, or at best to interpret them in an allegorical fashion, had called a halt. Never wholly forsaking his early political ambitions, Plato earnestly sought to combine his loftiest notions with plans for a social system or Republic wherein the human spirit, destined for immortality in another sphere, might develop its latent capacities.

In short, Plato's political theory was concerned not so much with a state that should promote the material well-being of its inhabitants (though he was interested, especially towards the end of his life, in this aspect also) as with a system capable of opening the way to the good life by providing the maximum incentive to it. Here again his attitude differs from that of most modern writers on so-called ethical questions. Today, a man's ideas of goodness and badness are generally supposed to be matters private to himself. The good life is something to be lived apart from, and often in spite of, the social system of the day. Religion, for instance, is a private affair, a matter for the individual conscience. To Plato, this division of life into a public and a private sphere was not to be tolerated. Politics and morals were the same. Bad politics lead to bad behaviour. The good life was possible only in the good state.[1]

Naturally, he was well aware how far short of this ideal of harmonious living his contemporaries and most of his predecessors had fallen: the extract from his letter already quoted shows that he had a shrewd idea what he was facing. But this yawning gulf between what was and what ought to be impressed him as something more than a mere accident of social life. It struck him as characteristic of life in general. It was part of the nature of things. Between the ordinary everyday world that we know and the world as it should be—between the information and knowledge with which we 'make do' in our normal routine of living and the true knowledge that should ideally be our guide—there is a serious discrepancy. At any given moment, we act not upon a true assessment of the situation but upon a rough compromise; we are content with beliefs and opinions. This is because the ordinary world in which we live is a world of imperfections and imprecisions, of half-lights and shadows.

These ideals, beliefs and opinions of ours are not necessarily to be regarded as the product of an inaccurate or distorted vision of the ordinary world; they represent a true and faithful reflection of it, such as it is. But this everyday world may not be the only world with which we can establish contact. It is simply the world which we perceive with our senses. In Plato's view, there is another and truer world, the world which we may perceive with our intellect. This alone is reality.

Plato is thus one of the first philosophers to assert and exploit the fundamental distinction between that which is perceived by our senses and that which is perceived by our intellect. Pythagoras, with his emphasis upon form and structure as opposed to matter or 'stuff', partially anticipated him; but Plato used the distinction as the basis for a theory which may be said to have exerted more influence upon later philosophical thought that any other: namely, his celebrated Theory of Ideas.

Plato's Theory of Ideas has frequently been misunderstood, or at least mis-stated, as a result of a failure to perceive how he arrived at it. In fact, there need be no mystery about it at all, for it developed logically and in-

[1] For Plato, the state signified the City State of his day.

evitably out of Socrates's technique of inquisition (though the influence of Parmenides is also apparent). Socrates's aim in discussing a subject was to reach agreement, by a series of interim arguments, upon what constituted the *essence* of that subject. Take, for instance, a virtue such as Justice. Socrates would try to establish what constituted the unique character whereby everything just was just. This was equivalent to establishing the Idea of justice. To arrive at the Idea of a thing was the final stage in any discussion upon which Socrates decided to embark.

Ideas, therefore, are the goal of our intellectual faculty; only by intellectual analysis can we arrive at a knowledge that they exist. With another bold stroke of originality, Plato then proceeds to explain how such analysis is made possible. In his view, the knowledge of Universals (as the Platonic Ideas are commonly called today) is the result not so much of learning as of re-learning. We do not acquire such knowledge; we recollect it.

This is above all the case with the truths of geometry (which is no doubt why Plato caused the famous inscription to be put up at the entrance to the Academy). In his dialogue entitled the *Meno,* he shows with extraordinary skill how an untutored slave-boy, questioned by Socrates, is able to discover and apprehend for himself the truth of a geometrical demonstration. How, Plato asks, can knowledge of this sort be completely new? If we set out to acquire a certain kind of knowledge, the knowledge we wish to acquire cannot be wholly strange to us; for if it were strange, how, once acquired, could we recognize it to be that which we were seeking? We cannot 'entertain' a complete stranger. Now it is clear that if there are certain truths of which we have instinctive knowledge (usually termed in philosophical textbooks *a priori* knowledge), we must surely have acquired that knowledge in some realm other than that into which we were born. Knowledge recollected here must have been collected elsewhere. What realm can this be, then, in which pure and perfect knowledge is eternally assembled? Moreover, how did the soul of man, once having known this state of perfection, ever become alienated from it?

Plato's answer to this fascinating problem is couched

in the language of myth. A myth, in the sense in which he uses the term, is an allegorical explanation, not a logical one. The myth to which we refer is an account of the 'history' of the soul, and we may retail this history in Plato's own words, taken from the dialogue called the *Phædrus*:

'The nature of the soul is altogether a subject for large and more than mortal discourse, but to say what the soul resembles is a briefer and human theme. Let me compare it to a pair of winged horses and a charioteer. Now the winged horses and the charioteers of the gods are all of them noble and of noble descent, but those of other races (*e.g.* human beings) are mixed. One human charioteer drives his in a pair; and one of them is noble and of noble breed, and the other is ignoble and of ignoble breed; and the driving of them is necessarily hard and difficult. I will try to explain to you how the mortal differs from the immortal creature. The soul in her totality has the care of all soulless being, and traverses the whole heaven taking different forms; when perfect and fully winged she soars upward, and orders the whole world; while the imperfect soul, losing her wings and drooping in her flight, at last settles on the solid ground—there, finding a home, she receives an earthly body which appears to be self-moved, but is really moved by her power; and this composition of soul and body is called a living and mortal creature. For immortal no such union can be reasonably believed to be. . . .

'And now let us ask the reason why the soul loses her wings! The wing is the corporeal element which is most akin to the divine, and which by nature tends to soar aloft and carry that which gravitates downwards into the upper region, where the gods dwell. The divine is beauty, wisdom, goodness, and the like; and by these the wing of the soul is nourished, and grows apace; but when fed upon evil and ugliness and the opposite of good, it wastes and is destroyed. . . . The reason why the soul exhibits this intense eagerness to behold the plain of truth is that pasturage is found there, which is suited to the highest part of the soul; and the wing on which the soul soars is nourished with this.

'And there is a law of Destiny, that the soul which attains any vision of truth in company with a God is preserved from harm until the next period, and if attaining always is always unharmed. But when she is unable to follow, and fails to behold the truth, and through some ill-hap sinks beneath the double load of forgetfulness and vice, and her wings fall from her and she drops to the ground, then the law ordains that this soul shall at her first birth pass, not into any other animal, but only into man; and the soul which has seen most of truth shall come to the birth as a philosopher, or artist, or some musical or loving nature; that which has seen truth in the second degree shall be some law-abiding being or soldier or ruler; the soul which is of the third class shall be a politician, or business man, or financier; the fourth shall be a lover of athletics or a physician; the fifth shall lead the life of a prophet or hierophant[1]; to the sixth the character of a poet or some other imitative artist will be assigned; to the seventh the life of an artisan or husbandman; to the eighth that of a sophist or demagogue; to the ninth that of a despot; all these are states of probation, in which he who lives justly improves, and he who lives unjustly deteriorates his lot.'

From the above account it will be seen that in the hierarchy of beings that are in contact with true reality, the philosophers and the 'good king' are those placed at the summit, with the philosopher definitely taking precedence. The mere politician comes third, along with the business man and the financier. We can therefore understand Plato's preoccupation with the problems of just and wise government; for he had become convinced that no good could come to mankind until the two highest callings, that of philosopher and that of ruler, were merged into one: in short, 'until philosophers are kings'.[2]

With Plato's theory of the 'transmigration of souls'—an idea which he almost certainly borrowed from Pythagoras—we are not concerned. What interests us rather is his belief, novel in its orientation, that man is, in the words appropriate to a later doctrine, a 'fallen' creature. Realizing his sorry condition, man strives to improve it; and he may, if supremely fortunate, arrive at true knowledge, as opposed to mere belief or opinion, by the technique of recollection or—to use Plato's term—*mimesis,*

[1] A priest of the sacred mysteries.
[2] This famous phrase occurs in *The Republic,* 473.

which 'brings to birth' the wisdom with which he was formerly endowed.

For, as Plato remarks further on in the same dialogue, 'a man must have intelligence of universals, and be able to proceed from the many particulars of sense to one conception of reason; this is the recollection of those things which our souls once saw when following God, when regardless of that which we now call reality she raised her head to Reality itself. . . . Once the beauty was clear to see, when in that happy company our souls saw the beatific vision and were initiated into what may be called the most blessed of mysteries, celebrated by us in our state of innocence, while we were untouched by evils to come, when we were admitted to the sight of visions innocent and simple, calm and happy, which we beheld shining in pure light; and we were pure ourselves and unstained by that which we carry about and call our body, imprisoned like shellfish in their shell.'

It is easy to dismiss such lofty passages as the outpourings of a mystic who was also a poet. A poet Plato most certainly was, in addition to being an inspirer of poetry in others. Wordsworth, writing two thousand years later, embodies such Platonic doctrines in his *Ode on the Intimations of Immortality*. But, even allowing for his superb use of imagery and metaphor, Plato is not indulging in mere rhetoric. He does not pile phrase upon phrase, period upon period, like the Sophists. He is not concerned merely to achieve an effect. He wants us to take his criticism of materialism seriously. He is inviting his contemporaries, and indeed all those who are to follow after him, to turn away from the kind of life which identifies happiness with indulgence in the pleasures of the senses, and to seek a more permanently satisfying mode of existence. No man had spoken quite like this before, except the man who had put him on the road to wisdom.

Plato's 'idealism' is nowhere more clearly revealed than in his account of the nature of art; for it is his contention that we come closest to apprehending the world of Forms when we gaze upon something or someone beautiful. Beauty, in other words, is the form most easily accessible to us, even to the least intellectual, because it manifests itself chiefly through the medium of vision.

'Of beauty,' Plato says, 'I repeat again that we saw her there' (*i.e.* in heaven) 'shining in company with the celestial forms: and coming to earth we find her here too, shining in clearness through the clearest aperture of sense. For sight is the most piercing of our bodily senses; though not by that is wisdom seen: for loveliness would have been transporting if there had been a visible image of her, and the other Ideas, if they had had visible counterparts, would be equally lovely. But this is the privilege of beauty, that being the loveliest she is also the most palpable to sight.'

Of the three noblest and most exalted Forms, Beauty, Truth and Goodness, the first is thus the doorway to the other two. If the eyes are the 'windows of the soul', then Beauty is the casement through which we are able to descry the more distant images of Truth and Goodness. Beauty, especially in its most exquisite natural manifestations, sets up an agitation in us that causes the baser souls to rush and possess, while it elevates those of clearer insight to a perception of that which lies beyond.

What, then, is the highest of the Forms, the goal of human aspiration? It is the Form or Idea of Goodness. The influence of this Form may be justly compared to that of the sun. The sun gives light, but at the same time it feeds and nurtures the world that enjoys its radiance: it is king and minister together, not merely ruling creation but simultaneously bringing it to fruition. Similarly with the Form of the Good. Goodness in its ideal manifestation causes the hierarchy of Forms to glow with celestial incandescence. It irradiates them, and at the same time it exercises an attractive influence. Thus, all the Forms approximate and incline to the Form of the Good; but this approximation or inclination does not imply a temporal growth or evolution. The world of the Forms is a timeless and eternal world, and the natural 'leading' of one Form to another is a logical or ideal process, of which the change and growth in the sensible world are but a shifting and shadowy copy. Time, in other words, is the 'moving image of Eternity'.

That Plato casts no doubt upon the existence or substantial reality of the natural world (the world of our body and its senses), we have already explained. But there appears to be a difficulty here. If the world open to our senses is merely the world of opinion and not of knowledge, how in fact can we penetrate from this shadowy, imperfect realm to the world of light and perfection? By our intellects, says Plato. Yes, but mere intellectual reasoning, though necessary to the achievement of supra-sensible knowledge, cannot function unless impelled by force of another kind. Before we can know, we must desire to know. Before we can ascend the scale, we must be possessed with the right kind of impulse. What is this impulse and where does it come from? Plato's answer is simple. It is Love.

Love is the medium or 'catalyst' whereby the soul, tied for the period of its natural life to the body, frees itself from passion and sensual desire and, with strengthening wings, ascends into the empyrean and gazes upon the divine Forms. In order to explain where this impulse of love comes from, Plato reminds us of his account of the 'pre-history' of the soul. Love, as human beings know it, is simply the memory, made poignant by a sense of loss, of the soul's previous communion with these same Forms. The 'twinge' of sadness rarely absent from human experience of love is therefore the nostalgia of a lover separated from the object of his complete devotion. Likewise, the sense of expectancy and fervour, uppermost at other times, is simply the lover's hope of recapturing in its fullness, and through attachment to some human object of desire, an experience of which he craves renewal. Love that is content to express itself solely upon the natural plane is doomed to perpetual frustration, for the mere satisfaction of the senses leads to early satiety and disgust. And this is the meaning of that much misunderstood thing 'Platonic love': not love that implies complete indifference to physical attraction, but love that has for its goal the satisfaction of the spirit in what Shakespeare termed 'the marriage of true minds'.

To sum up: Plato's theory of Ideas is the result of his attempt to do two things. It is first of all an attempt to show how knowledge of reality is acquired. Secondly, it is an attempt to show what reality is like. It is thus both a theory of knowledge and a theory of reality.

Plato's application of his theory to the problems of political and social life is very relevant for us today. In his book *The Republic,* he is engaged in discussing not merely the abstract idea of government, but the practical reforms needed to improve the Athenian state of his own time. He was worried about the way things were going, just as Socrates had been worried before him. We have shown already how fervently Plato desired to create a democracy fit for good men, and above all good philosophers, to live in. Now it seemed to him obvious that no state could be considered good and just that was not founded upon the Idea of the Good which the philosophers, as opposed to the Sophists, had apprehended in the course of their meditations.

In other words, what was good for society must follow from what was good in the realm of true knowledge. There was not one law for the world of Opinion and another law for the world of Ideas, because such order and logic as was manifested in the former must ultimately derive from the influence of the latter percolating through the intervening 'no-man's-land' of imperfection. How, then, could the influence of the Ideas be made to impinge more directly upon men's consciences? How could we 'let in the light', or induce men to raise their eyes to the source of divine energy? How could we cultivate in the soil of the spirit the love that, once inclined in the right direction, would put forth its leaves in a spontaneous effort to raise itself in the sun's face, there to burst into flower?

Plato's answer is pruned of all extravagant expectations. The way is difficult, and for many impossible. Those who cannot fare forward by their own unaided efforts must submit themselves to superior direction. Above all there must be a long and painful process of education.

When Plato ventured to speak of a 'philosopher King', therefore, he had in mind something more than a benign but rather ineffectual figure, given to meditation and study, but separated by his superior intellect and rarefied tastes from the common herd. His philosopher was to be a practical philosopher; his King was also to be a lawmaker, an active statesman. He was to lay down the law with the authority not merely of his regal office but of his philosophical insight. In obeying the laws he proclaimed, the common people would thus be acting in conformity with the supreme good of the universe. Some of them would no doubt obey willingly, conscious of the wisdom of the law-giver. Some would obey mechanically, conscious merely of the necessity of conforming to a common standard. Some would obey with an ill-grace, being so far corrupted and immersed in the natural world that the 'pull' of heavenly wisdom would be felt hardly at all. Plato's ideal Republic approximated in this respect more to an authoritarian system than to what we should call Democracy. In the last of his books, significantly entitled *The Laws,* he went to great lengths to show how rigid and disciplined must be the state of transition from the corrupt and chaotic system of his day to the ideal system of the future. This 'state of transition'—a phrase not unfamiliar to us—would be not so much the dictation of the proletariat as the dictation of an *élite;* and no one in his right mind would presume to say how long and with what degree of repression such dictation would need to be maintained.

The sub-title of Plato's book *The Republic* is *On Justice.* Now Plato employs the word Justice in a very wide sense. He identifies it with the Form of the Good, which is the same as God. (Plato's conception of God, incidentally, is very different from our own, and we shall examine this difference when we come to discuss the religious ideas of Aristotle.) He contends that by our just acts, rather than our 'good' acts (a vague term), we help to realize God's purpose in the world, because love of Goodness is after all a longing for order, proportion, measure, and symmetry—it is in fact 'the desire and pursuit of the whole'—and justice is nothing but the observance of order, measure, and symmetry in our dealings with our fellowmen.

Thus we talk of 'fair dealing', where the word 'fair' combines the notions of beauty and justice. To describe Justice as the 'mother of the virtues'—the human virtues, that is to say—is to come close to Plato's meaning: and in its capacity of progenitor, Justice provides each faculty of the soul with its appropriate offspring. To talk of 'faculties of the soul' may sound like philosophical jargon, and jargon it has become, because the distinction between thought, will, and feeling is frequently employed without due attention to the facts which it seeks to explain.

Among the faculties, Plato gives pride of place to Intellect or Intelligence because this faculty penetrates to the eternal Forms behind the shadowy world of sense. Now the 'justice' of Intelligence is wisdom; for a wise man is not one who knows many things but one who sees things in proportion. Second in order of importance comes the faculty of Will, of which the 'justice' is known as courage, because a will that is directed to noble ends must engage in ceaseless war against indifference and sloth, and this requires determination. Lastly comes the faculty of sensibility or Feeling. In this sphere justice takes the form of temperance: temperance, that is to say, not in its abused modern sense but in the sense of self-control or moderation (the 'nothing too much' of the French essayist Montaigne), because neither a starved nor a glutted sensibility is tolerable to the man of balanced mind.

This three-fold distinction between the faculties of the soul is applied by Plato to the constitution of society itself. Society is composed of three orders, or, as we should say today, classes. At the head is the class of philosophers or thinkers, who represent the Intelligence of the body-politic. Next come the warriors or military class, whose task is to defend the state from outside enemies, and whose virtue is courage. Finally come the merchants and artisans, the agricultural labourers, the slaves and the servants, who, being concerned with men's material needs, represent the most physical element in the system, corresponding to the most physical part of the mind, namely the sense-organs, whose virtue consists in submission to the higher faculties.

Even philosophers may rule unjustly, as Plato readily admits. Philosophers are men, and liable to make faulty judgments; and the very eminence of their position is such as to render them susceptible to pride and love of power. Long before Lord Acton made his famous statement that 'power corrupts, but absolute power corrupts absolutely', Plato, who had seen such abuses at first hand, observed that 'no human soul in its youth and irresponsibility will be able to sustain the temptation of arbitrary power—there is no one who will not, under such circumstances, become filled with folly, that worst of diseases, and be hated by his nearest and dearest friends; and when this happens his kingdom is undermined, and all his power vanishes'.[1]

Moreover, the achievement of the balanced and mature character is something much more difficult than is commonly supposed: 'Quick intelligence, memory, sagacity, cleverness and similar qualities do not often grow together, and persons who possess them and are at the same time high-spirited and magnanimous are not so constituted by nature as to live an orderly and peaceful and settled life. Their vivacity drives them this way and that, and they lose their stability. On the other hand, those steadfast natures which can better be depended upon, which are in battle impregnable to fear and immovable, are equally immovable when there is anything to be learned.'[2]

Although Plato frankly acknowledges the difficulty of living the philosophical life, and is not in favour of giving young people too much philosophical instruction in their early education—when, as he shrewdly remarks, 'the chief and special care should be given to their bodies that they may have them to use in the service of philosophy' (for 'youngsters, when they first get the taste in their mouths, argue for amusement, and are always contradicting and refuting others in imitation of those who refute them')[3]—he never loses faith in the importance of philosophy, because, as he points out in another part of *The Republic* (500), 'a man cannot help imitating that with which he lives in admiring communion; and the philosopher, in his communion with the divine order, becomes orderly and divine, as far as the nature of man allows: but, like everyone else, he will have his enemies'.

In order to reduce to a minimum the temptations of power to which the rulers or Guardians are subject, Plato proposes that they shall not merely be deprived of all personal property, but that even the blessings of family life shall be denied them. 'The community of wives and children among our citizens,' he says,[4] 'is clearly the source of the greatest good for the State. And this agrees with the other principle which we were affirming—that the governing class were not to have houses or lands or

[1] *Laws*, 691.
[2] *The Republic*, 503 ff.
[3] *Ibid.*, 539.
[4] *Ibid.*, 464.

any other property; their pay was to be their food, which they were to receive from the other citizens, and they were to have no private expenses; for we intend them to preserve their true character of guardians. Both the community of property and the community of families tend to make them more truly guardians; they will not tear the city in pieces by differing about "mine" and "not mine" . . . but all will be affected as far as may be by the same pleasures and pains because they are all of one opinion about what is near and dear to them, and therefore they all tend towards a common end.'

Thus it will be seen that Plato expounds a point of view diametrically opposite to that put forward centuries later by the economist and philosopher Adam Smith (1723-90), who declared that public benefit would automatically result from private interest. As for the system of Communism which Plato outlined in *The Republic*, this too differs from that which has been advocated by revolutionaries in our own time. For the communal life is intended only for the caste of Guardians, and has since been put into practice, if at all, by groups equally restricted in membership, such as certain religious communities. And in view of the past history and record of experimental communist societies, it is doubtful whether they can survive unless inspired by intense religious fervour, as Plato was careful to emphasize.

Even so there must be a long and arduous period of initiation. 'When our rulers have reached fifty years of age, then let those who have won through and have excelled in every sphere of action and knowledge be introduced at last to their final task: the time has now arrived at which they must raise the eye of the soul to the universal light which lightens all things, and behold the Absolute Good' (*i.e.* the Supreme Form). 'For that is the pattern according to which they are to order the State and the lives of individuals, and the remainder of their own lives too, making philosophy their chief pursuit, but, when their turn comes, toiling also at politics and ruling for the public good, not as though they were performing some heroic action, but simply as a matter of duty; and when they have brought up in each generation others like themselves and left them in their place to be governors of the State, then they will depart to the Islands of the Blest and there dwell.'[1]

That was all very well—in theory. In practice, as the ageing philosopher realized, men exhibit qualities that differ little as regards ferocity from those displayed by animals, and as regards cunning and duplicity have no parallel even in the brute creation. Naturally, some few persons of wisdom and integrity there will always be: 'those who belong to this small class have tasted how sweet and blessed a possession philosophy is, and have also seen enough of the madness of the multitude; and they know that no politician is honest, nor is there any champion of justice at whose side they may fight and be saved. Such a one may be compared to a man who has fallen among wild beasts—he will not join in the wickedness of his fellows, but neither is he able singly to resist all their fierce natures, and so seeing that he would be of no use to the State or to his friends, and reflecting that he would have to throw away his life without doing any good either to himself or to others, he holds his peace, and goes his own way.'[2]

Plato, for his part, would not hold his peace. He worked and hoped on until the end. But some part of him had died, and the generous enthusiasms of his youth were chastened. The writer of *The Laws* is a disappointed idealist, and the disappointed idealist is almost always a cynic. As we read that sombre blue-book, which is as dull and heavy in parts as a government report, we experience a feeling of having heard these maxims, these grim counsels, before. We are in a familiar atmosphere, the atmosphere of our own time. Here is the very breviary of dictatorship, with its minute directions for mobilizing, swaying, and snooping upon public opinion; with its prisons for political offenders and those found guilty of 'irreligion' (had Plato so far forgotten the accusers of Socrates?), its reformatories and concentration camps —'to be situated in some wild and desolate region in the centre of the country'—where a superinquisition called The Nocturnal Council exercised the functions of a Security Police; and with the forcible expulsion (already suggested in *The Republic*) of the poets and artists and all

[1] Ibid., 540.
[2] Ibid., 496.

those who flourish in an atmosphere of freedom of expression.

However near to despair this supremely endowed philosopher came, he never for an instant lost sight of the end to which human life should be directed. He remained in doubt only as to the means by which this end should be attained. Perhaps he hit the nail on the head most surely in a passage which occurs towards the end of *The Laws,* where he states the problem that in later ages was to become the chief preoccupation of all men of goodwill. 'In no very long period of time,' he observed, 'an autocrat, if he wishes, can change the manners of a State; he has only to go in the direction of virtue or of vice, whichever he prefers, he himself indicating by his example the lines of conduct, praising and rewarding some actions and rebuking others, and degrading those who disobey. The quickest and easiest way for a State to change its laws is through the leadership of its masters: such changes never have and never will come to pass in any other way.' So far, so good; but, he continues, 'the real impossibility, or difficulty, is of another sort, and is rarely surmounted in the course of ages; but when once it is surmounted, every kind of blessing follows. *The difficulty is to find a divine passion for rational and just institutions.*' That indeed was the purpose of his life; and if he failed to achieve it, his failure was touched with sublimity. From Socrates he had learnt that virtue was the child of true knowledge, and for himself he arrived at the idea that true knowledge issued from communion with the Supreme Good. The crucial question was whether mankind, left to itself and in the absence of some prolonged emotional stimulus, could ever be brought to desire this supreme communion for its own sake. That same question was later tackled by the Christian philosophers with an insight that Plato could not have possessed. But those later philosophers in turn looked back to him as the most inspired of the thinkers of the old dispensation, whose doctrine of the love of Good was the nearest approach to the Christian Gospel of Love.

Aristotle

'Almost all things have been found out, but some have been forgotten.'

—Politics

1

Plato had tried to reform a king who was already in his middle years. To Aristotle was given the privilege—if indeed he counted it a privilege and not an imposition—of supervising the youthful education of one of the world's greatest conquerors, Alexander of Macedon. It is not easy for us today to realize with what esteem and awe philosophy and philosophers were regarded in the ancient world, even by powerful rulers. Later philosophers enjoyed royal favour, and some, like Descartes and Leibnitz, entered into correspondence with kings and princesses; but to no subsequent thinker was accorded an opportunity so remarkable as that which offered itself to Aristotle.

Aristotle was born in either 385 or 384 B.C. in the town of Stagira, in Macedonia. This little place is situated on the peninsula to which the name Calchis still attaches. Aristotle's father, Nicomachus, was a doctor of considerable ability, who finally rose to be chief physician at the court of Amyntas II, King of Macedonia. While in the latter's service, he wrote a number of books on medicine and natural science. Aristotle's mother, Phœstis, was a native of Calchis. By reason of his father's profession, the young boy became a member of the guild of Asclepiadæ (named after Asclepius or Æsculapius, the Greek god of medicine), since the medical profession was hereditary in that confraternity.

This early acquaintance with natural science in its most practical aspect exerted a profound effect upon

Aristotle's whole life and way of thinking. Not merely did it turn his interests in a particular direction—the direction of analysis, experiment, and classification—but it caused him finally to strike out on an original line of his own. This new departure in thought has affected all subsequent enquiry, whether scientific, philosophical, political or ethical. For the ideas and conclusions of Aristotle have entered into our common traditions of thought, so that we speak with his idiom even though we may protest ignorance of his writings.

Concerning the youth of Aristotle we possess numerous odd scraps of information and much testimony of doubtful value. Some ancient biographers write as if the contemporaries of their hero, knowing him to be destined for fame, were constantly engaged in collecting evidence of that future achievement which they can at best have dimly surmised. The historians of antiquity were liberal in their use of anecdote. Consequently there have been almost as many anecdotes preserved about Aristotle as about Plato. We do not need to dwell upon the more ephemeral of these stories, which shed little light upon his boyhood and early youth.

For our present purpose, the age at which Aristotle becomes interesting is that of seventeen. It was then that he set out for Athens, with the intention, so far as we know, of entering the Academy of Plato (368 or 367 B.C.). In days when even a short journey was an adventure, this excursion by an unknown youth to the headquarters of the best-known teacher of the day was attended by many hazards. Moreover, it was an early age at which to secure admission to so select an institution as the Academy. Aristotle must already have shown evidence of marked, even precocious, ability in order to have been permitted by his guardian Proxenus (his father being dead) to undertake the journey at all. Then there was the question as to whether he would prove an acceptable pupil. On that score there seems to have been no doubt. He was at once admitted to the company. So the future 'master of those that know' was first of all a humble seeker after knowledge, content to sit at the foot of the man whom he was later to criticize, but whose memory he never ceased to reverence.

A man of such originality might have been expected

soon to weary of discipleship, and to seek the earliest opportunity of organizing an 'opposition' school of his own. But, as it happened, Aristotle was content to enjoy the status of pupil and imitator much longer and with a greater measure of self-effacement than many a thinker of lesser stature. The majority of scholars and intellectual leaders serve an apprenticeship of three, four or five years at some seat of learning. Aristotle served as many as twenty in the Platonic Academy. Finally he left it for the only reason that might have been expected to prompt his departure, namely, the death of Plato in 347.

It happened that he had chosen an interesting and even critical time to enter the Academy. For many years now the central figure of that institution, the spirit that animated its deliberations, and indeed the character whom Plato had invariably employed as a mouthpiece for his theories, had been Socrates. To Plato and his closest associates, the memory of Socrates was still the most vivid experience of their lives, just as his method was the most revolutionary that they had yet studied. But now a generation was growing up for whom the master was not Socrates but Plato, and to whom Socrates was scarcely more than a revered name, possibly somewhat too idealized to be quite credible. Although the figure of Socrates never gave place to any other in Plato's memory, there came a time when Plato's own thought began to develop in directions that Socrates had not merely failed to explore but regarded as definitely outside the scope of philosophy. In short, a new spirit was coming over the Academy, and Aristotle's arrival more or less coincided with its emergence.

If our chronology is not at fault, Aristotle must have put in his first appearance at Athens at a time when Plato was away at the court of Dionysius II. Thus he probably did not have an opportunity of meeting the master until he had already become a well-established academician. His first teachers of Platonism were among those members, who, like himself, enjoyed the status of disciples. Although Aristotle soon succeeded in proving his ability, the activities at which he excelled were not as yet (and were not for many years to become) those of original speculation; they were those of faithful interpretation of the master's own works. Aristotle's first writings, in fact, consisted not merely of dialogues in the Platonic manner but of expositions of Plato's ideas; and these expositions were so distinguished for clarity and persuasiveness that for many centuries after his death they were studied with greater eagerness than the works of Plato himself.

It seems probable that later thinkers, such as Epicurus (340-270 B.C.) and later still Cicero (106-43 B.C.), derived their knowledge of Platonism less from the works of the master, which were regarded as exceedingly abstruse, than from the works of the pupil, which were accepted as models of precise statement. We should give a great deal to be able to read these early dialogues today; but except for a few fragments and what can be deduced from a paraphrase here and there in the works of less gifted writers, they have all been lost: a fate which, as we shall see, nearly overtook the whole body of Aristotle's writings.

The change in spirit at the Academy was, to be precise, a change to a more complex and abstract point of view. Socrates always had his feet on the ground—his bare feet; and his aim was to discover exactly where he stood and where other people stood. He distrusted airy speculations. Plato was a more complicated person, with at least three aspects to his character. There was first the fervent disciple of Socrates, who endeavoured to continue his work of careful analysis and intellectual midwifery. Secondly, there was the ardent champion of social justice, who hoped to persuade reigning potentates to fashion their states according to eternal precepts. Finally there was the pure philosopher, who, disillusioned with politics and despairing of the efforts of enthusiastic reformers (himself included), sought to lift himself by intense mental concentration to a realm of perfection utterly removed from mundane affairs.

Nor is it true to assert that these three 'stages' of Plato's thought followed one another in strict succession. At some moments the Socratic element was uppermost; at some, the reformer; at some, the soaring idealist. Towards the end of his life, the two most 'contradictory' attitudes strove one with the other for dominance. For even the most earnest and high-minded person has his moods of reaction, depression and anti-climax. Thus the

Plato who composed such abstruse and lofty dialogues as the *Theœtetus,* the *Parmenides* and the *Philebus* was also the Plato who composed, and died while completing, the sombre treatise on *The Laws.* This was an object lesson for so observant a pupil as Aristotle.

The word 'abstract' fills certain people with alarm, though the literal meaning of the term—'to draw out'—need not suggest anything obscure. If 'abstract' is taken always to mean 'vague', then abstractions are to be shunned, since philosophical thought is above all an attempt to combat vagueness. In fact, however, the process of abstraction is one with which each of us is perfectly familiar and to which we have constant recourse. Whenever we make a general statement, we are distinguishing a number of instances from the rule or principle to which they conform. At a higher level, indeed, the distinction between the 'universal' and the 'particular' is constantly present in the kind of thinking that we call, sometimes with too great a sense of awe, scientific. The scientist is engaged in detecting the operation of uniform processes or laws in the natural world, and at the same time in recording such instances as are observed to conform to these laws.

Being ever in search of evidence of the truth of his theories, the man of scientific turn of mind is usually a great 'collector'. This applies even to such an apparently abstract thinker as the psychologist, who collects 'cases' as assiduously as the geologist collects specimens. Aristotle, one of the world's first collectors, and in consequence one of the pioneers of the science of classification, differed from most of his successors not so much in his methods of enquiry as in the extraordinary breadth of his interests. Here his early association with men of science must have stood him in good stead. He imposed no limits upon his investigations save those which Nature herself imposed by having made him mortal; otherwise he would have undoubtedly pursued his researches into every field of knowledge accessible to human curiosity.

As it is, he examined nearly everything that there is to be examined, and collected nearly everything that there is to be collected. He set out to classify animals, vegetables, minerals, as well as virtues, passions, and mental faculties. He collected the names of past rulers and winners of international gymnastic contests, and he collected and classified constitutions. In spite of this passion for detailed research and enquiry, however, he never allowed his interest to become a mania. He did not collect for the sake of collection. He was above all interested in tracing the operation of a general law in nature, both physical and 'human'. This was the law whereby one thing or being turns into another thing or being—in short, the law of organic development.

Preoccupation with the idea of growth and development was not something that Aristotle learnt directly from Plato, because Plato's world was essentially a static world. Yet it is possible to say that Plato's very indifference to this aspect of nature, his obsession with ideal perfection, was indirectly responsible for Aristotle's 'shift' of interest to that which, lacking perfection, strove to attain it through trial and error, perseverance and persistence. Now the sphere of nature in which such striving is most apparent is that of living organisms. Aristotle's aim, therefore, resolved itself into the reconciliation of Plato's theory of Ideas with the facts of biological development.

This digression concerning the difference in spirit between the work of Plato and Aristotle is introduced because otherwise the period elapsing between his first arrival at the Academy and the death of Plato twenty years later remains an unintelligible blank. To understand Aristotle's development as a thinker we need to use our imaginations to fill this blank. These, as the conventional biographies say, were the 'formative years': years during which he produced, if not his masterpieces, then the material out of which his masterpieces grew. Above all, it was during this period that he came into contact with the foremost intellects of the age: men who, like himself, had journeyed from other lands and who were thus able to put him in possession of facts of which he would otherwise have been ignorant.

Such a man was Eudoxus of Cyzicus, a distinguished mathematician, who had a store of information concerning the technical achievements of the Egyptians and the peoples of Asia Minor, and who was therefore a source of precisely the 'facts' of which Aristotle was in search.

Nor must we imagine that Aristotle, as leader of the younger generation, was engaged in the kind of study of which Plato and his bosom companions disapproved. 'Fact-finding' was in the air. Plato, as we have already remarked, had himself caught the contagion. The treatise on *The Laws* is in effect a concession to the new approach to the study of the world of man. Without it, Aristotle's treatise on *Politics* would probably never have taken shape as it did.

In the year 348-347 a great crisis occurred in Aristotle's life—or, to be more exact, a double crisis. First of all, Plato died. Almost at the same time, and more unexpectedly, a disaster overtook Aristotle's home town in Macedonia. During an attack upon the flourishing cities of the Chalcidic peninsula, Philip of Macedon gave orders for the complete destruction of Stagira, the philosopher's birthplace. Aristotle thus found himself suddenly isolated in both a spiritual and a physical sense. Although he had left Stagira as a youth with a feeling of exultation at escaping from a provincial atmosphere, he did not realize his affection for his birthplace until he was made aware that he could never find it as he had left it.

The young man who ventures into the world always has in mind to return, in the hour of success, to the place from which he set out unknown and underestimated; he even secretly entertains the hope that conditions will still be much as he left them, so that the contrast between his own achievement and that of his fellows will be the more pronounced. This ruthless act of Philip, with whose family Aristotle was later to become associated, affected him deeply for many years: until, by a turn of the wheel of fortune, he finally obtained restitution at the hands of the perpetrator himself.

The death of Plato plunged Aristotle into a mood similar to that which had overcome Plato himself at the death of Socrates: the difference being that while Socrates had been condemned as a dangerous criminal, Plato died full of years and honours. Nevertheless, the effect upon the most promising disciple was in each case the same. Plato left Athens, bound he hardly knew whither. Aristotle did likewise. His strongest tie with the centre of Greek learning had been snapped. Now an independent, free-lance philosopher, his precipitate departure marks a break not only with his mode of life but also with his mode of thought. Henceforth he was to become an original exponent of philosophy, critical of the work of his contemporaries and even of Plato himself.

If Aristotle was Plato's most famous pupil, why, it may be asked, did he promptly desert the Academy when the master died? Some historians have suggested that the two philosophers had already become estranged. There is little evidence to support this view. It is contradicted at least by the beautiful elegy written by Aristotle at this time, the occasion of which was the death of a great and honoured friend whose identity, seeing that Aristotle was not easily roused to poetic composition, can hardly be other than Plato himself.

Throughout Aristotle's later writings, the references to Plato, however critical, are marked by a special tone of veneration. Far from Plato's presence at the Academy becoming increasingly intolerable to Aristotle, it was probably the only thing that kept him there. For he was not always on such good terms with his fellow-disciples. One of the chief reasons for Aristotle's departure was doubtless the appointment of his chief rival, Speusippus, as head of the Academy: a position which, if Aristotle did not exactly covet, he would have derived some pleasure from being able to refuse. In the circumstances, however, the appointment of Speusippus was understandable, because his succession kept the Academy in Plato's family. Aristotle was an outsider.

Whatever the reasons for his departure, Aristotle, accompanied by his colleague Xenocrates of Chalcedon, set out in 347 B.C. on a journey to Assos, the Æolian town situated on the Troad. The choice of this locality as a place in which to settle was not made by accident. Two ex-members of Plato's Academy were already stationed there: Erastus and Coriscus from the town of Scepsis on Ida, of which we shall presently hear more. During the latter part of his life, Plato had devoted much energy to the founding of small colonies of scholars, or little Academies; and of these the community which had been started at Assos was one of the most flourishing. Moreover, it owed its continued prosperity as much to the patronage of the local tyrant[1] as to Plato's own encouragement.

This tyrant, Hermias by name, had been persuaded by Plato to study philosophy, geometry and dialectic, and had even introduced a measure of constitutional reform into his domain as a result of his 'conversion' to philosophy. It must be admitted that Plato was a great deal more successful with him than he had been with the younger Dionysius. Hermias was so thoroughly in earnest, indeed, that he virtually presented Assos to the group of philosophers who had assembled there; and it is interesting to read the letter addressed by Plato to Hermias and his protégés, in which he urges them, almost in the language of a biblical epistle, to co-operate in the great work of reforming mankind according to the principles of justice. This combined effort to unite thought and action was on a relatively small scale, as efforts of this kind are doomed to be. But events were to demonstrate in the most striking fashion that there was nothing artificial or unreal about it.

To Assos came the young philosopher Theophrastus, the 'Divine Speaker' a name supposed to have been conferred upon him by Aristotle himself), from Eresus in Lesbos. Theophrastus, once a disciple of Plato, was not merely one of Aristotle's most brilliant pupils but the faithful friend to whom the Aristotelian manuscripts were bequeathed in the master's will. This bequest was to exert an influence upon the history of philosophy that no one at the time could have foreseen.

Aristotle's relations with his patron were so friendly that the tyrant finally gave the philosopher his niece and adopted daughter Pythias in marriage. We know very little of Aristotle's married life, which suggests that on the whole it went smoothly. Pythias bore him a daughter to whom the parents gave her mother's name, and of whom we later hear in Aristotle's will. In endeavouring to make the philosopher's life appear somewhat more romantic than it really was—never did so extraordinary a man live so comparatively ordinary a private life—later writers spun tales out of their own imaginations about a dramatic elopement and flight from Assos. From recently

[1] In Greek history a tyrant usually means an absolute ruler or dictator who owed his position to usurpation.

discovered records, however, we gather that the alliance was concluded in the most orthodox manner, and that Hermias not merely approved but himself suggested it.

Sentimental historians actually diminish the romantic aspect of the marriage by making it out to have been an affair of secrecy and intrigue; for the romantic aspect of it surely was that a proud, if high-minded, ruler should have counted it an honour to link himself by marriage with a mere teacher of philosophy. Little did Hermias know that future ages would learn of his name solely as a result of this happy association, without which he would have remained undistinguished among a hundred other minor potentates.

Three happy years passed by, and then Aristotle undertook a journey to Mytilene in Lesbos, probably at the suggestion and invitation of Theophrastus, whose home country it was. Again, as always when Aristotle (or Plato) made a journey, rumours have later grown up about quarrels and estrangements. But whoever Aristotle may have quarrelled with, it was certainly not with his father-in-law Hermias, if the latter's subsequent conduct is any guide. The removal was merely to a neighbouring island; and it is probable that Aristotle went there in pursuit of one of his favourite hobbies, namely, collecting. Scholars have pointed out that his researches into marine biology, always thorough and accurate, are particularly illuminating in connection with the marine flora of the Æolic coast and its islands: so that if he did not go there with the express intention of exploring this aspect of nature, at least he appears to have occupied much of his spare time in such investigation.

In 343-342, however, an important and highly confidential message reached him which abruptly put an end to his stay in Lesbos, bringing him once more into the limelight and affording him opportunities such as few men of his calling have enjoyed.

The message in question was from no less a person than King Philip of Macedon, the ruler whose high-handed action at Stagira had caused Aristotle such grief. Philip had a son, Alexander, then thirteen years of age, of whom much was expected and to whom Philip, not himself an intellectual man, had resolved to give the best possible education. To whom, then, should he turn for help and advice but to Aristotle, already renowned throughout the Greek world for his skill as an instructor? Aristotle, after some thought, decided to accept the invitation. And so during four out of the seven years that he was to spend in Macedon, he was in charge of the studies of one of the most remarkable men in history.

Not long after his departure from Assos, an event occurred which caused Aristotle great anguish of mind. It concerned his old patron and friend, Hermias. Philip had for some time been preparing hostilities against Persia; and it seems highly probable that between him and Hermias there existed a secret treaty or understanding, since a tyrant of such limited authority as the latter was compelled by circumstances to seek support from one of the great powers. Suspecting that Hermias was in the opposite camp, the Persian general Mentor resolved to crush him before he had time to become more powerful. His forces surrounded those of Hermias at Atarneus; and there, on pretence of inviting Hermias to a parley, he treacherously kidnapped him. Renowned for neither magnanimity nor mercy, the Persians treated Hermias in the most vile manner. In order to extract from him the details of his supposed alliance with Philip, they put him to the torture, and finally, unable to make him talk, crucified him.

Before the end, the Persian King ordained that he should be asked to state his last wish. Hermias's answer caused mild astonishment. 'Tell my friends and companions,' he declared, 'that I have done nothing weak or unworthy of philosophy.' If this report is authentic—and our knowledge of Hermias's character suggests that it may well be—it reveals the extraordinary influence exerted by the members of the Academy and above all by Aristotle over men of different, and often opposite, temperament.

Hermias, for example, was a man of low birth and little education. In his youth he worked in a bank, probably as a money-changer. He had made his way in the world by sheer force of character. But he possessed qualities of moral greatness which his association with Aristotle brought out and developed in the most remarkable manner. He had little to lose by disclosing his alliance with Persia's enemy save the respect of the man to whom he owed the alteration in his outlook on life. Such high-mindedness was not commonly to be found among the rulers of antiquity; and many a nominally Christian monarch met the trials of his faith with less dignity. Aristotle was deeply moved.

At Delphi today there stands a cenotaph to Hermias, for which Aristotle wrote a dedicatory epigram. There is also extant a hymn to the ruler's memory which the philosopher composed at this time. To indulge one's emotions in the safety of a powerful court may be all very well; but we must not forget that Aristotle's vindication of Hermias was itself an act of moral courage, for the Greek nationalists, especially those at Athens who followed the orator Demosthenes, were violently opposed to Philip and his grandiose imperial schemes, and were therefore not disposed to think well of one suspected to be in sympathy with them.

The story of Aristotle's first arrival at the court of King Philip at Pella was until recently the source of much dispute among historians. A number of writers of antiquity suggest that Aristotle left Assos after Hermias's capture by Mentor and as a direct consequence of it. This would lend color to the idea that he ran away with Pythias, the tyrant's daughter. But we now have good grounds for thinking that he left Assos while Hermias was still living. Whether the 'alliance' between Hermias and Philip had anything to do with Aristotle's journey is of course a matter of conjecture. Possibly it had. It has also been pointed out that Aristotle, though already famous as a leader of thought, had family connections with the Macedonian court through his father; but this does not seem to have had much to do with his appointment. What we need to realize is that the Academy and those bodies associated with it had come in time to be world-famous institutions, like the old oracles. For the ancient world was a small world, and institutions of this kind have no exact parallel today; but that is not so much because the world has expanded as because wisdom has shrunk.

Although Aristotle had complete charge of Alexander during the latter's most impressionable years, it is easy to exaggerate the influence of master over pupil. Admittedly, with such a master and with such a pupil, a partnership unique in history might have been formed. There is no other record, perhaps, of a great man ever having been associated in this manner with a man equally great in a different sphere. How strange, therefore, that throughout Aristotle's writings there is a complete absence of enthusiasm for conquering kings of the type that his pupil ultimately became! If we are to judge from the scant attention he gives to them in his works, Aristotle might never have taken the smallest interest in the imperial developments occurring in his day. It is not that he was uninterested in political questions; he was passionately interested in them. Whereas his famous treatise on *Politics* is concerned with the structure of the Greek City State, however, he was living in an age in which much larger units of political allegiance were coming into being. These he mostly ignored; and when he did not ignore them, he disapproved.

To suggest that Aristotle exerted no particular influence upon the character of Alexander, however, would be untrue. Among the great conquerors of the ancient world, Alexander alone is distinguished for a breadth of character, a sense of high purpose, which seems to have been derived from the kind of philosophical training the Academy sought to instil. Like Hermias, but with greater opportunities, he tried to mould his conduct according to an ideal; and even if he were no more than a highly successful general, it was as the New Achilles—an up-to-date version of one of the great heroes of antiquity—that he saw himself. A man must be judged not merely by what he is but by the standard that he sets himself. Alexander may have been as much a 'scourge' to the countries he overran as Attila or Tamburlaine; but he believed himself to be the bearer of civilization and enlightenment.

The royal pupil never became his master's close friend or even confidant; but, except for one phase of their relationship of which we shall speak, they seem to have remained on excellent terms. Even when Alexander was engaged in the most gigantic of his military operations in the East, with princes bowing down to him and wealth and fame accumulating beyond his highest expectations, he did not forget the man who had tried to instruct him in logic and the nature of virtue.

Among other tokens of his respect and affection—tokens not perhaps untinged with irony—he gave instructions that Aristotle should receive all the interesting geological specimens collected on the various campaigns. There is no doubt, too, that Aristotle's astonishing researches into animal life would not have been possible without the discoveries made by Alexander's men, and the reports and specimens which, on Alexander's instructions, they sent home for study and classification.

As for Philip, he showed his gratitude to Aristotle in even more tangible ways. He caused to be built a delightful gymnasium, called the Nymphæum, in a quiet grove on the royal estates, where Aristotle could indulge in his reflections and investigations in peace, and where he could receive his young pupils (for we gather that, besides Alexander, several young noblemen had the honour to receive instruction from him during his sojourn in Pella). Of all Philip's acts of kindness, however, that which gave Aristotle the keenest pleasure and satisfaction was the rebuilding, under royal supervision, of the little town of Stagira. For thus was removed the one blot upon their friendship. It is almost a perfect act of justice for a man to be able to recompense another in the way that, being appropriate to his talents, best satisfies himself at the same time.

In 336 B.C., an act of violence put an end to their association. While walking in procession to celebrate the marriage of his daughter, Philip was fatally stabbed by a young man called Pausanias, who is thought to have borne him a private grudge. The King, then no more than forty-seven years old, died in the twenty-fourth year of his reign. He was succeeded by Alexander, and this put an end to the latter's period of tutelage. As for Aristotle, he remained in Macedonia for about a year, and then, feeling the urge to be on his travels again, packed up and returned to Athens.

After thirteen years' absence, he found a very different city and a very different intellectual atmosphere in the Academy. He returned with a great reputation, perhaps the greatest philosophical reputation of the time, certainly the greatest since Plato. But, as before, he was still to some extent the stranger, and it was not to be expected that he should be received by his colleagues of the Academy as a long-lost brother. Possibly, assuming that his leadership in philosophical matters would be openly acknowledged, he believed that he would step into the President's place without more ado. For it happened that Speusippus had just died, and the choice of a successor was due to be made from among those thought most capable of maintaining the Platonic tradition. As it turned out, the Presidency went not to Aristotle but to his old friend and companion, Xenocrates of Chalcedon; and Aristotle may well have experienced the sensation of finding it even more difficult to surrender a coveted office to a friend than to an enemy.

Whatever may have been his intimate feelings in the matter, the choice of another to do what he would have done equally well, if to the sacrifice of the leisure that he needed, no doubt proved a blessing in disguise. He resolved to devote himself henceforth to scientific pursuits. He could not wholly abandon teaching; for the itch to instruct, to enlighten, to arouse curiosity in others, was no less compelling than to indulge his own curiosity by research. But he found, as he grew older, that a teacher must adopt towards his pupils an attitude of increasing discrimination. On the one hand, there is a small circle that he can take into his confidence and treat as equals and friends. On the other hand, there is a much wider circle of disciples to whom he can communicate merely the superficial elements of his doctrines, without obtaining more than formal adherence. With the first group, the teacher is distinguished from the pupils merely by being the first among them; with the second, he remains the aloof leader while the rest follow—at some distance. Being engaged henceforth in research of the most specialized kind, Aristotle found himself under the necessity of giving two quite distinct series of lectures: one to his intimate disciples and the other to what we should today call the 'general public'. Hence arose the distinction between the 'esoteric' doctrines of Aristotle and the 'exoteric', the abstruse and the simple: which is not quite the same as the modern distinction between 'highbrow' and 'lowbrow'.

Although he never appears to have cut himself off from the Academy, Aristotle soon felt the need to set up an institution of his own. Near the beautiful temple of Apollo Lyceius in one of the north-east quarters of Athens stood a gymnasium, called appropriately the Lyceum, in which Aristotle proceeded to set up a kind of rival Academy. Needless to say, he soon attracted a group of enthusiastic followers, some of whom were apparently ex-members of the Platonic school.

We know something of the activities of the Lyceum. In the mornings, Aristotle used to lecture to a small gathering of his friends on such subjects as metaphysics. In the afternoons he concerned himself with the exposition of the simpler subjects, such as rhetoric and dialectic. It is traditionally held that he conversed with his friends walking up and down under the covered portico or *peripatos* of the gymnasium. Hence the name of 'peripatetic' was later given to the school that Aristotle founded.

Although he prospered and wielded considerable influence in Athens, Aristotle was not so secure in the esteem of his fellows as to be able to live without a patron, especially as Demosthenes and the Athenian nationalists were still hostile to one of his sympathies and past associations. The man who befriended him and who later became his executor was Alexander's own Commander-in-Chief and Regent in Macedonia and Greece, Antipater. With such a patron, Aristotle had nothing to fear. But naturally Antipater's power depended upon that of Alexander, and the day came when the Regent found himself deprived of authority; and that was an evil moment for Aristotle.

For many rich and productive years, however, Aristotle worked, experimented, collected, and taught; and the substance of what he taught is still preserved in the numerous treatises that bear his name. These treatises, such as they are, were not written for posterity. They represent in most cases the notes of lectures delivered to a particular audience at a particular time. We have referred to Plato's attempt at reproducing in prose an essentially spoken or argued (dialectical) philosophy; Aristotle, intent upon teaching, left nothing so sustained and perfect as Plato's dialogues. But what he has left us are his own, not other people's notes; and here and there we come upon passages of such transcendent clarity and beauty that we are able to form some notion of the literary skill at his command, and of which his 'lost' dialogues evidently provided striking examples. No thinker remained throughout his career so indifferent to posterity, and yet no thinker came to exert such tremendous influence upon it. Or perhaps we should say that no thinker was more anxious that philosophical thought should prosper, and less concerned with his own reputation as its purveyor.

Absorbed in the work that he relished, Aristotle continued to regard the spectacular achievements of Alexander with ironic detachment. To certain aspects of the conqueror's policy, notably that which sought to break down the distinction between Greek and Barbarian, he was definitely opposed, though he admired the attempt to establish Greek colonies in Asia and Egypt, and even wrote a book on the subject (the treatise *On Colonization*, subtitled *Alexander*). In 327, however, the relation between him and his old pupil became suddenly strained. A nephew of Aristotle, Callisthenes, had for some time been a member of Alexander's suite, with the office of recorder or historian of the conqueror's campaigns. He apparently performed this task very capably in a number of books that have since perished; but although he went out of his way to eulogize his master and to attack the old Macedonian conservatives at home who disapproved of the young King's foreign exploits, he seems to have been by nature rash and outspoken. He made no attempt, for instance, to conceal his scorn at Alexander's adoption of certain oriental customs, particularly that which required excessive adoration of the King's person; and this critical attitude finally brought him under suspicion.

When a plot to assassinate the King was later uncovered, he was immediately held responsible, though the true culprit turned out to be a page called Hermolaus. Alexander's execution of Callisthenes could not fail to anger Aristotle, since there had been little attempt to establish the victim's guilt. As it was suspected that Aristotle himself shared the opinion of Callisthenes regarding Alexander's conversion to oriental ways (which resulted in eighty of his generals being ordered at Susa to marry Asiatic wives, an example promptly followed by at least 10,000 of his Macedonian troops), the rumour circulated after the King's death in 323 that Aristotle had been concerned in a plot to poison him. No greater slander could have been circulated. Apart from the absurdity of attributing such base conduct to Aristotle, the death of Alexander was the last thing that, out of pure self-interest, he could have welcomed. It rendered his position extremely precarious. Indeed, it very nearly brought about his undoing.

No sooner had the news arrived that Alexander was dead than the Nationalist party at Athens, ever biding its time, rose up in rebellion. If Antipater had still been at Athens, Aristotle's prospects might have been a good deal brighter; but Antipater, having likewise incurred the displeasure of Alexander, was busy campaigning himself back to favour in Asia Minor. Knowing with what hatred the Nationalists regarded him, and what murderous passions the oratory of Demosthenes could on occasion arouse, Aristotle planned to make his escape from Athens. His flight was hurried, but not altogether undignified. He was as little concerned for his personal safety as Socrates; but, calling to mind the circumstances of Socrates's death, he decided that no good purpose could be served by his remaining in Athens, if the price of staying was the silence and censorship offered to his predecessor as an alternative to the hemlock. For he had a shrewd suspicion of what was coming.

In spite of rumours that had been deliberately put about, no evidence could be produced to show that Aristotle had engaged in political intrigues. He was a friend of Macedon, and that was enough to damn him in the eyes of the new rulers at Athens. As no particular crime could be attributed to him, the authorities resorted to vague and mischievous generalities. The ludicrous but familiar charge of 'impiety' was preferred against him by a demagogue called Eurymedon, who seems to have been as anxious to repeat the rôle of Anytus as he was confident of avoiding the latter's fate. The charge stung Aristotle to the quick. For this was more than a personal accusation; it was an attack upon his professional integrity. And, as he remarked at the time, '*he could not permit Athens to sin twice against philosophy*'.

He decided to retire to Chalcis in Eubœa, where he had inherited some property from his mother. His wife, Pythias, had died some years before, and he had since taken a slave-girl, Herpyllis, to live with him: a union which appears to have been as happy as that which preceded it, and which resulted in a son, Nicomachus. The daughter of his first marriage, Pythias, was still a young girl, but Aristotle had bequeathed her hand to Nicanor, the son of his foster-parents, and now his adopted child. From the will he composed about this time, we learn a great deal, not merely about Aristotle's character, but about the circumstances in which he was placed during the last period of his life. He cites Antipater as his executor, and gives instructions as to how he shall be buried ('with Pythias') and how his children shall be educated. There is an interesting passage relating to the second wife, Herpyllis:

'The executors and Nicanor, in memory of me and of the steady affection which Herpyllis has borne towards me, shall take care of her in every other respect and, if she desires to be married, shall see that she be given to one not unworthy; and besides what she has already received, they shall give her a talent of silver out of the estate and three hand-maidens whomsoever she shall choose besides the maid she has at present and the man-servant Pyrrhaeus; and if she chooses to remain at Calchis, the lodge by the garden; if in Stagira, my father's house, with such furniture as they think proper and as Herpyllis herself may approve.' As to his servants, he directs that 'none who waited upon me shall be sold but they shall continue to be employed; and when they arrive at the proper age they shall have their freedom if they desire it'. Finally, as we have seen, he left all his manuscripts to Theophrastus.

Just as the Academy became a kind of sacred shrine after the death of its founder, so the Lyceum inevitably became identified with Aristotle. And we may judge in what high honour his memory was held by the fact that the very ground on which he taught was later bequeathed, by a special legal concession, to Theophrastus, though the latter, being a foreigner or 'metic', was not strictly entitled to hold property in Attica. This bequest was made to Theophrastus by his pupil Demetrius of Phalerum; and it is reasonable to suppose that his intention was to ensure that the man who had 'inherited' Aristotle's ideas should also inherit the place associated with their germination. The property consisted of a garden and several buildings: there was a library, a room full of specimens of all kinds, with maps laid out on boards, and a museum in which stood a statue of Aristotle, forming a kind of sanctuary. It had been the custom to hold monthly meetings at the Lyceum, at which there would be philosophical discussions followed (and sometimes accompanied) by eating and drinking. Some of these parties appear to have been very elaborate and convivial, and we possess details of regulations drawn up to ensure that a high standard of philosophical as well as gastronomic decorum was maintained.

Although none of the Lyceum gatherings have been immortalized like that which Plato describes in his *Symposium,* we know that they were both select and successful. A later President, Strato, took care to list among the properties of that institution the linen, crockery, and drinking-cups used on festive occasions. The custom may often have led to abuse. Under Strato's successor Lycon, for instance, some of the poorer students made complaints that while they could afford the instruction, they could not always afford the junketing that went with it.

To turn from the cold, impersonal and objective style of the great treatises on Metaphysics, Ethics and Logic to Aristotle's practical and yet almost tender testament is to catch a glimpse of the generous personality of the man himself. No doubt he realized that he had but a short time to enjoy his 'hermit life', as he described it. A disease of the stomach from which he had suffered intermittently took a serious turn within a few months of his arrival in Calchis; and after a day or two's illness he was dead. He had reached his sixty-third year and was at the height of his mental powers; and who can guess upon what further works he would have embarked had worry and misfortune not accelerated his end? That he died at peace with the world—especially the little world of his family—we know; but his last months must have been clouded by certain slights which his enemies, now openly hostile, chose to level at him.

In particular, he must have been hurt by the act of the Delphians in cancelling the honours bestowed upon him as a result of his compilation of the list of Pythian warriors; but he bore the insult bravely, and there was a touch

of irony in his remark in a letter to Antipater: 'About
the voting at Delphi and the depriving me of my honours,
my feeling is that I am sorry, but not unduly so.' Delphi
was a revered name in philosophy, and the double sin
from which Aristotle had preserved Athens had now
been committed by the people whose oracle had hailed
Socrates as the 'wisest of men'. Fifteen hundred years
later, Dante in his great poem bestowed upon Aristotle a
title of almost equal majesty—*Il maestro di color che
sanno,* 'The master of those who know'. And that is how
the world has since regarded him.

2

None of the adventures that befell Aristotle equalled
those that befell his manuscripts after his death. When
Theophrastus, their first custodian, died in 287 B.C., he
left all his private papers to a relation and pupil, Neleus
of Scepsis. The collection included not merely the works
of Aristotle and Theophrastus themselves but the extensive libraries of these two writers. Neleus took good care
of his valuable property; and when he finally decided to
sell the books to King Ptolemy II of Egypt, as an addition
to the great library at Alexandria, he retained for himself
the original MSS., which were his special heirlooms.
These were passed on to his own heirs, who were subjects of a king of Pergamus.

Now this monarch's ambition was to build a library
surpassing in size that at Alexandria; and in order to
preserve the manuscripts from seizure by the bibliophile
king's special agents, Neleus's family hid them in a cellar.
Whether because they were too well concealed or because the owners lacked interest in their contents, they
remained thus entombed for the next two centuries, the
only attention paid them being that of the worms with
which the damp vaults were infested. Here they might
easily have perished altogether but for the zeal of
an Athenian philosopher and book-collector, Apellicon
of Teos, who, in the century before Christ, made a special search for the original works of Aristotle.

Having finally discovered where the manuscripts were
located, he entered into negotiations with the owners for
their purchase, and is said to have acquired them very

cheaply. With a view to producing a standard edition of
Aristotle's works he thereupon started to edit them himself. But the adventures of the manuscripts were not yet
over. When the Roman general, Sulla, captured Athens
in 84 B.C., he appropriated Apellicon's famous library
and took it *en bloc* to Rome. Here, in the new centre
of culture, another keen student of Philosophy, Andronicus of Rhodes, published an entirely new edition
of both Aristotle and Theophrastus, putting the manuscripts into the order in which they are now assembled.
Both Andronicus and the remarkable scholar, Alexander
of Aphrodisias, wrote detailed commentaries upon the
works of Aristotle, but those of the former have been
lost.

As for the Lyceum, its life fell far short of that of the
Academy; but it survived until the reign of the Roman
Emperor Marcus Aurelius (A.D. 121-180). Up to this
time and indeed for many centuries after, Aristotle,
though studied with attention, was regarded simply as
the most distinguished of the disciples of Plato. Not until his writings had penetrated the oriental world and
their influence had been reflected back to the West, did
he become a master-philosopher in his own right. But of
the history of his reputation we shall speak in due course.

Aristotle's numerous writings fall roughly into four
sections: (1) Works on Logic and Dialectics; (2) Theoretical Philosophy (*i.e.* Metaphysics, Mathematics and
Physics); (3) Practical Philosophy or Politics; and (4)
Writings on Art or Æsthetics. For reasons already
given, many of these treatises make difficult reading:
without a commentary, the ordinary student is bound to
find himself bewildered and befogged, not merely by the
terminology but by the extreme concentration of the argument. There are few purple passages in Aristotle; and
so he has never been able to command the degree of affection that Plato, with his superb gift of style, has inspired. Nevertheless, Aristotle has his moments; and
there are phrases, and often single terms, that have become part and parcel of our everyday vocabulary.

We have seen how Aristotle, after spending years as
a devoted disciple of Plato, broke away from the Academy
and gradually evolved a new philosophical method. People break away from the society in which they have

lived not merely because of some material compulsion but because they have come to think differently. Aristotle had come to think differently. And the subject upon which his thoughts had undergone change was nothing less than the cornerstone of Plato's philosophical edifice: namely, the theory of Ideas or Forms.

In defining the nature of the Ideas, Plato sought to emphasize their supremacy over everything else— *i.e.* their 'transcendent' character: Plato exalted the Ideal so far above the Actual that the latter, almost losing its reality, became a twilight sphere of imprecision. Aristotle, more of a realist by temperament, found this lofty idealism unsatisfactory. He wanted to demonstrate that there was reality on earth as well as in heaven. Furthermore, he wanted to prove that reality inhered in *particular* things, and that by examining such things the universal Ideas could best be apprehended. He believed he had discovered a technique or instrument by which these Universals could be elucidated, without dragging in a mystical sense or intuition such as Plato deemed necessary. This instrument was Logic. Logic, Aristotle sought to show, applied to everything. This, then, was the universal 'key' to truth which Plato had sought, and towards which his famous Dialectic was merely a groping.

Although Aristotle was disposed to accept Plato's theory that the nature of each particular thing depended upon its Form, his realism forbade him to maintain that the Form exerted its creative influence from outside— *i.e.* from some supernatural region accessible only to the purified soul of the philosopher. It was not, he held, a heavenly model which the material object sought, more or less successfully, to copy; it was already there, at work in the object, and by its influence serving to preserve that object as a unity. As Aristotle pointed out, we have no means of perceiving the Form of a statue—that by virtue of which it is a statue, and that by virtue of which it is *this* statue and not another—except by contemplating the finished work. The more 'finished' the work of art, the more completely does it succeed in embodying its Form. We must concentrate on the whole thing, the completed object, the fruition.

The effort manifested by each natural object to embody more completely the Form which determines it, is the cause of the pervading *movement* in nature. The early Greek philosophers, from Parmenides onwards, had been puzzled and often baffled by the problem of change. In our sketch of the philosophy of Socrates, we have mentioned some of the attempts made by his predecessors to explain this phenomenon. Aristotle explained it by the impulsion within each object to pass from one Form to another, by organic stages, until a phase of maturity or wholeness had been attained, after which a process of disintegration set in and the determining Form 'lost its hold'. This so-called determining Form is described by Aristotle as the Final Cause of the object, since it is the end to which the whole process is directed. The various stages preceding maturity are those in which the object is *potentially* that which it is striving to be, as a bud is potentially a leaf and a youth potentially a man.

We can understand each particular stage, therefore, only by perceiving that it is engaged in turning into something else, which realizes more of its potentialities. The end explains the beginning and all that lies in between, and the beginning already hints at the end. A 'promising' child is one of whom we expect great things, or who manifests earlier than his fellows the qualities we expect to find in a fully developed adult. Thus Aristotle arrived at a view of Matter which makes of it something different from just 'stuff', in the common sense of that word. Matter is never wholly formless, because that which is wholly formless cannot exist at all; and we know that Matter exists. Matter is therefore the unformed, or rather the half-formed. Pure Form, at the other extreme, is something immaterial; and Aristotle has a name for this perfect and supreme manifestation of Form. He calls it God.

Aristotle's theory of Form is not at all difficult to grasp once we realize the problem which he has set out to tackle. No philosophical theory—indeed no theory of any kind—can be grasped unless we understand that it represents the answer to a question or a series of questions. A philosopher, especially if he leaves us merely the notes of his conversation or lectures, does not always state explicitly what questions he is proposing to discuss: usually because he takes it for granted that his audience, having assembled to hear him, shares in some measure his interests, and therefore knows what questions he is likely to raise.

Aristotle's problem—his chief problem, that is to say —amounted to this. Here is a world of change, flux, and imperfection: a world to which part of us at least belongs, in so far as part of us (our physical make-up) is subject to the change, flux, and imperfection that we observe in nature. But there is another part of us, differently constituted, which possesses the capacity to make clear to us our shortcomings, and even enables us to prescribe remedies for them. This part of us we call our mind or spirit. Whereas our bodies belong to the natural world, derive their sustenance from it, and eventually perish in the manner of all natural things, our minds do not appear to be at home in this shifting unstable environment, even though they may be involved with it. On the contrary, they derive their nutriment from another and higher order of Being, which is subject to none of the deficiencies of the natural order. Plato had defined this higher world of Being as the realm of Forms; and with certain modifications Aristotle had accepted this definition. One modification, as we have seen, was that he regarded the Forms as *immanent* in nature rather than *transcendent*; another modification was that he held an entirely different conception of the nature of God.

It is a common belief that before the advent of the prophets of Israel, no one believed in the existence of God. This is a serious error. The difference between the pre-Christian and the Christian belief in God was not merely a difference concerning the divine nature; it was a difference concerning the relation between the divine nature and the world of man. A study of the history of religious thought reveals the interesting fact, not always sufficiently understood today, that the kind of God you believe in determines the kind of world you believe in. The early Greek philosophers held that the world in which they lived was a certain kind of world because they believed it to stand in a certain relation to the supreme Spirit, or God. The Christians, in their turn, held that the world in which they lived was a certain kind of world because they believed it to stand in a totally different relation. The transition between the early Greek view and the Christian view is best seen in Plato and

Aristotle; and that is the reason why certain Christian theologians agreed to admit Plato and Aristotle to the company of 'honorary' Christians.

According to Plato, God created the world on the model of the eternal Forms. The Platonic God is therefore a kind of Demi-urge, for whom the Forms represent the general principles upon which the work of creation is based. According to Aristotle, God's rôle is altogether different. He is not in reality a creator at all. He is rather the cause of all the movement in the world, while Himself remaining immobile and self-absorbed. In other words, He is the supreme Final Cause towards which the whole of nature is drawn; but He remains indifferent to this ceaseless striving on the part of nature, because He is engaged in an eternal self-communion.

Who, then, created the world, and how did it come into being? The answer, according to Aristotle, is that the world, by seeking to imitate God, is occupied in creating itself. There was no beginning to this process and there will be no end, though it is just possible (Aristotle suggested) that there may be a regular cycle of changes dependent upon the movement of the stars in their courses.

This aloof, metaphysical God was postulated by Aristotle for logical rather than for religious reasons. In order to account for the change and development in the world, there must first be something static, changeless and eternal: in short, there must be an Unmoved Mover presiding over everything else in lonely majesty. Such a God is not a being to be worshipped: He is a B°ing to be descried. He is not the object of the adoration of the devout: He is the object of the respect of metaphysicians. Meanwhile, the purpose of science is not to speculate upon the nature and characteristics of God, for these it can never know; the purpose of science is to study the developing world of nature. Aristotle's Unmoved Mover is therefore unmoved in two senses: He is unmoved by any other force in the universe, because there is no force in the universe equal to His own, and He is equally unmoved by the efforts and yearnings of the world in which He excites such commotion.

That such a view of God should have been seriously entertained may seem strange to us; but this is due largely to the spiritual insight of an obscure Semitic tribe which claimed to worship a God of righteousness and justice—a 'jealous' but not a self-absorbed God—and which looked for the coming of a Messiah who should demonstrate God's essential concern for the world He created. The Christian revolution infused the cold metaphysics of the ancient world with warmth and life; it clothed the Supreme Being of Aristotle with flesh and blood by what is correctly called the Incarnation. But even so it did not sweep the philosophy of Aristotle away. When the doctors of the Christian Church undertook to construct a complete and systematic philosophy of existence (a task not attempted on a grand scale until the thirteenth century), they found in the newly-recovered works of Aristotle a wealth of material upon which they drew heavily, and which they pronounced to be the greatest achievement hitherto of human reason unaided by divine inspiration.

Like Plato, Aristotle maintained that the highest object of our intellects is the contemplation of eternal truth; but he shared none of Plato's indifference to temporal matters. On the contrary, he bids us seek for truth in what lies around and about us, considering it no lapse from dignity on the philosopher's part to spend much of his time collecting and dissecting specimens, collating manuscripts, and rummaging among old archives and records. Socrates questioned men; Aristotle went on to question things. He questioned in all directions, being the first great thinker to seek for an underlying connection between the various spheres of enquiry in which he interested himself. In short, he was the first modern scientist.

It requires an imaginative effort on our part, almost a mental somersault, to realize that the early thinkers of the Western world did not take for granted the fact that the world they lived in was essentially 'one world'. If we believed in the existence of a multitude of gods—some more powerful than others and each occupying a special niche in a divine hierarchy—we should naturally tend to think of reality as being composed of a number of separate domains, access to which would depend upon our being content to wait upon the good pleasure of the presiding deity. Successful living, in other words, would depend upon our possessing not so much the master-key to reality as a number of different keys to a number of different locks. For in practical life, as we know, it is the minor officials that have to be encountered, the local powers-that-be that must be placated.

The writer, D. H. Lawrence, who often grasped the essence of a philosophy better than some of his academic contemporaries, stated in his own way the early Greek attitude in his book, *Apocalypse*: 'Today it is almost impossible for us to realize what the old Greeks meant by God, or Theos. Everything was Theos; but even so, not at the same moment. At the moment, whatever struck you was God. If it was a pool of water, the very watery pool might strike you. Then that was God. Or a faint vapour at evening rising might catch the imagination: then that was Theos. Or a thirst might overcome you at the sight of water; then the thirst itself was a God. . . . Even to the early scientists or philosophers, "the cold", "the moist", "the hot", "the dry", were things in themselves, realities, gods, theoi. And they *did* things.'

The belief or trust in minor deities or powers (modern writers talk of 'forces' in scarcely less anthropomorphic language) has never wholly died, though it has been driven underground, often into the subconscious; but the monotheism of Christianity has so shaped the minds of Western man that the idea of a 'pluralistic' universe, though frequently resuscitated, has never returned to favour. Nor can we imagine it doing so. Aristotle is half-way between the early Ionian thinkers and the Christian Fathers.

Although he personally practised the contemplative life that he enjoined upon other philosophers, Aristotle recognized that for the majority of men the intellectual vocation imposed too great a strain; besides which the ordinary man has a definite job to do. There are others, the slaves, who are by nature incapable of anything but manual labour. Plato, appalled by the frivolity and baseness of mankind, wished to guarantee freedom for the devotees of the spirit by subjecting the masses to iron discipline. He is not alone among the idealists of history who have ended by condoning a régime of censorship and compulsion, of the knout and the firing-squad.

Less exacting in his demands upon the run of men,

Aristotle preaches an ethics of compromise. Shun extremes, he urges. Observe the 'golden mean' in your behaviour. Happiness will result from the avoidance of excess. When action is undertaken from 'a balance of considerations' and virtue becomes a 'settled habit', the formation of character is merely a matter of time: for character, instead of being something that a man possesses ready-made, is simply the pattern formed by his good actions throughout life. Here, as elsewhere, Aristotle lays emphasis upon the fact of development. The world itself is a process, man a process within that world, and moral character a process within man. Everything, as Heraclitus correctly affirmed, flows; but the flow has direction, aim and purpose.

Just as Plato wrote the *Republic* and later the *Laws* in order to expound his views on the relation between the individual and the State, so Aristotle wrote his treatise on *Politics* in order to show that the good life is essentially a social life, since man is by nature 'a political animal'. Although the State of which he wrote was the City State of his time (we have remarked how indifferent he remained to larger units), his observations upon the various types of government, and upon the art of government in general, are in many respects still valid. Reading this work for the first time, the modern student may recoil from some of Aristotle's conclusions, especially that which suggests that certain men are born to be slaves; and he may well be surprised to find democracy denounced as a form of tyranny, along with absolute monarchy and self-seeking oligarchy; but if he carefully follows Aristotle's argument, he will observe that the aim of the book is precisely to pursue a middle course between extreme forms of government, and to arrive at a conception of the state which is neither exclusively monarchical, nor oligarchical, nor democratic, but a blend of all three. This balanced state Aristotle calls a 'polity'.

Not content with analysing the conditions of the just society, Aristotle, like Plato, describes in detail the kind of education that its citizens should receive. Plato recommended the explusion of artists from his ideal Republic; his argument was that artists, being concerned to depict the world as it is, are responsible for beguiling men's minds with that which is imperfect and compounded of illusion. (It has been pointed out that this indictment refers only to the so-called 'representative' artists.) In his treatise on *Poetics,* Aristotle dissociates himself from this attitude to art and artists. Art he holds, and above all the art of Drama (of which his time saw many splendid examples), may fulfil an important and indispensable social function. In portraying human beings engaged in acts of heroism, villainy, justice and violence, and in revealing now their sublime qualities and now their ridiculous, the artist is able to exercise a most salutary effect upon the feelings and emotions of his audience. He does not merely excite to admiration or pity, pleasure or disgust; he purifies these emotions by a process akin to 'earthing' them. The ordinary man is usually inarticulate as regards feeling: the function of art is to enable his pent-up emotions to discharge themselves in the manner least likely to cause damage to his fellow-beings. This process of spiritual release Aristotle called 'catharsis', and his theory has exerted a profound influence upon art, literary criticism, and even psychology. Thus the liberating effect that Socrates ascribed to the dialectical method of philosophy, Aristotle extends to the sphere of imaginative creation.

A final word about the influence of Aristotle's writings. Of their effect upon the oriental world we have already spoken. The last of the Neo-Platonists paid particular attention to Aristotle's views on Physics, and some of the Neo-Platonic manuscripts at length came into the hands of Jewish and Moslem thinkers, chiefly by way of the Christian communities in Syria. Thence, via Baghdad, they circulated to Cordova, as a result of which they began to exert an influence upon Latin Christianity. Towards the end of the twelfth century and at the beginning of the thirteenth, Greek texts and Arabic translations of Aristotle's treatise on *First Philosophy* and other writings were studied by the doctors of the Catholic Church. The official Catholic attitude remained one of extreme reserve, however, until Albert the Great and Thomas Aquinas, authors of exhaustive commentaries, demonstrated that the metaphysical views of Aristotle were, with due modification, a reasonable basis for Christian theology.

Although Aristotle's influence became thenceforward more widespread than it had ever been, it did not exercise quite the 'dictatorship' that some popular histories of thought, whether philosophical or scientific, would suggest. With thinkers such as William of Ockham (*d.* 1350), John Buridan (*d.* 1360), Nicholas Oresme (*d.* 1382), and Albert of Saxony (d. 1350), a definite reaction against Aristotle's theories of physics set in; and out of this reaction developed the movement known as modern thought. Thus we have Francis Bacon (1561-1626) describing Aristotle as 'the vile plaything of words'; a most ungenerous phrase to use of one who, like Bacon himself, was passionately devoted to research and experiment. But a man cannot be held responsible for the extravagances of his disciples and commentators, who often endeavour to prove themselves more orthodox than the master.

Of some great men it has been said that they 'rule from the grave'; but even the most salutary exercise of mortmain cannot prevent their tomb from becoming a gaudy shrine, decked with the trappings of those who, out of misplaced zeal, confuse idolatry with deference. If Aristotle went into hiding, it was not for the first time; and he has always managed to issue forth again. If he has been misunderstood, he has survived the most absurd travesties. His thought has thus become intimately bound up with the fortunes of our civilization, so that to eject him would be equivalent almost to dropping the pilot.

From Stoicism to Neo-Platonism

In sketching the life and thought of the philosophers that follow, we shall be building upon the foundations already laid. The great philosophers of mediæval and modern times make no attempt to conceal the debt which they owe to Socrates, Plato and Aristotle, even when they join issue with them most fiercely; for although their problems are so different, the methods they use and the very terminology they employ are those invented and worked out by the early Greek masters. This applies not merely to the sphere of metaphysics proper but to that of ethics or morals, political theory, education, economics, literary criticism, and above all the physical sciences. Even those who deplore the excessive attention still paid to 'the classics' in education, and who would substitute a more 'modern' scientific form of instruction in our schools and universities, do not deny that this 'classical tradition' is intimately bound up with what is known as Western civilization, and that the abandonment of this tradition (assuming such deliberate jettisoning to be possible) would leave a void not easily filled.

Today we realize more clearly than ever that civilization is not so much a material as a spiritual or intellectual inheritance; that we can ignore this inheritance at our peril; and that the decline and fall of empires has something to do with the 'morale' of the people composing them—this morale being strengthened or impoverished according to the grip maintained upon certain principles which have formed the basis of communal life. Hence the importance of that branch of history which is concerned with the history of speculative thought; and hence the interest that must centre round the lives of those who have revolutionized our mental conception of the world.

The death of Alexander the Great in 323 B.C. marks roughly the end of an era. The philosophical tradition that had grown up in the free City States of Greece now assumed a new guise. During the next few centuries, the

Greek spirit of enquiry pervaded the whole of the Mediterranean region, and 'Hellenism' became a kind of world culture, though we should bear in mind that the world in question consisted of the area covered by the Macedonian Empire and later the Roman Empire. Naturally, the break-up of the old order, and the merging of small political units into a larger whole, profoundly affected and disturbed the life of the thinking individual. There were many who felt, not perhaps always consciously, that they had lost their bearings. The old traditions of local civic patriotism were falling into neglect. New principles of conduct were needed. Strange and novel religious cults sprang up, and from them a handful of earnest devotees derived a transient satisfaction of the spiritual hunger within them. Even the rulers themselves felt the need of moral backing for their own achievements and experiments in government; for the most humble and obscure inhabitant of a great and far-flung empire is not so lonely at heart, or so much a prey to inner doubts and misgivings, as the man at the head of it.

To meet this need for guidance and certainty on the part of the individual, great or small, the Stoics and the Epicureans propounded their philosophies of life. Led by Zeno of Citium in Cyprus (*d*. 260 by his own hand[1]), Cleanthes from the Troad and Chrysippus of Tarsus, the Stoics were men of the world who endeavoured to influence the great ones of the age. They taught with equal zeal the importance of effort and that of indifference in face of both success and failure. Happiness consisted in accepting one's destiny, for there was an inner harmony in the universe which the truly wise man will discern and approve. The Epicureans,[2] on the other hand, while not advocating unlimited or habitual indulgence (as the term 'Epicurean' has since come to suggest), believed that pleasure was the goal of human endeavour; but only the sage will know which among the pleasures of life are those most worthy of pursuit, his preference being for such as agitate the soul least and enable us to live in tranquillity.

[1] But at the age of ninety-eight years.
[2] Epicurus was born on Samos in 341 B.C. and died in Athens in 270.

Both Stoics and Epicureans succeeded in grasping half of the truth while convinced that they possessed the whole of it; and thus their doctrines were attacked from various angles by a group of thinkers who, abhorring all dogmatism, maintained that happiness was to be derived solely from the suspension of all judgment. In this group were such men as Anaxarchus and Pyrrho of Elis (born 365; hence 'pyrrhonism'), who were later to influence the sceptics Timon of Phliasius (c. 300 B.C.) and later still Sextus Empiricus (A.D. 180-210). There were others whose approach was more direct: Aristippus of Cyrene, for instance, who pointed out that if the Epicureans were right to suppose that pleasure was the end of life, they were implicitly justifying suicide, since the end of life, thus defined, is unattainable. Indeed, Pyrrho (so Epictetus records) used to say: 'There is no difference between living and dying.' A person asked him: 'Why, then, do you not die?' 'Because,' answered Pyrrho, 'there is no difference.'

The problem of how the world came into being had puzzled the Greek thinkers, who never really succeeded in answering it except in terms of myth (as in Plato's *Timæus*). There was another people, however, which believed itself to be specially gifted with insight into the way the world had originated and how it was related to the Supreme Spirit. This people, the Hebrews, believed that God had created the world out of nothing; that He was particularly interested in the work of His creation; and that He would one day announce His solidarity with mankind by sending a Messiah to assume the leadership of the chosen people. This 'Creation Myth' was outlined in the book of *Genesis,* and the idea of the coming of the Messiah found expression in a series of prophetic utterances for which no other religion has an equivalent. What the Greeks found intellectually unacceptable, if not inconceivable, the Hebrews believed with passionate intensity; but when the Christian Faith later began to win converts among every class of people, the need became apparent for a reasoned theology. Thus is was natural to have recourse to Greek categories of thought, because these were the forms in which reasoned argument most naturally found expression.

Some of the 'philosophies' produced at this time were

a peculiar hotch-potch of pagan and Christian ideas: the most interesting being that of Philo the Jew, who developed the Greek notion of the 'Logis' or creative-principle in such a way as to foreshadow the 'Word-made-Flesh' theme of the Fourth Gospel of the New Testament. A group of philosophers and teachers who put up a determined resistance to the new faith was that of the Platonic Academy. They felt they had nothing to learn from a religion of such humble origins and dubious intellectual credentials. If men required an other-worldly faith, a liberation from the flesh and the devil, Plato had already supplied the answer. Not 'forward with Christ' but 'back to Plato' should be the watchword.

The thinkers of this group of 'Neo-Platonists', as they were called, were Platonists with a difference. In philosophical thought there is no 'going back' to anyone. The point of view that finds sympathy with a past thinker is itself the product of a new climate of thought. Whereas Plato never loses sight of the fact that his ultimate aim is the betterment of society, Plotinus (203-270), the greatest of the Neo-Platonist philosophers, ignores the social needs of man and concentrates upon the mystical union of the soul with God. He is concerned less with justice or happiness on earth than with ecstasy in heaven—an ecstasy which is the product of mystical contemplation rather than (as with Aristotle) of intellectual research into causes. In his pantheism, Plotinus is a pagan; in his emphasis upon love and self-discipline he comes near to the Christianity which, in its orthodox forms, he rejected.

St. Augustine

'Wherever we are, there is no place where He is not whose we are.'

—Augustine: last letter.

1

By far the most dramatic example of a pagan thinker who arrived, step by step and after many backslidings, at an acceptance of the Christian faith is that of Augustine. The personality of Saint Augustine, one of the most attractive in the history of thought, has cast a spell over thousands who have neither the capacity nor the inclination to study his writings on theology. Born at Tagaste in Numidia (North Africa) in A.D. 354, he came of a family which, though probably Roman, contained some Punic or Numidian blood, and was by tradition thoroughly Africanized. This fact is not without significance; it throws light upon Augustine's ardent and passionate temperament, his stormy youth, and also his energetic old age.

Determined to give him the finest education available, his parents sent him at the age of twelve to the Grammar School, or its equivalent, at Madaura, where a community of Roman veterans had settled. Here he received a thoroughly Roman education, for it was the principle in the colony that, being away from Rome, it was the more important to do as Rome did.[1] Five years later he was sent to Carthage, where, assisted financially by a wealthy patron named Romanianus, he took a course in Rhetoric, a subject then considered as useful to an enter-

---

[1] Augustine's later friend St. Ambrose was, incidentally, the author of the famous phrase *Si fueris Romæ, Romano vivito more* —'If you are at Rome, live in the Roman style'.

prising young man as Social Science or Economics is to-day.

Carthage was the metropolis. Attracted by its wealthy, colourful, and by no means straitlaced society, Augustine at once fell a victim to its allurements. That he was by nature vicious we have no reason to believe. He was certainly no worse than the majority of his contemporaries. Nevertheless, his lapses were a source of constant pain to his mother, Monica, a Christian from birth and tireless in her efforts to rear him in the same faith. He formed a number of attachments, one of which resulted in the birth of a son, Adeodatus. In his later *Confessions* we find him bitter with self-reproach at these youthful indiscretions, from the consequences of which he was to suffer for many years. Recalling the days of his first contact with the follies and snares of an essentially pagan society, he uttered the famous words: 'To Carthage then I came, where a cauldron of unholy loves sang all about mine ears.'

For all his social entanglements, he was not an idle student. Thirsting for knowledge and intent upon discovering a faith to live by, though unwilling as yet to embrace the religion of his mother, he fell in with a group of clever but wayward intellectuals known as Manichæans. The Manichæans entertained the belief that good and evil, being equal in power, were engaged in a perpetual struggle from which evil, in this world, tended to issue triumphant: and for this reason it was prudent to placate the dominant force. Such a belief gave rise to abuses both of logic and of conduct; it was particularly demoralizing to a man of Augustine's temperament. So far involved did he become with the society of the Manichæans, and so persuasive were the arguments they used to compel his adherence, that he remained for the next nine years under the spell of this stupefying heresy, clinging rather to what appeared to excuse his dissolute habits than to what satisfied his pressing mental needs.

Then, at long last, came release. Faustus, the master exponent of the Manichæan doctrine, paid a personal visit to Carthage. Hoping to extract from him the answer to certain intellectual difficulties, Augustine eagerly sought his company and listened to his conversation. He was thoroughly disillusioned. The man was not so much an imposter as a simpleton—though an exceedingly pompous and plausible one. Augustine at once saw through him and his facile logic. But, having escaped his influence, he arrived no nearer to the solution of his problems. He had torn one veil aside but without revealing anything likely to point him on the right way. At least the Manichæan teaching had provided some sort of mental nourishment, however mediocre. Now he was left with a jaded palate and no sustenance at all.

Unable to stay longer in Carthage, where, as he confesses, he had lived 'seduced and seducing, deceived and deceiving, in divers lusts:—openly, by sciences which they call liberal; secretly, with a false-named religion; here proud, there superstitious, everywhere vain', he decided to make a journey to Rome. His motives for taking such a step were mixed. He wanted a change of scenery, but above all he wanted to taste the intellectual life of the great metropolis, which, as a Roman by sympathy, he regarded as his spiritual home. His family, except for Monica, accompanied him. For some months after their arrival Augustine sought an appointment in which he could exercise his now highly developed talents in Rhetoric. Disappointment attended him at every step; and, as he laconically put it, 'I found other offences committed in Rome to which I was not exposed in Africa.' By good fortune, however, or by what he termed the Providence of God, a post of teacher of Rhetoric fell vacant at that time in Milan. Augustine put in for the job, requesting the prefect of Rome, Symmachus, to set him a subject upon which to display his ability. He passed the test brilliantly and was appointed.

Installed at Milan, where his mother soon joined him, Augustine came into contact with one of the most influential figures of the age, Bishop Ambrose, who, after Monica herself, was the first upright Christian he had known. The teaching and preaching of Ambrose attracted him as no other teaching and preaching had done: not at first because of its matter, which he largely ignored, nor on account of its polish, which he admitted to be inferior to that of Faustus, but on account of the obvious sincerity of the man, and the friendship which, in spite of differences in age and status, grew up spontaneously between them.

Gradually, as their intimacy increased, Augustine was moved to accept as valid much that in Ambrose's teaching he had previously dismissed as mere poetry or self-delusion. 'While I opened my heart to admit "how eloquently he spake", there also entered "how truly he spake"; but this by degrees.' It dawned upon him, though no less gradually, that he must on no account force the pace of his own conviction. In this state of semi-belief, he decided to assume the status of a catechumen, that is, one studying for admittance to the Church by baptism, which Monica and her husband (who accepted the faith later than his partner) had long before arranged for him. He desired salvation; but the old life still held its attractions and caused him to falter more times than he cared to recall. 'Make me pure,' was his prayer,'—but not yet.' As for Monica, she realized that it would take time for him to pass 'from sickness unto health', and that such convalescence would most probably result from 'the access, as it were, of a sharper fit, which physicians call "the crisis".'

The crisis, in his case, was somewhat long in coming, perhaps because he awaited it too complacently instead of plodding steadily forward in search of truth. For at this stage it was honour, gain and happiness, instead of true sanctity, that he desired most fervently. The pursuit of happiness led him, as it has led others, into curious reflections. One day he noticed a beggar in the streets of Milan joking and laughing. The contrast between this simple wretch on the one hand and himself and his friends on the other, engaged in incessant mental stress and torment, made him realize how 'for that by all such efforts of ours, as those wherein I then toiled, dragging along, under the goading of desire, the burden of my own wretchedness, and, by dragging, augmenting it, we yet looked to arrive at that very joyousness, whither that beggar-man had arrived before us, who should never perchance attain it'.

Even the privileges of his office as Professor of Rhetoric sickened him. 'How miserable was I then . . . when I was preparing to recite a panegyric to the Emperor (Valentinian the Younger), wherein I was to utter many a lie, and lying was to be applauded by those who knew I lied.' He toyed with the idea of marriage—

a rich marriage, it went without saying—and, in other moods, of becoming a hermit or member of a monastic community. He separated, not without some measure of regret, from the mother of his child, only to form a liaison with a woman less worthy and by no means as constant.

Of his industry at this time there was no doubt. He was overflowing with energy. He studied the scriptures with growing zeal, and also such philosophers as Plato. His Christian friends, and particularly the learned Simplicianus, were gratified that his tastes in pagan philosophy were as refined as this, for, as he said, 'the Platonists in many ways led to a belief in God and his word'. From Simplicianus he learned of the conversion of the great teacher Victorinus, who, having risen high in the esteem of his fellow Romans, even to the extent of being honoured with a statue in the forum itself, showed his courage by one day professing his new faith to the multitude. Here, then, was a man for whom honour and reputation, both so dear to Augustine, counted as nothing in comparison with the obscure blessing of humility. What prevented him, who had so much less to lose, from following this great example? Nothing but the sloth and paralysis that still held his will: 'for,' as he later wrote, 'of a froward will was a lust made; and a lust served became custom; and custom not resisted became necessity. By which links, as it were, joined together, a hard bondage held me enthralled.'

At length a day came when a friend, Pontitianus, paid a casual visit to Augustine and his friend Alypius. By birth an African like himself, but now a convert to Christianity, Pontitianus held high office at the Roman Emperor's court. Noticing a book lying upon Augustine's table and supposing it to be some text used by him in the course of his teaching, he turned over the pages and found it to be the writings of Paul the Apostle. This discovery, for which he had not been prepared, moved him to speak of the life and work of more recent followers of Christ, above all of Anthony, the illiterate monk of Egypt (born A.D. 251), and of his companion desert sages.

These revelations of contemporary sanctity, achieved without the aid of subtle arguments and ponderous learning, shamed Augustine into a recognition of the great contrast between his own intellectual gifts and his spiritual poverty. A feeling of intense humiliation and anguish followed; and then, as if the scales had fallen from his eyes, he saw plainly and for the first time his cardinal error. His extravagant intellectual pretensions were, it seemed, the primary obstacles to his acceptance of the Catholic faith. The weapons of dialectic and logic, wherewith he had hoped to argue himself into certainty, had brought him nearer and nearer to complete scepticism. Turning impulsively to his companion Alypius, he exclaimed: 'Are we ashamed to follow, because others are gone before, and not ashamed not even to follow?' His friend became conscious of a great change in the speaker, who hurried out into an adjoining garden and there, with Alypius following, sat down.

For some moments Augustine remained completely inarticulate. In his mind the phrase 'Be it done now' echoed again and again, and, from the other side of his nature, the leering words 'Think you that you can do without us?' The inward tension then resolved itself in a flood of tears, during which he became conscious of another voice, as it were of a young boy or girl, saying gently: 'Take up and read. Take up and read!' Returning, now somewhat calmer, to where Alypius was sitting and seizing the volume of Paul which he had brought with him, his eyes fell upon the text beginning 'Not in rioting and drunkenness . . .' He felt his doubts already receding; and Alypius, continuing the same passage as far as the striking and appropriate words 'Him that is weak in faith, receive', experienced a similar sensation of release from perplexity. Their joint impulse, needless to translate into speech, was to go indoors and tell Monica what had happened. This was the moment which she had long awaited. For, as Augustine put it, his own sudden conversion was responsible for another in her: namely, 'the conversion of her mourning into joy'.

As a result of this momentous turning-point in his life, Augustine decided to abandon the profession of instructor in Rhetoric. He went into retirement in the country to make himself ready for baptism, Ambrose giving him the advice he needed. About this time his health broke down, so that the continuance of his profession might in any event have been rendered impossible. With him stayed Alypius and the boy Adeodatus, whose mental gifts, at barely fifteen years of age, were already remarkable: he and his father wrote a book together called *The Master*. All three were baptized by Ambrose in 387. Soon after they decided to return, with Monica, to Africa.

The little company had travelled no further than Ostia, the port of Rome, when Monica fell ill. She was then in her fifty-sixth year. Her peaceful death soon after removed the best and most lasting influence upon Augustine's life. Not merely did she enjoy the good fortune of witnessing his entry into the Church; shortly before her death she found in him the companion that her husband, though nominally turned Christian, had never proved equal to being. Her patience and suffering received their due reward at the last in an experience which, though Augustine was to live to a great age, he himself treasured as the most precious of his life, and for which his own words must suffice:

'It came to pass, Thyself, as I believe, by Thy secret ways so ordering it, that she and I stood alone, leaning in a certain window, which looked into the garden of the house where we now lay, at Ostia; where, removed from the din of men, we were recruiting from the fatigues of the journey for the voyage. We were discoursing then together, alone, very sweetly; and forgetting those things which are behind, and reaching forth unto those things which are before, we were enquiring between ourselves in the presence of the Truth, which Thou art, of what sort the eternal life of the saints was to be, which eye hath not seen, nor ear heard, nor hath it entered into the heart of man. But yet we gasped with the mouth of our heart, after those heavenly streams of Thy Fountain, the fountain of life, which is with Thee; that being bedewed thence according to our capacity, we might in some sort meditate upon so high a mystery.

'And when our discourse was brought to that point, that the very highest delight of the earthly senses, in the very purest material light, was, in respect of the sweetness of that life, not only not worthy of comparison, but not even of mention; we raising up ourselves with a more glowing affection towards the "Self-Same", did by degrees pass through all things bodily, even the very heaven; yea, we were soaring higher yet, by inward musing, and discourse, and admiring of Thy works; and we came to our own minds and went beyond them, that we might arrive at that region of never-failing plenty, where Thou feedest Israel with the food of Truth, and where life is the Wisdom by whom all these things are made . . . and while we were discoursing and panting after her, we slightly touched on her with the whole effort of our heart . . . when my mother said: "Son, for my part I have no further delight in anything in this life. What I do here any longer and to what end I am here, I know not now that my hopes in this world are accomplished. One thing there was for which I desired to linger for a while in this life, that I might see thee a Catholic Christian before I died. My God hath done this for me most abundantly, that I should now see thee withal, despising earthly happiness, become His servant: what do I here?" '

A few days later she was dead.

The fame that Augustine had sought in youth and renounced upon seclusion, came to him, though in different guise, in old age. Having spent three years as a recluse, he was ordained priest in 391 by Valerius, Bishop of Hippo. Four years later he succeeded Valerius to the episcopate—a promotion as swift as it was merited. In 397 he began the composition of his *Confessions*, one of the most moving records of its kind ever written, and from which the passages quoted above are taken. Not that this autobiography was the only great work that he produced. He wrote numerous sermons, commentaries and treatises, some expository and others directed against heretics such as the Donatists and the Pelagians. Finally, about 413, he began to write the monumental work called *The City of God,* wherein he expounded his plan for a Christian Commonwealth sufficiently stable and enduring to survive the internal decay of the Roman Empire. As he grew older, so his rule tended to become more autocratic; but, as far as his spiritual life was concerned, he never turned aside from the path upon which, following his conversion and his mother's death, he had set his feet. He did not lack enemies, even among the ranks of Christians, the most cruel being those who took delight in reminding him of his youthful errors. Such

taunts he bore with true humility, ever ready to acknowledge his faults and of sufficient uprightness not to repeat
them.

He died in Hippo in 430, having completed *The City
of God* four years earlier, with the Vandals already surg-
ing at the gates. Since his acceptance of the Faith of his
mother, forty-three eventful years had passed; but, to
the end, his attitude to the Church was summed up in
the moving words from the 10th Book of the *Confessions*: '*Sero te amavi pulchritudo tam antiqua et tam
nova, sero te amavi*' ('Too late have I loved thee,
O Beauty most ancient and most new! too late have I
loved thee').

2

For reasons already given, it was to Plato rather than
to Aristotle that Augustine, seeking for a philosophical
basis for his maturing religious beliefs, instinctively
turned: for indeed there was hardly anything of importance, or realized importance, of Aristotle to turn to.
Apart from the subject-matter of his philosophy, Plato
exhibited the qualities of mind that Augustine most admired and in great part shared: above all, a passionate
desire to make contact with a reality transcending that
perceived by the senses. Like Plato, he held that the
function of science, or ordered knowledge, was to render
us more capable of sanctity and hence salvation: *nulla est
causa philosophandi nisi ut beati simus.* He echoed the
words of the Apostle that the truth, as revealed in the
Son of God, should make men free. Unlike Plotinus, for
whom God was so transcendent a Being as to be beyond
the reach of thought altogether, Augustine maintained
that human reason, notwithstanding its limitations, was
at least *capable* of apprehending God, though not necessarily of understanding Him.

To assert otherwise was unduly to belittle the faculty
of Reason, and therefore to cast doubt upon the value
of a gift of God. Indeed, this gift of Reason was the most
precious with which man had been endowed, since it
marked his superiority over the rest of creation. If, however, Reason occupied a position of such eminence in
man's spiritual make-up, what of that other faculty upon

which theologians were accustomed to place such emphasis as almost to accord superiority to it: namely, Faith? Augustine, be it noted, refused to regard Reason and Faith as faculties opposed one to the other, as certain theologians have done both before and since, and as Augustine himself is sometimes credited with doing. To Faith, admittedly, he accorded some primacy, as well as a certain priority in time; we must believe a thing—or rather believe *in* it—in order fully to understand it. *Credo ut intelligam.* Everyone has experienced the mental condition of being intellectually satisfied but not emotionally satisfied. But the condition in which the mind is completely at ease with itself and with the world is that of *knowledge:* and knowledge is a blend of both Faith and Reason, or rather a state in which these two are merged into a larger whole.

In maintaining that the human intellect could comprehend but not fully understand God, Augustine had in mind the fact that, in thinking of God, we become involved in a series of contradictions or, as they are sometimes termed, 'antinomies'. Thus God is the cause of all change, but He is immutable. He exists but inhabits no particular place. He is living but not in time. This is the consequence of our finite mind endeavouring, and failing, to grasp the nature of an infinite and immaterial object. It is precisely because God is immaterial (a 'spirit') that no material image, or set of material images, can do justice to Him. Hence the danger of interpreting the Trinity in a literal manner. God is Three Persons and yet One Person, just as a human person is compounded of thought, will and feeling—distinct but united faculties. Augustine's most serious charge against the upholders of the Arian heresy was that they converted a *distinction* into a *separation*.

Unlike the Greek philosophers of antiquity, Augustine insisted, as his Christian beliefs obliged him to do, that God created the world by an act of free-will. That such creation presupposed a previous eternity of inactivity on the part of God, Augustine denied, though his non-Christian critics had put forward this hypothesis as an insuperable objection to Catholic theology. Prior to the act of divine creation, there was no 'duration', infinite or otherwise, because the creation of the world involved the creation of time as well: indeed, movement, which is time, cannot exist apart from finite things, and therefore in eternity there can be neither movement nor duration. This, as the reader will recognize, and as Augustine was ready to acknowledge, is pure Plato.

Where Augustine parted company with Plato was in his view of the Fall of Man and (of course) the Incarnation. Concerning the Fall of Man Plato speaks in the language of myth; but he clearly believes that such an event took place—or how do we account for the condition of imperfection in which man, despite his momentary glimpses of true reality, finds himself? As to whether Plato conceived the possibility of an Incarnation, it is difficult to say, though there is a passage to suggest that he thought the perfect man would, like Socrates, be done to death by his fellows. Augustine held that before the Fall man was guided solely by his reason; since then, this 'inner light' has been increasingly obscured by sin. Had man's soul remained thoroughly transparent to reason, the revelation of God in Jesus Christ would not have been necessary. Those who persist in maintaining that Reason alone can save the world (*i.e.* the so-called Rationalists) are those who either ignore the fact of sin or explain it in terms of something else ('environment', 'heredity', etc.).

Oppressed by a sense of impending doom as a result of the degeneracy of the Roman civilization of his day, Augustine emphasized to a degree that some of his followers found excessive the absolute dependence of men upon divine grace. If man has become the slave of vice and sin, salvation could come only through a definite act of liberation. Thus, towards the end of his life, Augustine tended to adopt a more and more fatalistic attitude to men and affairs. The phrase 'O Lord, thou pluckest me out' summed up his philosophy of salvation. It may be that he never forgot how near to being engulfed in the abyss of error he himself had come.

Peter Abelard

'The only way to return to God is by neglecting the creature we have adored, and adoring the God whom we have neglected.'

—Abelard to Héloïse.

The story of Abelard is well known (though not always accurately known) by millions whose acquaintance with philosophy is of the slightest, and who are totally unaware of the part played by purely philosophical controversies in his stormy career. Few people likewise realize how far his innovations in thought have since been accepted as just and reasonable, even by the Church whose representatives repeatedly condemned him for heresy. In writing of Abelard, therefore, we shall be writing of a man who lived in days when the correct formulation of a doctrine was a matter about which men not merely quarrelled but were prepared to shed blood (their own and other people's); when a philosophical definition or distinction was thus literally a matter of life and death; and finally when a man who had something to teach attracted pupils from far beyond the borders of the country in which he lived.

Today, it is possible for a man's words to be broadcast to all nations of the earth. In the twelfth and thirteenth centuries, with none of these means of diffusion at his disposal, a great teacher might exert an influence upon his contemporaries greater than that which is wielded by the most eloquent of modern publicists. And this influence was primarily of an intellectual character. The demagogue's success was purely local.

Born about 1080 in Pallet, near Nantes in Brittany, Peter Abelard came of noble stock. His father and mother seem to have been persons of culture and refinement, and to Peter, their eldest son, they gave the best education they could afford. We know little of Abelard's childhood and youth; but it is obvious that he grew up with a strong sense of independence and marked intellectual ability. His desire for learning finally became so inordinate that he resolved, after the manner of the time, to set out by himself in quest of those who could put him in the way of further instruction: for in those days education was a thing to be sought by travel and pilgrimage, not something accepted as a right. In quitting his home Abelard abandoned not merely his family but his own right of primogeniture; and like any other wandering student, he travelled light, though he had the advantage of a heavier purse than most of his companions.

The goal of all young men with his particular leanings was Paris; but it appears that before arriving at the capital, Abelard spent a year or two studying at Locminé under a well-known teacher, Roscellinus, canon of Compiègne. Roscellinus taught philosophy or dialectics. He taught it well, but he did not always teach what the Church approved. He had in fact already been condemned for heresy both at London and at Soissons. This made him something of a notoriety; but he was not on that account deprived of influence, or of the wealth that came from having many pupils. Abelard was later to enjoy a similar status. Undoubtedly his contact with Roscellinus sharpened his independent spirit, for thereafter orthodoxy could never contain him. He studied everything, mastering all branches of enquiry save mathematics, for which he never displayed the smallest aptitude. At music he excelled; and he soon made a name for himself as a composer of songs.

We next find this talented, well-favoured young man sitting at the feet (the phrase is to be taken literally, for the students reclined on the straw-covered floor of the lecture-room, resting their notebooks on their raised knees) of another distinguished teacher, William of Champeaux, who at that time occupied the Chair at the episcopal school at old Notre Dame. William was a teacher of great influence not merely with his students (who were of all nationalities) but with the powers-that-be. His orthodoxy was unquestioned. Abelard recog-

nized this, and immediately proceeded to question orthodoxy.

As it is impossible to treat Abelard's career apart
from the philosophical disputes that served so largely to
shape it, we shall here discuss the two together. Considerable mental adjustment is needed for us today if we
would understand how it came about that a particular
philosophical problem, seemingly so barren and superficial, should plunge the whole of Christendom into bitter dissension; but this is because our own quarrels and
controversies are conducted upon a plane that obscures
the clash of ideas at the basis of every problem, even the
'impersonal' problems of economics. The particular
problem that agitated the minds of the thinkers of the
twelfth century was a development of a logical argument
already elaborated by Aristotle. This argument was concerned with the relation between *genera* and *species*—
a subject innocent enough in appearance, but bristling
with difficulties once we examine its implications. Briefly,
it may be stated as follows. While there are individual
beings called men, that by virtue of which they are men
is not something individual but universal. The question
is whether the universal 'Man' enjoys an existence similar, if not superior, to that of individual men.

Plato, it will be remembered, answered this question
in the affirmative; he believed, in other words, that Universals or Ideas inhabited a region of their own—
a region of pure, timeless Being—from which the world
of sense was separated by a gulf. Aristotle, realizing the
disadvantages of such a theory, contended that the Ideas
were already in contact with natural things, providing
them with a kind of internal impulsion to realize their
fullest potentialities.

Abelard and his contemporaries knew nothing of
Aristotle save that which they could derive from
Porphyry's *Introduction* (translated from the Latin) to
his works; but the logical problem of Universal and Particular struck them as especially relevant to the discussion of the central dogmas of the Christian Faith, such
as the Trinity, Original Sin, and indeed the nature of
the Church itself. Were the Three Persons of the Trinity
separate entities, or three aspects or attributes of one en-

tity? Was Original Sin simply a 'name' for a collection of individual sins, or did it refer to an essential Sinfulness characteristic of and pervading all human shortcomings? Was the Christian Church merely an assembly of individual churches—an ecclesiastical federation—or was it Catholic or Universal in the true sense, an ideal entity from which each individual church derived such spirituality as it possessed?

Roscellinus, who declared that Universals were simply empty names (the standpoint of the Nominalist), was promptly accused of heresy for denying the central dogmas of the Faith. William of Champeaux, on the other hand, was a stout defender of the Realist view that Universals enjoyed a reality of their own. Abelard, while rejecting Nominalism, found the Realist doctrine frankly incredible. Within a short time of entering the philosopher's classes, he therefore began openly to defy his master. To everyone's astonishment, William was first indignant, then baffled, and finally overwhelmed, though not convinced. Abelard's moral victory caused a major sensation; but, like all his victories, it was to recoil upon the man who achieved it. 'This,' he wrote many years after, 'was the beginning of my calamities.'

The view put forward by Abelard in contrast to that held by the Nominalists and the Realists is now known in the text-books as Conceptualism. It is a reasonable doctrine, easily comprehensible to the ordinary man. The Universal, said Abelard, exists, but only *in* the individual. Every person partakes of the nature of Man, but we arrive at the idea of Man through studying this man and that man. Outside the individual, this universal man is merely an intellectual *concept*. The human mind is so made that it can entertain such concepts as if they enjoyed an abstract being. They do indeed enjoy such a being, but it is a mental being, an *ens rationis*. The glory of our human Reason is that it can deal in such abstractions, manipulating them at will. And since Reason is a gift of God (as Augustine himself affirmed), we should not be afraid to subject everything in heaven and earth to its impartial scrutiny.

Abelard's contentions, inoffensive as they seem to us, were regarded in his day with the utmost suspicion. In claiming so high a place for the human intellect, he was said to be crediting the finite with the capacity to understand the infinite. That was blasphemy. Whatever Augustine's attitude to Reason, he had firmly believed in the primacy of Faith. Abelard was virtually saying: 'I understand in order that I may believe.' This was rationalism, and through rationalism lay the way to atheism.

Although scholarship exhibited considerable vitality at this time, its academic organization was much inferior to that of the present day. A teacher had to live by his wits; and if his pupils drifted away, he was usually ruined or at least thrown temporarily out of employment. William of Champeaux, however, was the adviser of princes as well as the instructor of youth. To incur his disfavour, as Abelard had done, was to run great risks. Not for the last time in his life, Abelard decided to quit the scene of his momentary triumph. He moved to the little town of Melun, thirty miles away, and there set up a rival school of Dialectics. Many of Williams's pupils followed him with enthusiasm. A little later, plucking up courage once more, the young rebel moved his informal 'Chair' nearer to Paris by about fifteen miles. His popularity increased daily, as did the flow of disciples, now only too eager to 'make a day of it' by walking to and from the village of Corbeil, the Opposition Headquarters. The roads and lanes echoed to the sound of youthful voices, with the clash of dialectical rapiers and the din of logic-chopping.

The strain of holding his own in the learned world, even though he had hitherto proved so successful, soon told upon Abelard's health, and he was obliged to retire to Brittany. He stayed in seclusion, though not in idleness, for some years. When he returned to the fray, he found William of Champeaux in retirement too, probably because he felt that his fighting days were over. Nevertheless the old man continued to teach Rhetoric in the priory of St. Victor, and thither Abelard used to pay occasional visits, no doubt with the object of continuing the heckling he had employed to such effect in Paris. This time he was no less successful. Indeed, he succeeded better than ever. One day, to the astonishment of the learned world, William of Champeaux—it does credit to his intellectual honesty—announced that, after due reflection, he had decided to change his mind upon the subject of Universals. That he agreed wholeheartedly with Abelard he would not admit; but it was clear to everybody that his change of viewpoint was, if not a surrender to Conceptualism, then at least a compromise with it. Abelard's reputation soared. So did his ambition. Claiming the Chair at Notre Dame as part of the spoils of victory, Abelard actually occupied it for a brief period before being ejected by William's friends. To Paris he had come, however, and at Paris he intended to stay: and so, as he later wrote, 'we pitched our camp' —the expression is more than justified—'on the hill of St. Geneviève.' [1]

Here stood an abbey already famous, or infamous, for the independent views and free behaviour of its inmates. Later critics and puritans spoke scathingly of the wealth, merriment and good living of the monks, who appeared to be on excellent terms with the 'cannonesses' of the nearby convent. In Abelard's time, the place was merely a trifle bohemian—a characteristic for which the locality (the modern 'Latin Quarter') is still distinguished. Abelard's temperament found just the stimulus there that it needed, though not for very long. As he was again on the point of scoring a dialectical victory over the orthodox teachers of Notre Dame, his mother summoned him to Pallet, this time to inform him of her resolve to adopt the religious life following her husband's decision to enter a monastery.

When, in somewhat sadder mood, Abelard returned to Paris, he hesitated to resume the controversies for which he had now become famous throughout Europe. Instead he began to devote himself to the detailed study of theology. His motives are not easy to analyse. He may have been seeking ecclesiastical preferment. He may have been genuinely 'converted', though he was not known to be anything but a believer. Possibly he considered it wise to become master of a subject about which his orthodoxy was beginning to be questioned. He knew that his enemies, who were multiplying in high places, had only to trump up a charge of heresy against him for his career to be changed from success to failure. If once he were to learn the rules of the theological game, he was confident of his ability to beat the so-called professionals at it. Soon he was lecturing to enthralled audiences at

[1] *I.e.* where the Lycée Henri Quatre stands today.

Laon, and proving a match for his master, Bishop Anselm, who promptly suspended him.

But it was too late. By universal acclamation he was appointed to the Chair at Notre Dame, which had now fallen vacant. His magnificent oratory, his ready wit, his huge learning (not by any means confined to the works of Christian writers), his fine presence, his high birth— all these combined to make him an object of attraction more dazzling even than a royal personage. Thousands of students assembled to hear him (the great expansion of Paris during this century is said to have been due chiefly to the increased student population), while his reputation as a 'wizard', 'smiter', 'Proteus', and 'Prometheus' grew among those who had never entered a lecture hall in their lives. For he seems to have exercised a general fascination over women as well as men.

Did success turn his head? To some extent it may have done so. In his later autobiography, he speaks of being swollen with vanity and pride, thinking himself to be 'the only philosopher in the world', and fearing 'no further menace' to his position. Certainly he was not given to underestimating his abilities, or he would not have risen to the position of first teacher in France. There is no evidence to suggest that his private life was anything but blameless. Had it been otherwise, he would undoubtedly have added this to the other items of reproach which he later enumerated in an agony of self-chastisement. If we take into account the moral standards of the time, even in respect of the ecclesiastical hierarchy, he might almost be considered a paragon of virtue. Later writers, and also some of Abelard's reputedly pious contemporaries (including St. Bernard of Clairvaux), represent Abelard as consistently a reprobate in both thought and deed. But the language of abuse at this time was much inflated, and intellectual heresy was usually associated with depraved conduct.

Possibly because he had devoted so much energy to intellectual matters, the emotional side of his nature seems to have lacked sufficient outlet. He was now in his thirty-ninth year, an age when many of the 'great lovers' of history have begun to weary of successive infatuations; but we gather that Abelard had hitherto known no woman either casually or in consequence of an 'af-

fair'. A man of his tastes and temperament was not likely
to fall victim to common women; but amid so much flattery and attention from female society, it was to be expected that he should become increasingly susceptible
to feminine charm. The remarkable circumstance in
Abelard's life was not so much that he should suddenly
have fallen in love, as that the object of his love should
have happened to combine precisely the qualities, mental and physical, that he most admired. Héloïse, even
when Abelard first beheld her among the concourse of
his students, was intellectually the match for all the
women and most of the men of her day; she was also
possessed of dignity and beauty. Even if not so dazzling
as later writers have tried to suggest, she was clearly a
woman of more than usual attraction.

A girl of about eighteen, Héloïse had received her
education at the Benedictine nunnery at Argenteuil, near
St. Denis, and also from her uncle (or reputed uncle),
Canon Fulbert. We do not know precisely where or when
she and Abelard first met: possibly a meeting between
two such paragons of learning was deliberately arranged
by parties wholly innocent of ulterior motives. All we
have to go upon is Abelard's own confession that within
a short time of seeing her he was 'wholly afire with love
of the maid'; that he sought her company; and that
finally, to cultivate her further aquaintance and no doubt
with the express object of winning her hand, he went to
lodge at her uncle's house. The initial arrangement was
that Abelard should receive board and lodging in return
for a small sum, and a few hours' weekly instruction of
Fulbert's niece.

Closer contact served but to increase Abelard's ar-
dour. He admits that neither the expression of his affection nor the welcome it found in the heart of his pupil
were long disguised. As he later put it, their lessons began to consist more of 'kisses than theses', being maintained with a thoroughness and regularity that his public
discourses soon lacked. There were raised eyebrows,
then whispered communications, and finally open gossip.
No longer able to listen to his voice expounding divinity
and logic, the swarm of pupils and admirers, crowding
to Fulbert's house, rehearsed the songs that the master
now composed in honour of a woman of unparalleled

virtue and sweetness. 'Every street, every house, re-sounded with my name,' wrote Héloïse long years after.

Proud to be associated with the 'wizard of the Schools' and to have secured for his niece such a unique teacher, Fulbert may have mistaken the tenor of the public gossip; or he may have been unusually stupid. One day, probably as the result of a friendly tip, he suddenly realized what was taking place under his own roof. His fury knew no bounds. Abelard was driven from the house, and forbidden re-admission. The association was to terminate at once.

So, indeed, it might have ended—at least for the time —had not Héloïse, seeking for an explanation of her condition from a treatise of Aristotle, realized that she was pregnant. Judging from the way in which she managed, by secret means, to convey the intelligence to her lover, this discovery delighted her beyond measure.

No doubt it would have delighted Abelard too, if he had had time to examine his feelings; but the expulsion from Fulbert's house had placed him in a dilemma. To marry Héloïse was to risk his whole career: for although Abelard was not at that time an ordained priest, it would seem that he was intent, as already hinted, upon ecclesiastical preferment. That Héloïse herself, a prisoner in the house of an outraged guardian, should regard marriage as the most desirable way out, seems obvious enough. But apparently she did not. This fact has puzzled both historians and psychologists. In spite of her strict upbringing and undoubtedly virtuous character (judging from her manner of life before and after the love-episode), she declared until the end of her days that marriage with Abelard was, in her opinion, less honourable a status than that of remaining his mistress. She admits it openly, and Abelard himself so reports it.

Directly he learnt of her condition, Abelard decided to take action. One night he managed to remove Héloïse from her uncle's house and carry her off, in nun's attire, to his home at Pallet. It appears that they stayed there together, free and undisturbed for the first time until Abelard felt that some sort of reconciliation with Fulbert was worth attempting. He set out, alone this time, for Paris; but needless to say, he greatly overestimated Fulbert's willingness to let bygones be bygones.

The suggestion put forward by Abelard for Fulbert's consideration was that a secret marriage should be arranged. Besides appealing to the sense of decorum of both, the idea opened the way to the resumption of Abelard's triumphal career. Fulbert appeared to be co-operative. But both parties had again reckoned without Héloïse. She objected outright to the proposal, preferring, as she put it, to be united with Abelard 'by love alone, not by the compulsion of the marriage vow': a sentiment from which the birth of her child in no way deflected her. In spite of her earnest entreaties and learned arguments (she instanced the married life of Socrates as a warning to every true philosopher), Abelard remained firm. They must return to Paris, be married, and endeavour to start life afresh. Héloïse finally assented. Leaving the child Astrolabe behind with Abelard's sister, they eventually arrived in the capital, where they were formally united in marriage, with Fulbert and a few trusted friends as witnesses.

The plan, having begun well, miscarried. With so many idle tongues wagging, it was necessary for husband and wife to meet rarely and in secret. Their nerves were rapidly becoming frayed when Fulbert, whom Héloïse had always distrusted, began to gossip about the marriage. Asked point-blank by friends whether or not she was Abelard's wife, Héloïse continued to deny the fact vehemently. Her attitude infuriated Fulbert and his former doting was exchanged for open abuse. Abelard could endure the tension no longer. He made another rescue attempt, this time carrying his wife away to the convent at Argenteuil, with which she had been familiar from her childhood days. Here she assumed the conventional habit of the Benedictine nuns, except for the veil.

Abelard admits that their relations continued during this period, as the discipline of the convent was lax; and such behaviour was not the most shocking that had been known to take place there. The same life of subterfuge continued, with few compensations for the couple apart from that of being temporarily out of Fulbert's clutches. In fact, however, no arrangement was better calculated to inflame Fulbert's wrath; for directly he learnt that Héloïse had been confined to a convent he jumped to the conclusion that Abelard, who had originally wished to keep his marriage secret, now desired to terminate it. He resolved to take revenge upon the man who had deceived and now proposed to dishonour him.

Finally he fixed upon a plan that would put an end, as he thought, to Abelard's association not merely with Héloïse but with any woman whom he had in mind to put in her place. He hired some desperadoes, squared Abelard's valet, and instructed them to gain access one night to Abelard's bedroom. There, as the unsuspecting man lay sleeping, they entered and brutally emasculated him. Short of actual murder, no more fiendish act could have been perpetrated. In a single night, Abelard's life—and indeed his whole personality—underwent a complete and permanent transformation.

It was natural that a blow of this nature should have plunged Abelard into the deepest anguish and despair. In an agony of repentance for sins committed and presumed to be receiving divine punishment, he decided to enter a monastery. This decision was understandable. Less understandable and praiseworthy was his desire that Héloïse, having once taken the nun's habit in dire emergency, should now take it in earnest and for good. The girl's distress was acute enough without this added imposition, since hers was a temperament not easily subdued. Nevertheless, as her love underwent no change in consequence of the forced change in her husband, she obeyed. At the final ceremony in the convent chapel, her closest friends made a last bid to prevent her taking the veil; but in vain. Approaching the altar to receive it from the Bishop, she recited not a prayer but the words of the heroine of Lucan:

> 'Why hapless did I wed,
> If this the fruit that my affection bore?
> Behold the penalty I now embrace
> For thy sweet sake!'

The idyll was at an end. Sombre tragedy followed, and continued more or less unrelieved until the end of Abelard's life. But it was a tragedy not without episodes of majesty, and the story of Abelard and Héloïse was more remarkable perhaps after they had gone their separate and solitary ways than when they were together.

For Abelard, life was to consist of one long battle with those who, fearing the power of a mind now concentrated upon questions of faith, sought more energetically than ever to silence and subdue him. For Héloïse, henceforth a figure of heroic dignity, the battle was primarily an interior one, of which we have some record in the brief confessions of her letters.

During his retirement in the abbey of St. Denis, Abelard set to work upon a treatise entitled *De Trinitate*. He also began to lecture again, finding that his old skill had not deserted him, but that on the contrary he had acquired an added subtlety. The students flocked in as eagerly as ever; the authorities pricked up their ears with the same attentiveness. Two other works, *A Dialogue between a Philosopher, a Jew and a Christian,* and a treatise on the works of the Fathers called *Sic et Non* ('Yes and No') made their appearance, both being characterized by the same impulse to submit even the most subtle articles of Faith to the scrutiny of Reason. The latter works achieved a fair measure of popularity, but the great book on the *Trinity* attracted most attention of all. Indeed, it attracted so much attention that its author was summoned to Soissons to answer for some of the more daring statements that it contained. His enemies had at last succeeded in pinning him down. It was now for him to extricate himself.

Abelard had hoped that the Council of Soissons would become the scene of his triumph. He would show the world that his spirit, unlike his body, was far from being maimed. The event turned out differently. He had no opportunity to defend himself. The verdict was a foregone conclusion. Accused roundly of 'tri-theism' (*i.e.* of believing in the separate deity of the Three Persons of the Trinity), he was compelled to consign his own book to the flames.

After a period of virtual confinement in the abbey of St. Medard, not far from Soissons, Abelard was allowed to return to St. Denis; but before long his enquiring mind rendered him so unpopular with the monks that he was again indicted for impiety and was obliged to flee the abbey. As a deserter, he incurred still further ecclesiastical displeasure, and in desperation he journeyed to Paris, hoping to find sufficient friends at court to shield him from the malice of his colleagues. Finally, after appearing at what amounted to a mock-trial, with Louis the Fat presiding, he was 'pardoned' on condition that he consented to adopt a hermit life. This at least spelt freedom: and freedom was all that he desired.

In complete solitude, living in two huts and a small oratory built entirely by hand, Abelard spent a period of comparative rest at Nogent-sur-Seine, feeling that he had at last escaped from the persecution of the righteous. Again he was sadly mistaken. Directly his whereabouts became known, the influx of students and disciples began as usual, and the hermitage soon became the centre of a thriving community. And as his reputation was gradually rekindled, so the rumours spread of further heresies and forbidden practices. 'I had one enemy—echo,' wrote the distracted man in his later *Memoirs*. These rumours came to the ears of Bernard of Clairvaux and Norbert of Prémontré, stern watchers over orthodoxy. Abelard, his peace of mind once more broken and fearing another Council or synod, contemplated flight from the 'Paraclete', as his hermitage was called; he even toyed with the idea of deserting Christendom altogether and fleeing to the realm of the Crescent.

Then, as luck would seem to have it, he was offered a way of escape. The monks of the monastery of St. Gildas in Brittany, having lost their abbot, invited Abelard to fill his place. He accepted. At the same time a happy thought struck him. He would install Héloïse, now prioress of Argenteuil, in the Paraclete hermitage, which was his own legal property. In 1131, he was instrumental in raising her to the status of Abbess. Whenever he could, he visited the flourishing community, glad to absent himself from his own boorish flock at St. Gildas, where, feeling the atmosphere appropriate, he had begun to write the *Story of My Calamities* for the consolation (as he tells us) of a friend.

It has been suggested that this remarkable document may have been written in the hope that its perusal by influential persons would lead to the author's restoration to favour. Whatever the truth of the contention, the MS. was circulated widely: and into whose hands should it eventually fall but those of the gentle Abbess of the Paraclete. Hence the famous *Letters* of Abelard and Héloïse, the only classic example of love-letters written from wife to husband after so broken a marriage. In this correspondence, first with reserve and later with a torrent of passion, Héloïse reveals the true state of her heart after years of self-abnegation and devotion to duty: and it is a heart that has not changed.

'*I have not looked to the marriage-bond or dowry; I have not even yearned to satisfy my own will and pleasure, but thine, as thou well knowest. The name of wife may be the holier and more approved; but the name of friend—nay, mistress or concubine, if thou wilt suffer it—has always been the sweeter to me. . . . . I should deem it more precious and more honourable to be thy mistress than to be the queen of a Cæsar.*'

So wrote the Reverend Mother Abbess of the Paraclete to the man whom she knew to be incapable of the response she still dared to solicit. Abelard's replies, though not what she craved, show some measure of alarm at the violent emotions that he has caused to awaken and urge her to fix her thoughts upon other matters. The correspondence ends on a calmer note; and we find a concluding epistle addressed by Abelard to 'the virgins of the Paraclete' in which, having enclosed a number of hymns and sermons of his own composition (very different hymns, we may suspect, from those secular outpourings of his youth), he congratulates them upon having a 'mother' who is versed in Latin, Greek, and Hebrew. He also sends detailed and reasoned replies to forty-two 'problems of Héloïse' derived from the Scriptures. Some of these have a very modern ring.

The atmosphere of St. Gildas becoming intolerable and even dangerous, Abelard left the abbey; and we are not certain of his movements until in 1136 he turns up once more at Paris. Again he is the centre of attraction. He finds the ancient skill unimpaired. And, as of old, he cannot keep his mouth shut. It is Bernard of Clairvaux who once more raises the alarm. Since no amount of admonition will serve to restrain him, the heretic must be finally crushed. This time Bernard is in deadly earnest. He sends for Abelard's new works—his *Theologia Christiana* and his *Commentary on the Epistle to the Ro-*

mans—studies them, decides they are the voice of Satan, and resolves to obtain Papal condemnation of their reprobate author. Arraigned before the Council of Sens in June, 1141, Abelard himself decides to appeal to Rome, and sets off to obtain justice at the hands of the Supreme Pontiff. On 16th July, probably as a result of Bernard's letters of denunciation, Abelard is excommunicated at St. Peter's, and condemned to imprisonment.

On the way to Rome, however, Abelard, now much broken in health, stopped at the great Benedictine abbey of Cluny, where the abbot, Peter the Venerable, received him with great kindness and at once interceded with Bernard (who had not yet published in France the Pope's indictment), so that the latter finally agreed to stay the persecution of his already failing enemy. Probably he was softened by an *Apology* which Abelard wrote to him from Cluny, where he also wrote a final and most tender letter to his 'sister Héloïse, once dear to me in the world, and now most dear in Christ'.

So Abelard became a monk at Cluny and passed out of men's sight. On 21st April, 1142, aged sixty-three, he died. Héloïse, who supervised his interment at the Paraclete, survived her husband by twenty years. Many centuries afterwards, the remains of these two courageous souls were removed; and in 1817 their ashes, commingled, were buried at the cemetery of Père Lachaise, on the outskirts of Paris, where they have since been preserved. In one of his last letters Abelard had written: 'I hope you will be willing, when you have finished this mortal life, to be buried near me. Your cold ashes need then fear nothing, and my tomb shall be then the more rich and renowned.' The inscription on the tomb reads as follows:

'Here, under the same stone, repose, of this monastery the founder, Peter Abelard, and the first abbess, Héloïse, heretofore in study, genius, love, inauspicious marriage, and repentance, now, as we hope, in eternal happiness, united. Peter died April 21st, 1142. Héloïse, May 17, 1164.'

Moslem and Jewish Philosophers and the Revival of Aristotelianism

In our account of the life and work of Aristotle, we have emphasized the extent to which Moslem thinkers were responsible for stimulating a new interest in the works of the master. Today we may tend to underestimate the part played by Orientals in precipitating a renaissance of Christian thought in the West. Between the death of Mohammed (632) and the tenth century, the Crescent had extended its Empire from Spain on the one hand to Turkestan on the other. This expansion without parallel in history of a militant religion was accompanied by a cultural renaissance no less remarkable. In course of time, the old division between the Christian West and the Moslem East lost its sharpness; for certain areas of Asia remained and still remain Christian, while Islam extended its influence to the borders of France. Greek thought infiltrated into the Orient by way of towns such as Edessa (the modern Urfa in Turkey), which was a veritable clearing-house of Hellenic culture. Baghdad was likewise a flourishing cultural centre where Oriental Christians engaged in Arabic translations of works on Greek science. In 832, the enlightened Abbasid Caliph, Al Mamoun, founded in that city a 'House of Wisdom': here learned doctors translated into Arabic the works of Plato, Aristotle, Euclid and Galen. At the heart of Islam there was an intellectual ferment which often brought about fierce conflict between the new spirit of enquiry and the upholders of Koranic orthodoxy. Men of learning proceeded to submit to the rest of reason the most sacred articles of religion, thereby employing the pagan doctrines of Aristotle to disturb the consciences of the faithful. In general, the spirit of rationalism, often regarded as an exclusively Western product, proved a vital force in the Islamic world well before it began to play its part in the evolution of Christian theology.

Of the great Moslem students of Aristotle from whom the Western world derived profit, the most famous were Alkindi (*d.* 873), Alfarabi (*d.* 949), Avicenna (980-1037), doctor as well as philosopher, and finally Averroes (*b.* Cordova, 1126). Averroes, the 'Great Commentator', maintained that truth could be reached upon three separate planes: that of philosophy, which was in touch with absolute truth; that of religion, which sought to interpret truth in terms of mythical imagery; and that of ordinary common sense, which attained the truth through faith or natural piety. Origen, the Christian philosopher, had stated similar views several centuries earlier in relation to Christian thought.

The contribution of the Jews was no less important in assisting the emergence of the scientific spirit from within the bosom of religious mysticism and dogma. In Egypt, in Spain, in Morocco even, Jewish thought flourished, sometimes in close contact with Moslem thought, sometimes with that of Christianity or such pagan survivals as Neo-Platonism, rarely in isolation. The *Kabbala*, for instance, was in essentials the Jewish version of Neo-Platonic mysticism, in contrast to the Talmud, which was the orthodox commentary upon the Law. A most notable attempt to 'reconcile' science and philosophy with the teachings of the scriptures was made by a Jewish Rabbi, Maimonides, born (like Averroes) at Cordova in 1135. Maimonides likewise invoked the work of Aristotle, but for the purpose of giving rational basis to Holy Writ. He is thus the true precursor of Thomas Aquinas (1227-74), the greatest of the so-called 'Scholastic' philosophers.

The word 'scholasticism', which has been revived in our day, is frequently misunderstood. Scholasticism, as originally conceived, was not a dry quibbling about theological subtleties; it was an attempt, and on the whole a successful attempt, to demonstrate that Faith and Reason, Religion and Science, complemented each other. Previously, attempts had been made to demonstrate either that the two were opposed or that they were identical. Both arguments broke down. That St. Thomas was able to effect a reconciliation (but not a compromise) was due to the extraordinary breadth of his mental outlook, his huge learning, and above all his sense of logic and precision, the latter being the fruit of a close study of Aristotle. Indeed, Scholasticism was the marriage between Christianity and Aristotelianism.

Today it is the practice of nations to 'export' their cultures, because each feels, rightly or wrongly, that it has something to give to the world. In the mediæval period, it was rather the practice to 'import' culture, because in Europe at any rate the centre of culture was the Catholic Church, with its great and pervasive spiritual authority. The exaggeration of the mediæval unity by some historians has given rise, especially in our day, to its belittlement by others; but to say that Europe was united by a common faith is not to say that it was free from dissension.

An international language manufactured from synthetic counters, such as has frequently been suggested in modern times as the cure for international misunderstanding, will fail of its purpose because it lacks roots; the international use of Latin in mediæval times was based upon a common culture, uniting all Christians without distinction of nation or class. The mediæval unity was an ideal unity, or a unity of ideals, from which there were in practice many departures; but at least the offender, in breaking the laws, knew that he was offending, the blasphemer that he was blaspheming, the heretic that he deserved the title of apostate. In this awareness, the orthodox structure was indirectly honoured and preserved. What politics divided, culture unified. And the unification of culture was made possible by a theology and philosophy which embraced, for the first and in some ways the last time, the whole of human experience.

St. Thomas Aquinas

'God is known through all things and yet apart from all things; and He is known through knowledge and through ignorance.'

—Commentary of 'The Divine Names'.

1

Thomas Aquinas was born in 1225 or 1227 at the castle of Rocca Secca, a few miles from the town of Aquino, after which he later took his name. Like Abelard, he came of noble stock. His father was Count of Aquino, a fief within the kingdom of Naples, and nephew of Frederick Barbarossa. His mother, Theodora of Theate, was descended from the old Norman Kings of Sicily. Thus Thomas came into the world blessed with every material advantage. Like Abelard in one other respect, he early signified his wish to renounce these inherited privileges and to devote himself exclusively to a religious calling.

Thomas's parents were resolved to give their son—the youngest and most promising of their seven sons—a thorough education. The youngster's uncle was Abbot of Monte Cassino, home of the Benedictine Order, and a name familiar to the present generation. To the care of this wise and learned man, Thomas was entrusted at the tender age of five. He did not prove exactly a brilliant pupil, if by brilliant we mean 'bright' or 'quick-witted'; he was rather a plodding, receptive, assiduous type of student, who, if we are to believe contemporary witnesses, never forgot anything once he had learnt it. Both his parents and his teachers were anxious that he should enter the University of Naples, for they felt that a great career lay before him either in the field of learning or in the ecclesiastical hierarchy; and at that period the vocation of scholarship, like that of the priesthood, was held in far higher esteem than it is today. So to Naples Thomas was sent at the age of fourteen.

By the time that Thomas Aquinas had reached the age of sixteen, his mind was quite made up on the subject of what he wanted to do. He wanted to acquire learning; but he wanted to acquire it in obscurity. Now a robust, large-limbed lad, almost a giant in stature, friendly in manner but not a social 'mixer' in the ordinary sense, he was nei-ther unhappy nor misplaced at the University; but the kind of fraternity for which he longed was not that of scholars but that of the devout. From the first moment of his acquaintance with it, the white and black habit of the Dominican Order, then commonly seen in the streets of Naples, had exercised a strong fascination over him: not for its austere appearance, but rather for the ideals for which it stood—chastity and poverty. A life of humble obscurity in the service of a Mendicant Order was not, it need hardly be said, the kind of ecclesiastical career to which his parents, in planning his future, had looked for-ward. On the contrary, they fancied him as a rich and powerful Church dignitary, achieving rapid and well-mer-ited promotion, and perhaps ending up as the Supreme Pontiff at Rome. He had influence; he had the brains; if necessary, he had the means. Aquinas knew this. But he also knew his own mind. And so, without divulging his intention to his family, he quietly took the vow of men-dicancy and joined the Dominican Order in 1244.

When his mother discovered what he had done, she was at first surprised, though not perhaps so displeased as her husband; but when she later found that she was not to be permitted to visit her son, her approval turned to open hostility. In banning visitors, the Dominicans were ensuring that their protégé should not be persuaded (as if he could be persuaded) to change his mind about his vocation; but Theodora was resolved not to allow them to monopolize the son upon whom she had set such hopes. Thomas had brothers in the upper ranks of the army of Frederick II. When their mother confided to them her fears about Thomas, they unanimously decided to remove him by force from the clutches of the monks. Al-though they succeeded in waylaying him on the road to Paris, they failed to shake his decision to remain attached to the Order. For more than a year they kept him a close prisoner in the castle of Rocca Secca. He did not object. He used the seclusion and ample leisure at his disposal for unremitting study of the Scriptures.

In trying to dissuade him from adopting the monastic life, his family had merely succeeded in making him more of a hermit than ever. Indeed, some of their attempts to divert him from his purpose were both frivolous and stupid. On one occasion they even resorted to the expedient of introducing an attractive and flashily-dressed young woman into his cell. The inmate, who was for once roused to fury, seized a flaming brand from the fire and drove her screaming from the room: after which, with two mighty strokes, he marked the door with the sign of the cross. This particular stratagem was not repeated.

In the end his mother repented of her thoughtless, if excusable, behaviour. Her son was so obviously fitted to be a hermit-scholar that it was better, as she now realized, to enable him to follow his inclinations in freedom rather than in servitude. One day, with her connivance, he managed to let himself down from the castle window by means of a rope, and make his way back to his Dominican friends. Outwitted, his brothers took no action. Besides, Thomas was as strong as an ox—a 'dumb ox', as he was called by one of his masters; and they did not fancy provoking him further. After a brief spell in Naples, he set out, this time unmolested, for Paris again, where his fame as a scholar soon grew.

In 1248, accompanied by Johannes Teutonicus, Thomas took the road to Cologne. The intention of the two scholars was to put themselves under the tuition of Albert of Bollstadt (1206-80). Albert, later named 'The Great', was a scholar of distinct originality. He was convinced that the difficulties encountered by the theological thought of his time could be solved only by reference to the work of Aristotle—that is, the 'complete' Aristotle. Perhaps the 'greatness' of Albert of Bollstadt lay in the fact that, while seeking to resurrect a pagan thinker, he lost hold of no single element of the Christian faith. For Thomas and Johannes the journey to Cologne was both long and tedious; it took them three months to accomplish. No sooner had Thomas begun to receive instruction from Albert, however, than the latter, discounting his pupil's bovine appearance, realized that he had met a genius. Master and pupil soon fell into that most perfect of scholastic relationships in which the 'rôles' were reversible at any moment. In Albert, Thomas recognized a spiritual leader as well as a teacher. In Thomas, Albert recognized an original and even daring thinker as well as a disciple. Together they would effect the 'conversion' of Aristotle, defying the official ban on his works of 1215.

Not merely did Albert and Thomas recognize each other's ability; the university and other authorities at Cologne could not but perceive how ably they worked in unison. Universities in those days often needed capable spokesmen for both scholastic and diplomatic reasons; and the relationship between scholarship and diplomacy was a great deal closer than it is now, owing to the importance of maintaining theological orthodoxy. Thus it came about in 1245 that the Chapter of the Dominican Order at Cologne dispatched Albert and Thomas on a kind of academic mission to Paris, still the great centre of learning of Europe. Here they remained for as long as three years, during which time Thomas not merely eclipsed his master in reputation as a teacher but proved himself a great intellectual force among the youth of his day. Many other philosophers have held their audience spellbound with original and startling 'ideas'. Thomas Aquinas acquired (and still maintains) his great reputation by the exposition and demonstration of clear, dry, logical propositions concerning Nature, man and God, presented without verbal flourishes, purple passages, or personal allusions, and set out like a legal treatise or a scientific blueprint. So much for the 'reactionary' influence of Aristotle on the mediæval mind!

Although his stay in Paris was successful beyond his expectations, he returned in 1248 without having had any degrees or honours conferred upon him. There was still much prejudice in high quarters about members of the Mendicant Orders. In 1252, however, he was encouraged to set out once more for Paris, ostensibly in order to obtain the official academic recognition that he deserved, but primarily in order to establish an independent school there. From this course he was soon diverted by a problem which seemed at the time to be of greater importance, if not for Thomas Aquinas, then at least for the Dominican Order. A bitter quarrel had broken out between the Mendicant Orders and the University of Paris concerning precisely that 'recognition' over which Thomas had already experienced a limited rebuff in the case of his own academic honours.

The Dominicans had decided, after careful consideration, to appeal to the Pope. This was a bold and usually expensive step, and no organization was advised to embark upon it unless it were either sure of its case or confident in the skill of the man it had selected as emissary. The Dominicans were doubly convinced. First of all, they had a good case; and secondly, they had a spokesman whose ability was universally recognized, not least by those who were called upon to put it to the test. For when the Dominicans asked themselves whom they should send to intercede with Pope Alexander IV, they had no hesitation in choosing the 'dumb ox', Thomas Aquinas.

Thomas's plea to the Pope was successful: so successful, indeed, that he was able to return in triumph to Paris in 1256, to be granted, without the least grudge on the part of the authorities, the degrees of Licentiate and Master in Theology. These honours were conferred in recognition of his brilliant teaching and theological studies, which already included a Commentary on the Bible and on the *Sentences*, or works of the Fathers, and the treatise *On Being and Essence* which scholars now regard as the key to his whole philosophical system.

Between 1259 and 1268, Thomas Aquinas, now occupying a status similar to that of Abelard in his day, lectured and composed treatises upon all the major theological topics of the age. He was now an international figure. To him, kings, prelates and men of learning referred the problems that confronted them, putting the great man to the kind of use that is not common in our day, when wise men write books in the hope of creating an audience or 'public' rather than in the knowledge that such an audience is ready to hand. Some modern philosophers—Earl Russell is the latest offender—enjoy pointing out the triviality and frivolity of some of the problems with which Aquinas concerned himself; but this is to forget both the origin of most of these problems and the necessity that Aquinas was under to deal politely and diplomatically with his correspondents or interlocutors. Most of these were sincere but some were clearly indulging in the favourite mediæval game of heresy-hunting. In any case, the majority of Aquinas's pronouncements were masterpieces of diplomatic skill, and worthy to be compared, at least in their form, with the more celebrated utterances of the classical oracles.

When asked, for instance, whether the names of the elect were written by the hand of God in heaven and whether there was an equivalent list in hell, he answered simply: 'For all I can see, it does not seem to be true, but there is no harm done in saying it.' Given conundrums of such relative puerility, this was a typical reply. Naturally he was frequently consulted upon questions of more serious import. Hugh II of Cyprus requested him to lay down the duties of a ruler; the Duchess of Brabant, faced with an age-old problem, consulted him upon the best way of handling Jewish subjects; the Pope repeatedly sought his advice upon matters of theology (it was at the request of Gregory X that he wrote the great *Summa Contra Gentiles,* as a compendium of arguments to be used against infidels). He had indeed become a kind of oracle. And in some quarters he is still treated as one.

To have written thirty large volumes in the space of forty-eight years was an achievement which, taking into account his heavy public duties and frequent journeys abroad, is almost without parallel. But Thomas Aquinas possessed the type of mind that is never at rest. His occupation was thought—directed, energetic thought, not reverie; his mysticism was a discipline, not a relaxation. His one aim was not to 'lose himself' in the divine but to find himself in it. There are anecdotes, indeed, concerning his absent-mindedness (a form, as Chesterton pointed out, of presence of mind). One day, it is recorded, he was dining with St. Louis, King of France, in a great company of nobles and ecclesiastics. The problems of the *Summa Theologiæ* were at that period uppermost in his mind. After remaining for some time in a fit of abstraction, he suddenly pounded the table with his heavy fist and exclaimed: 'That settles the Manichees!' His companions, much embarrassed, nudged him to recall him to his outer senses; but St. Louis, with great tact, put everyone at ease by summoning a secretary and begging Aquinas to record, for the benefit of Christendom, the idea that had occurred to him.

During these productive years, Aquinas taught at such centres of learning as Ostia, Viterbo, Anagni, Perugia, Bologna, and Rome itself. Pope Urban IV, who welcomed his presence, was determined to raise him to high office in the Church. It was not common that a scholar of such profound learning and original mind could be relied upon to uphold, whatever the problem under discussion, the orthodox point of view; it was less common still to find that, after such rigorous and logical enquiries, orthodoxy appeared more firmly entrenched than ever. Yet that was precisely the effect of Aquinas's analytical researches: he succeeded, as few have succeeded since, in enlarging men's capacity for orthodoxy. When, later on, the French philosopher Descartes set out to apply the sceptical method to every sphere of thought, he found that most theological writings failed to stand up to the strain imposed upon them. But there was one exception: the works of Thomas Aquinas. St. Thomas appeared to have an answer to everything, for he had thought of every possible objection, pushed through it, and made his way out the other side.

Although every inducement was offered Thomas to accept high office, and although he undoubtedly possessed gifts of administration and leadership as far above the average as he excelled his fellows in scholarship, he steadfastly refused to seek such preferment. No doubt it was with his own case in mind that he remarked in his Sermon for the Feast of St. Martin that 'the episcopal state, for all its greatness, is not to be sought out; if a man says "I want to be a learned man, that afterwards I may be the wise ruler of a great church", his plan is not good. Augustine says: "It is not fitting for a man to aspire to that high place which is needed for the governance of the people, even though he may occupy it fittingly. . . . If no man put upon you the burden of this charge, give your time to the search for, and the gathering of, truth." '

In 1268, we find him back once more in Paris. During the next few years he was engaged in high controversy with a number of persons of whose growing influence the Church went in fear; for a heretic, especially an eloquent heretic, is the most plausible of men. There were in fact two sorts of heretic whose errors Aquinas was invited, and indeed urged, to confute: those, like Siger of Brabant, who followed the ideas of Averroes to the point of placing the authority of Aristotle above that of divine truth, and those, like some of the Franciscans, who adopted a one-sided Augustinianism and thereby upset the balance between Faith and Reason. Both in effect were covertly destroying that unity and harmony of thought which the Scholastic doctors were striving to preserve. Out of these resounding controversies issued that gigantic synthesis of Christian thought and apologetic, the *Summa Theologiæ,* in which Aquinas constructed a 'cathedral' of reason as perfect and comprehensive as the edifices of stone that were raised, by a like impulse, in his century.

Feeling that their champion had had enough of disputation, the Dominican Order recalled him—it is said at the wish of the King of Sicily, brother of St. Louis of France—to teach once more at Naples. But a man's reputation, once securely established, will not let him be. Summoned by Pope Gregory X to the General Council of Lyon in 1274, Aquinas, accompanied by Reginald, a brother of his Order, set out on muleback to put his wisdom once again at the service of the Church. This time his task was that of reconciling the differences between the Greek and Latin Churches, and also of organizing another Crusade. Although Aquinas was thoroughly overworked and already ailing, such business could not be neglected and he refused to send excuses. When they had reached the castle of Magenza, however (the property of his niece, the Countess Ceccano), the doctor underwent a sudden change. He fell into what his companions and hosts called 'an ecstasy' in which he remained absorbed for a considerable time; and when he came to himself, almost as if he were revisiting the earth, his health was observed to have broken down beyond restoration.

Of his failing condition he was as conscious as his friends; and he at once expressed an earnest wish to be allowed to die in a house belonging to his Order. An attempt was made to comply with this desire; but the party that escorted him, realizing that further travel would be useless, decided to stop at the Cistercian Abbey of Fossa Nuova near Terracina, where he died on 7th March, 1274. Until the last moment, except for periods of rapt meditation, he was in full possession and exercise of his faculties. A demon for work, if for nothing else, he continued to dictate to his secretary a commentary upon *The Song of Songs*, which his hosts had requested him to undertake. He had reached the passage beginning *'Filiae Jerusalem dicite dilecto meo, quia prae amore morior'* ('I charge you, O daughters of Jerusalem, if ye find my beloved, that ye tell him that I am sick of love') when he suddenly collapsed and died within a few minutes.[1]

At the time of his death, the fame of Thomas Aquinas had become so widespread that different Orders quarrelled fiercely for the possession of his mortal remains. The chief dispute was between the Dominicans and the Cistercians; and this undignified squabble, so alien to the spirit of the man over whom it had arisen, was still continuing when, fifty years later, Thomas was canonized by Pope John XXII. Nor was the dispute over the body finally settled until Urban V, issuing a special Bull in 1368, ordained that the saint's remains should be handed over to the Dominicans of Toulouse. At Toulouse stood the mother church of the Dominican Order. Even so, the surrender was not complete: to the Convent of St. Jacques at Paris, where both Thomas and his master Albert had once taught, an arm was presented.

More than two centuries after his canonization, Pope Pius V proclaimed Thomas Aquinas 'Fifth Doctor of the Church' (1567), thereby making his festival equal in rank with that of the four Latin Fathers, Ambrose, Augustine, Jerome and Gregory. Not until the nineteenth century, however, did the Roman Church pronounce

[1] After his death a rumour began to circulate that Aquinas had been poisoned by Charles of Anjou. Dante, who accepted Aquinas as his philosophic master, apparently believed this charge, for in the twentieth canto of the *Purgatorio* (line 67) he writes:

'Carlo venne in Italia, e, per ammenda, Vittima fe' di Curradino; e poi ripinse al ciel Tommoso, per ammenda.'

'Charles came to Italy, and, for amends, made a victim of Conradin; and then thrust Thomas back to heaven, for amends.'

the 'Thomist' philosophy to be the basis of Catholic theological teaching. Today, both Catholic and non-Catholic philosophers recognize in the enormous achievement of the 'Angelic Doctor' (as he came to be called) the most complete synthesis of speculation concerning the natural and spiritual world that has yet been constructed. Just as Dante had referred to Aristotle as 'the master of those who know', so also he referred to Aquinas, whom he naturally placed higher in status than Aristotle, as a 'flame of heavenly wisdom'. It is therefore fitting that at the close of Dante's journey, as unfolded in the third part of the *Divine Comedy*, both Thomas and Albert should be encountered among those nearest to the Divine Presence: 'I was of the lambs of the sacred flock,' Aquinas is made to say, 'that Dominic leadeth upon the way where is good fattening if there be no straying. This, who most neighboureth me upon the right, brother and master was to me, and he was Albert of Cologne, I Thomas of Aquino' (*Paradiso*, X, 94-99). Thus, while Beatrice is the guide upon whom Dante relies during his final journey, Thomas Aquinas is the real successor of Virgil, in that he fulfils the function of interpreter of the spiritual mysteries into which Dante is being initiated.

To the Middle Ages, the intellect was not a dead, lifeless instrument, but a light to wisdom and faith. Consequently, Aquinas, the philosopher and poet (he wrote some very beautiful hymns, of which the most famous is that contained in his Office for the Feast of Corpus Christi, written at the request of Urban IV), represents for Dante the human reason at its highest level of perfection. The philosophies of a later age, in which Reason is contrasted with Sense, Instinct or Intuition (as if the latter alone possessed warmth, life and radiance), would have been as unintelligible to Dante as to Aquinas himself.

2

We have said that the aim of Scholasticism was to demonstrate the harmony or compatibility between Reason and Faith. What St. Thomas succeeded in doing was not merely to prove such compatibility but to codify all knowledge in the light of it. Being an exceedingly careful and precise thinker, he avoids the pitfalls into which so many religious philosophers have sunk: he seeks not to 'spiritualize' everything, but, by recognizing what his modern disciple Maritain has termed the 'primacy of the spiritual', to define with accuracy the boundaries and 'rights' of the natural realm. Studying Aquinas for the first time, modern thinkers have been surprised and impressed to find that, austere and high-minded man though he was, he fully recognized the part played in human conduct and motive by such natural forces as sex. What he did not do was to attribute to such impulses a power and supremacy out of all proportion to their nature.

With the exception of the sermons, hymns and devotional works, the writings of St. Thomas are composed upon a pattern which the ordinary reader may find a trifle uninviting: either they are short essays or *opuscula* upon a particular philosophical problem, which is 'argued out' much like a problem in mathematics, or they take the form of ten-volume treatises, divided into sections and subsections and resembling a legal digest rather than a work of literary exposition. Hence the student who—fired by what he has heard of the 'majesty' and 'profundity' of the Angelic Doctor—sets out to peruse what he actually wrote, will soon find himself wading through pages of syllogisms and propositions without encountering a single brilliant metaphor or anecdote; still less will he come upon anything resembling a personal confession or *cri de cœur*. Aquinas is a thinker; Augustine was a thinker who happened also to be a great literary artist. Hence those who refuse to study anything that cannot be 'read as literature' (which usually means read for its emotional rather than its intellectual appeal) will compare the humanity and warmth of Augustine with the cold, passionless intellectuality of Aquinas. The comparison is unjust. Aquinas is not without passion, but he is passionate in a different way from Augustine. And we know that the Thomist philosophy can inspire passion in others, for there is the *Divine Comedy* to prove it.

Not merely is the *form* of St. Thomas's philosophy unfamiliar to most modern students; its *content* is also. As a result of certain developments of modern thought usually labelled 'idealist', philosophy has come to be regarded in many quarters as a vague, abstract, ethereal study, quite beyond the mental grasp of ordinary and (it is sometimes added) normal people. With St. Thomas, philosophy was not like that at all. He begins at the beginning. We know something, and a thing is what we know; to deny that we have any reliable knowledge, as the sceptics do, is itself to make an affirmation and therefore to climb out of scepticism forthwith.

Aquinas follows Aristotle in asserting that the 'form' is that which gives being to a thing and makes it what it is; further, that all forms are in some way linked with matter, except the form of God, the Form of Forms. Thus we come to know God by and through the world of matter, which manifests a hierarchy of Forms; and since the more perfect a form is the more it increases its individuality, God is the supreme unity and supreme individual at once. For St. Thomas, the natural sphere has both meaning and purpose. He is not the kind of philosopher who claims to know God in some direct fashion, and whose primary task is therefore to explain away the existence or 'illusion' of Matter.

St. Thomas held that the human mind was committed to a standard which prevented our intellect from being converted into something different, and possibly mischievous. That standard was Reason. In the same way, the human will was committed to a standard which, as long as it remained uppermost, preserved the will as a free instrument. That standard was the Good. The onset of sin was due entirely to our natural and sensual nature rising up and suspending the will's operations. St. Thomas refused to entertain the paralysing notion which Augustine came to embrace with excessive fervour: namely, that human souls were predestined to salvation or damnation. So great was his respect for Reason, and so ample his conception of it, that he held the Divine Will itself to be motivated by Reason. If there were any predestination to sin, it was not of the deterministic kind of Augustine; it was a moral predestination. The sinner ultimately comes to *choose* damnation. Otherwise it is not his sin that condemns him, but somebody else's; and that is to drift once more into the heresy of the Manichees.

Since the intellect necessarily has Reason for its guide, it can know and understand the world of nature without any illumination from outside; but as both the intellect and the world of nature are, as it were, orientated towards God, philosophy inevitably leads on to theology and is completed by it. Thus St. Thomas wishes to apply his important (and in its origin Aristotelian) distinction between 'potentiality' and 'actuality' to every sphere of existence. Since nature is a hierarchy of Forms, each stage in the hierarchy is the 'form' of the stage next below it and the 'matter' of the stage next above it. Thus Matter is potential Spirit, the natural man a potential Christian, philosophy a potential theology, and the State a material version of the Church.

St. Thomas did not complete the *Summa Theologiæ*. Great master of synthesis and codification as he was, he was content to leave his finest work unfinished, not because of age (for he died comparatively young), nor because of the sudden visitation of death, nor because of the magnitude of the task—he would often employ four secretaries at a time, dictating to each a different composition. It was because of his consciousness that no single book and no single man could attempt to embrace all the mysteries of nature and God; and also because, as he confessed to those friends who questioned him on this point, 'all that he had written so far appeared to him as nothing in comparison with the wonderful things that God had been pleased to reveal to him recently'. Hence it is clear that those critics, and also those over-fervid adherents, who believe that Thomism represents a 'closed system' of philosophical theology, not to be added to and not to be subtracted from, are possessed with an idea foreign to the intention of its author.

Scholastic Decline and
Scientific Advance

Those who have formed the impression that the Middle Ages were a time of order, unity and social stability have often been deeply distressed to discover, on inspecting the facts more closely, that this much-idealized period was in fact no less agitated, violent and confused than any other: with the result that they dismiss such works as Aquinas's *Summa Theologiæ* and Dante's *Divine Comedy* as exhibiting a purely fictitious unity, and end by transferring their affections to some other historical epoch, either before or since, which they proceed to endow with the characteristics of enlightenment or re-birth. Historical disillusion of this kind is due to a failure to perceive that every unity or order in society is engaged either in coming to be or in passing away; it never permanently crystallizes. Thus the mediæval synthesis of reason and faith, Empire and Church, was at all times a precarious synthesis: it contained within itself, as every unity must do, the seeds of its own dissolution.

We soon pass, in other words, from the age of St. Thomas to an age of open conflict and scepticism and infidelity. How was this change brought about? There were various long-term causes: the appalling strain and misery of the Hundred Years' War (1337-1453), the disintegration of the Empire, and the ecclesiastical schisms that deprived the Papacy of its power and reputation. Christendom was split up into principalities or nations; or rather, principalities or nations were the only authorities that survived the collapse of the European order. Not Christendoms but kingdoms became the centres of stability. We find lawyers beginning to argue seriously about the supremacy of the Royal power, so that kings (including the English Henry VIII) who wanted formal authority for their strengthened prerogatives found it already propounded for them by their own jurists. At the same time the prestige of the European universities was beginning to grow, chiefly perhaps because of their independent status and their wealth. At Oxford and at Chartres, for instance, distinguished schools of theology flourished, while the study of mathematics induced in such men as Robert Grosseteste, Bishop of Lincoln (1175-1253), and the monk Roger Bacon (*c.* 1210-*c.* 1292) an appetite for exploring the secrets of the natural world which anticipated by several centuries the scientific humanism of the Renaissance.

Within the universities themselves a celebrated controversy arose, that between the 'Ancients' and the 'Moderns'. The Ancients clung to Aristotle as the final authority upon most branches of knowledge; the Moderns, seeking to divest themselves of traditional theories, studied 'facts' alone. Duns Scotus (1274-1308), a Franciscan monk who was also professor of philosophy and theology at Oxford and a critic of Thomism, Raymond Lull (1234-1315) of Palma, theologian, naturalist, troubadour and devotee of Arabian mysticism, and finally William of Ockham (1280-1350), reflect each in their different ways the 'modern' spirit: and this tendency gave rise in turn to a new movement of Nominalism, according to which (as we saw in the work of Abelard) general terms or universals were held to be 'fictions'.

The rise of experiment and scepticism did not necessarily bring about a weakening of religious faith among the common people. While philosophy and theology, as today, were matters for the schools and universities, traditional beliefs and likewise superstitions maintained a firm hold upon the laity. But even traditional faith was stirring with new impulses, largely under the influence of the monks and friars. The aristocratic scholasticism of the intellectuals seems to have called into being, by way of reaction, a revival of mysticism and the cult of inner illumination. Eckhart (*d.* 1300) the Dominican, Tauler (*d.* 1361), one of Luther's teachers, Ruysbroeck of the Netherlands (1293-1381), and Thomas à Kempis (1379-1471), author of the famous *Imitation of Christ*, widened still further the division between Reason and Faith that opened as the influence of the Scholastic philosophy declined.

The reaction in so many quarters against Aristotelianism caused a revival of interest in Plato; but just as the Aristotle of the Middle Ages had been an Aristotle converted, without permission, to Catholicism, so the Platonism of the Renaissance, as manifested in the work of thinkers such as Nicholas of Cusa (1401-64), Marsilio Ficino (1433-99), Pico de la Mirandola (1463-94), and Paracelsus (1493-1541), was Platonism permeated with Christian ideas. Plato had regarded the natural world as a world of half-truths and imprecision; men such as Leonardo da Vinci (1452-1519) assumed that Nature obeyed uniform laws which the scientist could both descry and tabulate. This conception of an ordered, reasonable world was ultimately derived from Christian teaching: for God, having created the world, 'saw that it was good', *i.e.* intelligible, harmonious and in conformity with the divine Logos or Reason.

The seeds of the new scientific spirit had been present, as we saw in the speculations of the English Franciscan monk, Roger Bacon. In the work of his later namesake, Francis Bacon (1561-1626), Chancellor to King James I, the new spirit is in full bloom. Bacon was one of the first declared enemies of *verbiage;* he believed that science had hitherto been rendered sterile because it had occupied itself with definitions and distinctions of a purely abstract or verbal kind. Experiment was the clue to the *Advancement of Learning* (the title of one of his works). Having experimented, the task was to organize research, to promote team work among scientists; hence the *Novum Organum,* the new technique or logic designed to supersede that of Aristotle. To apply such a technique was to acquire control over Nature. Science for Bacon is not merely true knowledge; it is power. What Bacon asserted as a revolutionary fact we tend to accept today as a commonplace.

Bacon was a man of extraordinary learning and culture, as his *Essays* alone reveal; but he was an inspirer of ideas in others rather than a practitioner of what he preached. His experimentation was fragmentary and 'rule of thumb'. Dismissed from high office on a charge of corruption, the indefatigable old man died from a cold caught one day while carrying out an experiment in refrigeration by stuffing a chicken with snow.

Bacon had dreamed dreams of a New Atlantis, a scientific Brave New World; René Descartes worked out the theoretical principles upon which scientific progress has since largely been based. With the Cartesian philosophy, modern thought is born.

René Descartes

'In our search for the direct road towards truth, we should busy ourselves with no object about which we cannot attain a certitude equal to that of the demonstrations of arithmetic and geometry.'

1

Born at La Haye in Touraine on 31st March, 1596, Descartes was the third son of a doctor and of the daughter of a Law Officer of Poitiers.

His family included numerous men of learning; it is not now agreed (as used to be maintained) that he came of military ancestry. He was a thoughtful, delicate boy, to whom the nickname 'little philosopher' easily attached itself. At the age of eight he was sent to a school for which he ever after preserved an affection: the Jesuit college at La Flèche in Anjou. Here the Rector, Father Charlet, a relation, and his tutor, Father Dinet, supervised his studies with particular care. Descartes seems to have been a model pupil, though not a mere bookworm; he it was who, on the assassination of King Henry IV, was deputed to receive the royal heart for burial at the church of La Flèche (1610).

The Jesuits taught Descartes the classics and poetry for five years, after which he proceeded to ethics, logic, mathematics, physics and metaphysics. This order, based upon the *trivium* and *quadrivium* of mediæval times, developed his sensibility along with his intellect, and must have aided the evolution of his superb power of literary expression. His health seems to have remained extremely delicate. Much of his time, then as later, was spent in bed. Here he learnt to meditate, developing the taste for reflection upon mathematical problems that never left him.

From school he went direct to the University of

Poitiers, where in 1616 he graduated in Law. Contrary to expectations, he rejected the idea of a legal career. Instead he began to contemplate one for which his early training seemed to have rendered him least fitted, that of soldiering. Nevertheless, he proceeded to devote his time to both riding and fencing; and upon the latter art he was even moved to compose an essay. To gain practical experience, he left France for Holland and forthwith became a gentleman volunteer in the army of the Stadt-halter, Prince Maurice of Nassau, at Breda. The change of scene and manner of life turned out to be most beneficial. The sickly youth was now mixing with men, and exercising both mind and body in an atmosphere free from constraint.

From another point of view, the career he had chosen gave him valuable and practical scope for his mathematical interests, as these were called into play by the problems in military engineering with which the officers were frequently confronted. In fact, the solution of tricky mathematical problems had become a popular pastime at Breda. The statement of a problem would be posted, for interest, upon one of the city walls, and anybody who wished could submit his idea of the solution. Descartes, though not yet proficient in Dutch, rarely missed an opportunity of exercising his ingenuity in this field.

One day, as he was puzzling out a particularly abstruse problem, he turned for help over the translation to a man who happened to be standing at his side. It proved to be the great Dutch mathematician, Beeckman. The latter challenged Descartes to go home, solve the problem, and bring him the answer. Descartes worked it out in two days, and as a result a great friendship was established. Two works of Descartes, an *Essay on Algebra* and a *Compendium of Music*, were dedicated to Beeckman about this time (1618), for the Frenchman had already developed the habit of pursuing his speculations along several different paths simultaneously. From Beeckman, Descartes derived something more than the incentive to pursue his mathematical researches; he derived, for the first time, friendship with a man of his own sympathies and of at least equal intelligence.

Pleasant as his life had been in Holland, Descartes soon realized that his military aspirations were simply a cloak for the desire to live at liberty with his own thoughts, and also for his impulse—often said to find satisfaction in a military career—to see the world. He formed a resolution to go to Germany. Whether owing to the sudden change of scene or to some inner compulsion which the move laid bare, Descartes now became conscious of a kind of acceleration of his mental processes, an intellectual excitement which he had not previously known.

At the start it took the form of mystical possession (he is said to have enrolled himself among the Rosicrucians at this time). Then on 10th November, 1619, being rapt in meditation of a deeper kind than usual, he conceived in a flash of inspiration the outlines of what he believed to be an entirely new science of nature and thought. An experience very similar to that which befell Archimedes, when he exclaimed 'Eureka' ('I have found it!'), followed. This moment of intense exhilaration in turn gave place to a series of prophetic dreams. In the first, so he records, he dreamt that he was lame and seeking shelter in a church after a storm. In the second, he was again aware of a violent storm, with thunder and also showers of sparks. In the third and last, he dreamt that, having opened a book of Ausonius, he came by accident upon the phrase: *Quid vitae sectabor iter?* ('Which way of life shall I follow?'). This series of inner illuminations exerted the most profound alteration in his outlook. He instantly made a vow to undertake a pilgrimage of gratitude to Our Lady of Loretto: a resolution that he fulfilled during a visit to Italy two years later.

The eight years following upon his mystical experience were years of deep, and for the most part solitary, meditation. He may have seen some action during his stay in Germany; but historians now incline to the view that he never took part in any serious military engagement. In 1624 we find him once more in Italy: but although he must have passed through Florence while Galileo was living there, no record exists of a meeting between the two. Back in France, now feeling the iron hand of Richelieu, he realized that a man of his tastes needed a settled life in a settled country. He therefore sold up his estates and left for Holland, calculating that he now had enough to support himself without hardship.

The record of his life in Holland is not very full, though this was the most productive period of his career. He seems never to have ceased to be a loyal member of the Catholic Church; but of his precise relationship with a woman called Hèlene, who bore him a child in 1632 (it died five years later), we know little. We do know, however, that a second crisis in his mental life occurred in the following year. He had almost completed a treatise called *The World*, in which he had accepted the Copernican thesis that the earth moved round the sun, when the news reached him of Galileo's condemnation by the Inquisition. For motives which have been severely criticized, not altogether with justice, he immediately abandoned work on his book. He may have feared persecution; it is more likely that, as a devout Catholic, he was reluctant to offend ecclesiastical authority upon an issue which still needed clarification.

He did not altogether escape persecution himself. At Leyden, he published the famous *Discourse on Method* (1637) and *Meditations* (1641), which embody in clear simple prose the ideas he had been elaborating since his illumination. The reception was enthusiastic in many quarters, but the conservative thinkers attacked him viciously. He became involved in public and private controversy. A denunciation by one of his enemies finally brought a summons to appear before the Magistrates of Utrecht on the charge of atheism. Descartes did not attend in person, but sent a letter of explanation. There was a further summons; and the situation was looking ugly when some of his powerful friends came to the rescue. The magistrates, having taken up the issue, were now in a dilemma as to how they should retire without loss of face. A solution worthy of the ancient oracles was finally hit upon: the authorities solemnly proclaimed that, as regards the new Cartesian philosophy, nothing was to be published either for or against it. And so the hubbub mysteriously died down.

Among the good friends upon whose loyalty Descartes was able to count at this time was the talented and intelligent Princess Elizabeth, daughter of Frederick V of Bohemia, now exiled in Holland. To her, he dedicated his *Principles of Philosophy* (1644), and in her he found a kindred soul. The two were constantly in each other's company, when not engaged in learned correspondence; but there is no reason to suppose that their relationship was anything but Platonic, or rather Cartesian.

As a result of repeated invitations, Descartes decided in 1649 to go to Sweden. He had now lived in Holland for twenty years; but owing to the covert hostility of certain officials, both civil and ecclesiastical, his life had latterly become uneasy there. The invitation to Sweden originally came from the remarkable Queen Christina, and Descartes felt the honour all the more keenly as it indicated his growing international fame. The journey was nevertheless a risk. Descartes was not old; but after such intense intellectual labours he lacked the resilience of men even several years his senior. Upon arrival, he found the climate particularly trying. The timetable to which, as royal guest, he was expected to adhere was still more taxing. The Queen, having heard vaguely about the New Philosophy, insisted upon being given formal instruction in it. The philosopher was to be put to work. Regularly three times a week, at the unpropitious hour of five in the morning, Descartes was obliged to visit the Queen in her bedroom to expound his ideas. He started off with enthusiasm, fulfilling his engagements conscientiously; but after a few weeks of such exertion, combined with strenuous public engagements during the day, his health broke down. On 1st February 1650, he fell desperately ill, and on the 12th he died. 'Well, my soul, we have to part company,' he is supposed to have murmured resignedly on his death bed. Descartes lived all his life a solitary; and patronage, when it came, was more than he could either comprehend or endure.

2

The *Discourse on Method* was the product of Descartes's interior conflict. He felt a duty towards orthodox belief, and he felt a duty towards his own ideal of the Sage or *Savant*. In this short essay, deliberately written in French to enable it to be read by all (such works were usually in Latin), Descartes delivers an attack upon the Scholastic method, with its sacred texts, its authorities, and its subtle definitions. His aim is to demonstrate, by citing his own experience, how the ordinary individual should arrive unaided at truth. What, in other words, will both satisfy our minds and enable us to know that such satisfaction is identical with truth? Is there some *criterion* that we can adopt whereby our beliefs and ideas can be tested without reference to external authority?

Today these questions seem banal. They were not so in Descartes's time. They were revolutionary questions. To ask them, however politely and reasonably, was to incur the suspicion of the established organizations of society. For Descartes was inviting his readers to approach the great questions of philosophy from an angle diametrically opposed to that of orthodoxy. The Scholastics, especially the later ones, had tended to assume the truth of their dogmas and had then proceeded to classify and codify them; such doubts as they raised were stated for the purpose of spectacular demolition at the hand of skilled dialecticians. According to Descartes's New Method, the test of a truth was not whether it had been enunciated by Holy Writ, or St. Augustine or St. Thomas, or stated *ex cathedra* by the Supreme Pontiff, but whether it was coherent with itself and above all whether it was 'clear and distinct'. In other words, the Method which Descartes proposed to apply to every sphere of knowledge was that which was best exemplified in analytical geometry. The stages and procedure used in a geometrical problem could surely be made to yield results of equal certitude in the sphere of metaphysics, logic, and ethics. That was Descartes's conviction, and the substance of his mystical revelation.

What he was in fact struggling to work out was something very like a universal mathematics. The idea that everything was susceptible to measurement, and that what eluded measurement was unreal, had been stated for the first time by Galileo. 'Philosophy,' Galileo had observed, 'is written in that vast book which stands ever open before our eyes, I mean the universe; but it cannot be read until we have learnt the language and become familiar with the characters in which it is written. *It is written in mathematical language.*' Descartes, though he claimed to owe nothing to Galileo, would have approved that statement. In his time, such a view was both novel and heterodox. What recommended it to Descartes was the fact that it revealed the interconnection between everything in the universe. In spite of its apparent lack of system and its teeming detail, the world exhibited a fundamental order; and that order was a mathematical order.

Descartes claimed that his Method was not a something to be learnt by the mastery of a few rules; it was a thing to be lived, to be grown into. Reflection must become a habit. Men must discover, by disciplined thought, what ideas are fundamental to their minds in the sense of being 'innate', like those of mathematics; for such ideas are superior in status to those either derived from sense or conjured up by the imagination.

How, therefore, can we eliminate the unreliable, the vague, and the illusory elements from our minds? By systematic scepticism or, as Descartes called it, 'methodic doubt'. Take nothing for granted; demand the production of its identity card, and examine that too lest it should prove to be a forgery. To take nothing for granted, however, is still to take something for granted: namely, the fact that you yourself are engaged in thinking and reflecting. And that is simultaneously to take for granted the fact that you, the thinking and reflecting being, exist. 'I think, therefore I am.' Descartes climbs out of doubt by certifying his own existence as a doubter. That is the first step towards knowledge.

I exist, argues Descartes, but in the capacity of a doubter; I am an essentially imperfect being, and I realize it. But unless I possessed at the same time some idea of the infinite and perfect, I should not have acquired this consciousness of imperfection. My reason tells me, therefore, that I am the creature of an all-wise, all-seeing, all-powerful God. Without the certitude of God's existence, I should not possess any guarantee that the deliverances of my Reason were such as could be relied upon; 'an atheist cannot be a geometrist'.

By this argument, as we have seen, Descartes reverses the Scholastic method. The latter began with matter and sense and argued itself up to God; Descartes, as it were, begins with God and argues down to matter and sense. His repudiation of authority, his emphasis upon Reason, his insistence upon logical clearness and distinctness, his interest in the developing sciences of physics and physiology, make him one of the pioneers of the great scientific movement which, during the next two centuries, reshaped the world.

The *Discourse on Method* is the Charter of scientific humanism. No philosophical or scientific writer has escaped its influence. As for its effect upon the civilization of France, that has been incalculable. More than a century later it inspired another book of equal influence, Rousseau's *Social Contract;* and it is no exaggeration to say that the 'reasonableness' still associated with the French mind at its most cultivated level is by nature Cartesian.

Against Descartes's method there have been several reactions, even within France itself. A Frenchman of remarkable intellect, Blaise Pascal (1623-62), whose death was even more lamentably premature than that of Descartes, underwent an experience very similar to the mystical revelation of the latter but opposite in significance. A mathematician of genius, Pascal records that one night he beheld a vision in which it was made clear to him that the true God of religion was not a 'God of philosophers and mathematicians' but 'the God of Abraham and Jacob': a revelation which, as he recorded on a parchment which he caused to be sewn into his clothing, caused him to weep 'tears of joy'. Pascal helped to redress the balance between the Cartesian or rationalist viewpoint and the sensitive, intuitional approach of the poets and mystics: between the *esprit de géomètre* and the *esprit de finesse.* He is the greater character of the two; but Descartes excelled him in capacity for systematic and original thinking.

Benedict Spinoza

'This man, from his granite pedestal, will point out to all men the way of blessedness which he found; and ages hence, the cultivated traveller, passing by this spot, will say in his heart: "The truest vision ever had of God came, perhaps, here."'

— Renan, at the dedication of Spinoza's statue
at the Hague, 1882.

1

The most remarkable fact about Spinoza is that although he was personally the most aloof and isolated of beings, his chief aim was to show how men could make the universe their home and acquire a feeling of kinship with all its creatures. Exiled at an early age from his own community, Spinoza sought communion with a society more permanent than that of man, and one which was based upon the order of Nature and of God. In return for his devotion to Nature and to God, however, he did not suppose that either the one or the other should condescend to take any particular interest in his own welfare. To expect such attention was to love selfishly: 'He who truly loves God cannot wish that God should love him in return.'

This was a new note in philosophy. Such, the reader might say, is the attitude not of a Cartesian philosopher, a lover of clearness and distinctness, a devotee of enlightened Reason, but of a mystic, or even a religious fanatic. That occasional remarks of Spinoza recall those of the Spanish mystic St. John of the Cross (1542-91) has more than once been pointed out: the German philosopher Novalis (1772-1801) likewise once referred to Spinoza as *Ein gottbetrunkener Mensch,* 'a God-intoxicated man'. Certainly Spinoza lived a most pious, upright, and—except in this one particular—sober life.

146

But his thought is the very reverse of vague or confused. It is as transparently clear as that of Descartes; if possible, it is expounded with greater economy of word. What makes Spinoza a difficult philosopher for some people is not so much the manner of his exposition as the conclusions which he urges his readers to accept. These conclusions were hard, frigid, and uninviting.

What were the origins of this strange man, perhaps the most solitary figure in the history of philosophy? A flood of light upon Spinoza's thought is thrown by the circumstances of his birth and upbringing. Born at Amsterdam on 24th November, 1632, he came of Portuguese-Jewish parentage. To be precise, his father and mother were not so much Jews as 'crypto' Jews: that is to say, they were descended from Jews whom the Inquisition had forced to accept the Christian faith. When Holland proclaimed toleration for all religions, many of these uneasy badgered folk did their best to seek asylum there (from about 1593 onwards). They brought with them their trades and their wits; and so they prospered. But they were still not citizens in the full sense. They resided, but they did not belong. Their religion, which they now practised again openly, made such absorption impossible. Hence the peculiar isolation of their position: they were avoided, as men usually avoided those who have suffered prolonged persecution.

Spinoza was sent to the Jewish school at Amsterdam, which had been founded in 1638. Here his education was confined exclusively to Hebrew subjects: first, the Jewish sacred books, such as the Talmud and the Hebrew Codes, and secondly, the Hebrew philosophers, such as Ibn Ezra, and Maimonides, whom we have mentioned as being a precursor of St. Thomas Aquinas. Such was the basic education given to Jewish boys at the time. Outside school-hours, however, Spinoza received instruction in secular subjects, and for these he showed great powers of assimilation. He also proved quick at learning languages; besides Spanish, which was spoken in his home, he learnt Latin, Portuguese, French, Italian and Dutch.

The first notable event in his life, after leaving school, was the death in 1654 of his father, a wealthy and respected man in the Jewish community. This event gave rise to family troubles, as Spinoza's step-sister laid claim to the entire estate. In consequence of a law-suit, Spinoza was pronounced the rightful heir; but for reasons which seem to have been genuinely altruistic, he waived the greater part of his claim in her favour, and prepared to work for his living. As an occupation, he chose the sedentary art of grinding, cutting and polishing lenses for spectacles, telescopes and microscopes; and in this art, to which he devoted the rest of his life, he came to exhibit considerable skill.

Although at school he had been given a thoroughly orthodox education, his reading of such philosophers as Maimonides had early stimulated his critical faculty. In his celebrated *Guide to the Perplexed*, Maimonides, besides drawing attention to a number of inconsistencies in the Bible, had implied that the ultimate court of appeal in theological matters was not so much Faith as Reason; that if verbal inspiration conflicted with what was reasonable, so much the worse (he hinted) for verbal inspiration; and that the faithful, however complete their devotion, were not absolved from treating the Scriptures as documents to be studied with discrimination and judgment. Spinoza, though a regular patron of the synagogue, boldly voiced his approval of this way of thinking. The Jewish leaders pricked up their ears. Such talk was doubly dangerous: it was calculated not merely to undermine the faith of the orthodox but to excite the suspicion of the Dutch Calvinists, at whose good pleasure the refugees were allowed to remain in Holland. For Spinoza was attacking beliefs common to both guests and hosts.

Although the Jews in Holland had fled from persecution, they exhibited a regrettable tendency, there as elsewhere, to persecute each other in exile. The leaders felt it incumbent upon them to suppress demonstrations of infidelity. Occasionally, in order to hush up a scandal they would endeavour to buy the silence of a heretic by means of bribery. We have evidence to suggest that Spinoza was offered money in this way. His stubborn refusal to be silenced caused him to be excommunicated by his community in 1656. Allegedly this was because he advanced the view that God had a body (by which he was referring to the world of matter); that angels were probably figments of the imagination; and that the

Bible had nothing to say upon the subject of immortality. As a precaution, his exclusion from the synagogue was formally reported to the Dutch civil authorities; and Spinoza, much against his will, was given a term of exile. He was barely twenty-four years old. It is said that at this time a fanatical Jew made an attempt upon his life.

During the years of exile, Spinoza made the acquaintance of a number of learned Christians, and through them came to study the new philosophy of Descartes. He also applied himself to physics and mathematics, and, like Descartes himself, probably familiarized himself with various types of theosophy. When he returned to Amsterdam in 1660, he already regarded himself, and was regarded by others, as a free-thinker; and although he is said to have put in an appearance at the synagogue and even to have written an Apology for his so-called heresies, his speculative mind could now no longer be bound by a 'closed' system of dogma and ritual. Besides the trade which he had adopted, he supplemented his income by teaching; the subject most in demand at this time was Hebrew, since both Christians and non-Christians were becoming increasingly interested to discover, amid the disputes of religious sects, what the Bible 'really said'. That Spinoza should have supplemented his instruction by exposition of the meaning of the text itself, was inevitable; and he soon became a recognized leader of study circles at which religion, philosophy, ethics, and natural science were discussed with a freedom rarely permitted even in the comparatively enlightened atmosphere of Amsterdam. It is possible, perhaps, to trace the origin of what is today called the 'higher criticism' of the Bible to these quiet, communal researches conducted by Spinoza.

Although he had studied the writings of Descartes with great eagerness, he was now beginning to experience a feeling of dissatisfaction with certain aspects of the new philosophy. A system of his own was simultaneously beginning to crystallize in his mind. Solitary as his manner of life had become, he felt the need for even more prolonged solitude; and the impulse to write down his thoughts in systematic form was becoming more insistent. He therefore moved to Rijnsburg, a town six miles from Leyden, where he took up lodgings with a doctor named Hermann Homan. Here, in congenial company, he wrote an essay entitled *A Short Treatise on God, Man and his Well-Being*, which was first discovered in 1852, and also began the book in which his genius is most fully manifest, namely, the *Ethics* (1661-65).

By his influence upon his distinguished friends and also by the letters he wrote to thinkers and scientists of the day, Spinoza slowly began to acquire a reputation abroad. His letters to the famous physicist Oldenburg, whom he met in 1661 and who later became associated with the Royal Society in London, brought him in touch with English scientists; and some years later he began a correspondence with Leibnitz, from which the latter profited more than he cared to acknowledge. About the year 1663 he was given a pension from the great Dutch patriot John De Witt. The two remained fast friends until a terrible tragedy parted them.

Spinoza was engaged between 1665 and 1670 upon the composition of a work in which he evidently meant to dispose once for all of the accusation, so frequently levelled against him, of atheism. This was known as the *Tractatus Theologico-Politicus,* an essay in which he expressed his feelings with unaccustomed passion. Unhappily the very aim he had set before himself was frustrated; he bowed to the advice of his friends not to publish such inflammable material under his own name. The book therefore appeared anonymously in 1670, and went through edition after edition within a short period. In the year of its publication, Spinoza moved to Voorburg, near the Hague, where he finally took up residence in the house on the Paviljoensgracht belonging to the painter Van der Spijck, remaining there until his death. His life at Voorburg seems to have been that of a complete recluse; but although he rarely ventured out of doors, he enjoyed the company of visitors, and with his artist-host Spijck he appears to have been on terms of great intimacy.

Two events occurred in the brief interval before his death, either of which may well have had the effect of hastening the end. One was the brutal assassination of his great patron De Witt. For the first time in the experience of his friends, Spinoza became convulsed with indignation, and was with difficulty prevailed upon not to fix a notice containing the words *Ultimi barbarorum* upon the prison in which the outrage had been committed. The second event is still a source of some mystery to historians. The Prince of Condé, who had established his winter quarters not far from Utrecht, apparently invited Spinoza, under promise of safe-conduct, to pay him a visit. Although by the time Spinoza arrived Condé was away, someone with sufficient authority evidently received him and offered him a pension on behalf of Louis XIV. This he refused, as was to be expected in view of the state of hostilities between France and Holland; but he did not reckon upon the bitterly hostile reception his fellow-townsmen were to accord him upon his return. Denounced as a spy, the mob very nearly tore him to pieces; and although he managed to reach his house unhurt, Spijck expressed the fear that the place would be raided that night. Spinoza reassured him. If necessary, he would go out, face the people, and die the death of John De Witt. From what we know of Spinoza's character, it is probable that, if necessary, he would have done so.

The explanation of this episode may be that the Dutch, realizing Spinoza's international reputation, used him to conduct certain peace negotiations which they could later repudiate. His journey seems to have been known to certain high officials—or so Spinoza claimed at the time. Moreover, on the French side there was a certain Colonel Stoup, commander of one of Condé's Swiss regiments, who played an ambiguous part in the proceedings—some say in order to discredit Spinoza and cause his arrest by the Dutch as a traitor: in which aim he nearly succeeded.

As time went on, Spinoza's occupation, though congenial to one accustomed to meditate for hours together, began to have a deleterious effect upon his health. It is said that the glass-dust in his workroom injured his lungs and induced consumption. In November 1677 he suddenly became very ill. Schuller, his doctor friend, was summoned, but on the 20th of the month Spinoza died. It was later suggested that, fearing a lingering death, the philosopher had called Schuller in order to arrange for a euthanasia; but this is hardly compatible with the calm and brave character that we know Spinoza to have possessed.

The man who had renounced his right to his father's fortune in youth left so few material possessions at death that his sister did not trouble to put in a claim for them. As for his writings, they were on the whole vilified and condemned for at least a century afterwards. Only with Lessing, Goethe and Coleridge did the serene philosophy of the short, swarthy Jewish exile from Portugal and from Zion come fully into its own. And today Spinoza is universally regarded as one of the great philosophers of the Western world.

2

To understand the philosophy of Spinoza is to appreciate its blend of Christian, mystical and Jewish thought. It is Christian in its serenity and compassion, mystical in its visionary character, and Jewish in its spiritual 'obstinacy': Spinoza resembles the Old Testament prophets in nothing so much as in his insistence that 'you cannot serve two masters'. If we are to love God, he maintains, there must be no compromise, no *quid pro quo;* but once we have surrendered ourselves to Him, we shall find that 'his service is perfect freedom'. In a sense, however, we have no choice in the matter. We are by nature linked with God, as 'modes' of the Divine Substance; to become *conscious* of this dependence is what is meant by freedom and liberation.

The object of the treatise on Ethics is to show, by a kind of mathematical analysis, how the soul of man is necessarily attached to its Creator. Although he rejects many of Descartes's conclusions and also some of his arguments, Spinoza retains the Cartesian Method, and the ideals of clarity as typified by the procedure of mathematics and physics. He describes his Ethical treatise on the title-page as being *ordine geometrico demonstrata* ('proved in geometrical order'); hence the aversion that some readers have shown for its aridity and coldness, as if philosophical arguments must necessarily be dressed up as fine literature before they can be accepted. By his emphasis upon necessity and the fact that man's duty is to pursue divine and not human ends, Spinoza seeks to explain—or explain away—the evil, ugliness and inexplicability that confronts us in the world. 'Whenever anything in nature seems to us ridiculous, absurd, or evil,' he writes in the *Tractatus Theologico-Politicus*, 'it is because we have but partial knowledge of things, and are in the main ignorant of the order and coherence of nature as a whole, and because we want everything to be arranged according to the dictates of our own reason: although in fact what our law pronounces bad is not bad as regards the order and laws of universal nature, but only as regards the laws of our own nature taken separately'. That last statement is an admirable summary of the philosophical attitude of Spinoza. When man 'takes himself separately', he takes himself solemnly and therefore creates triviality; whereas if he realizes his dependence upon what is greater than himself, he attains to true dignity and peace of mind.

Spinoza's theory of Substance has proved a stumbling-block to philosophical students. But the idea which he is trying to put forward is really quite simple. If, as he says, there exists a truly Substantial Being, that Being or Substance must be *causa sui;* that is to say, it cannot have been produced by something other than itself, or it would not be a true substance. Likewise it must be infinite; if it were not, it would be in some way limited, and such limitation would be due to the existence of other substances. In short, if there is a substance at all, it must both depend upon itself and provide the ground of everything else. Such a substance must therefore be equivalent to God, for only God possesses the characteristics of being at once self-caused and the cause of everything. God, therefore, is the entire universe, since everything that issues from Him is a part of Him; and so Spinoza is accustomed to refer to the one universal Substance as *Deus sive Natura*, God or Nature, according as to whether he wishes to refer to its spiritual or to its material aspect. Such a theory is called in technical terms *monistic;* what Spinoza was endeavouring to do was to overcome the Cartesian division, or *dualism*, between mind and body, whereby there existed two different substances, a thinking and a non-thinking one, giving rise to the tricky problem as to how they worked together in harness.

That freedom results from a clear and dispassionate awareness of our dependence upon universal and divine laws is the cornerstone of Spinoza's ethical teaching. Freedom and understanding are thus as closely identified for Spinoza as they are for Socrates. Obstacles to freedom of thought must be eliminated from society: for bigoted ecclesiastics are wrong in supposing that piety and morality will increase with the introduction of spiritual 'controls' and inquisitional practices. The object of the *Tractatus Theologico-Politicus* was precisely to show 'that not only is perfect liberty to philosophize compatible with devout piety and the peace of the state, but that to take away such liberty is to destroy the public peace and even piety itself'. And in the course of the same work Spinoza flares up suddenly with indignation at the thought of how the world has treated so many of its great men, and how it had nearly treated him. 'What greater misfortune for a state can be conceived than that honourable men should be sent like criminals into exile, because they held diverse opinions which they cannot disguise? What, I say, can be more hurtful than that men who have committed no crime or wickedness should, simply because they are enlightened, be treated as enemies and put to death, and that the scaffold, the terror of evil-doers, should become the stage where the highest examples of tolerance and virtue are displayed to the people with all the marks of ignominy that authority can devise?'

This passage, which might have come straight out of Plato's *Apology of Socrates*, reveals the *saeva indignatio* of a great but passionate nature. Few men have preached so uncompromising a doctrine and yet practised it so uncompromisingly themselves. Spinoza is no hasty reformer; the way to blessedness, which is 'virtue itself', remains obscure. 'If the road I have shown to lead to this is very difficult,' he says at the conclusion of the *Ethics,* 'it can yet be discovered. And clearly it must be very hard when it is so seldom found. For how could it be that it is neglected practically by all, if salvation were close at hand and could be found without difficulty? But all things excellent are as difficult as they are rare.'

Gottfried Leibnitz

'You will find that when you are admitted to the heart of nature, the further you go the greater will be your delights, because you will be only at the beginning of a chain that goes on to infinity.'

—Philosophical Dream.

1

Leibnitz might have been a greater philosopher, and perhaps a greater man, if he had needed to struggle to greatness. As it was, he achieved reputation and honour, in more fields than one, with an ease that astonished his contemporaries, and in some respects turned his head. He was at one and the same time a mathematician, a lawyer, an historian, a diplomat—and a philosopher. Of the ignominy and obscurity that drove Spinoza into Stoic seclusion, he knew little until his last years. He never had cause to fear persecution, like Descartes and Locke. Even professional jealousy left few marks upon him. For he had enough confidence in his own powers not to feel it, and sufficiently established prestige never to become the object of it. In short, with so many gifts and with such opportunities, he ought to have cut a greater figure in the philosophical pantheon than he has done. In the 'best of all possible worlds' (to employ his own description of this earth), he ought to have become the best of all possible philosophers. There is something poignant about the opening of the essay from which an extract is given at the head of this chapter: 'I was happy to be among men, but not happy about human nature.'

Gottfried Wilhelm Leibnitz was reared in an atmosphere of learned speculation. His father was Professor of Moral Philosophy at Leipzig. Born on 21st June, 1646, in the latter city, young Leibnitz displayed remarkable precocity; for his father, realizing the boy's appetite for learning, decided to give him the run of his library before the age of six, using the words *tolle, lege* ('take, read'). The little fellow not merely devoured the classical philosophers and historians, but even ventured upon the Fathers of the Church. At the age of twelve, he could read Latin and Greek with ease. The next subject to absorb his attention was Logic, in which he claimed to have introduced reforms at an early age, for he became immediately dissatisfied with the scholastic approach. His parents and overseers found this avidity for learning a trifle overwhelming. They feared that he would turn into a bookworm or pedant. But they were wrong. Leibnitz wore his erudition lightly. If he was a scholar among courtiers, he was a courtier among scholars.

When Leibnitz was fifteen, he entered the University of Leipzig as a law-student. The first part of his course, which occupied a period of two years, consisted chiefly of philosophy. His masters belonged to the old school; their pupil, already bursting with knowledge, soon found that he belonged to the new. He discovered, largely for himself, the works of Francis Bacon, Campanella (1568-1630), Galileo and, above all, Descartes. Admittedly, his revolt against Scholasticism was not accomplished without some mental turmoil. No subtle revolution of this kind ever is. Leibnitz has left us an account of his final conversion, which, like most conversions, took place out of doors in the course of a walk (even Augustine had to run into his garden to be converted). 'I remember walking alone,' he writes, 'at the age of fifteen, in a wood near Leipzig called the Rosenthal, to deliberate whether I should retain the doctrine of substantial forms. At last mechanism triumphed and induced me to apply myself to mathematics.' Thus he joined the band, headed by Galileo, of those who believed that the book of nature was written by God in the language of mathematics. The next problem was to put himself under an efficient tutor in this difficult but fascinating subject. Most of the summer of 1663 he spent at Jena, and there took lessons from Weigel, whose reputation as a mathematics teacher was at its height; but this was only his initiation into a sphere of enquiry to which he was later to make some original contributions.

If Leibnitz had been seduced by the subtle charms of mathematical philosophy, he did not remain wholly unfaithful to the law. Indeed, he had a particular reason for pursuing his legal training: for he had decided to adopt the profession of Assessor as being that most likely to fit his temperament and in particular to give him scope for private reflection. He therefore became a candidate in 1666 for the degree of Doctor of Law. His one handicap was his comparative youth; he was only twenty years old. There were candidates in the field much older than he; and it is to be feared that their covert opposition was responsible for the official refusal to grant Leibnitz the honour which, in every other respect, he had merited. The affront nettled him. If his native town would not recognize his ability, he would see what redress could be obtained elsewhere. He left Leipzig—for ever, as it proved—and applied for admission to the University of Altdorf (the academic seat of the free city of Nuremberg). Here, as a result of a dissertation that won immediate approval from authorities more than three times his age, he was asked to stay and accept the vacant Professorship of Law. This was justice indeed. But the inviting gesture was all that Leibnitz, at his time of life, wanted. He politely but firmly refused the offer; for he had by this time begun to entertain higher ambitions than could be satisfied by a mere professorship. He wanted to be an international figure.

At Nuremberg, where he now decided to stay, he began to move in society for which he was more suited. Like Descartes and Spinoza, he was for some while attracted to the doctrines of the Rosicrucians; and as Nuremberg was a Rosicrucian centre, he was able to mix freely in their society and even to take part in their activities. Of more material benefit to him, however, was his meeting with Johann Christian von Boineburg, who had had a distinguished career as first minister to the Elector of Mainz. Boineburg encouraged the young man to print some of his essays, above all that entitled *Nova Methodus docendi discendique juris*, with which he had been particularly impressed; and he suggested that the book should be dedicated to the Elector himself. Following this advice, Leibnitz decided to present his work to the great man in person; and the Elector was so favourably struck with the young lawyer's ability that he forthwith offered him a government position revising the Statute Book. Such intricate work being well within Leibnitz's capacity, he tackled it with confidence; but it soon became evident both to the Elector and his advisers that the new official was equal to much heavier responsibilities. Soon, therefore, he was commissioned with the task of doing battle, with his ready pen, on behalf of the candidature of a German prince for the throne of Poland, which had become vacant in 1669. This, his first political treatise, is unique in history as being the only diplomatic argument to submit mathematical proofs for its statements. Still it did not prevent the throne of Poland from being occupied once more by a Polish prince.

Another direction in which Leibnitz was called upon to use his literary and forensic skill was that of exposing France's aggressive designs in Europe. In an essay entitled *Thoughts on Public Safety*, Leibnitz advocated a 'Rheinbund' or league against Louis XIV for the defence of Germany, against which France seemed to be preparing for war. This document is interesting for a further suggestion that it contained: namely, that European nations, instead of attacking each other, should seek to revive the crusading spirit by uniting together in an expedition against some non-Christian state. What about Egypt, for instance, 'one of the best situated lands in the world'? Would not France do better to attack and conquer such a country than despoil her Christian neighbours? The French Secretary of State, commending this essay to Louis XIV, and deciding to solicit the author for further views on the subject, invited him to Paris. Leibnitz set out, with great expectations, on 18th March, 1672. He never obtained the royal audience to which he was looking forward; but both his journey and the composition of a further treatise seem to have given Louis food for thought, and he might well have put Leibnitz's grandiose plan into operation had not relations between France and Turkey (then in control of Egypt) suddenly taken a turn for the better. More than a century later, Napoleon, on entering Hanover in 1803, unearthed documents in the government archives relating to this scheme. He then made the interesting discovery that the idea of a French expedition to Egypt, such as he himself had undertaken in an atmosphere of tragi-comedy in 1797, had been proposed originally by a German philosopher.

Philosophically, if not politically, Leibnitz profited from his journey. Politics and diplomacy were not allowed to crowd out mathematics and philosophy. In Paris he met the philosopher Malebranche, a religious Cartesian (1638-1715), Arnauld, the author of an anti-Cartesian treatise (1612-94), and the great philosopher and astronomer Huyghens (1629-93). To each he expounded his developing ideas and discoveries in such diverse fields as logic, natural philosophy, mathematics, mechanics, optics, and hydrostatics, together with his novel opinions on law and theology. Above all he outlined his famous philosophy of Monads, of which we shall speak later. His mind, now in its full maturity, seemed to be teeming with original suggestions, reforms, improvements, solutions. Nor were his ideas confined to the plane of theory or hypothesis. He showed himself to be an inventor too, having a peculiar genius for the construction of machines and gadgets. Most striking of his inventions at this period was a new type of calculating machine, which excelled that of Pascal to the extent of being able to multiply, divide, and extract roots. After having been exhibited at Paris, this machine was displayed on the premises of the Royal Society in London, of which Leibnitz became a member in 1673. His election to the French Academy as a distinguished foreign member did not take place until 1700.

When in January, 1673, he came to London as the special envoy of the Elector of Mainz, Leibnitz hastened to make acquaintance with the better-known English scientists and mathematicians. He met and (like Spinoza) corresponded with Oldenburg, then secretary of the Royal Society. He met the chemist Boyle and the mathematician Pell, who introduced him to the discoveries of Mercator as outlined in the latter's treatise called *Logarithmatechnica,* which to some extent Leibnitz had himself anticipated. When he returned to Paris, he began to pursue his mathematical speculations with even greater energy, profiting meanwhile from the tuition of Huyghens; and in due course he worked out that system of differential and integral calculus, which is generally regarded as his particular discovery in the field of mathematics.

A change now came over Leibnitz's fortunes which was thereafter to determine the course of his life. For some while he had been engaged in frequent and learned correspondence with Duke John Frederick of Brunswick-Lüneburg. In 1673, having entered the Duke's service, he went to Hanover (travelling, incidentally, via London and Amsterdam, which enabled him to pay a visit to Spinoza), and there assumed charge of the family library. Although he held the post of librarian for the next forty years, the work he was called upon to do went far beyond the confines of librarianship. He was expected to be at once champion of the rights of the Brunswick family and what amounted to Public Relations Officer for the State of Hanover. One of his numerous tasks, that of compiling a history of the Brunswicks, involved rummaging in the archives of towns as far separated as Vienna, Modena, Venice and Rome. In Vienna the wealth of material put at his disposal kept him occupied for nine months. In Rome, where his reputation had preceded him, he was diplomatically asked whether, assuming that he entered the Catholic Church, he would accept the custodianship of the Vatican library.

Although he was not disposed to change his creed, least of all on such a pretext, Leibnitz had been much preoccupied in the past by the question of Catholic and Protestant reunion. It was not the least of his attempts to arrive at a unity transcending differences. To demonstrate that some sort of reconciliation between the two faiths was not merely desirable but feasible, he wrote in 1686 a *Systema Theologicum*, but this was not published until long after his death. At first he met with a good deal of co-operation and encouragement from elements on both sides; but when it came to thrashing out the real issues and discussing particular dogmas, the debate soon assumed a tone of bitter controversy, it being further realized that each side secretly hoped to achieve reunion by the wholesale reconversion of the other. When in 1688 the English revolution occurred and the Protestant Succession was established, the balance of spiritual power in Europe was permanently upset; nor did Leibnitz fare any better in his attempt, made a little later, to bring about a working alliance between the Reformed and the Lutheran churches.

Despite these setbacks, Leibnitz continued to prosper as few philosophers have prospered before or since. In 1690, he was appointed librarian at Wolfenbüttel by Duke Anton of Brunswick-Wolfenbüttel, and increased a reputation already well established for learning, wisdom and inventiveness. He made close friendships at the highest social level. With the Electress Sophie Charlotte of Brandenburg and Princess Sophie of Hanover, her mother, he became so intimate that in 1700 he was invited to Berlin for the purpose of establishing there an Academy of Learning, plans for which he had been working upon for some years. The institution was formally opened on 11th July, Leibnitz being elected its life-president. From then onwards public distinctions were conferred upon him with a liberality seldom enjoyed today except by successful politicians or sportsmen. The Elector of Brandenburg conferred upon him the title of Privy Councillor of Justice in 1700: which title he was to receive from two other patrons, the Elector of Hanover in 1704 and Peter the Great in 1712. (Leibnitz had sent him plans for an Academy at St. Petersburg.)

At Berlin, Leibnitz spent some of the happiest years of his life. Only the death of the Electress Sophie Charlotte, to whom he had taught philosophy in circumstances rather more congenial than those in which Descartes instructed Queen Christina of Sweden, put an end to his inner contentment, though it failed to halt his public advancement. He visited Berlin on the last occasion in 1711, after which he left for Vienna with the intention of setting up another Academy. Although the opposition of the Jesuits prevented him from making much headway, his services to learning were rewarded by two further honours, an Imperial privy councillorship and a barony of the Empire. From a material point of view there were not many worlds left to conquer. During his absence from Hanover, however, the Elector George Louis had been invited to England to become King, and it was with genuine regret that Leibnitz, his Brunswick researches still unfinished, was not permitted to join him. In fact he never completed the family history upon which he had laboured for so many years, and his huge MS. was not published until 1843.

Until his death in November, 1716, Leibnitz occupied himself with ceaseless correspondence, devoting his attention to almost every field of learning that scholars of the day considered worthy of cultivation. But the very successes of his early and middle life were responsible for a contrasting negligence by the public as he grew older. His health began to give him trouble, and he was involved in futile arguments with critics, which exhausted his time and patience. It would be incredible, if it were not true, to say that he died practically unnoticed, even in the circles in which he had moved as a leader and guide. At his funeral, which took place at Hanover, his secretary Eckhart alone followed him to the grave. There never was a philosopher whose death presented so complete a contrast to his life; but in pondering that unlamented end we perceive that throughout the whole of his successful career Leibnitz remained essentially a lonely figure, happy in a few attachments, which, once broken, left him, like the musician Schubert, with nothing but his genius. He was 'the man with a load of talent'; and we feel that he had not the opportunity, in one lifetime, to unpack and set in order all that he had brought with him.

2

The difference between Descartes, Pascal and Spinoza on the one hand, and Leibnitz on the other, is at bottom a difference in temperament. Of Spinoza we have used the word 'obstinate'. That quality of non-compromising obstinacy is characteristic of Descartes and Pascal, too; and it is not altogether absent from the work of Locke. Each of these thinkers wishes to accord universal applicability to a single principle—be it reason, intelligence or observation. This principle is regarded as the key to all problems. Being conciliatory by temperament and willing to learn from both sides, Leibnitz displays a contrasting attitude. He seeks to maintain a standpoint in which justice is done to all extremes. To adopt a one-sided point of view is equivalent, in his opinion, to adopting a false one. Leibnitz was as anxious to further the cause of unity within the theoretical sciences as he was anxious to further it in politics and religion. And for this reason he distrusted the rationalism of Descartes as being too productive of *distinctions*, of fissures and divisions in thought.

Leibnitz employed a phrase in connection with the Cartesian philosophy which has become famous. He said that it represented the 'ante-chamber' of truth. The truth lay just beyond it, after a partition had been penetrated or broken down. To Leibnitz, the philosophy of Spinoza was likewise open to objection, because Spinoza had merely clamped together in one Substance that which Descartes had forcibly separated. What needed to be revised, and if necessary jettisoned, was the current notion of Substance. Leibnitz's theory of Monads was an attempt to replace this notion by something more satisfactory and in harmony with modern scientific ideas.

The true constituent of reality, argues Leibnitz, is not so much a particle of matter as a centre of force. This centre of force he calls a monad. A monad is an individual thing capable of self-activity and self-subsistence; its very individuality and unity render it both independent of other monads and representative, as it were, of the whole world. Thus, in Leibnitz's words, the monads composing reality, though 'without windows', form a 'mirror of the universe', just as a truly individual thing, simply because it is complete and self-sufficient, enjoys universal characteristics. For example, a real, complete, unified *personality* is a better representative of the genus Man than an unbalanced immature one.

Leibnitz is careful to distinguish his monads from atoms, in the accepted sense. It is true that, in one of his works, he writes that 'the monads are the very atoms of nature—in a word, the elements of things'; but he does not understand them to be pieces, however tiny, of matter. They are not physical at all; they are rather metaphysical entities, local embodiments of force, varying one from the other in power. It is the graduation or hierarchy of monads, beginning with the simplest elements in nature and ending with God Himself, the Monad of Monads, that explains the universe in which we live. Cartesianism can never explain it, because Cartesianism invokes force from outside in the person of an intervening God.

According to Leibnitz, even the simplest of monads is endowed with the faculty of perception. At first this perception is both elementary and confused; later it expresses itself more perfectly in thought and finally in self-consciousness. Similarly, every monad possesses its own *vis motrix* or motive force; and as we ascend the hierarchy, this motive force becomes first instinct and later will. Thought and will, operating in concert, produce freedom and therefore happiness; there is no happiness where there is uncontrolled submission to passion. Thus, Leibnitz, like Spinoza, believes that man's highest goal is to render himself capable of *amor intellectualis dei*, the intellectual love of God.

Much that Leibnitz asserted has been taken up, with renewed interest, by the philosophers of our own time. He started a great many hares, and could follow but few of them. One aspect of his system, however, has puzzled and dissatisfied even the most earnest of his disciples. So concerned is he to show that his universe of monads will not merely hold together but function dynamically by itself (whereas Descartes had dragged in God at every point) that he leaves us wondering how it is that the whole affair originally began. If the monads are 'windowless', individual, and infinite in number, they must clearly have started in good order, otherwise the result would have been not the 'best possible world' (as Leibnitz claimed) but the worst possible chaos. Who, therefore, lined up and graded the monads? God did, says Leibnitz. He pre-established their harmonious arrangement. They continue to pursue, each in its own direction, their pre-ordained course. Consequently, they are a team, but without a conscious team spirit. 'According to my system,' writes Leibnitz in his essay *The Monadology* (§ 81), 'bodies act as if there were no souls, and souls act as if there were no bodies, and both act as if each influenced the other.' In reality there is no interaction; merely the impression of co-operation as the result of God's original dynamic scheme.

This, the reader may say, is all very clever; but is it in fact very different from the gambit adopted by

Descartes? Yes. Descartes said that God, with unceasing care, kept the world going. Leibnitz said that God, with remarkable ingenuity, set the world going. Descartes postulated an active God in a passive universe; Leibnitz postulated a passive God in an active universe. Leibnitz's chief disciple, Christian Wolff (1679-1754), failed to recognize the importance of Leibnitz's dynamic conception of the world; and perhaps that is why the philosophy of Leibnitz, so soon to be overshadowed by the gigantic structure of Kant, did not come into its own—if indeed it has yet come into its own—until a much later period.

Religious Conflict and the
Rise of Rationalism

In the century that followed the death of Descartes, the European order underwent many violent changes. On the continent, the religious quarrel between Catholicism and Protestantism appeared no nearer solution, though Protestantism as a political force began slowly to gain the ascendancy. The problem for men was how to live, or to carry on social and international life, in a world thus racked and dislocated by religious passions: in short, the problem was one of toleration. Now an intellectual problem may well agitate a thousand or a million minds at the same time; but only among a few, a sensitive and cultivated minority, will there be an awareness of that problem's true meaning. The philosopher is one who *abstracts* the real issue from the tangle of emotions that cling round it; consequently, as with the philosophy of Spinoza, his work often seems hard and cold, especially to those eager to plunge into battle armed with some provocative slogan or resonant war-cry. Such an apostle of calm and toleration was Pierre Bayle (1647-1706), a French Protestant, exiled, like Spinoza, in Holland; while another Frenchman, Fontenelle, distinguished from his fellow philosophers by his longevity (1657-1757), and inferior in versatility to Voltaire alone, did much to foster that new critical spirit which, as he claimed, would render the human mind capable of a gigantic 'spring forward', not least in the realm of the physical sciences. In this prophecy concerning the future of science he was not mistaken.[1]

There were those who, aware of the new critical forces at work, shied at the prospect of a great and perhaps disastrous intellectual upheaval. Thomas Hobbes, born in the year of the Great Armada (1588), delivered a

---

[1] His greatest remark was made on his deathbed. A friend enquired: *'Qu'est-ce-que vous sentez, Monsieur de Fontenelle?'* To which the old man replied: *'Je sens . . . une certaine . . . difficulté . . . de continuer . . . d'être'*.

counter-attack against the new libertarianism in his book of political philosophy, *The Leviathan* (1651). An apparent atheist, he feared, like many of his kind, the decay of those absolute standards in thought and life which religion formerly upheld. 'For if men were at liberty to take for God's commandments their own dreams and fancies, or the dreams and fancies of private men,' he writes (*The Leviathan*, Chapter XXVI), 'scarcely two men would agree upon what is God's commandment; and yet in respect of them, every man would despise the commandments of the Commonwealth.' That is true; but it was a risk which the advocates of toleration were prepared to run. At the close of the seventeenth century, indeed, a school of moral philosophers arose which openly preached a morality of personal sentiment. Shaftesbury (1671-1713), while agreeing with Hobbes that men were by nature egoists, yet posited the existence of a 'moral sense' which prevented them from becoming incurably anti-social. Hutcheson (1694-1746), pursuing this line of thought, endeavoured to represent the moral sense as being independent of all supernatural sanction, while Mandeville (1670?-1733), in a celebrated work entitled *The Fable of the Bees,* broke through the partition between private morality and public service by proclaiming the plausible but dangerous doctrine that the pursuit of private advantage was conducive to the public interest.

For the most part these are small men, skirmishers on the flank of the philosophical caravan. An Englishman, John Locke, stated the anti-Cartesian viewpoint more clearly and in a manner that influenced thinkers all over Europe.

John Locke

'If I have anything to boast of, it is that I sincerely love and seek truth with indifference whom it pleases or displeases.'

—Letter to his friend Anthony Collins.

1

Born at Wrington in Somersetshire in 1632, Locke came of Puritan parents, and was for fourteen years educated in his own family circle—a little pocket of peace in a restive country soon to be plunged into civil war. In 1646, he went to Westminster School. Here, a Puritan in a Puritan stronghold, he might have been expected to flourish and distinguish himself. In fact he did neither. Judging from some of his observations in a later essay entitled *Thoughts on Education*, he was most unhappy at school, forming a poor opinion not merely of Westminister but of public schools in general.

At Oxford, whither he went in 1652 and stayed for thirty years, he found an atmosphere more congenial to his already precocious mind. John Owen, the Puritan, who was both Dean of Christ Church and Vice-Chancellor of the University, was appointed Locke's tutor at The House. Governed by Independents and crowded with Presbyterians, Oxford was becoming a hot-bed of fanaticism and heresy-hunting; and although Locke was by upbringing favourable to Puritanism, he found a great deal less liberty in the new régime (especially in Presbyterian circles) than he had expected. 'The popular assertors of liberty,' he wrote of this period, 'were the greatest engrossers of it too, and not unfitly called its keepers.' Nevertheless, such men as Owen and Godwin were advocates of genuine religious liberty, and inspired in Locke that devotion to the idea of Toleration upon which he was later to write with such eloquence.

Recounting his early career to his patroness, Lady Masham, Locke later confessed that he was far from being a model student. Nevertheless, he studied in his own way, read widely, including the works of Descartes and Hobbes (*The Leviathan* had but recently appeared), met and corresponded with distinguished men of learning, participated in the chemical and meteorological experiments of the Royal Society, which was founded at Oxford in the Restoration Year (1660), began to study theology with a view (some say) to taking Anglican Orders, and finally, realizing that ecclesiastical advancement was not compatible with the kind of research that he favoured, decided to become a doctor. In his profession, despite his nickname 'Doctor' Locke, he obtained no academic distinctions; but he seems to have practised medicine at Oxford around the year 1666, abandoning it only when his own health broke down. Thereafter he never knew the meaning of physical vigour. He seems to have suffered from chronic asthma, and later developed some form of consumption, though neither seems to have curtailed his mental energy.

Indeed, he was seeking new outlets for this energy. Having accompanied Sir Walter Vane on a mission to Cleves in 1665, he developed a deep interest in diplomacy and politics. On his return to Oxford, he happened to meet Lord Ashley, afterwards famous as Earl of Shaftesbury. The two men formed an immediate and, as it turned out, life-long friendship. Two years later we find Locke settled at Exeter House, the London residence of Ashley, as his private secretary. Locke was now caught up, for better or for worse, in the political life of more than one nation. In 1673, he emerged as a public figure, since in that year he was appointed, on Ashley's influence, Secretary to the Council of Trade and Plantations.

This immersion in public life was undoubtedly beneficial both to Locke and to philosophy; he was never to suffer from that ingrown academic mentality which afflicts so many scholars and otherwise able thinkers. At Exeter House, where he met persons of every sort, he could select at will those with whom he wished to form lasting associations. Like many others who are surrounded by a throng of people, he enjoyed best the company of a small group of intimates. Out of a little 'study circle' at

Exeter House in 1671 developed the greatest enterprise of his life. 'Five or six friends' had assembled, at Locke's invitation, to discuss the 'principles of morality and religion'. They were soon baffled by 'difficulties that arose on every side'. Locke suggested that, as a prelude to such discussion, the members should think out for themselves the limits of man's capacity for knowledge. At first he believed it possible to jot down on 'a single sheet of paper' what these limits were; but he soon found the task more arduous than he could have dreamed possible. Thus 'what was begun by chance was continued by entreaty, written by incoherent parcels, and after long intervals of neglect resumed again as humour and occasions permitted'. Twenty years were to pass before the great *Essay Concerning Human Understanding* was finally completed, but such were its small beginnings.

Well might he describe this work as 'written by incoherent parcels'. Upon Ashley's fall from favour, Locke's career was seriously interrupted. He was obliged to go into retirement for a few years, choosing as his place of exile Montpellier and Paris, where he established a considerable reputation among men of learning. Here he jotted down more notes upon the human understanding, and looked after his precarious health. When in 1679 there was a change in the political atmosphere at home, Locke returned to London. It was a brief respite. Shaftesbury soon got into trouble again, was placed in the Tower, released after trial and once more exiled (he died in Holland in 1683). Locke, who spent most of the time either at Beluton or Oxford, kept his mouth shut. He knew enough of political intrigue to realize that he was being watched closely by government snoopers. We know that this was so. A report from Oxford in 1682 says: 'John Locke lives a very cunning unintelligible life here'; and the Dean of Christ Church, writing to Lord Sunderland, confessed that 'there is not anyone in the college who has heard him speak a word against, or so much as censuring, the government'.

Finally, the strain began to tell even upon this 'master of taciturnity'. So in 1683 he quietly slipped over to Holland, still as much the land of freedom and home of exiled intellectuals as it had been in Spinoza's day. Bayle, the French philosopher, was an exile there at the time.

Locke's sudden departure from England fanned the suspicion that his discreet conduct at home had served to allay. The British Government endeavoured to secure his arrest. He was deprived of his Studentship at Christ Church. Even his return to Oxford itself was prohibited by order of the King.

These cruel slights, which turned a voluntary into a compulsory exile, failed to reduce him to despair; they even roused him to greater exertions. He finished the *Essay*, contributed articles to Le Clerc's *Bibliothèque Universelle* (these latter were his first publications), and thus embarked at the age of fifty-four upon the career for which he had been so long preparing, that of authorship. It was the turn of the tide, both for Locke and for his country. In February, 1689, the philosopher experienced the exhilaration of returning home in the ship which brought the Princess of Orange to join her father, who had been crowned king of England the previous November.

The next two years were occupied in consolidating his fame. He had a large number of manuscripts ready for the press, which were issued one after another to a now eager and receptive public: the *Letters on Toleration*, the two *Treatises on Civil Government* (published anonymously), and the *Essay Concerning Human Understanding Itself* (1690). After the excitement of home-coming had subsided, Locke, partly from inclination and partly on account of his health (which the climate of London had never suited), decided to retire to the country. This was to prove the most pleasant exile of all that he had experienced. His hosts, Sir Francis and Lady Masham, were the embodiments of hospitality and, what was much to Locke's taste, of human understanding. And so Locke spent the last years of his life at the little village of Oates, conveniently situated twenty miles out of London, in the heart of Essex.

Retirement for Locke meant the reverse of idleness. Not merely did he spend much time in answering letters and pamphlets, many of them hotly controversial, concerning the *Essay*; he also produced new works on economics, finance and theology. An essay entitled *The Reasonableness of Christianity as delivered in the Scriptures,* published at first anonymously in 1695, brought him into collision not merely with obscure rectors, anxious to demonstrate their polemical gifts, but with well-known bishops, anxious to preserve public orthodoxy. Among the latter was Stillingfleet, Bishop of Worcester, with whom he exchanged some of his most vigorous letters. In the following year Locke was obliged to interrupt his retirement by making regular visits to town in discharge of his duties as Commissioner at the Board of Trade, an office conferred upon him in recognition of his experience and ability in public work. Meanwhile, new editions of the *Essay* had to be prepared (the fourth appeared in 1700), and there were translations into French and Latin to be supervised.

As the century turned, Locke, now a very tired but on the whole a contented man, began to prepare himself for death. He abandoned public work, rarely ventured outside Oates, and spent most of his working hours meditating upon the Scriptures. When he heard that the authorities at Oxford had decided formally to condemn his *Essay*, he was not greatly distressed. The dignitaries of Oxford had once refused admission to his person; it was not surprising that they should now ban his masterpiece. (The University has since done full justice to his memory, and the John Locke Scholarship in Psychology is a much coveted award for those wishing to pursue higher studies in that subject.) Commenting on the academic anathema, Locke remarked to a local friend: 'I take what has been done rather as a recommendation of the book, and when you and I next meet we shall be merry on the subject.'

In 1704, while still engaged upon an answer to an attack upon his views on Toleration, he began to decline rapidly in health; by the autumn he was clearly dying, and the end came on 28th October. It was a peaceful release, and, to quote the words of his will, he died 'in perfect charity with all men, and in sincere communion with the whole Church of Christ, by whatever names'—a typical phrase, this—'Christ's followers call themselves'. He was buried in the parish church at High Laver, near the Masham family grave. Unhappily, the manor house at Oates no longer stands to commemorate the idyllic retirement of the man most distinguished in British philosophy for calm, sober, and solid judgment.

2

It is frequently maintained that Locke, in endeavouring to analyse the human understanding from the point of view of common sense, was adopting a point of view typically British. The tradition of common-sense philosophy, which begins with Thomas Reid (1710-96) and the Scottish school of thinkers, and still flourishes in Britain, is something to which no other European country presents a parallel; but the very predominance of such a tendency at certain periods of history is indicative of an opposite movement, against which it is pitted and from which it derives its momentum. Thus the materialism of Hobbes and the criticism of Locke are counter-balanced, and from certain points of view overshadowed, by that extraordinary flowering of religious genius both in poetry and in prose—in Lancelot Andrewes and Jeremy Taylor, as well as in Vaughan, Traherne, and Herbert—for which seventeenth-century England is famous. And it is impossible to understand the problems which Locke is tackling unless we realize the kind of world—the highly complicated world—in which he marshalled his thoughts.

No doubt it was from his study of medicine that Locke became convinced that the traditional methods of scientific enquiry needed to be overhauled. From the time of Plato to that of Descartes, the assumption had remained unchallenged that truth, or at least the truth of metaphysics, morals and religion, were somehow *innate* in the human mind; you had simply to examine your mind, to wait upon your thoughts, for the fundamental principles of life and conduct to disclose themselves. Socrates had not merely enjoined his fellows to 'know themselves'; he had declared that only by introspection could knowledge of any value be obtained. Plato invented the technique of Dialectic to bring such knowledge to birth; Aristotle, though more experimentally-minded, based his logic upon the same foundation. And what of Descartes himself and his so-called New Method? Even he, too, for all his distrust of Scholasticism and love of 'clearness and distinctness', had failed to dissociate himself altogether from an *a priori* attitude. His 'ladder' from self-knowledge to knowledge of God passed through a kind of intellectual limbo, never touching sense-experience at any point. No wonder Descartes was accused of having preluded his thinking by 'closing his eyes and stopping his ears'.

In his *Essay Concerning Human Understanding,* Locke launches a frontal attack upon *a priori* thinking in general. If truth is native to our minds, he says, observation and experimental enquiry will lead us nowhere; at best they can merely confirm our knowledge, never add to it. And it is doubtful whether, taking the word confirmation literally, they can even confirm such knowledge; because an indubitable 'inner' conviction of the kind furnished by Descartes's *Cogito,* for instance, needs no additional evidence in its favour. In Locke's opinion, however, we arrive at knowledge by a method which is the reverse of that of the spider, who spins its web out of its own bowels. We do not nurture ideas from within; we acquire them from without. There are no 'innate ideas'. All our ideas (*i.e.* all our knowledge) are acquired through and in sensation.

Having laid down this challenging proposition, Locke proceeds to answer three questions that arise out of it. The first is: where do our ideas, if assumed not to be innate, come from? The second is: how do we know that our ideas, thus originating, are true? The third is: how much can the human understanding comprehend, and what sort of knowledge remains beyond its reach?

To 'know', in Locke's view, is to perceive a relation between ideas. Now ideas are of two kinds. There are first simple ideas, derived either immediately in sensation, or by a kind of 'inner' experience called reflection. Secondly, there are complex ideas, which are no more than combinations of the first. The mind or spirit of man originally resembles an empty tablet; experience is that which writes upon it. Before we admit sensation, we cannot engage in thinking: *nihil est in intellectu quod non antea fuerit in sensu*—'there is nothing in the intellect which was not previously in the senses'.

That which causes an idea to be produced in our mind is, in Locke's terminology, the 'quality' of the external object. And here Locke introduces a distinction which has played an important rôle in all later philosophical thought.

Qualities such as solidity, extension, form, number, etc., are all constant qualities: to whatever alterations the body or object is subjected, these qualities suffer no change. Such qualities Locke calls 'primary'. They are to be distinguished from what he calls 'secondary' qualities, which, though not to be found in the object itself, are the result of the impact of some power in the primary qualities upon our sense-organs. Such secondary qualities are colours, odours, sounds, tastes, etc.; qualities occasioned by the object, but *produced* as a result of something which we, as observers, contribute. Without human sense-organs, colour and sounds, odours and taste would simply not exist.

Granted that we know all things from sensation, what guarantee have we that the object, the material body, the originator of all these ideas wherewith we form a picture of reality, is really *there*? That, admittedly, was a source of difficulty for Locke. It is part of his 'platform' that we have no immediate knowledge of anything but our own ideas. If experience simply means 'sensuous experience', the problems seem insoluble. Locke, to be fair to him, does his very best to provide a solution to this problem. He points out, for instance, that an actual sensation is accomplished by pleasure and pain. These are feelings which never attach themselves to the memory of that sensation, or, if so, with never the same degree of intensity. Moreover, we find by experience that one of our senses, if suspected of a 'false report', can be corroborated by the testimony of another. Perceiving a fire, a man awaits the report of his tactile sense before concluding that his visual sensation was genuine. These are indisputable facts; but as proofs of the existence of an object external to, and productive of, our ideas, they are frankly subjective; that is to say, they prove nothing at all, but merely suggest very great probabilities. And they suggest probabilities only if we are disposed, in the first place, to believe in the existence of an external world. Locke did so. But supposing we do nothing of the kind—what then? A most ingenious answer to that question was given, as we shall see, by Bishop Berkeley.

It is interesting to draw attention to two notions which Locke shared, however reluctantly, with the Cartesians. The first is the notion of cause. Locke assumes the existence of an object external to our senses, endowed with primary qualities and capable of stimulating in us secondary qualities. This means that he believes in the causal nexus: a relationship which, as we shall see, gave a good deal of trouble to later philosophers. Secondly, as he believes that our ideas are caused by *something*, that something must be a passive *substratum*, which, if endowed with primary qualities, cannot be resolved into such qualities. This is Substance; and we know nothing more about it than that it is an 'unknown somewhat' outside the scope of our faculties.

At this point, therefore, Locke sets up a kind of mental frontier commission. Philosophy, he says, must not presume to enquire into realms that cannot be explored by the well-tried scientific methods of observation and induction, comparison and experiment. The problem of Substance, the problem of Essence (*i.e.* what constitutes the inner character of a thing), remain outside the scope of philosophy. If a mediæval science called Metaphysics claims to explore these things, then we should have nothing to do with the mediæval science called Metaphysics. It has brought us nowhere. From now onwards we must adhere solely to the evidence of our senses: that is to say, we must be rigorous *empiricists*. In Locke, therefore, we have a modern restatement of the theory of Nominalism (*cf.* the chapter on Abelard) as first asserted by Roscellinus and developed by William of Ockham. And, in a sense, the controversies of the next two centuries on this subject were just as vigorous as those which agitated the ecclesiastics and heretics of the mediæval Church. Nor are we, in the mid-twentieth century, at the end of them.

George Berkeley

'My speculations have had the same effect upon me as visiting foreign countries: in the end I return where I was before.'

—Commonplace Book.

1

The term 'freethinker', of which we hear a great deal today, became current, in England at least, during the latter half of the seventeenth century. Toleration was in the air. After 1688, England became, with the Dutch Republic, a refuge for the persecuted and the heterodox, the religious refugee and the philosophical sceptic. From that time onwards no one was obliged, though he has remained free, to leave England on account of his beliefs; and today it seems virtually impossible that so benign and moderate a spirit as that of Locke should ever have needed to go into exile.

The progress of free-thought in England can be judged to some extent from the titles of books published in the years following the so-called Glorious Revolution of 1688. There were John Toland's *Christianity not Mysterious* (1696), Arthur Collins's *A Discourse of Freethinking* (1713), Thomas Chubb's *A Discourse concerning Reason with regard to Religion* (1730), and many other significant titles, to mention only minor works. Some of this 'free-thought' was merely destructive and mischievous, though less mischievous perhaps for being permitted open expression; some of it was combating both ignorance and superstition. In orthodox quarters it often provoked unmannerly replies, the more so as it reached its mark or touched a sore spot; but there were masterly counter-attacks as well, witness that of Bishop Butler (1692-1752), author of *The Analogy of Religion*, one of the finest theological treatises in any language.

The thinker best remembered for his wholesale and uncompromising attack upon materialism, however, is George Berkeley. In Berkeley, British philosophy possesses a figure as versatile and revolutionary as that of Descartes in French philosophy and Leibnitz in German philosophy. It is a measure of the breadth of the British tradition that a thinker like Locke can be followed by a thinker like Berkeley, and that a thinker like Berkeley can be followed by a thinker like Hume, and that both kinds of thinkers can claim to be speaking in the name of common sense. Nevertheless, Berkeley's extreme position—for it is an extreme, though not a preposterous, position—has given rise to much unnecessary mystification. The ordinary reader may feel, on reading his works, that he is being hoodwinked by someone much too clever to be allowed to run amok among fundamental truths. And, though Hume's reversion to brute materialism may not be any more attractive, the usual reaction is that it is preferable to a skylarking idealism.

Who was this extraordinary man Berkeley, and how did he come to the belief that there is no such thing as 'matter'? Was his disbelief in the independent world of nature just a pose, or was it based upon reasonable and logical argument? Was Bergson right to declare that modern philosophy begins not so much with Descartes as with Berkeley? Was this man an incurable dreamer and mystic, or was he in fact a person of sound sense and practical ability?

Although he was born at Dysert in the county of Kilkenny in Ireland (12th March, 1685), Berkeley came of an ancient English family. Of his early childhood in Ireland we know little, except that he entered the second class of Kilkenny School on 17th July, 1696. Four years later we find him enrolled as an undergraduate at Trinity College, Dublin. At Trinity he had a long and brilliant career. During the latter part of his twelve years' stay he was Fellow and Tutor of the College; and this is the period in which he conceived, wrote and published the most famous of his works on philosophy. We lack information about his private life during these busy, formative years. Judging from one anecdote that has been recorded, however, he was a man of extreme curiosity. One day, it appears, he saw a man hanged. When he returned to his lodgings, he persuaded a friend of his, Contarini, uncle of Oliver Goldsmith, to 'hang' him as an experiment. Being unloosed from the halter nearly unconscious, all he could murmur was: 'Bless my heart, Contarini, you have rumpled my band.' Apart from this incident, which may not be authentic, his life seems to have been singularly free from the grim and sordid, though not from disappointment.

During his years at the university, Berkeley kept a Common-place Book. This volume was discovered long after his death and published in 1871. From it we see that as early as 1705 he believed himself to have arrived at a new philosophical principle—an answer, as he supposed, to the problems raised but not solved by Descartes, Locke, Spinoza and Leibnitz. In 1705 he formed a Discussion Group at which these new ideas were debated. Four years later appeared his first important work, *An Essay towards a New Theory of Vision,* to be followed in 1710, when he was only twenty-five, by his *Treatise concerning the Principles of Human Knowledge.* The latter is a landmark in philosophical thought.

Since these urbane compositions contained many novel doctrines, Berkeley naturally expected them to make a considerable stir. The reception accorded them, however, was disappointing. Where they were not ignored, they were for the most part misunderstood. In order to present them in more attractive guise, Berkeley sat down to write the three *Dialogues between Hylas and Philonous,* which are among the most readable expositions of philosophical ideas. Here, more than anywhere else in his works, he displays his wit, his capacity for high controversy, and his translucent prose style. They are in some respects a reversion to the Platonic form of dialogue, except that they assume a rather more propagandist air, being directed primarily against 'Sceptics and Atheists'. Naturally they were directed also against persons of even greater respectability: for Berkeley was distressed to find that his new principle was travestied and misunderstood by persons for whose intelligence and character he had the highest regard.

For reasons of health and also because he wanted to

broaden his horizon, Berkeley came to London in 1713. He quickly made a name for himself in intellectual circles, meeting Steele, Addison, Swift and Pope. To Swift, a fellow ecclesiastic with Irish associations, he owed his introduction to the eccentric but well-disposed Lord Peterborough, Ambassador to the King of Sicily and the Italian States, whose private chaplain Berkeley became on an extensive tour through France and Italy. Foreign travel proved much to the young philosopher's taste. In 1715 he was off again to Italy, this time as tutor to the son of Dr. St. George Ashe, Bishop of Cloyne, Clogher and Derry. His diary of the tour, together with a *History of Sicily,* have been lost; but we see from his correspondence that few things escaped his notice, whether the subject was some natural curiosity, such as the Tarantula spider, or a social or political problem. The 'dreamer' or 'visionary', as his critics were accustomed to call him, was by no means unaware of what was happening in the world about him. On returning to England in 1721, just after the South Sea Bubble incident, he showed the measure of his concern for the welfare of the country by writing an *Essay towards Preventing the Ruin of Britain.*

In the year of the publication of his essay, Berkeley returned to Ireland, this time as chaplain to the Duke of Grafton. His great intellectual gifts were soon put to use at the university again, where he became both divinity lecturer and official preacher. He took his D.D. on 14th November, 1721. Preferment swiftly followed in both the ecclesiastical and the secular spheres: in 1722 he became Dean of Dromore—an office that did not consume much of his time, even as Deaneries then went—and Senior Proctor of the University. Then, with his career mapped out before him, and his attention concentrated upon his new system of philosophy, an unexpected event occurred. A woman with whom he had come into contact but once—no less a woman in fact than Miss Vanhomrigh, Swift's friend Vanessa—bequeathed to Berkeley, without warning or explanation,[1] half of her considerable fortune.

Whatever else may be said about the sudden acquisition of money, it unsettles. Berkeley's wealth, soon to be

[1] Possibly she was jealous of Swift's attachment to Esther Johnson ('Stella').

augmented by the emoluments attaching to the Deanery of Derry (about £1,100 a year), turned his mind to schemes which were temporarily to deflect the whole course of his life.

From 1724 onwards, then, Berkeley concentrated his mind upon a project which, though somewhat fantastic in retrospect, seemed to its originator eminently practical. Briefly, the idea was to establish in the Bermudas a missionary college from which to conduct evangelistic campaigns in America, particularly among the negro population. Without Berkeley's enthusiasm and powers of persuasion, public interest in such a scheme could never have been enlisted; that Berkeley was able to extract a promise from the government of £20,000 towards meeting the expenses was even more remarkable. The money was indeed promised; four years passed but not a penny was handed over. Meanwhile Berkeley worked, persuaded, argued, canvassed, waited. Twice a week he attended the tea parties given by Princess (later Queen) Caroline, less for the enjoyment such functions gave him than for the opportunity they afforded of making contacts likely to further his project. How thoroughly he was in earnest may be judged from a passage from a letter written on his behalf by Swift to Lord Carteret:

I do humbly entreat your Excellency either to use such persuasions as will keep one of the first men in this Kingdom for learning and virtue quite at home, or assist him by your credit to compass his romantic design, which however is very noble and generous, and directly proper for a great person of your excellent education to encourage.

Nothing, as regards material help, was forthcoming. Rather than abandon the project, however, Berkeley resolved to go without the money, feeling that if he could furnish more direct evidence that the scheme was feasible, he would be able to shame the government into honouring its promises. A Royal Charter for the College (to be called St. Paul's) had already been granted; the royal bounty must surely follow. Resigning his rich Deanery, Berkeley set sail with his newly-married wife, daughter of Judge Forster, in the autumn of 1728. A small group of loyal friends accompanied him, all of them at some personal and material sacrifice.

Berkeley spent three years away from England. Pending a decision from London, he settled at Newport, on Rhode Island, where he purchased a farm of about 96 acres and built a house which he named, perhaps not without irony, Whitehall. Frustrated as he might be, he was not idle. In the intervals between drawing-up plans and reports, he continued his studies and worked on a philosophical dialogue directed against freethinking. This book, which he entitled *Alciphron, or the Minute Philosopher*, was a long essay in the style of the *Dialogues between Hylas and Philonous*. He wrote it at leisure, so he records, on a 'natural alcove' of rock on the island coast. It was not published until he returned home.

At length it became obvious, if not to the trustful Berkeley, then at least to his friends, that the government subsidy would never be paid at all. In a revealing letter, Walpole wrote that while as an official he was bound to say that the money, being already earmarked, would materialize, his advice as a friend was that Berkeley and his followers should dismiss the subject from their minds. We know now that the sum in question had already been diverted elsewhere. Disappointed, but not in despair, Berkeley resolved to return. Before doing so, however, he arranged for his large collection of books to be presented to Yale University, and for his farm to be sold for the purpose of founding scholarships there. And so he bade farewell to his pleasant homestead, his slaves (in whose material and moral welfare he had always taken the greatest interest), and the many friends that he had won during his residence. Typical of his character was his insistence, once back in London, that all the subscriptions which his enthusiasm and eloquence had drawn from private purses three years before should be returned.

Berkeley's imperturbable character, his warm and generous disposition, and his genius for friendship, had long won him the respect and admiration of the most hardheaded of men—and this was an age of hardheaded men. He was again received in high society; and soon the promotion which he had formerly renounced, if not forfeited, caused him to be raised to the Bishopric of Cloyne, which office he retained almost to the day of his death. Once settled at Cloyne, Berkeley decided to content himself with episcopal duties and meditation, and to plan no further excursions, save into the realm of theoretical philosophy. As for his office, he appears to have been a model Bishop. His private life was rigorous in its severity. He usually rose as early as three or four in the morning for purposes of study. His encouragement of local industries by patronizing the neighbouring workmen for all his needs meant dressing in the coarsest of clothes. He still devoted much time to literary work; in 1735 appeared *The Analyst*, an attack upon the extravagances of mathematical theorists, and shortly afterwards *The Querist*, which was concerned chiefly with questions of social reform. Then followed a pause of some years during which he turned his attention to a subject which, next to the Bermuda project, seems to have engrossed him more than any other, but in which posterity has been accustomed to see little but a waste of energy and talent. The result of his researches were finally published in a work for which there is no parallel in philosophical literature: *Siris: A Chain of Philosophical Reflections and Enquiries concerning the virtues of Tar Water, and divers other subjects connected together and arising one from another*.

Although a man of robust and handsome appearance, Berkeley's manner of life had not always been conducive to the maintenance of physical fitness; and it is clear that as he grew older he developed a tendency towards hypochondria. 'My own sedentary life,' he wrote in *Siris* (§ 119), 'has long since thrown me into an ill habit, attended with many ailments, particularly a nervous colic, which rendered my life a burden, the more so because my pains were exasperated by exercise. But since the use of tar water, I find, though not a perfect recovery from my old and rooted illness, yet such a gradual return of health and ease, that I esteem my having taken this medicine the greatest of all temporal blessings, and am convinced that under providence I owe my life to it.'

In *Siris* Berkeley has not merely given us a treatise on medicine; he has produced at the same time a remarkable philosophical essay, for the 'chain of reflections and enquiries' leads him to speculate upon the nature of existence itself, beginning with the simplest considerations and ending with a mysticism which is both Christian and Platonic in inspiration. In the properties of tar, he claimed to detect the fundamental constituents of matter—or, if it is preferred, the vital elements which compose organic nature: thus he leaps from one subject to another, much as the spirit prompts him, throwing out a series of illuminating remarks rather than a consistently logical argument. *Siris* excited sufficient interest among a public always receptive of new 'cures' to prompt its author to issue, after an interval of eighteen years, an essay entitled *Further Thoughts on Tar Water*. Such was the measure of his confidence in that simple remedy.

In the year of the publication of this last essay, which was little more than a tract, Berkeley decided to remove to Oxford in order to be near his son George, who was an undergraduate there (his eldest son had died the year before). Although he was fully prepared to resign his Bishopric, he was granted special permission by the King to retain episcopal status. One Sunday evening in January, 1753, while listening to a sermon being read by his wife, he died peacefully. He was buried in Christ Church.

Two spontaneous testimonies from his friends sum up Berkeley's character and the influence it exerted. The first is from Francis Atterbury, Bishop of Rochester: 'So much understanding, so much knowledge, so much innocence, and such humility, I did not think had been the fashion of any but angels, till I saw this gentleman.' The second is from Alexander Pope, a man not much given to flattery:

'To Berkeley every virtue under heaven.'

2

The history of Berkeley's reputation has been to some extent the history of the way in which he has been misunderstood. And the misunderstanding has arisen as much from the thoughtless admiration of friends as from the deliberate detraction of enemies. The question to be asked in outlining the thought of Berkeley is first—what did he in fact say? The second question, issuing out of the first, is—why did he say it?

First, then, as to what Berkeley actually said. Whereas Locke had introduced a distinction between 'primary qualities' and 'secondary qualities', maintaining that the latter inhered not in the perceived object but in the perceiving subject, Berkeley begins by declaring this distinction to be invalid. Just as a colour cannot exist apart from the sensation of a perceiving subject, so the 'primary qualities' of extension, form and motion are, in Berkeley's opinion, equally dependent upon perception. When we talk of an object, we are talking invariably of the object of a *subject*; the former cannot exist, and cannot be imagined as existing, without the latter. Now the object of the mind is, as Descartes, Hobbes, and Locke agreed, always an *idea*. Therefore, all objects, all 'things', indeed 'all the choir of heaven and furniture of the earth', are nothing but ideas. In spite of the difficulties inherent in his view, Locke had resolutely maintained that our ideas, to be true, must be 'of' something. Berkeley regards this as an absurdity. An idea, in his view, is not 'of' anything but another idea. The world is composed of minds on the one hand and ideas on the other. An 'outside' or 'external' world is therefore inconceivable.

So far, so good. But—and this is the point to be stressed—Berkeley never meant to assert that, as a consequence of the non-existence of matter, natural entities such as the earth, sun, stars, chairs and tables, were nothing but *illusions*. He was as completely aware of their existence as was Dr. Johnson, who thought to dismiss Berkeley's philosophy by kicking a stone with 'mighty force' and saying 'I refute it thus!' In the *Principles of Human Knowledge* and again in the Dialogues, Berkeley does his best to clear himself of the charge of denying the *reality* of the natural world. 'I do not argue,' he explains, 'against the existence of any one thing that we can apprehend, either by sense or reflection. That the things I see with mine eyes and touch with my hands do exist, really exist, I make not the least question. The only thing whose existence we deny is that which philosophers call matter or corporeal substance. And in doing of this, there is no damage done to the rest of mankind, who, I dare say, will never miss it. The atheist indeed will want the colour of an empty name to support his impiety; and the philosophers may possibly find they have lost a great handle for trifling and disputation.'

Berkeley's position is as hard to refute as that of Locke is to prove. But there remains a difficulty for which there appears at first sight to be no solution: namely, if existence depends upon being perceived (if *esse est percipi*), what happens to things when in fact no one is perceiving them? Berkeley, it must be admitted, was plagued with questions of this kind, which usually resulted from a failure to grasp the fundamentals of his position: but just as he held that we know reality *because* it is composed of ideas present to our minds and is inconceivable except as thus present, so he held that the world of nature is permanent *because* there is always in the last resort a mind to perceive it, namely, the mind of God. 'So long as (objects) are not actually perceived by me, or do not exist in my mind or that of any other created spirit, they must either have no existence at all or else subsist in the mind of some Eternal Spirit: it being perfectly unintelligible and involving all the absurdity of abstraction to attribute to any single part of them an existence independent of a spirit. To be convinced of which, the reader need only reflect and try to separate in his own thoughts the being of a sensible thing from its being perceived.' Berkeley's view is thus seen to approximate to that of Malebranche, who declared that 'we see all things in God'. Berkeley, incidentally, had visited Malebranche in his cell in Paris, and the two had engaged in some heated argument. The report that Malebranche died as a result of an illness brought on by the excitement caused by Berkeley's polemics is now generally discounted.

A philosopher of Berkeley's proved sincerity and eminence does not adopt an extreme view without good reason. In every generation there are wiseacres who enjoy bewildering the public with far-fetched systems, just as there are poets and painters whose one ambition is to *épater le bourgeois*. Berkeley did not try to bewilder and astonish; he was out to combat what he believed to be the most dangerous tendency of his age, namely, the drift towards materialism. Nor is it strictly true to say that he associated materialism merely with the belief in matter; what he regards as pernicious in the thought of his time is its addiction to *abstractions*. To Berkeley, the interposition of the artificial 'idea' between the perceiver and the object perceived is simply one among other examples of this abstractionist tendency. Thus empiricism, which claims to keep rigidly to the brute facts of experience, inevitably becomes involved in the most complicated word-spinning.

To those who accused him of making nonsense of such notions as the uniformity of nature and the sequence of cause and effect, Berkeley answered that such regularities were better explicable on his idealist view than on that of materialism: for 'whenever the course of nature is interrupted by a miracle, men are ready to own the presence of a superior agent. But when we see things go on in the ordinary course, they do not excite in us any reflection; their order and concatenation, though it be an argument of the greatest wisdom, power, and goodness in their creator, is yet so constant and familiar to us, that we do not think them the immediate effects of a free spirit: especially since inconstancy and mutability in acting, though it be an imperfection, is looked on as a mark of freedom.'

The Precursors of Hume

Berkeley had few disciples, for not many philosophers were vigorous enough to follow him all the way; and you cannot be a true Berkeleyan unless you follow the master all the way. His colleague, Arthur Collier, is perhaps the only other orthodox Berkeleyan: in 1713 he published a book entitled *Clavis universalis, or a New Enquiry after Truth, being a Demonstration of the Non-existence or Impossibility of an External World*. A thinker who owed nothing directly to Berkeley, and who had probably never heard of him, was the Italian Giambattista Vico (1668-1744), an idealist of great originality who applied his theories to the problems of society and history, and outlined the principles of a New Science from which modern philosophers, particularly the Italian idealists Croce and Gentile, have drawn much inspiration. Vico, who laid stress upon the historical evolution of the human mind, lived an obscure but intensely busy life in Naples at a time when the chief centres of learning were London and Paris. Another contemporary, Montesquieu (1689-1755), a Frenchman, also set out to philosophize about society; but Montesquieu tended to look upon society as a mechanism with which human reason could at best 'tinker', not as the product of man's developing consciousness. His thought is static; that of Vico is dynamic. Meanwhile, thanks to the versatile Voltaire, France had been made acquainted with the ideas of Locke. Pushing empiricism to its logical conclusion, philosophers such as Condillac, Abbot of Mureaux (1715-80), and La Mettrie, the doctor-author of *L'Homme Machine* (1748) and *L'Homme Plante* (1748), ended up by denying the existence of mind altogether, and thereby anticipated the theories of modern Behaviourism.

The French critic, Rémy de Gourmont, observed that 'very simple ideas are within the reach of very complicated minds only'. This is especially true of philosophy. We have seen how Berkeley, realizing that perception is always of the concrete and never of the abstract, concluded that perception and existence involved each other, and that in consequence there could be no such thing as a world outside or external to our minds. What makes Berkeley a thinker of such stature is not so much his original idea, however, as the way in which he sticks to it, analyses it and develops it. There is all the difference between the thinker possessed with an *idée fixe* which he enunciates as a dogma, and the thinker who, like Berkeley, is prepared to defend his thesis by argument step by step. As we know, Berkeley regretted that his critics should have shown such constant reluctance to cross swords with him; for while he was not seeking to provoke astonishment or dismay, he considered that his original notions deserved more than a passing gesture of contempt. A man of very different temperament from Berkeley, but resembling him in his addiction to an intellectual passion, was the Scotsman, David Hume. In spite of the hostility which his views have provoked (especially in orthodox circles), Hume deserves without question to be numbered among the important philosophers of the Western world. Berkeley's philosophy is a triumph of belief; Hume's philosophy is a triumph of disbelief. For if it is hard to believe, it is equally hard to maintain a consistent attitude of scepticism.

David Hume

'If I must be a fool, as all who reason or believe anything certainly *are, my follies shall at least be natural and agreeable.'*

—Treatise of Human Nature.

1

If we are right in assuming (as he himself assumed) that the family of Hume can be identified with that of the Homes, who had been associated for centuries with Ninewells, Edinburgh, David Hume came of a line of both substance and tradition. He was born on the 26th April, 1711. As for his early education, he tells us that he passed through 'the ordinary course with success'. We know that he matriculated, under the name of 'David Home', at Edinburgh in February, 1723, which is evidence of no mean ability. His first intention was apparently to study law; but already at the age of 16 he had set his heart upon becoming a philosopher. By 'philosopher' he did not mean to imply a professor or instructor in philosophy—which is what a philosopher means today, if it does not mean a man who makes the best of a bad job, or takes the rough with the smooth; he meant to imply a devotee of the philosophical or contemplative *life*, a kind of religious or philosophical ascetic. The crisis came at the age of eighteen. It was then, as we learn from a letter written many years after (probably to the physician George Cheyne), that Hume believed himself to have arrived, like Berkeley at the same age and Descartes somewhat later in life, at a new discovery in thought, a new principle of philosophy.

Whatever the precise nature of this revelation, it was sufficiently compelling to cause him not merely to renounce the formal study of law but to embark upon research into the classics, English literature and philosophy itself. By 1729 the strain of such unremitting application had begun to affect his health. He suffered what we to-day call a nervous breakdown. Fortunately, he went the right way about curing it. He reformed his diet, took regular exercise, especially riding and walking—and, perhaps wisest of all, continued gently to pursue his studies. Such, we gather, was his manner of life for the next few years. Absorbed as he was in intellectual matters, he was still not absolutely sure what form his life's work should take: whether he should retire to some secluded spot and write down his thought in systematic form, or whether, having for so long studied in solitude, he should return to the world of men, and particularly of worldly men. He seems, at the critical moment, to have felt the 'pull' of society; we do not know precisely what were his motives in trying his hand for a period at commerce in Bristol. We may surmise, however, that this experience, though brief, decided him for good and all. It was now philosophy or nothing. In the summer of 1734 he was off to France. On 12th September he arrived at Rheims. Finally he decided to halt at La Flèche in Anjou, where for the next two years he was to make his home.

La Flèche, as the reader may remember, was a spot already sacred to philosophy, for it was there that Descartes had received his Jesuit education. There the New Method had germinated. Hume had not long settled in his new home when he experienced, with unconcealed delight, the first stirring of his creative powers—a moment for which he had waited so long as almost to have despaired of its arrival. The immediate stimulus (and there must always be an immediate stimulus) was an argument in which he became involved one day with a local Jesuit father. The subject was the reality of miracles. Dissatisfied with the orthodox view presented to him, Hume sat down to write a philosophical essay which, as he warmed to his theme, came to embrace most of the problems of natural and revealed religion. Admittedly it represented no more than an experiment, though an experiment worth making; but it cleared the stage for the more ambitious works upon which, now that his faculties were aroused, he felt ready to embark. The first of these works was entitled *A Treatise of Human*

Nature, and Hume confessed that he intended by its composition to 'produce a total alteration of philosophy'. The claim, as it turned out, was not altogether extravagant. For some thinkers, of whom one at least was to prove Hume's superior, it came to represent a decisive turning-point in thought.

In return for £50 down and twelve bound copies, Hume agreed to have the *Treatise* issued anonymously in 1739. Meanwhile, having returned to Ninewells, he awaited publication with high hopes. He was confident that his views, displayed with tantalizing anonymity, would cause the kind of uproar for which all philosophers wish to provide occasion but so few arouse. Like Berkeley, he expected to precipitate a mild intellectual revolution; but, like Berkeley, he was sadly disappointed. A 'revolutionary' or 'advanced' author tends to forget that, being far ahead of the public, he must expect recognition only from those who, by great mental effort and adjustment, can keep up with him. From the public as a whole he must anticipate nothing but indifference or hostility, atoned for scarcely at all by the placid recognition of later generations. In Hume's own words, 'the book fell dead-born from the press'. Not that it was completely ignored; one reviewer paid him the doubtful compliment of comparing this first composition to the 'crude attempts' of a Milton or a Raphael. Deserved or not, the slight roused Hume to such fury that he is said to have considered challenging the writer to a duel; but the story is in keeping neither with what we know of Hume's character nor with his ideal of philosophical conduct.

At any rate he pushed ahead, still hopeful of success, with the second volume, which the firm of Thomas Longman agreed to publish in 1740. Again the work excited no particular interest. But the completed treatise, which was duly recognized to be a literary as well as a philosophical masterpiece, gradually began to make its way in the philosophical world: until, like the works of Locke and Berkeley, it came to form part of the tradition not merely of English but of European philosophy.

This does not mean that the philosophy of Hume is a satisfying philosophy. It is not. It does not even form a satisfactory philosophical *system* such as the work of Plato, Aquinas, or even Leibnitz. Yet that, if nothing else, is the reason for its importance: it represents the first ambitious attempt to establish a basis from which other philosophical systems may be criticized. In short, it inaugurates the modern tradition of philosophy as a technique for the criticism of other philosophy, particularly that form which is known as metaphysics.

After the publication of the *Treatise of Human Nature*, Hume produced a number of shorter works which were later assembled under the title of *Essays Moral and Political*. An application for a Professorship at Edinburgh was unsuccessful. Being in need of employment, he obtained in 1745 the lucrative but otherwise not very satisfactory position of tutor in the family of the Marquis of Annandale. The Marquis, who had already been declared by Chancery to be incapable of managing his own affairs, was almost a complete lunatic; nor was Hume slow to perceive that his estate, as supervised by a certain Captain Vincent, was showing good profits to everyone save its nominal master. Hume was not devoid of moral courage: and his plain expression of disapproval of what was going on cost him his job the following year. In these circumstances, he felt obliged to close with an offer, made soon after, to act as secretary to General St. Clair for the duration of an expedition to Canada. This particular expedition did not materialize: instead it was diverted to an attack upon Port Lorient. Hume impressed his commander sufficiently to gain the appointment of Judge-Advocate. Soon afterwards he was appointed member of a diplomatic mission to Vienna and Turin, sporting a uniform which lent him the appearance, so it is said, of 'a grocer in the train-bands'. Hume seems never to have been wholly at ease in high society, and his manners possessed none of the grace and polish of his own prose style.

When, in 1749, Hume returned to Ninewells, he had in his pocket 'near a £1,000', not a bad capital sum in those days upon which to retire for the purpose of writing philosophy, which is not as a rule a paying business. Seclusion had once more exerted its attractions over him, and indeed the next few years proved that he had made the best use of it. In 1751 was published the *Political Discourses* and the *Enquiry concerning the Principles of Morals*. Upon a work of more controversial matter, to which he gave the title of *Dialogue concerning Natural Religion*, he had spent much labour; but realizing that its publication would draw upon him fierce accusations of infidelity and atheism, he finally decided to hold it back until such time as the public mood, easily disturbed in those days, grew calmer. As it was he became the object of a great deal of abuse, which he held chiefly responsible for his failure, for the second time, to obtain a university professorship.

In spite of these attempts to blacken his reputation (there was never any insinuation regarding his personal conduct), he finally succeeded in obtaining a position which, besides carrying a good measure of prestige, was to prove of great convenience to himself. This was the post of librarian of the Advocates' Library at Edinburgh, among the 30,000 volumes of which (it was the largest collection of its kind in Scotland) he was in his element. The pay, by contrast, was shocking: a bare £40 a year.

Although still as interested as ever in matters philosophical, and hoping one day to produce something more deserving of the name of 'system' than anything he had so far assembled, Hume had long been toying with the idea of writing a history of the United Kingdom. There have been several reasons suggested why, in middle life, his interest should thus have shifted from the theoretical to the practical, from the abstract to the concrete. That a professional thinker should 'change his direction' in this way is usually not an accident; there is some problem that he feels an urgent need to solve, and he will not rest content until he has devoted all his attention to it.

In the course of his travels abroad, as well as in his own country, Hume had developed an interest in public affairs. Being hardly at all adulterated by motives of ambition (for he did not aspire to shine in the world, other than as a figure of academic distinction), this interest was on the whole sincere. The difficulties and disturbances of his own age needed, in his view, first to be understood in order to be cured. When and how did these troubles begin? Hume realized that the key to the understanding of present social stress lay in history, in the chain of events that have led up to the present. And to pursue the kind of detailed research needed to satisfy his new mental curiosity, he could not have been better placed.

The first volume of what was to prove an epoch-making work appeared in 1754. It began with the reign of James I, which its author, after much reflection, pronounced to be the period from which the prevailing discontents dated, though he later saw reason to change his mind. This first volume had a poor reception. An author accustomed to initial disappointments ought not, on finding this first instalment a 'flop', to have allowed himself to be so dejected. The book represented, as Hume prided himself, a new departure in historical writing. The public does not collectively take to new departures. The public must be persevered with. Fortunately Hume pushed steadily on with his studies until, by the year 1762, he had completed five volumes. With gratification he began to realize that his patience was being rewarded. The copies began to melt from the bookshop shelves. Money flowed in steadily, increasingly: until Hume, who had never before believed such a thing possible, discovered that he was not merely a rich man, but something far more unique in those days, a man enriched by literary achievement. Hume's history was almost the first serious 'best-seller'.

For a good many years after its author's death, the *History of England* remained the standard work of its kind, the scholar's classic, enjoying the distinction common to such classics of being referred to not by its title but by its author. A man who declared that he was 'reading Hume' might confidently be supposed to be reading the History, not the *Treatise of Human Nature*, nor the *Enquiry concerning Human Understanding*. Today, such as is the changed estimation of these two branches of his work, the presumption would be otherwise, the History being relegated to the background and rarely consulted save out of curiosity. Nevertheless, it forms a landmark in historical writing in that it concerns itself as much with social and literary as with political affairs.

For reasons largely dictated by Hume's peculiar temperament, the more he progressed with his history the more he allowed personal bias to influence his judgments. Hume the philosopher stepped down some way to meet Hume the historian. Just as Dr. Johnson confessed to have made sure, in writing his disguised parliamentary reports, that 'the Whig dogs had the worst of it', so Hume made no disguise in this book of his intransigent Toryism. Nor was he any kinder to the English people, whom he repeatedly accused of an anti-Scottish bias and a desire to ruin Scotland. Thus we have vituperative references to the 'barbarians on the banks of the Thames', and, on the party side, to 'the villainous seditious Whig strokes' or 'plaguey prejudices of Whiggism', which increased in violence as the story proceeded and infuriated a large section of the public. But the book still sold and sold, as infuriating books will do.

No doubt some of Hume's anti-Whig fury was due to his mounting hatred of Puritanism and bigotry. Royalism in the past seemed to him to have stood for a broader, more tolerant tradition, which he believed to be seriously in peril. Whatever his political views, however, he cannot by any stretch of imagination be described as orthodox in matters of religion. During the composition of the History, he turned aside more than once to write on philosophical subjects; in 1757, resuming the theme of his earlier *Dialogues concerning Natural Religion* he produced a highly controversial study entitled *The Natural History of Religion*. His main contention was that polytheism represented the most natural, as well as the earliest, form of religious belief, while monotheism was the result of custom and habit not necessarily superior either to the former or to downright scepticism. In this work in particular, Hume, feeling moderately secure in his position, makes little or no attempt to conceal his own lack of faith. Not that he wished to advertise himself as an atheist; atheism, in his opinion, was a point of view to which no one wishing to avoid dogmatism could subscribe, for you could no more deny the possibility of a supernatural God than you could be sure that such a God existed.

Nevertheless, Hume could not resist the temptation to indulge in ridicule at the expense of orthodox and conventional religious beliefs, which in one place he describes somewhat uncharitably as 'sick men's dreams'; and in consequence his books have been listed by certain institutions as unfit for the devout. The truth is that Hume was temperamentally a man too much given to intellectual curiosity to find repose in any convenient formula of belief; but he recognized that in this respect he and his kind were not typical of the human race, and he was anxious not to disturb any man's convictions so long as they were free from fanaticism and intolerance.

The year after completing the History, Hume was invited to accompany Lord Hertford to Paris as secretary to the Embassy. He went in the capacity of a subordinate; by Parisian society, on the other hand, he was received as a man of the highest distinction, for his works were by then well known there. When the Foreign Office sent Hume to Paris, the French, quicker in these matters than other peoples, reminded England by their adulation what an important man she had chosen as representative. With Dalembert, the philosopher (1717-83), and Turgot (1717-81), the statesman-economist, Hume formed immediate attachments, for his point of view was very similar to their own.

In society itself (insofar as that could be separated from intellectual circles; the division was not so complete as it is now) the British philosopher shined less brightly. A contemporary witness has recorded how oddly his 'broad, unmeaning face' contrasted with the flower of French beauty, though Hume, as we shall see, now considered himself to be a dashing courtier, and lost no opportunity of participating in entertainments and charades for which his presence was requested by the ladies.

He made a good and discreet secretary; and when, later, General Conway wanted an assistant at the Foreign Office, Hume was considered the best man for the job. That was in 1767. After two years of responsible work, he began to feel that his interests and health required, as his pocket now permitted, a rest from professional labour, and a return to that part of the world in which he was most at home. He therefore decided to settle in Edinburgh, taking a house at the corner of St. David's Street sufficiently large to enable him still to entertain the best society. He could well afford it. His pension and other earnings now brought him in £1,000 a year. He had comparatively few commitments, though he was exceedingly generous to friends and struggling authors. Smollett, the novelist, was one of those to whom he gave timely assistance.

The most ungrateful beneficiary was a man of established, indeed international, reputation, Jean-Jacques Rousseau. Rousseau, for whose writing Hume had a high regard, had been expelled from one country after another, as much because of his own quarrelsomeness as because he as a writer of 'dangerous' or seditious books. Hume was anxious for him to be given asylum in England. Arrangements were therefore made to bring Rousseau and his mistress, Thérèse le Vasseur, over to that country, and Hume even went so far as to persuade the government to grant the Frenchman a small pension, on the understanding that the matter was to be kept secret. The ramifications of the story are very complicated; but it appears that Rousseau, learning of the proposed pension, and at once identifying secrecy with conspiracy and intrigue, wrote, as was his habit, a ferocious letter to the one man who had tried to help him. Hume, rightly indignant, replied asking Rousseau to explain himself. Once labouring under the delusion of persecution, however, the latter was beyond the control of any man and all but one woman; and the plan of providing him with an asylum of peace was wholly frustrated, though Rousseau spent long enough in England to write the first six books of his *Confessions*. As to Hume's handling of the affair, it was creditable throughout.

On 25th August, 1776, after an illness of some length which he bore without complaining, Hume died, having reached the age of sixty-five. He has left us his own view of his character and achievements which, allowing for a slight element of complacency, is as good a summoning-up as he deserves at the hand of others. It is also a fine example of his supple, urbane, exquisitely clear prose, and with it we conclude this sketch of his life, almost as if he were speaking, disembodied, from behind that veil of sensation which he never thought to penetrate:

'I am, or rather was (for that is the style I must now use in speaking of myself, which emboldens me the more to speak my sentiments), I was, I say, a man of mild disposition, of command of temper, of an open, social, and cheerful humour, capable of attachment, but little susceptible of enmity and of great moderation in all my passions. Even my love of literary fame, my ruling passion, never soured my temper, notwithstanding my frequent disappointments. My company was not unacceptable to the young and careless, as well as to the studious and literary; and as I took particular pleasure in the company of modest women, I had no reason to be displeased with the reception I met with from them. In a word, though most men, anywise eminent, have found reason to complain of calumny, I never was touched, or even attacked, by her baleful tooth; and though I wantonly exposed myself to the rage of both civil and religious factions, they seemed to be disarmed in my behalf of their wonted fury. My friends never had occasion to vindicate any one circumstance of my character and conduct; not but that the zealots, we may well suppose, would have been glad to invent and propagate any story to my disadvantage, but they could never find any which they thought would wear the face of probability.'

2

Although Hume differed in outlook from Berkeley as radically as a sceptic must necessarily differ from a convinced believer, there was one point upon which they were in whole-hearted agreement. This was the question of abstract ideas. Hume declared that of all the discoveries of modern thought, Berkeley's demonstration of the unreality of abstract ideas was by far the most important. But whereas Berkeley, criticizing Descartes and Locke, had argued that no idea was 'of' anything but another idea, thereby demonstrating the unreality of an external world, Hume introduced a distinction between ideas and what he called 'impressions'. The latter were defined as actual physical (or mental) *percepts,* i.e. things in their natural state as our senses perceived them. If, therefore, Hume had been asked to say what an idea was 'of', he would have replied that it was 'of' a previous impression. Any idea of which the previous impression or group of impressions could not be traced was to be judged a false or fictitious idea.

The multiplication of more or less subtle 'distinctions' has long been regarded, not without cause, as the curse of philosophy. When the spurious thinker runs up against a difficulty, he makes a distinction, thereby trying to encircle the obstacle on either side. If the two branches of enquiry do not manage to meet, a further bifurcation occurs, creating four questing antennae and so on until the enquiry has become altogether too involved for the lay mind to grasp. The great philosophers are distinguished for their capacity to keep their ultimate end in view; consequently when they introduce a distinction, it is usually with great care to explain why it should have been necessary at all, and upon what particular aspect of the enquiry it is designed to throw light. This applies above all to Hume's impression-idea distinction.

Having maintained that every genuine idea is a copy of a previous impression, Hume is still faced with the task of explaining how it is that we have, or appear to have, 'complex' ideas—genuine complex ideas, that is to say, as opposed to false or fictitious ones. It is here that Hume unfolds that part of his philosophy which has caused greatest controversy, and from which Kant, as we shall see, was to derive the stimulus to embark upon his own profound line of enquiry.

The transition, according to Hume, from our simple ideas to those of a complex character is not a logical or rational one at all: at least no logical or rational connecting-link has so far been traced. It is purely one of imaginative association or habit. From the observed succession of certain ideas to others, or certain groups of ideas to other groups of ideas, we build up what we call our knowledge of matters of fact. The recurrence of these various successions impels us to attribute a greater or lesser measure of certainty to facts or events. This is true not merely of such facts as that the sun rises in the east and will set tonight, but of the observed succession of every set of 'effects' to an apparent set of 'causes'. All we are entitled to say is that we observe the *succession*, several times or continually repeated, of the latter to the former. Of the necessary connection or link between one and the other we have no impression at all. To assert that such a connection exists is to assert something for which there is no warranty in science and no justification save in custom.

If we bear in mind the theory of ideas advanced by Berkeley, we shall remember that he, like Hume, was obliged to explain how it is that our ideas, being the sole constituents of our minds and of the world itself, come to be arranged in a certain way, namely, the way in which we find them arranged. Berkeley's answer, perhaps the least satisfactory of all the explanations put forward by him in justification of a most ingenious theory, is that God has so arranged them. To this assertion Hume's reply is characteristic. If you believe in God, he says, well and good; your belief will permit you to believe in practically anything. But supposing you do not (and it is a matter of temperament, after all)? In that case, you can hazard no reasonable explanation as to why things are as they are. All you know is that in the course of normal living you come to rely upon events assuming direction, order, recurrence and regularity. Meanwhile, whether or not you discover the true explanation of such patterns, you must go on living as if such an explanation were forthcoming. Instinct will not wait for reason to catch up. Thus Hume would maintain that the entire assemblage of our knowledge—including the existence of an external world, the idea of personal identity, indeed the idea of knowledge itself—depends upon our trust in certain instincts. Against these, as he himself had good cause to know, the whole armoury of philosophical scepticism cannot prevail.

Believing as he does that 'all our reasonings concerning causes and effects are derived from nothing but custom, and that belief is more properly an act of the sensitive, than of the cognitive part of our natures', Hume comes to the conclusion that, as human creatures compelled to live and work as well as speculate, we must in essential matters, and for the greater part of the time, 'follow our instincts'. 'For I have already shown,' he observes, 'that the understanding, when it acts alone and according to its most general principles, entirely subverts itself, and leaves not the lowest degree of evidence in any proposition either in philosophy or in common life.' What, then, should we do to avoid intellectual suicide? If such are the consolations of philosophy, how has that exalted subject managed to acquire its reputation as a solace? Hume's reply reveals the kind of man he was rather than the kind of comfort philosophy may be expected to confer upon its devotees: 'Most fortunately it happens,' he says, 'that since reason is incapable of dispelling these clouds, nature herself suffices to that purpose, and cures me of this philosophical melancholy and delirium, either by relaxing this bent of mind or by some avocation and lively impression of my senses which obliterate all these chimeras. I dine, I play a game of backgammon, I converse, and am merry with my friends; and when after three or four hours' amusement I return to these speculations, they appear so cold and strained and ridiculous that I cannot find in my heart to enter into them any farther.' There are many to whom such sedatives, even if accessible, would be wholly ineffective. And there are many to whom the very idea of taking them would seem like intellectual cowardice. Hume's curiosity was extreme; but it was a broad rather than a deep curiosity. We can hardly imagine an Aristotle, a Spinoza, of a Kant speaking in this urbane but superficial manner.

In general it may be said that the materialism of Hume is nothing but the 'immaterialism' of Berkeley with the lights switched off. It was the *reductio ad absurdum* of what has been called, with reference to the course of philosophy from Descartes onwards, the 'way of ideas'. Our natural reaction to the study of Hume is to conclude either that philosophy, *i.e.* metaphysical philosophy, is nonsense, or that Hume's premises are seriously open to question. In both cases the reaction is bound to be somewhat violent. In England and France, many thinkers, rebelling against orthodoxy in both politics and religion, saw in Hume an apostle of liberation from superstition, an extirpator of absurd and outmoded fancies in theology and metaphysics. Others, less iconoclastic by temperament but genuinely desirous of salutory reform, were shocked thereby into rethinking their whole philosophical position from the beginning. Among these latter was a man of immense intellectual capacity and erudition: Immanuel Kant.

Encyclopaedists and Romantics

In fifth-century Athens philosophy was regarded as something in the nature of a divine gift. In the Middle Ages it became an intellectual discipline subordinated to its superior director, theology. In the sixteenth and seventeenth centuries it was an interesting, though sometimes also a dangerous, hobby. But in the eighteenth century it first became a profession.

Towards the end of the eighteenth century—one of the most crucial epochs of the world's history—a group of thinkers flourished in France under the title of '*philosophes*'. A '*philosophe*' was a man who, by proclaiming himself a thinker by profession, believed it his mission to apply reason to the problems of society, and to act as a kind of mental physician to the body politic. Among these apostles of reason were some who, though appalled by the flagrant abuses of the time, believed that the next few decades would see the establishment of a new form of society, based upon reason and justice, leading to a new order of civilization throughout Europe. With the object of compiling a modern equivalent to St. Thomas Aquinas's *Summa Theologiæ,* and intending to codify the new knowledge at the disposal of enlightened men, these *savants* drew up plans for a gigantic Encyclopædia. Hence the title 'Encyclopædists', which was applied to a circle of writers of whom Denis Diderot (1713-84), founder of the Encyclopædia project, was the acknowledged leader.

Diderot was a man of extraordinary versatility: philosopher, scientist, mathematician, and novelist (his remarkable story *La Réligieuse* would be regarded, if first published today, as a work of unusual sophistication and psychological precocity). His chief collaborator was Dalembert, with whom, as we have seen, Hume became acquainted during his stay in Paris. Excelling his contemporaries in breadth of vision and profundity, Voltaire (1694-1778), himself a contributor to the Encyclopædia, directed the whole weight of his wit, learning, and eloquence against the ignorance, superstition and cruelty of his time. Sharing the current belief that the eighteenth century represented, at its best, the highest reach of which civilization was capable, he persisted in the hope that by the steady application of reason to the problems of society, public enlightenment might be achieved within the space of one or two generations. His attraction to British philosophy, increased by his own residence in England, was due to its emphasis upon experiment and practice, and its distrust of metaphysical abstractions. Voltaire's passion for exactitude, clarity, and order (characteristics of the French mind at its best) confirmed him in a prejudice against everything that was half-formed, in process of formation, or lacking in precision; and this slight mental inflexibility tended to blind him to two great factors in human development— first, the influence of sentiment and emotions in human conduct, and secondly the concept of evolution in history. The latter, he held, had no real place in a view of the world according to which all ages prior to the eighteenth century formed one long night of superstitious barbarism. For of darkness there can be no history; and if the millennium is due to dawn tomorrow, there is no scope for future eras of historical development.

To the apocalyptic visions of Voltaire, which the brave old man entertained to the end of his long life, when, as he declared, he 'left off dying' to come to Paris for the last time, Rousseau (1712-78) provided the most violent antidote. Instead of a millennium of reason, Rousseau preached the necessity of recapturing primitive innocence. This was possible, he held, only by recovering that spontaneity of sentiment which civilization and the progress of physical science had tended to desiccate. Rousseau's emphasis upon man's inner life of imagination and sentiment, as expounded in *Emile* and *Julie*, exerted the most powerful impression upon Kant, whose whole philosophical position might well have been different had he not, at an early and critical stage of his career, made acquaintance with Rousseau's writings. That Rousseau's temperament made him the most unmanageable of men, setting an example of romantic irresponsibility which cast its spell over many later generations, we have already observed. Hume, who received first-hand evidence of his incalculability, summed up the French writer succinctly: 'He has only *felt* during the whole course of his life. He is like a man who was stripped not only of his clothes, but of his skin, and turned out in that situation to combat with the rude and boisterous elements.' [1] Nevertheless, Rousseau must not be dismissed as an effeminate dreamer. Like many others who have preached the brotherhood of man, he could speak with the tongue of devils as well as angels (as his *Confessions* amply show), and he was a shrewd, if unbalanced, critic of his fellows. He was not in himself a particularly original thinker, even in *The Social Contract*; his function was rather to redress the balance of thought.

[1] *Cf.* 'You would say that my heart and my mind do not belong to the same individual. Feeling fills my soul more quickly than a flash of lightning; but instead of enlightening me it burns and dazzles me' (*Confessions*, Book III).

Immanuel Kant

'You will not learn from me philosophy, but how to philosophize—not thoughts to repeat, but how to think. Think for yourselves, enquire for yourselves, stand on your own feet.'

1

The story of Kant's life is so difficult to separate from his philosophy that we shall here revert to the method already adopted on occasion, and discuss the two together. Of the importance of Kant's contribution to thought, everyone who possesses the slightest knowledge of the history of philosophy is in some degree aware: if asked to give the names of five philosophers, or at least of more than three, the ordinary man will almost certainly include Immanuel Kant. There are at least two good reasons why Kant should be recognized as a great figure even by those who, if challenged to expound the essence of his thought, would be hard put to it to do so. One is that he made gigantic and lasting contributions to all the major problems of philosophy; the other is that he came very near, in his own individual way, to living the genuine philosophical life. The number of so-called 'practising' philosophers is not large: there is Pythagoras, there is Socrates, there is Aquinas, there is Spinoza—and there is Kant. If Spenser is the poet's poet, then Kant is surely the philosopher's philosopher.

The career of Immanuel Kant provides a striking demonstration of the capacity of genius to overcome limitations. At a time when it is an accepted axiom that 'travel broadens the mind', and that the 'conquest of distance' has tended to further international understanding, we may well ponder the fact that Kant, who knew so much and commanded (at any rate in his later years) such widespread public attention, never once crossed the frontiers of East Prussia, nor showed any inclination to make such an excursion in the interests of either recreation or learning. To speculate whether a more cosmopolitan Kant would have produced a system less rigid in certain of its aspects is futile; what we should find sufficiently remarkable is that his philosophy, thus conceived in a limited though active environment, has influenced thinkers in every part of the world.

Kant's father, Johann Georg Kant, was born in Memel but finally settled in Königsberg. He persisted in the belief, which his son shared all his life, that his family came originally from Scotland. This is not at all unlikely. There had been an influx of Scottish immigrants into Poland during the seventeenth century, and Kant himself drew attention to the prevalence in East Prussia of such names as Douglas, Simpson, Hamilton, etc. Although some of the immigrant families accumulated power and riches, a great many pursued humble trades. Kant's father was a strap-maker, who, marrying the daughter of a fellow-craftsman, begot nine children of whom Immanuel was the second (born 22nd April, 1724). The five children to survive were brought up in the extreme of austerity. According to Kant's own testimony, his father and mother were model partners. 'Never,' he says, 'not even once, have I had to hear my parents say an unbecoming word, or do an unworthy act.' Kant always speaks of his father with respect. To his mother he seems to have been particularly attached, and such early education as she was capable of giving him (and she seems to have taught him a great deal) moulded his outlook for life. By nature a devout woman, she was much influenced by the religious reform movements of the day. This was known as Pietism, and its emphasis was upon faith and sentiment as opposed to reason and dogma. The Pietistic movement was started in Germany by Jacob Spener about 1670; in Kant's day its chief representatives in Königsberg were J. H. Lysius and F. A. Schultz. The latter was both director of a college patronized by Freidrich William I and pastor of the church at which the Kant family worshipped. Ever willing to help the poorer members of his congregation, Schultz remained for many years a real friend to the Kant household. On one occasion Kant remarked that Schultz was perhaps the only person who really understood his philosophy: a high compliment indeed.

After a brief period at a local Hospital School, Kant entered the *Collegium Fridericianum* (the institution over which Schultz presided) at the age of eight, staying there until he entered the university in 1740. His schooling was as strict as the puritan foundation could make it; and the habits of regularity, punctuality, frugality and hard work thereby inculcated, combined with early home influences to form a character almost too rigid and unbending to be attractive.

Kant's mother died of rheumatic fever when he was thirteen years old. Life thereafter proved very difficult for the family. The funerals of both parents were those of paupers, as the churchyard register shows. Kant's education thenceforth became a matter for his own exertions. From 1740 to 1746 he studied diligently at the university; and although he seems to have long remained uncertain of his true vocation, the influence of a remarkable young professor, Martin Knutzen, who put him in the way of the works of Isaac Newton, evidently first aroused his curiosity regarding metaphysics. Kant's associates during this period of preparation were students scarcely better off than himself. Two friends with whom he lodged, and in company with whom he is supposed to have earned a casual penny at billiards or cards, Wollner and Heilsberg (both Lithuanians), ended up the one as Finance Minister at Berlin and the other as War Minister. Kant also augmented his income in the way more usual to the indigent student, namely, by doing odd jobs of tutoring and finally by taking a permanent post as tutor. He lived with the family of a Reformed Church Pastor at Judschen, a village situated sixty miles from Königsberg, this being the absolute limit of his wanderings. He acted as tutor to two other families before becoming, in 1755, a licensed but unpaid lecturer at the university of Königsberg; by which time he had published sufficient papers on scientific and philosophical subjects to qualify as Doctor of Philosophy (the equivalent of our Master of Arts).

Largely owing to political intrigues, his efforts to obtain a professorship failed; but the government at Berlin, having heard of his ability as teacher and scholar, directed in 1766 that he should be appointed sub-librarian in the Schloss Library, the emoluments of which amounted to about £10 a year. Kant found the work trying, let alone ill-paid, and he soon resigned. Not that his work at the university, both official and unofficial, seemed likely to lead to prosperity. He was extremely hard up. He wore his clothes out until his friends, much embarrassed, begged him in vain to accept money to buy new ones. He moved from lodging-house to lodging-house, usually impelled to leave by the disturbances to which he was perpetually subject—at one house near the river it was the raucous boatmen, at another an intolerably vocal cock. Thus he struggled on, living so plainly as to succeed finally in accumulating a reserve fund of twenty sovereigns. By 1770, when he had reached the mature age of forty-six, he had established a reputation both as writer and as lecturer on such various themes as mathematics, physics, logic, metaphysics, ethics, geography, anthropology, and even military pyrotechnics and the science of fortification (the latter courses being attended by members of the Russian garrison). Like Francis Bacon before him, he seems to have made up his mind to 'take all knowledge for his province'. To have massed such a fund of knowledge and achieved such authority upon such meagre resources was to come near to being the most underpaid man in the world.

Twelve years after first applying for a professorship at Königsberg he was offered the Chair he had almost given up hope of obtaining, that of Logic and Metaphysics. His position was at last stabilized; and with stability came comparative financial ease—that is to say, his income rose to £60 a year (roughly what Wordsworth was earning at the height of his fame), together with some small 'extras' for academic services. Later he was given an additional subsidy, and at the end of his life his salary amounted to about £100 a year. The greater portion of this income he invested with an English settler in Königsberg, Green, at six (later five) per cent. The result of this judicious saving was that he left in his will the respectable sum of 21,539 thalers, and that in spite of his yearly outlay upon charitable purposes.

Professor Kant worked fully as hard as the earnest *privat-dozent* who had been obliged to exercise such self-denial. But his work was more profitably distributed, and he had much more leisure. Nevertheless, his time-table remained extremely rigid, and for the next quarter of a century he rarely departed from it. Admittedly, he was occasionally indisposed, and one afternoon he missed his customary walk through absorption in Rousseau's newly-published *Emile*. If Blücher is said to have invented punctuality by arriving at the right time on the field of Waterloo, Kant may be said to have invented *routine* in the streets and lecture-rooms of Königsberg.

Kant's day, details of which have been carefully recorded, was planned as follows. Punctually at five minutes to five in the morning, his devoted servant Lampe, an old soldier from Würzburg, used to rouse him. At five o'clock sharp, the Professor, presumably in his dressing-gown, was installed at the desk in his study. While making notes for his lectures, he would drink a cup of tea and smoke one pipe. He was in the lecture-room promptly at seven, where he discoursed for an hour on Logic or Metaphysics followed by an hour on some less abstract theme. During the remainder of the morning he worked at his manuscripts. Halting at precisely 12.45, he announced the time to the cook, who would depend upon this verbal signal to make ready for lunch. Guests to the number of five (Kant's stock of plate would not accommodate more) might be expected daily, each invitation being issued that same morning in order to secure immediate acceptance or otherwise. Nor was any guest likely to receive a second invitation who appeared late for the first. Abstemious though he was in his habits, Kant enjoyed nothing better than to extend hospitality to his friends; and having sat down to a three-course lunch, he liked to linger as much as four hours over the dessert and the wine. He was himself a good conversationalist, and was not without a sense of humour, though he maintained high standards of decorum. It was his maxim that conversation at mealtimes should pass naturally through the three stages of narration, discussion and jest. In his own case, the two themes upon which jest was debarred were metaphysics (a subject which, being the occupation of the rest of his life, was banned altogether from meals) and his own bachelor status, to which he rarely made reference. (The two women in whom he appears to have taken more than casual interest were, we gather, unable to preserve their single state long enough for the philosopher to calculate whether or not he should invite them to change it.) Once the conversation had passed the third stage, Kant did not hesitate to make clear to his companions that it was time for his afternoon walk. In the case of this regular promenade, the word 'constitutional' was particularly appropriate. Kant was far from being robust, and, like some other confirmed bachelors, he displayed a tendency to hypochondria. As he was convinced that every possible anti-germ precaution should be observed, he rarely departed from the practice of taking his walks unaccompanied, thereby enabling him to keep his mouth firmly closed. For the same reason he studiously refrained from indulging in exercise violent enough to induce perspiration, of which he had a particular dread. Thus, except towards the close of his life, he succeeded in keeping physically fit to a degree which, taking into account the intensity of his sedentary labours, was remarkable. The mind being in his case driven harder than his body, it was not surprising that the former should have been first to show signs of collapse.

His walk over, Kant would spend an hour or two reading the newspapers—his very isolation from the world made him an avid collector of news—and also such books and journals as he considered worth a professional philosopher's scrutiny. Having refreshed his mind with new matter, he would turn once more to the particular philosophical problems which held his attention. In the winter season this reflective mood would seize him about the hour of darkness. It was then his custom to fix his eye, as an aid to concentration, upon the tower of Lobernicht Church, just as during his lectures it had been his habit to stare at a particular button on the coat of one of his regular pupils. One season, it appears, the rapid growth of some nearby poplar trees obscured the view upon which he had come to depend, just as one day the particular button he habitually kept in view was found to be missing. In both cases Kant suffered genuine mental torment; nor was his peace of mind restored until in the one case the trees were cut by the kindness of a neighbour and in the other the button was replaced.

It is not possible here to cite all the various idiosyncrasies that have been attributed to Kant: his habits of dress (and in particular the elaborate mechanism whereby his stockings were suspended) and his peculiar mannerisms. Suffice it to say that such details are all in keeping with his meticulous unbending character. The witty account by Heine (1799-1856), the German poet, sums up the impression made by Kant upon his fellow townsfolk:

'The life of Immanuel Kant is hard to describe; he has indeed neither life nor history in the proper sense of the words. He lived an abstract, mechanical, old-bachelor existence, in a quiet remote street in Königsberg, an old city at the north-eastern boundary of Germany. I do not believe that the great cathedral clock of that city accomplished its day's work in a less passionate and more regular way than its countryman, Immanuel Kant. Rising from bed, coffee-drinking, writing, lecturing, eating, walking, everything had its fixed time; and the neighbours knew that it must be exactly half-past four when they saw Professor Kant, in his grey coat, with his cane in his hand, step out of his house door, and move towards the little lime-tree avenue, which is named, after him, the Philosopher's Walk. Eight times he walked up and down that walk at every season of the year; and when the weather was bad, his servant, old Lampe, was seen anxiously following him with a large umbrella under his arm, like an image of Providence. Strange contrast between the outward life of the man and his world-destroying thought. Of a truth, if the citizens of Königsberg had had any inkling of the meaning of that thought, they would have shuddered before him as before an executioner. But the good people saw nothing in him but a professor of philosophy; and when he passed at the appointed hour, they gave him friendly greetings—and set their watches.'

2

Of Kant it may justly be said that the first half of his career was made up of two closely-interrelated struggles: the struggle to gain sufficient means to live and the struggle to set his mental house in order. As an unpaid lecturer, he devoted himself with great earnestness to the study of past and contemporary philosophers; and it was fully in the spirit of Galileo and Descartes—indeed of the 'new philosophy' in general—that he wrote that 'in every branch of natural science there is only so much strict and proper science as there is of mathematics'. Kant's study of Newton, together with his interest in scientific discovery in general, had gradually induced in him a deep dissatisfaction with the subject which, from 1770 onwards, he was obliged to teach. He was not even sure that metaphysics, divorced from the experimental sciences in general, had any right to exist. That such was his mood about the year 1765 may be judged from a remark made in the course of a letter to the young mathematical philosopher Johann Heinrich Lambert, who had written to him suggesting collaboration in tackling the new problems of thought raised by the progress of scientific discovery: 'After many and many a tack', Kant wrote, 'I have at last reached a firm conviction as to the method which ought to be employed if escape is ever to be made from the illusory and pretended knowledge known as metaphysics.' What, we may well ask, was in his mind?

In maintaining that metaphysics, as commonly understood, represented nothing but 'illusory and pretended knowledge', Kant was not advancing anything original. As we saw in the last chapter, Hume had entertained a view of metaphysics very similar to this; and we have Kant's own admission that it was in consequence of his perusal of Hume's *Enquiry concerning Human Understanding* (apparently he never set eyes on the *Treatise of Human Nature*, though the *Enquiry* was a re-issue of part of it) that he was 'awakened from his dogmatic slumber'. But whereas Hume was an avowed enemy of metaphysics in all its forms, Kant, concentrating upon the question as to what constituted true knowledge, refrains from dismissing metaphysical knowledge as utter nonsense. He leaves us always in some doubt as to how far he wishes to 'search for a proper method of metaphysics' and how far he wishes to supersede metaphysics by a new 'critical philosophy' of his own. In 1770, we find him again confiding to Lambert that 'It is nearly a year since, as I flatter myself, I reached a conception, which I feel sure I shall never change, though I may extend it: a conception which enables us to test all sorts of metaphysical questions by perfectly certain and easy criteria and to obtain a decision as to how far they are soluble or not.' In 1771, another 'year since', he writes to his friend Marcus Herz of Berlin that he is occupied with a work on the subject of the 'boundaries of Sense and Reason'. In February, 1772, again, he declares himself to be 'in a position to propound a criticism of the pure reason'. And so he goes on, making announcement after announcement, year by year, working on short essays and beginning longer ones, revising his views almost weekly, but always returning once more to the task of erecting what he well describes as 'an architectonic of pure reason', until, in 1780, at least a decade later than he originally intended, fearing that unless he marshalled his maturing ideas he would leave nothing to the world save a stack of miscellaneous notes written on the oddest scraps of paper, he devoted five busy months to the composition of the *Critique of Pure Reason*, one of the greatest, if least commonly read, of philosophical treatises. From the first edition of this substantial production, Kant received a payment of £30.

We have already hinted at the general problem with which Kant, in preparing for the *Critique*, was chiefly concerned; but a philosopher, like an artist, does not occupy his mind with a problem unless, in a sense, he is obliged to—unless, that is to say, it has become an 'irritant' that he feels the need to expel from his system, and unless he is endowed with the self-awareness to perceive what it is that, being troublesome, needs to be ejected. Moreover, the greater the thinker, the more he will reflect in his own individual experience the problems of his fellow-men: the more, indeed, he will think on their behalf and show them, by his superior gift of insight, what they themselves only dimly perceive.

If Hume may be called a 'rigorous' thinker, in what sense was Kant's approach more rigorous still? To study Kant's development is to observe that he was early perplexed by a contradiction in the thought of his time, which he realized must be resolved if philosophy were not to lay itself open to the charge of casuistry. The contradiction, in Kant's view, was between the thoroughgoing scepticism of Hume and the Newtonian view of the universe as a vast, intricate but fundamentally intelligible mechanism. Having begun to study Newton, Kant realized that the one principle or relation upon which the whole structure depended was that of cause and effect. Moreover, this principle, as understood by Newton himself, was nothing if not an *objective* principle. The relation really did operate and was observed at work in the world of nature. For Hume, on the other hand, the so-called relation of cause and effect was nothing more than a habit of our imagination. Instead of being a truth subsisting independently of our minds, a necessary and universal nexus based upon reason, the causal relation was a truth (if indeed it could be called as much as that) without any external foundation at all. Here was a violent contradiction between science and philosophy. Although by profession and inclination a philosopher, Kant was passionately interested in the methods and achievements of physical science. If, however, he was right to suppose, with Descartes and his successors, that a science became increasingly scientific the more it approximated to the condition of mathematics, then it followed that science was bound to affirm the objective certainty of the relation of cause and effect. Thus philosophy, having arrived at the parting of the ways, must choose between the way of Newton and the way of Hume.

Such was the problem which Kant endeavoured to solve in writing the *Critique of Pure Reason*. First of all, we may ask, why *pure* Reason? Kant's reply to this question was as follows. The primary task of philosophy since the time of Socrates, and even among Socrates's predecessors, was to arrive at a basis of certainty; to distinguish between the contingent and the necessary; to learn to distinguish the deliverances of reason from the deliverances of sentiment and emotion. Every age, every generation almost, views this crucial problem from a different angle. For Kant, the problem was to discover how the certain, necessary and universal judgments of science —the whole structure of scientific thought linked together by the causal relation—were *possible*. Hume had pointed out that such judgments could not be arrived at by mere analysis of our own ideas. Agreed; but that did not prove their irrationality or impossibility. Of their existence in experience there was no doubt; but, as Kant went on to observe, that which we observe to operate in experience need not itself have originated in experience. We must ask ourselves, as Hume never satisfactorily asked himself, what precisely we mean by experience. For the word is often employed very loosely. In short, there is a difference between 'experience' used to connote 'all experience whatever' and experience used solely to connote 'sense-experience'. Failure to observe this important distinction has been responsible for much confusion and obscurity in modern philosophy.

Kant therefore begins the *Critique* by advancing the following proposition: the perception of objects—common, everyday sense-perception, that is to say—is not a direct process, but rather a process which demands that the object shall already have been subjected to what he terms, somewhat formidably, 'the *a priori* conditions of all scientific knowledge', including that of causation. This explanation may appear unnecessarily abstruse; but if we are sufficiently patient with Kant, our efforts will be rewarded. What does he mean by this novel account of the perceptive process? First of all, we must remove a possible misconception. He is not describing the physiological or psychological mechanism of perception. His enquiry is conducted a stage farther back. In order to analyse knowledge—knowledge in general—he naturally begins with the most elementary form of knowledge. And the point he is trying to make is that, during the act of perception, we are concerned with something already organized, already in a condition to be perceived, already 'worked up' into something *perceptible*. In other words, the object, in order to be an object at all, has to undergo such treatment as will give it sufficient rudimentary form to bring it within the purview of the higher faculties of our intelligence.

To provide this 'treatment' is the initial act of our sensibility. It is an act which involves a synthesis of what would otherwise be (and otherwise is) utterly formless, disparate, and miscellaneous—a 'manifold', as Kant calls it, without cohesion. Now the initial act involves a great deal more than setting things in good order; it effects a definite transformation, except that the latter word presupposes the exchange of one form for another, while this process consists in bringing order out of chaos. Here Kant introduces a new conception, which some have described as the most revolutionary discovery in modern philosophy. Our perception of objects as disposed in space and enduring through time is the first and most important achievement, he holds, of this initial act of sensibility. Space and time, that is to say, do not characterize the world, if it can be called a world, external to our minds; they are contributed by ourselves in our act of observing it. They are 'ideal' or subjective. In the framework that they provide, we build up, with the aid of our understanding, a coherent picture of the world.

The world, observe; not reality itself. Our understanding, resting upon the foundations laid by our sensibility, succeeds only in apprehending *phenomena*. To grasp the nature of things as they are in themselves is an entirely different matter. Kant does not deny that such apprehension is possible; all he maintains is that it is achieved, though rarely, by a faculty distinct from our ordinary understanding.

To sum up Kant's position: whereas philosophers have tended in the past to suggest that the mind's function is to 'conform to' reality, to register accurately and impartially what it perceives to be 'there' (*i.e.* 'over there', in a world standing apart from the mind), Kant advances the view that the world of phenomena enjoys existence only in so far as we ourselves participate in its construction. (Such a view is very different from that suggested by Berkeley, who maintained not simply that the mind imposed form upon a chaos of impressions, but that the whole world of phenomena, consisted of ready-made ideas.) Hitherto, he says in effect, it has been contended that our knowledge is determined by the object; henceforth, as a result of his 'Copernican Revolution' in thought, it will be necessary to maintain that the object is largely determined by our knowledge.

Impressive as this philosophical revolution may be, we must bear in mind that we are still speaking of knowledge of phenomena, of appearances, of the outside of things. So far and no farther can our reason proceed. Let it once attempt to probe into deeper matters—for instance, the nature of the self, or the problems of God, human freedom, and the immortality of the soul—and it will involve itself in untold difficulties. The history of philosophy is very illuminating in this respect. For centuries, Kant points out, philosophers and theologians have endeavoured, no doubt with the best of intentions, to unravel the deeper problems of life and thought according to a method which is frankly inadequate. To apply the methods of reason to that which by hypothesis evades reason at every turn; to apply intellect to spirit; to endeavour to rationalize religion—these, the aims of the great scholastic philosophers, Kant considers to have been gravely mistaken. By refusing to repudiate such aims, orthodox theologians had rendered a marked disservice to mankind. Being increasingly unintelligible to the masses, their teaching had provided an excuse for casuistry, clap-trap and pedantry. As for the humble and poor in spirit, they were usually content to accept a simpler faith. Hence the great rift of the Reformation, followed by the mushroom growth of 'inferior religions' of the heart instead of the head, of the emotions instead of the intellect. In the atmosphere of such popular illuminism Kant himself had been born and bred; and though not a regular churchgoer, his religion throughout life was in spirit identical with that of his humble parents. Thus his philosophy of knowledge, like his philosophy of ethics and of art, was essentially the product of his own experience. Of the intellectual problem, the mental 'irritant', with which he began, we have already spoken; but we must not forget that every intellectual problem, every conscious questioning, is shadowed by a deeper, emotional problem, of which it is an articulation. Naturally the degree of articulation or self-consciousness attained depends upon the degree of genius with which the thinker is endowed.

His claim that human reason, operating alone, is incapable of understanding the nature of 'things-in-themselves' leads Kant to repudiate as outmoded and mischievous the traditional science of metaphysics. That is the reason why he refers to his own thought as 'critical philosophy'. Such a conclusion proved startling to many; even Kant himself appears to have found in it an element of paradox. He had set out to examine and exalt pure reason. He had ended by restricting the scope of that same faculty. He had set out to reform the science of metaphysics. He had ended by exposing it as a sham. Where, as a professional philosopher paid to give instruction in 'Logic and Metaphysics', was he to go for a solution to this dilemma?

He was to go in a direction which, since his time and under his spell, many others have followed. For Kant's 'next step', whether a step in the right direction or a step in the dark, has affected the whole course of human thought.

Having quashed the claims of metaphysics (with whose fate he links that of theology) to penetrate reality as well as the world of phenomena, Kant adopts an attitude very different from that of Hume, who, having made a similar repudiation, merely throws his hand in. No one was a greater champion of the rights and powers of the human mind than Kant; and if he felt obliged, for the reasons we have cited, to circumscribe the powers of reason, he was the more persuaded that truth, ultimate truth, could be reached by another and deeper channel of intelligence. Here again Kant's pietistic upbringing asserted itself. What, he asks, is the most profound experience that we can have? In what sphere of life, for instance, do we feel ourselves to be in contact, however intermittently, with the essence of things? What is deeper than science and more compelling in its influence than art? Some philosophers would have answered 'love'. Kant, less sentimental, answers 'duty'—moral duty or the exercise of our ethical will. That, he says, is the channel whereby we make contact with the thing-in-itself. That is the experience in which we see beyond reason and enter the world behind appearances, the world of which metaphysics is dimly conscious but essentially ignorant.

Such is Kant's philosophy in outline in so far as it is expounded in the first of the Critiques. Its initial reception was moderate; it could be called disappointing only if Kant, who knew the meaning of obscurity, had been foolish enough to entertain excessive expectations. Like Hume's *Treatise of Human Nature*, the book made its way gradually, silently, creating its own audience in the manner, as Proust later maintained, of a great work of art. It received one or two appreciative reviews, followed by a long period of silence. Kant was as grateful for the latter as for the former, since, as he remarked a year later, 'this silence at any rate evinces a suspension of judgment, and a suspicion that after all, in a work which abandons every accustomed path and strikes into a new one which at first feels strange, there may be something calculated to give new life and fertility to an important, but now dead, branch of human knowledge—evinces, in short, an anxiety not to break off and to destroy the yet tender shoot by a premature judgment'.

The conclusions at which he had arrived in the *Critique of Pure Reason*, especially on the subject of moral judgment, prompted him to devote his attention next to ethical questions. In 1785 appeared the essay entitled *Foundation of the Metaphysic of Ethics* (a typical Kantian title: how many potential readers must this great man have alienated first by his titles and secondly by his terminology!) This, as well as his later ethical treatises, achieved something very like popularity; there was a zeal and fervour about their composition that made them more readable than his previous works, and their message was more easily intelligible.

The message was simple: a good act, says Kant, is one that can be 'universalized'—that is to say, if you are in doubt as to whether a course of action is good or not, ask yourself whether it could be made, without danger to mankind, a universal law. Secondly, treat every man not as a means, but as an end. And why an end? Because 'a good will is that by which alone man's existence can have absolute value; and in relation to it the existence of the world can have an ultimate purpose'. Duty, therefore, is a 'categorical imperative'. Do not ask *why* it should be obeyed: 'We cannot comprehend the practical unconditioned necessity of the moral imperative; we can only comprehend its incomprehensibility'. This was a stimulating doctrine in a day much given to moral lethargy and materialistic ethics. Moreover, it is a doctrine, Protestant in its inspiration, which has since influenced the lives of thousands to whom the name of Kant has meant little or nothing. Although the 'moral law' appears formidable and despotic in its operation, the existence in man of a moral consciousness, a sense of duty, is the surest evidence of his freedom. As an element of the world of nature, man is merely one among a number of other *phenomena*; as a member of the world of spirit, or of what Kant called 'the kingdom of ends', he is a free self-motivated being. In the one case, he is subject, like any other material thing, to the law of cause and effect; in the other case, he is his own master, endowed with self-consciousness, and bound by nothing but his own choice. Thus Kant found a 'way out' of the blind determinism of Hume.

3

Not until he had reached the age of 66 was Kant content to regard his exposition of the Critical Philosophy as complete. Two more Critiques, the *Critique of Practical Reason* (1788) and the *Critique of Judgment,* a treatise on æsthetics (1790), followed that on Pure Reason. Now a rapidly ageing man, Kant confessed that 'it is only for between two or three hours in the forenoon that I can persistently devote myself to headwork'. Nevertheless, he continued not merely to lecture but to write papers on various philosophical questions. On one occasion he received an official rebuke for his supposed unorthodoxy from the Government at Berlin (1794). His reply was a trifle abject. Meanwhile, his reputation not merely in Germany but in the outside world was growing. To some it seemed as if the Kantian doctrine, especially as regards morality, was destined to become a new gospel, almost a successor to Christianity; 'In a hundred years,' one of his most enthusiastic disciples exclaimed, 'Kant will have the reputation of Jesus Christ.' At any rate, he was great enough and sufficiently well known to receive a fan-mail. From 1792 onwards, a certain Maria von Herbert, suffering from the effects of a love-affair and (judging from what is known of her) of a good deal else, wrote him a series of letters with the object of 'drawing him out' on the subject of love and marriage. In a year or two she was hinting at the desirability of a meeting, so that she might ascertain, among other things, 'whether it would not be worth your while to take a wife, or devote yourself to someone with your whole heart, and leave an image of yourself behind'. (The poor lady, given no encouragement in Kant's lifetime, committed suicide six months after his death.) Pilgrims, not less earnest but more philosophically inclined, visited the sage of Königsberg and have left us interesting accounts of him. Among these was a young man called Fichte, of whose work we shall later speak.

Kant abandoned his still heavy programme of lectures in the summer of 1795, but he continued to discourse for one hour each day on Logic and Metaphysics. Nor was he content thenceforth to sink into obscure idleness. On the contrary, he took greater interest than ever before in public affairs, especially in the course of the French Revolution, which he had hailed at its inception with as much enthusiasm as Charles James Fox: 'I can now say like Simeon,' he had exclaimed, ' "Lord, let thy servant depart in peace, for mine eyes have seen thy salvation." ' By 1795, it seemed as if, to use Tom Paine's phrase, a 'morning of reason' had dawned in Europe; and Kant, blind to the catastrophes to come, wrote an essay on *Perpetual Peace*, the prospects of which seemed then brighter than ever before. During the next two years he collected together a number of essays and lectures for publication, but in 1797 he decided to abandon public work altogether. This withdrawal from active academic life was marked by a special ceremony and procession. Forty-two years of continuous and active teaching could not be allowed to pass without some sign of appreciation from students, both young and old. Kant was wise to make this decision to retire. His faculties, and above all his memory, were showing signs of failure. He realized that while his life might be prolonged for some few more years, his brain was already worn out. It was better to spare an admiring public the sight of humiliating dotage.

Owing to the detailed memoirs of an old pupil, Wasianski, we know much more about Kant's last years than about his youth and middle-age. It is in many ways a pathetic story. We learn, for instance, how failing memory caused the great man to write everything down, however trivial, on scraps of paper. A scribbled sentence—'the name Lampe must be completely forgotten' —reveals, apart from the oddity of such a memorandum, how deeply he had been attached to his old servant, whom he was obliged eventually to dismiss for drunkenness and general unreliability, but whom he remembered in his will. A feeling of tension in his head grew more trying from about 1796 onwards. Attributing it to electricity in the air, Kant convinced himself that the forces responsible for his distress were identical with those reported to have caused the death of a number of cats in Germany about the same time. From such obsessions he could not be shaken, and his friends were obliged to humour him as best they could.

In a condition just short of complete senility he lingered on for several years. At moments he was perfectly himself again, though conscious of reduced vitality. 'Sirs, I am old and weak:' he said one day to a small gathering of friends, 'you must treat me like a child. I am not afraid of death. If I felt this night that I should die, I would lift up my hands, fall down and say, God be praised.' He lingered on, but several times his weakness nearly precipitated his end. One day he stumbled and collapsed in the street. Two ladies, running to his assistance, were surprised to receive from the old man, his balance scarcely restored, the rose he was wearing in his buttonhole. The regular supervision of his private affairs was now beyond his capacity. Wasianski assumed charge of the household, and a new servant, Johann Kaufmann, succeeded the unsatisfactory Lampe. Very occasionally the old man went out, or sat in his garden; but his nights were restless, and the enjoyment of life began to diminish with the onset of an old complaint, flatulence of the stomach. On 22nd April, 1803, his birthday, he laboriously penned the words: 'According to the Bible our life lasts seventy years, and at the most eighty; and when it is at its best, it has been labour and sorrow.' That autumn he had become so utterly helpless that his sister, then living in an almshouse, arrived to look after him. She proved a very capable housekeeper; and Kant, while he grew no better, at least was able to make ready for the end in an atmosphere of domestic peace.

In the early part of 1804 Kant's faculties no longer displayed that recuperative power which had enabled him, even in his seclusion, to state his views on subjects of current interest, whether it was the composition of the university senate (from which an attempt was made to oust him), the virtues or otherwise of inoculation, or some moral problem about which his advice was sought. He became blind, partially deaf, and generally decrepit. On a sunny day in February (the 12th) he died. His body was placed on a bier in his own dining-room, and for sixteen days the mourners of his native city passed through to pay their respects. He was buried in the University Church in what is called the Professors' Vault. Some years afterwards his bust in marble was placed above his grave, to be moved later to the New University.

To conclude our account of Kant by lingering over his final dotage is to run the risk of forgetting what an extraordinary influence he exerted up to and even including his last years. Let us revert for one moment to those days of power and success, not forgetting that a thinker of Kant's type finds the rapt attention of a few more rewarding than the formal respect of a multitude. This, at least, is how he appeared to a young student as late as 1795: 'His delivery has quite the tone of ordinary conversation, and can scarcely be called elegant. Imagine to yourself a little old man' (Kant was not much above five feet in height), 'bent forward as he sits, in a brown coat with leather buttons, with wig and hair-bag to boot; imagine further that this little man sometimes takes his hands out from the close-buttoned coat where they lie crossed, and makes a slight movement before his face as a man does when wishing someone else quite to understand him. Draw this picture to yourself and you see him to a hair. Though all this can scarcely be termed elegant, though his words do not ring clear, still, everything which his delivery, if I may say so, wants in form, is richly compensated by the excellence of the matter. . . .'

Kant once remarked that two things in life moved him above all else: the first was 'the starry heavens above' and the second 'the moral law in my heart'. To those—and there are many—who find his writings ponderous, his arguments tortuous, and his conclusions repellent, the reply may be given that, whatever the difficulty of his works, they are monuments of sincerity, patience and application. He abhorred false simplification, without delighting in obscurity for its own sake. He attacked metaphysics not so much because he desired to abolish the study of ultimate reality as because he hated the mumbo-jumbo that often goes with 'transcendental' studies, the casuistry of the 'philosophaster'. At his best he speaks with a sublimity reminiscent of Plato himself, and his deepest words on the subject of the meaning of life (with which every philosopher worth the name is ultimately concerned) belong to what may be termed the *philosophia perennis*:

'It is difficult to suppose that a creature whose life has its first beginning in circumstances so trivial and so entirely dependent upon our own choice, should have an existence that extends to all eternity. As regards the continuance here on earth of the species as a whole, this difficulty is negligible, since accident in the individual case is still subject to a general law, but as regards each individual it certainly seems highly questionable to expect so potent an effect from causes so insignificant. But to meet these objections we can propound a transcendental hypothesis, namely, that all life is, strictly speaking, intelligible only, is not subject to changes of time, and neither begins in birth nor ends in death; that this life is an appearance only, that is, a sensible representation of the purely spiritual life, and the whole sensible world is a mere picture which in our present mode of knowledge hovers before us, and like a dream has in itself no objective reality; that if we could intuit ourselves and things *as they are,* we should see ourselves in a world of spiritual beings, our sole and true community which has not begun through birth, and will not cease through bodily death—both birth and death being mere appearances.'

German Romantic Philosophy
from Fichte to Hegel

Kant was a thinker of such comprehensive vision that his disciples, of whom there were many, tended to concentrate upon and develop certain aspects of his system to the neglect of others. Such are the drawbacks of discipleship; the applause of enthusiastic followers drowns many a great man's true message. A philosopher whose emulation caused Kant some embarrassment during his lifetime was the young Fichte, to whom we have already been introduced. Fichte claimed to have developed Kant's theory of ethics in such a way as to transform it into a philosophy of action—of revolutionary action. Born in 1762, he was the son of a Saxon linen-weaver. In 1793 he was appointed Professor of Philosophy at the University of Jena; but was obliged in 1799 to resign his Chair as a result of charges, in themselves quite false, of atheism. For the next decade he lived from hand to mouth, barely earning sufficient to maintain his family; but in 1809, having regained popularity as a result of his *Addresses to the German Nation* (1807-08), he was made professor at the University of Berlin. Fitche's philosophy, not immediately easy to grasp, may be summarized as follows. Agreeing with Kant that man's will is the highest value in the universe, and that practical reason enjoys primacy, Fichte maintains that the business of mankind is self-realization. The thing-in-itself is not 'unknowable'; it is our own ego, our ideal self. To realize oneself is to become free. But freedom is not attained without struggle, opposition, conquest: the ego thus attains freedom by overcoming all that is not itself—the non-ego. The latter it creates in order that it may engage in such struggle. This Non-Ego is mere appearance, phenomena; and while the understanding perceives and assists in constructing the world of phenomena, the Will or Ego uses it as a kind of improvised pontoon to reach the reality behind it. This dialectic, active in the individual, is also active in society and indeed in all history. History is nothing but the history of freedom, the story of man's struggle for liberation, the story of the vicissitudes of liberty. Fichte's *Addresses* to his countrymen, in which he expounded his ideas in words of great patriotic fervour, undoubtedly had a great deal to do with the uprush of German nationalism at a time when the French army, sweeping over Europe, had occupied and dismembered Prussia.

To Fichte's lofty idealism was opposed, as might be expected, a movement of practical scientific thought for which the German people have since been distinguished. Simultaneously, but again not unexpectedly, a remarkable revival of another kind took place. Schiller and Goethe are universal figures. Novalis, Friedrich Schlegel, Tieck and above all Hölderlin, are the great German romantic writers. Schelling and Hegel, at least at the beginning of their careers, were 'romantic' philosophers. And just as the Romantic writers of this period were the first, or among the first, to develop a new interest and insight into history, so Hegel, as his thought grew to maturity, turned his attention and that of all subsequent philosophy to the problems of historical development. Of the importance of this new vista of thought, hitherto explored only by the isolated genius of Vico, we shall have something to say later on. For it may be that the concept of History is that which is most characteristic of our era, as the concept of Nature was that most characteristic of the era preceding it.

The philosophy of Schelling (1775-1854), in its first phase, was a curious blend of mysticism, poetry, and almost magical science. He called it the Philosophy of Nature, and it would seem to have its origins in the early speculations of the German-Swiss philosopher Paracelsus,[1] as well as in the more recent 'illuminism' of the 'unknown philosopher' Saint-Martin (1743-1803). At this stage Schelling was preoccupied with the problem of the reconciliation of 'contraries': in nature, the contraries whereby thought develops into consciousness, and in spirit, the contraries whereby thought develops into self-consciousness. In his second and revised view of philosophy—that to which he gives the name of the Philosophy of Identity—he explains this process of antithesis

[1] See p. 136.

and synthesis in terms very similar to those employed by Fichte in his Dialectic. Here the goal to which the whole process is moving is the Absolute, which Schelling defines as something that survives all the changes manifested in nature and spirit (hence the use of the word 'identity' to describe it). In the Absolute, which is the highest manifestation of Will (and this distinguishes it from an entity such as Spinoza's God), the Ego and Non-Ego of Fichte, otherwise in combat, are reconciled.

Upon further reflection, however, his somewhat abstract standpoint satisfied Schilling as little as that with which he had begun: it dissatisfied him, indeed, because his development in the meantime had caused him to sacrifice the element of mysticism. At the close of his career, he came to the conclusion, as have so many of his kind, that the pursuit of mere speculative or rational philosophy led to profitless hair-splitting and futile argumentation; that it was useless as a guide to action; and that it failed even to stir the emotions. He therefore sought to evolve a philosophy which should grasp, instead of evading, reality, and which should have some message for the individual. Thus he turned his mind to the concrete thought of history: to the life of ordinary men, who, while philosophers are engaged in their lofty discourses, must meanwhile live, work and shape the future. Only by becoming concrete, full-blooded, historical and topical could philosophy henceforth justify itself. Having thus stated the problem, Schelling passed it, ripe for solution, to his young colleague, Georg Wilhelm Friedrich Hegel.

With Hegel, philosophy renewed itself. And no one is entitled to say that he understands modern philosophy unless he has grasped, at least in outline (for there is much detail of a less apprehensible kind), the thought of this 'Aristotle of modern times'. Hegel has received less than the justice due to him, especially in the English-speaking world, owing to the impression, current since the beginning of the First World War, that he is one of the forerunners of Prussianism and later Nazism; that he identifies might with right and therefore exalts the will to power; and that he was himself an obsequious, if learned, servant of the Prussian military hierarchy of his day. None of these accusations is altogether without basis: but their preferment has tended to obscure, if not for some people completely to obliterate, the great originality and value of the Hegelian system. In tracing so-called 'fore-runners', it is easy to find in abundance what is being sought: a passage here, an emphasis there, a reported anecdote—and the case is considered proved.

One of the reasons why Hegel is so noteworthy a figure in philosophy is that he broke with the tradition of thought initiated by Descartes. Descartes, as we saw, claimed to have overcome scepticism by asserting his awareness of himself as a thinker. As a thinker, too, he recognized his contact with the truth by the clearness and distinctness of his own ideas. The Cartesian Method was the Charter of Human Reason; and Reason in the seventeenth century was regarded in much the same light as Faith during the Middle Ages: it was capable of moving mountains.

The result of the Cartesian approach was, as we said, a new attitude to knowledge and scientific method. This attitude can be summarized as follows: first ideas, then things—first thought, then action. And what was so very original about that? Do not we all think first and act afterwards, even if we think hastily and inadequately? Agreed: but behind this 'rhythm' of knowledge was an assumption that was not often brought into the light. The assumption was that ideas and things, thought and action, were somehow 'outside each other'; they acted and reacted one upon the other, but from different sides of the stage. It was also assumed, however covertly, that when (if such a thing were imaginable) the rhythm of knowledge came to a halt or a temporary rest, the two partners would retire to their separate spheres, the one to commune with itself in a world of spirit and the other to repose inert and lifeless in a world of matter.

This general idea was the result of an attempt, made by a process of abstraction, to arrive at the basic assumptions that men, when engaged in thought of any kind, are bound to make. A better word than 'assumption' would be 'presupposition'; a presupposition is that which a man holds to be true before he 'supposes' anything. The externality or mutual exclusion of thought and action was, we may therefore say, a presupposition of the thought of philosophers from the time of Descartes until the time of Hegel. We recognize this fact in everyday speech: the influence of 'mind' over 'matter' is a subject about which we never weary of talking.

To say that such a presupposition was entertained throughout the period we have specified does not imply that its limitations were never recognized. Spinoza, for one, recognized them. He therefore posited his single Substance which could be regarded, according to the point of view taken, as both thinking and non-thinking. Kant recognized them, and therefore advanced the view that human reason, in looking outwards, never contacted the 'object' at all but merely a set of 'appearances' in the construction of which it played a considerable part: it succeeded, that is to say, in acquainting itself with that which it had itself introduced. The thing-in-itself evaded it; and to weigh in, as Kant did, with the assertion that a faculty other than our understanding—namely our moral sensibility—was capable of penetrating to the heart of reality, much as heart speaks to heart, was, from a strictly philosophical point of view, something very like treachery. It was there that Hegel took up the challenge. With his assault upon the problem, a whole tradition of thought was brought to an end. Either reason enjoyed primacy, or it did not; but if it enjoyed primacy, it did not lie outside its object, it 'generated' that object.

Georg Wilhelm Hegel

'One man has understood me, and even he has not.'
    —Attributed to Hegel.

1

Few thinkers have taken longer to arrive at maturity than Hegel; but few, having once developed, have exhibited such extraordinary insight into so many spheres of thought. Kant's outlook was astonishingly broad for one whose personal experience was in a sense so confined. Hegel possessed more than a wide outlook; he had grasp, or, if it is preferred, 'inlook', intuitive penetration into the spheres of science, art, philosophy, and above all history such as no later philosopher has possessed.

Born at Stuttgart on the 27th August, 1770, Hegel came of an unpretentious middle-class family. His father was a revenue officer; his mother, from whom it would seem that he inherited his chief abilities, was both well-educated and intelligent, and taught her little son all the Latin that he ever knew, which was quite considerable. Later he went to the grammar school at Stuttgart, where he remained, a scholar of average ability, until he had reached his nineteenth year. Without distinguishing himself, he was an industrious pupil, though busier at outside activities than at his prescribed lessons. Among his hobbies, for example, was the collecting of many hundreds of extracts, from books, newspapers, and other sources, which, with a hint of his future efforts at systematization, he arranged carefully in alphabetical order. We also know that from an early age he read the classics with mounting enjoyment and increasing understanding; and this love of the humanities, which Kant possessed to nothing like the same degree, may account for the quality of dignity and balance with which his work as a whole, in spite of serious defects of exposition, is graced.

It was as a student of theology that in 1788 Hegel entered the University of Tübingen. His choice of theology is not very easy to understand, because at this stage he showed no particular aptitude for the subject. Probably he put his name down for theology as some modern students put their names down for teaching; they can think of nothing better to do. No doubt Hegel excelled least at those aspects of his training upon which the greatest importance was placed; he seems to have made no great impression as a preacher, whatever the quality of his sermon-notes. Nevertheless, he plodded on with his studies, determined to complete the course and qualify for a degree. This he did, with fair success, in 1790. Nevertheless, the report upon his work and character given at the end of his stay at Tübingen was, if not absolutely damning, far from encouraging; and a less obstinate student would no doubt have been inclined to renounce academic aspirations for good and all. According to his supervisors, he was a young man of good ability, moderate industry, and average knowledge: the subject in which he exhibited least talent was, they took the trouble to emphasize, philosophy.

If Hegel was not a model student, he was at least a normal one. The beer-parties, escapades, and even the amorous adventures characteristic of undergraduate life occupied as much of his time as he needed rest from his work, but not more. He was a popular person, though not particularly youthful in either manner or appearance: his companions nicknamed him the 'old man'. As for his closest friends, some idea of his leanings and enthusiasms may be judged from the fact that he was almost immediately attracted within the cultivated circle of Schelling and Hölderlin, whose genius he recognized sooner than they recognized his. From Hölderlin especially he acquired considerable knowledge of the classical authors, thus increasing the regard in which he already held them.

Having left the university a certificated, adequately-trained, but in no way outstanding young man, convinced of nothing so much as his unfitness for the Ministry, Hegel was obliged to follow in the footsteps of Kant and secure a post as private tutor. The first position he ob-

tained was with a family at Berne; but although he benefited from the change of scene, he hankered after the congenial company he had left behind. Being thrown for long
hours each day upon his own resources, and deciding to
engage in literary work and research, he soon completed
a detailed treatise on *The Fiscal System of the Canton of
Berne*. But as his real interests lay deeper than economics,
he began to reflect seriously upon those subjects which,
when imposed upon him as a duty at the university, had
left him so completely cold. Encouraged to study Christianity from the original sources, he began to gather material for a new and original Life of Christ. At this period
of his life he sought to eliminate as far as possible the
miraculous element in Christianity, and to present Christ
as merely the best of good persons. In the Christian faith
he claimed to have found the answer to the problem for
which even the greatest of Greek philosophers had discovered no solution: the problem, already spoken of in connection with Aristotle, concerning the exact relation between God and the world that He created. Only later did
he perceive that this problem was insoluble save on the
understanding that Christ was not merely the best of good
persons, but the incarnation of the Divine Logos.

During his stay abroad Hegel had been careful not to
lose touch with his friends. To Hölderlin he owed it that
in 1797 he secured a more congenial post: this was with
a Frankfurt merchant, Herr Gogol. Wherever he went
he took the greatest interest in his surroundings, and
thus we find him absorbed once more in economic problems. In order thoroughly to master the general
principles of economics and politics, he had already
made himself acquainted with the works of Hume (on
economics), Montesquieu, and Gibbon, and had tried
to keep abreast with social changes in other countries
(he sought all the information he could, for instance,
concerning the English Poor Law Bill of 1796). The result was a number of studies on European social problems, including one on the Constitution of Germany and
another *On the Internal Conditions of Wurtemberg in
Recent Times*; but the latter, owing possibly to its drastic criticism of the magistracy, did not get as far as publication. Not that he neglected his philosophical studies;
he merely found, as have others, that philosophical prob-

lems have a way of working themselves towards a solution while the mind, at its topmost layers, is concentrated upon matters of quite another order. There are in existence a number of MS. notes made by Hegel at this period which foreshadow, like Berkeley's Commonplace Book, the whole of his philosophical system.

When in 1799 his father died, Hegel inherited a sum of money which, though exceedingly modest, filled him with hopes of being able to continue his researches without slaving for a living as only a hack-tutor need slave. By 1801 he was already settled at Jena, at this period a centre of great cultural activity. Schelling himself, now grown to eminence as a philosopher with a 'message', was the social lion. Hegel, won over to philosophy for good, now began to seek an academic 'platform' from which to expound his own ideas; and finding much in the teaching of Schelling of which he thoroughly approved, he collaborated with the master (1802-03) in a periodical entitled *The Critical Journal of Philosophy*. Meanwhile, he submitted to the authorities an original essay, *De Orbitus Planetarum,* and was made a *privat-dozent* at the university. He was now on the first rung of the academic ladder.

It was a ladder that he was slow to climb. He was conscious of having something to say; he had not yet learnt how to say it. For four years he continued to expound philosophy; and although at the end of that period the number of his pupils had more than doubled (he had begun with eleven and he now had thirty!), the future seemed to hold little promise of improvement. All this time, however, he was increasing his knowledge, especially of the ancient Greek philosophers; and if he failed to achieve popularity among the younger generation, he was steadily gaining the respect of his academic colleagues. The extent to which he had come to occupy a niche in the philosophical world, indeed, may be judged from the fact that in 1805, having made a formal application, he was appointed to the high post of Professor Extraordinarius at Weimar. Apart from the distinction of such an appointment, Hegel, now thirty-five years old, had the satisfaction of knowing that he was now able to command a regular income. His stipend amounted to one hundred thalers a year.

The new professor had occupied his Chair but a short time when political trouble broke out. Prussia, feeling her independence to be threatened by the formation of the Confederation of the Rhine, decided to declare war on Napoleon, with whom she had entered into alliance less than a year before. As a result, the French armies turned upon Prussia and inflicted upon her two simultaneous defeats in October, 1806, one at Jena and the other at Auerstädt. Hegel's reaction to this violent reprisal was very similar to that of Goethe. Without allowing national sentiment to becloud his judgment, he felt that the disaster was deserved. Of the bureaucratic system of Prussia, with its petty tyranny and corruption, he had always entertained a low opinion, and he did not trouble to conceal his satisfaction at the prospect of its being swept away. Loyalties at the period of which we are speaking were still not so much international as supernational. Beethoven dedicated his Eroica '-phony to the man who, if not an open enemy o. ..s country, had done nothing to show himself its friend. And Hegel, with the sound of the cannonade at Jena in his ears, could write of the 'world soul' Emperor whose armies he frankly hoped would prevail over those of his own country.

The defeat at Jena, if welcomed by a minority of intellectuals, brought nothing but ignominy in its train. Two weeks later, Napoleon, having entered Berlin itself, was issuing the famous 'Decrees' wherein he announced his schemes for the defeat of the last enemy, Britain. Those who had somewhat recklessly displayed their admiration for the conqueror's 'civilizing mission' were not rendered more popular by the revelation of what that mission entailed; and Hegel found that such little popularity as he enjoyed was fast dwindling. Once more driven in upon himself, he worked hard upon the first book of any magnitude that he had projected, and in 1807 published the *Phenomenology of Spirit*.

The *Phenomenology* was described by Hegel himself as his 'voyage of discovery'. It was a word of great originality and scope. Hitherto he had regarded himself as a devoted, if discriminating, pupil of Schelling. But the thought of Schelling was ceasing to satisfy him. The chief objection to a man with a 'message' is that he is constantly in receipt of new ones, each of which he feels obliged to pass on to his disciples with the same air of conviction. So it was with Schelling. He got through philosophies as a man might get through successive suits of clothes. What alienated Hegel was the manner in which he introduced, at the appropriate moment, an Absolute so comprehensive as to envelop the whole collection of problems that were awaiting analysis. This, in Hegel's view, was cheating. Philosophy must not expect outside aid from mysticism; it must work its own passage. And in the 'voyage of discovery', that is what philosophy was supposed to be doing.

The voyage was an adventurous one. From the most elementary forms of sense-experience, knowledge is shown as developing step by step to the highest form of consciousness, which, in Hegel's view, is philosophy itself. Never before had the *panorama* of knowledge been set out in such fullness and at the same time with such minuteness of detail. The *Phenomenology* is the dress-rehearsal for the astonishing performances of the *Logic*, the *Philosophy of Nature,* and the *Philosophy of Mind*.

As Hegel's thought was the most exciting thing in an otherwise comparatively uneventful and sedentary life, an account of how his system developed is here in place. The life of a statesman is an account of his diplomatic master-strokes. The life of an actor centres round his most successful rôles. The life of a soldier is concerned with his successive battles, with special regard for his victories. The life of a philosopher, on this analogy, must include his adventures in speculation.

Hegel's early admiration for Schelling did not blind him to the fact that the last great philosophical leader was Kant. Kant had claimed to criticize metaphysics out of existence, or at least out of harm's way; and neither Fichte nor Schelling, acute though they were, had succeeded in rehabilitating that unpopular and frequently execrated science. To Hegel—the student so 'deficient' in (academic) philosophy—must be given the credit for restoring metaphysics to its rightful heritage. And to Hegel, for that same reason, must be given the credit for raising the prestige of philosophy higher than it had been for many years. To those who claimed that the meaning of life, the nature of existence, was a matter for science or for art or, as the sceptics and agnostics said, for dismissal as beyond human comprehension, Hegel replied that it was, as ever, a matter for philosophy. By philosophy he meant the science which, by taking all experience for its province, defined the limitations of the various 'sciences', exposed the presuppositions upon which they were based, and thereby freed the mind from the tyranny of *abstractions*.

In thus defining the task of philosophy or metaphysics, Hegel did not mean to imply that the individual abstract sciences represented so much hocus-pocus. On the contrary, he believed them to form necessary and indispensable steps on the road to self-knowledge. The error was to 'pause' at one or other of these stages, imagining the journey to have been already completed. The error, in short, was to mistake the abstract for the concrete. If, for instance, an artist believes that his imaginative world is the only real world, or a scientist that his measurable facts are the only facts of significance, the result will be disastrous. But let the artist and the scientist but realize that their particular medium affords an intimation of true knowledge—let them but realize that, in addition to being artist and scientist, they are human beings needing to be fed upon more concrete food than images and symbols—and they will preserve their sense of proportion and thereby their humanity. Kant criticized metaphysics by reference to the sciences; Hegel, more orthodox, criticized the sciences by reference to metaphysics.

The view of knowledge that Hegel began to work out in detail owed much to that of Plato. The latter had expounded the theory that knowledge, being a process of recollection, was achieved in a series of stages culminating in the soul's final communion with the Form of the Good. Between the state of primal innocence and that of final redemption lay the 'vale of tears' which is life on earth. Hegel's theory is based upon a similar assumption. What distinguishes his thought from that of Plato is the fact, not always sufficiently appreciated by modern philosophers, that he accepts as philosophically significant the Christian doctrines of the Fall, the Incarnation and the Redemption. There is a common impression that no great philosopher has ever adhered to an orthodox religious faith. Hegel's Christianity is not merely a private conviction but an integral element in his philosophical system.

One implication of the view that knowledge (*i.e.* self-knowledge) is achieved by stages is that the human mind is unable to know itself in a direct fashion. It is obliged, in consequence, to create for itself a series of spheres, each more 'transparent' than the last, through which it can bring itself, as it were, to a new and maturer vision of its nature. These spheres are precisely the 'forms' of knowledge with which we are familiar: art, science, history, etc. Our school *curricula* dimly reflect this necessity. The mind must pass through one sphere after another, surrendering itself temporarily to the influence of each, until it sees its own face in the mirror that it has constructed for itself. In a word, the mind learns to know itself through communion with its own spiritual offspring.

Hegel's terminology and method of exposition have not been calculated to endear him to the ordinary reader. Both are difficult, sometimes aggravatingly so. But the fact to which he is endeavouring, here and elsewhere, to draw attention is a very simple one. We come to know ourselves through contact with other people. As Hume took pains to point out, there is no direct or immediate knowledge of the 'self'. The chief source of difficulty in Hegel's theory, however, is that he is referring not so much to the ordinary, individual mind, as to Mind in general—the 'transcendental' Mind of which Kant spoke. Put a word in capital letters and use it always in the singular, and you will automatically scare half the readers in the English-speaking world. Nevertheless, if we are to understand Hegel, we must first discover what it is that he is trying to do. What Hegel was principally trying to do was to represent reality as the development, by a timeless process of dialectic, of an Absolute Mind, or, as he called it, the Idea. Only in the light of some such idealist theory, he claimed, could we understand both the relation between Nature and Mind and the whole course of human history. For that is the task which Hegel, in restoring to philosophy its legitimate subject-matter, had set out to accomplish. The *Phenomenology* is thus a great deal more than a cruise undertaken in home waters; it is a voyage through all the oceans of the spirit. The history and nature of civilizations, the characteristics of nationalities, the limitations and errors of thought in each epoch, crowd together in a work that is more ambitious in scope than the *Critique of Pure Reason.*

In a phrase that has since become famous, Hegel referred to the Absolute of Schelling, as 'a night when all cows are black'. A static, immovable, featureless concept of this kind was incapable, in Hegel's view, of explaining either the oppositions that Schelling wished to explain or the logical development of Nature and Mind. The Absolute is simply the God of philosophy, and as such must display the characteristics of deity in intellectual guise. Now whereas Schelling sought to represent Nature and Mind as proceeding from an immobile Absolute, Hegel sought to represent the Absolute itself as active, not in the sense of being the principle of Nature and Mind but in the sense of being the very process whereby Nature and Mind turn the one into the other. The kind of view that he wished to avoid, in other words, was that which pictured Nature and Mind as a façade behind which the Absolute brooded in lonely majesty. Instead of being the principle from which things proceeded, the Hegelian Absolute or Idea was *the process itself.*

Another difference between the Absolute of Schelling and the Thing-in-Itself of Kant on the one hand and the Idea of Hegel on the other was concerned with the goal to which they were leading. Schelling's mystical Absolute and Kant's Thing-in-Itself transcended both reason and logic; Hegel conceived his Idea to be the very embodiment of such reason and logic. The Absolute and Reason were identical. The Process itself was the unfolding of Reason first in inorganic matter, then in living matter, and finally, having become self-conscious, in man. Unlike the eighteenth-century 'rationalists', for whom Reason implied merely a series of principles or rules of thought, Hegel looked upon Reason as permeating concrete things as well. For the Ideal Reason not only conceives things, it also generates things. The science of Reason is therefore the one universal science. Now Hegel gives this science a name. He calls it Logic.

2

In 1807, the year of the publication of the *Phenomenology*, Hegel was invited to become editor of the *Bamberger Zeitung*. He accepted the offer less because of its congeniality than because he wished to maintain his material position, now that the university was temporarily closed. So far as we know, he wrote little original work for the paper, and in the following year he resigned his post for one that seemed more attractive. This was the Rectorship of the Ægidien-Gymnasium in Nuremberg. As principal of the College, Hegel proved an unexpected success. For work of this kind his character and temperament showed themselves to be entirely suited. He kept order, but he permitted a greater measure of freedom than was customary in such institutions. Years of dogged perseverance, likewise, had greatly improved his ability as a teacher. He now began to 'hold' his audiences, and so to increase them. There was even talk of a second and greater Kant.

A free house and 1,500 gulden (about £130) a year income may have turned Hegel's mind to establishing what he lacked all his adult life, namely, a home. In 1811, he decided to get married. Marie von Tucher was twenty-two years younger than the prematurely aged, quiet but kindly man with whom she decided to share her fortunes. She gave him the home he wanted, two sons, one of whom became a well-known historian, and such companionship as a philosopher has rarely been allowed to enjoy. If we were engaged upon a history of sentiment, we might hazard the suggestion that Hegel's was the happiest marriage in philosophy. But among the great philosophers, only a minority have ventured upon the married state; for it would seem that thinking for thinking's sake is largely a celibate occupation.

Having reached the conclusions outlined on the subject of the Absolute Idea, it was natural that Hegel should next proceed to work out the details of that new science of Logic of which he had stated the general principles. In 1812 appeared the first two volumes of the *Science of Logic* (the third appeared in 1816), and this time the learned world sat up and took notice. Ponderous, turgid, abstruse, prolix—all these derogatory adjectives have been applied to this immense production; it is these and much more, especially for students obliged to read it in translation. But, allowing for such defects, the *Logic* remains a work of speculative genius ranking among the world's greatest philosophical treatises. To ignore its towering presence in the landscape of modern philosophy is like visiting a cathedral town and omitting to view the sacred edifice.

The central argument of the *Logic* is one of such abstract character that even the most persevering student is apt to find it baffling. In such a case, the best way of approach is to revert for a moment to Hegel's criticism of the inert Absolutes of both Kant and Schelling. The latter, it will be remembered, maintained that the Absolute (or the Thing-in-Itself) was unknowable by human understanding. To Hegel such a statement was absurd. The Thing-in-Itself, far from being inaccessible or unknowable, was easily the most knowable thing in all human experience. For the Thing-in-Itself was simply another word for Being as such, or Pure Being. But that is surely not such a familiar thing? Too familiar!— Hegel would answer. For Being is everything, and everything is a mode or aspect of Being. Pure Being is simply that which is left when every possible qualification of Being has been removed. To imagine such an unqualified entity may be difficult; but that does not prove its unreality. The mind breathes the atmosphere of Being as the body breathes air. Being as such is therefore the common source of all the categories and concepts of our thought.

From this general root-idea Hegel builds up the hierarchy of concepts which forms the Logic. Having once and for all disposed of the scepticism which denies our capacity to contact Being—a scepticism which, if persisted in, makes nonsense not merely of philosophical thought but of thought in general (a fact which Kant failed to realize, though his ambiguous attitude to physics implied that he half suspected what he had done, or left undone)—Hegel proceeds to ask the apparently simple question: how, if every single thing is a qualification or modification of Being, did the articulation of Being as such into individual 'beings' ever take place? A simple question indeed, and therefore in philosophy a question that may easily cause us trouble. Neither here nor elsewhere is Hegel discussing the problem of Evolution, which is a process in time; he is discussing a purely logical process, a process out of time. In short, he is asking how the multitude of entities both spiritual and material can be deduced from that undifferentiated ocean of Being which logically presupposes them all. (The Evolutionist asks a similar question, but about things in time: and incidentally Hegel, to whom the problem presented itself more than once in the course of his *Philosophy of Nature*, dismissed as untenable the thesis elaborated by Darwin half a century later.)

Hegel's answer to this question introduces an idea fundamental to his thought, namely, the idea of contradiction. Why does anything turn into anything else? Because, says Hegel, it 'itches' to. In other words, there is an irritant or rift in it, which, once exasperated (to use Bergson's term), causes it to take measures to transform itself into something capable of healing that rift. In the sphere of thought, this rift takes the form of a contradiction. What contradiction is inherent in the idea of Pure Being that it should ever become anything else? The answer is simple. Pure Being is the most universal of notions; there is nothing so utterly and unequivocally comprehensive. But for that same reason it is the notion most completely deprived of content. There is nothing in it because everything has been removed from it. To be a house, or to be a green, or to be dishonest—to be all these things is to be *something*. But to be just Being is to be nothing at all. And that is the contradiction to which Hegel refers. Pure Being has only to be examined, to be pinned down, to be focused, to disclose the fact that there is nothing there. As we bring to bear our minds upon it, it slides away and vanishes.

A thing that simultaneously is and is not cannot therefore stay still. It must move on, budge, develop. The pitting of Being and Not-Being one against the other therefore generated a third notion, the notion of development itself, or Becoming. For what constitutes Becoming? Clearly two things: Being itself and Not-Being in the sense of that which is not yet Being but will be. Becoming therefore 'contains' the two contradictory notions with which we set out, and in so doing resolves the tension between them. Within the new concept of Becoming they are now engulfed; but the truth is that they never enjoyed independent existence. They were, and will ever remain, abstract notions from what is *the first concrete concept*, Becoming. Thus we return to the central idea of Hegel's philosophy, which is the idea of Process as that which permeates and informs reality as a whole.

To trace the stages whereby Hegel mounts from the concept of Becoming to that of the Absolute Idea would take too long. All that we need to bear in mind is that each unity or synthesis, save the last of all, reveals an element of contradiction (the same contradiction but in a new form) which is in turn reconciled in a higher unity, and so on. Nor must we fall into the error of supposing that the contradictions are simply and solely in our minds (*i.e.* that they are 'subjective'). They exist in the things themselves. Whereas Plato said that reality was a world of half-truths, Hegel said that reality was a world of conflicting truths.

To Hegel, then, the fact that Nature contained an element of contradiction proved not that Nature was not real but that it was somehow incomplete. It was incomplete because it was all the while undergoing the process of transforming itself into something else. This process of transformation was not something that would one day be finished; it was a perpetual transformation. That into which Nature was transforming itself was Mind. Nature kept on throwing up or precipitating Mind; Mind kept on being thrown up and precipitated by Nature. This was a logical and not a temporal process. To consider Nature apart from the fact of its being turned into Mind was to consider an abstraction. The reality was, as ever, the process itself, the process of Mind-manufacture. To use Hegel's own phrase, this development and passing away was a process that would never itself develop or pass away.

The dialectical process of 'thesis' versus 'antithesis' to be resolved in 'synthesis' was an exceedingly fruitful one; and Hegel was able to use it to illuminate many aspects of human experience. But it must be admitted that he tended to overdo it. This 'panlogism', as it has been called, has been responsible for much of the discredit into which the Hegelian philosophy, and the various schools that grew out of it, have since fallen. Nature, he maintained, is that phase in the development of the Idea (or God) in which the spirit 'externalizes' itself: that is to say (and this suggestion is a very original one), the natural world is the world in which everything is outside every other thing. But Nature, as we saw, is not merely engaged in externalizing itself; it is engaged simultaneously in the opposite process, a process of internalization, a process of becoming Mind. Now the process of becoming Mind is that at which a transition occurs between natural science and history; for whereas natural science is concerned with measuring and descrying order and uniformity in an external world, history is concerned with exploring the inward significance of human actions, which is an investigation of the internal realm of spirit. Such things as consciousness and freedom, which are characteristics of mind, do not bring history into being; they are themselves brought into being in history. What in Nature is mere instinct and blind passion becomes in history Reason and Will, which in turn give rise to Law and the State. But it is important to remember that since Nature never finally gives place to Mind, but is merely always engaged in turning into it, Law and the State never finally supersede instinct and passion, though they are always engaged in the attempt at such supersession.

So far, so good; but Hegel's attempt to apply the Dialectic to the course of history itself is not so fortunate. He ends up by proving that the Germanic world is the synthesis of the Oriental world and the Classical world; that Berlin is the centre of the earth; and that the State is the higher unity in which both the family and civil society are synthesized. This latter proposition is one that has exerted great influence upon political thought. We shall have more to say of it in connection with the two schools of Hegelianism which flourished after the master's death.

It is sometimes asserted that Hegel's philosophy culminates in the idea of the State. True it is that he defined the State as the 'march of God in the world'; but in the course of that divine progress much else of value was achieved. The human spirit, he rightly insists, is not satisfied with the activities of political life; it must go on to explore those realms which are more congenial to its nature. These are art, religion, and philosophy, regarded as purely intellectual activities: activities which, though possible only under good and strong government, are not the less individualistic and personal for that. For if history is that phase in the development of spirit in which the Idea 'turns back upon itself', it is likewise that phase in which for the first time it engages in self-communion. Such introspection discloses three fundamental ideals in the recesses of the soul: the ideal of the beautiful (art), the ideal of God (religion), and the ideal of truth (philosophy).

In art the human mind foreshadows the final triumph over matter but does not achieve it; or rather it achieves it in imagination only. Not that the artist will necessarily recognize this; he believes his world of imagination to be the only real world, and his work of art to possess a value in itself. This tendency to materialize the work of art, to set it up as an object of intrinsic value—a tendency particularly strong in the most primitive forms of art, but manifest at every level—is that which links the artistic impulse with the religious. The particular connection is idolatry. Whereas idolatry is characteristic of primitive religion, however, the higher religions begin with the elimination of idolatry. Hence the iconoclasm of Moses is the beginning of purified, spiritualized religion; but idolatry and superstition are continually creeping back into their former position, and can never be wholly abolished. Religion assumes many forms. There is the religion of the Hindu which exalts God and debases man. There is the religion of Greece, which exalts man and tends to debase God. Finally (we observe once more the use of the triadic form), there is the Christian religion in which the divine and the human, instead of being considered in separation, are synthesized in the God-Man, Jesus Christ. This is the Logos of which both Plato and Aristotle spoke and which the author of the Fourth Gospel interpreted in philosophical terms. Christianity, therefore, is the Absolute Religion.

What, in Hegel's view, is the difference between religion and philosophy? It is simply a difference in form. They are about the same thing: God or the Idea. But while there is in religion a necessarily authoritative element, philosophy can accept no authorities of any kind. It is the voice of Reason, and Reason ceases to be such unless it is free. Philosophy, therefore, states in *conceptual* terms that which religion, even the highest religion, states in imaginative terms. But we must guard against a possible misconception. Philosophy, with its conceptual approach, is not an abstract thing. It is a concrete thing, for it is an offspring of history. Philosophy is therefore best regarded as the History of Philosophy. We cannot think about the present unless we know that which has led up to it.

3

We have outlined the ideas of the *Logic* at some length because Hegel's whole philosophy is contained in it. Its first publication brought him immediate recognition as the foremost German philosopher of his time. Three universities, Erlangen, Berlin, and Heidelberg, offered him Chairs. After some deliberation, he accepted Heidelberg, where he stayed until 1818. During his time there he prepared a work of considerable size, to which he gave the title of *Encyclopædia of the Philosophical Sciences*. This he wrote largely as an accompaniment to his lectures, which, though never rising to the level of great oratory (he was hampered by a chronic cough), were attracting more and more students by their wealth of learning and masterly exposition of difficult theories, not least his own. In 1818, the University of Berlin again extended its invitation; and Hegel, proud to succeed the last incumbent, Fichte (since whose death the Chair had remained empty), accepted it.

From his arrival at Berlin until his death, Hegel enjoyed a reputation without parallel in the history of modern philosophy. With the German government he was on the best of terms. No reprimand needed to be issued on account of heterodox thought; Hegel seemed to express the very sentiments of the new German imperialism. This may be seen in particular from his treatise on political theory entitled, *The Philosophy of Right* (1821). His lectures were now received as the final word on their respective subjects: Æsthetics, the

Philosophy of Religion, the Philosophy of History, the History of Philosophy. These latter lectures were not issued by Hegel in book form; but from notes made by himself and his students they were later 'written up' and published. At the conclusion of the series on the Philosophy of History, the old man looked up from his desk (his snuff-box as usual before him) and declared roundly: 'Knowledge has reached *this point* in its development.' As the old distinction between 'facts' and theories was one that he particularly abhorred, the final conclusions of his own thought constituted for him the latest information on the subject. There is a story told that on being informed that certain of his theories were incompatible with some new scientific facts that had been adduced, he replied characteristically: 'So much the worse for the facts!' It must be admitted that the great esteem in which he was held in his later years rendered him increasingly dogmatic; but in spite of this rigidity of thought, his mind was by no means closed to new influences. He speculated until the end.

That a man in his established position should have been seriously perturbed by the liberal movement which, never long in abeyance, rose up again in 1830, was to be expected. In *The Philosophy of Right* Hegel had set out to prove that the continuous life of the State was maintained not through parliaments but through the monarchy. He sincerely believed the Prussian absolute monarchy to be the most enlightened in the world. But, as he should himself have been aware, liberalism could not be prevented from asserting itself, for every 'positive' element will eventually make itself felt, if life is indeed the dialectical struggle that Hegel declared. It was nevertheless a worried, querulous old man who received from Frederick William II a decoration in 1831 for services to learning. A tired old man, too, who on being led out one calm, clear night to look at the stars, remarked that he found the sight 'boring'.[1]

Hegel's last work of importance was, interestingly enough, an essay on the British Reform Bill, passed in 1832. Considering his attitude towards Reform in his own country, it is odd that in this work he should have criticized the slowness with which the English govern-

[1] *Cf.* Carlyle in similar circumstances: 'Hech! it is a sad sight'.

ment had suppressed abuses. In the same year another disruptive and democratic force invaded Europe. This was the cholera. Hegel moved out of Berlin into the suburbs. The infection caught up with him. A day's illness and he died. It was at his own wish that they laid his body next to that of Fichte in the cemetery near the Oranienburg Gate.

The Marxist Philosophy

The Germany in which Kant was born was a 'crazy quilt' of more than three hundred independent States, each with its own particular system of government, its own tariffs, and its own army. The idea of a united Germany, even if entertained, was regarded as altogether outside the scope of practical politics. Such a man as Lessing (1729-81) could say with complete sincerity that 'the love of country is a sentiment which I do not understand'. Possibly the isolation of these little principalities encouraged the pursuit of abstract studies; for among the huddled roofs and spires of their picture-book towns there was usually a university, with its learned professors, its crowd of ardent students, and occasionally its genius. No wonder the saying arose that whereas England ruled the sea and France ruled the land, Germany ruled the clouds. The idea, still current, of metaphysics as a 'heady' nebulous subject is no doubt largely the result of its intensive cultivation in German seats of learning during the eighteenth and nineteenth centuries—the forced growth of so many academic hot-houses.

Over this busy, divided land, there appeared, to the foreign visitor at least, to hang an atmosphere of peace and almost smug contentment. When the remarkable Madame de Staël wrote her book on Germany, Heine, never uncritical of his country, described her as 'eddying about like a whirlwind through our tranquil Germany, exclaiming everywhere delightedly, "O how sweet is the peace that I breathe here!" She had got overheated in France and came among us to cool off. The chaste breath of our poets was so comforting to her boiling and fiery heart. She looked upon our philosophers as so many different kinds of ices; she sipped Kant like a vanilla sherbet and Fichte like a pistachio cream. "O what a charming coolness reigns in your woods!" she kept constantly exclaiming; "what a ravishing odour of violets! How peacefully the canary-birds twitter in their little German nests!" '

But this tranquil country concealed beneath its surface much potential unrest. It was the liberation movement during the Napoleonic wars that first aroused the German people to a sense of nationality; for common humiliation is a powerful unifier. The movement in its intellectual aspect was led, as we saw, by a university professor. As Fichte told his countrymen, there existed in the German language no specific word for 'character', because to be German was automatically to be endowed with character. The Germans, he said, were an *Urvolk*, the Chosen People of Nature. There was no need for them to learn to be civilized; they had an obligation to teach others their own 'natural' civilization. To realize their world-mission, however, they must fulfil their mission as a nation; they must first become the nation that they naturally are.

The German Confederation formed after the Napoleonic wars, with Austria as its president, was little more than a group of absolute monarchies. One by one the liberties gained in the struggle against Napoleon were extinguished. Once you have liberated, you must govern; and to govern a liberated people is at once to come into conflict with the various 'resistance-groups' that were previously such an asset. Youth movements such as the *Burschenshaft*, formed to continue the struggle for liberty within the new political framework, were suppressed. Literature was censored. Even university professors—or, to speak more accurately, university professors in particular—were told to watch their step on pain of dismissal, fine, or imprisonment. In Prussia itself the Chief of Police was an agent of Metternich, whose policy of repression and reaction throughout the Confederation remained unchallenged.

As for Kant, he had received in his day but one official rebuke, and his answer, though dignified, was somewhat servile; he promised not to embark upon further public discussion about matters of faith. Such accusations of impiety were not infrequently made by secular bodies: for if it can be suggested that a man is already a moral reprobate, it becomes easier (if the occasion arises) to represent him as a public nuisance. Fichte was the victim of such persecution; Hegel, as we have just seen, was all that the secular authorities asked for, and more. But what was true of Hegel as a person was far from being true of the philosophical system that he left behind. As soon as the master was dead and the reconciling hand removed, all the latent ambiguities of that vast system of thought came creeping out of the clefts and cracks in its dialectic, and precipitated the most violent controversies, not all of which were confined to the plane of theory.

One of the presuppositions upon which Hegel's thought is based is that 'the real is the rational and the rational is the real'. Applied to political thought, this presupposition admits of two interpretations. If you say that the real is the rational, you are tending to imply that what exists is all that it should be: in which case you will do everything possible to maintain the *status quo*. This was the standpoint adopted by the so-called Right-Wing Hegelians, or conservatives. If, however, taking the formula in its alternative phrasing, you maintain that 'the rational is the real', you are at liberty to suggest that the present system, not being rational, ought to be transformed into something that is. This was the standpoint adopted within a short period of the philosopher's death by the so-called Left-Wing Hegelians, or radicals. In their view, all the historical institutions regarded by Hegel as sacred and more or less eternal—the Prussian State and the Christian Church in particular—were considered as obstacles to progress. At first the controversy was conducted purely on the intellectual plane, centring around the theological criticism of Strauss, Feuerbach and Bauer. All of these were opponents of orthodoxy and the last was a thoroughgoing sceptic. When Frederick William IV ascended to the throne of Prussia, however, he took steps to terminate the controversy, having decided that Hegelianism itself was a bad influence. Accordingly in 1841 he summoned to Berlin the ageing Schelling (at that time adviser to the ruler of Bavaria) for the purpose of obtaining guidance on the subject: an invitation which the veteran thinker is said to have accepted with some relish, presumably by way of reprisals for having been so long excluded from the limelight. But the controversy continued as bitterly as ever, and for a good reason. The very essence of the Hegelian philosophy is that no such thing as an absolute natural truth exists, and that no institution is perfect: truth and fact are not static but dynamic. Consequently Frederick William IV was not far wrong in supposing that the danger lay not with the Left-Wing Hegelians alone but with the Hegelians in general. And it might be added of Hegel himself, that though a Right-Wing Hegelian by temperament, he was a Left-Wing Hegelian by example.

In the Philosophy of History as Hegel conceived it, 'we have to do with individuals that are peoples, with wholes that are states'. Only one other thinker, Giambattista Vico, had turned his attention to this gigantic theme; but after Hegel had treated it (he remained ignorant of Vico's achievement), a great revival of historical studies took place in Germany, and thence elsewhere, which diverted and invigorated the whole course of modern thought. For the next century and more there were two marked but related tendencies in thought: a tendency to regard history from a philosophical point of view and an even more significant tendency to regard philosophy from a historical point of view.

While the study of history was being pursued upon the academic plane by such men as Ranke, and later Mommsen and Treitschke, a more practical attitude was being adopted by a group of Left-Wing Hegelians whose interests had brought them in contact with the common people to a degree not usually permitted to men of their origin. Of these, the two most famous were Frederick Engels and Karl Marx (1818-85), collaborators in the *Communist Manifesto* published in 1848. Engels was the son of a wealthy German cotton manufacturer. Marx, a German Jew of humbler origins, having taken part as a revolutionary in the uprisings of 1848, sought refuge in London in the same year, and remained there until his death. Living in lodgings in Bloomsbury and working daily in the library of the British Museum, he slowly amassed the material for the book which was to turn a great part of the world upside down. This was *Capital*, the first volume of which appeared in 1867. A book need not be read, or read by more than a select few, in order to exert powerful influence; few books of Marx have enjoyed a large circulation and yet their collective impact upon their time and later has been incalculable.

What they have done is to 'touch off' the impulses towards change in a few select and remarkable individuals; but at the same time—for these changes are never wholly the result of accident—they have themselves expressed in forthright terms the inarticulate feelings of the masses.

Capital is a book almost as difficult to describe as it is to read. A text-book of history, a précis of government blue books, a prophetic denunciation of social evils; it is all these, and its style is successively the style appropriate to all these. It is therefore best read in extracts, as any other Bible is read by the faithful. For while its every word may be regarded as sacred, not even the most ardent disciple will regard it as evenly inspired. What is important for the student of thought is the general philosophy underlying it: and if it is agreed that the philosophy was a species of Hegelianism, the question arises as to how far its author can claim to have been an original philosopher.

Dialectical Materialism is today the official philosophy of one-sixth of the world, and Dialectical Materialism was the invention of Engles and Marx. How did it come to be formulated? A clue is to be found in an early work of Marx on the subject of Feuerbach. 'Philosophers,' says Marx, 'have hitherto interpreted the world in various ways; the thing is to change it.' The Real must be transformed into the Rational, if necessary by revolutionary action. What is wanted therefore is a philosophy of action, an active philosophy, a unity—hitherto never achieved—between theory and practice.

As a student of Hegel, Marx early began to ask himself the question: why should the processes of nature and history necessarily be regarded as the finite reflection of a timeless dialectic of Spirit? What, in other words, is this transcendent Idea of which, Hegel assures us, the dialectic is merely the eternal self-revelation? Why all this metaphysical mumbo-jumbo about an Entity which, whatever it may mean to philosophers spinning their complicated systems in the seclusion of their studies, has no significance for the common man? Even if the common man knows or thinks he knows what is meant by God, he can neither know nor pretend that he knows what is meant by the Idea. In the interests of common sense and for the welfare of humanity, can we not bring philosophy down to earth, and if necessary plant it firmly there? Of the nature of the Spirit, we finite creatures know nothing. To us, the one demonstrably real entity is Matter. A realistic philosophy, and still more an activist philosophy, will be based upon the twin notion that Matter is the fundamental reality and that such changes as take place in the universe are primarily material changes. A realistic philosophy will be a dynamic—or, to continue to employ the favourite word of Hegel—a dialectical materialism.

This was Marx's so-called 'inversion' of the Hegelian dialectic. This was his way of bringing it down to earth. But it still remained a dialectic. Like the Idea, Matter underwent changes according to the process of thesis—antithesis—synthesis; unlike the Idea (and this is one of Marx's most radical departures from Hegelian orthodoxy), it underwent this process *in time*.

An understanding of the downtrodden, the persecuted, and the exploited came much more naturally to Marx than to Engels, because Marx belonged to a race which knew at first hand the meaning of oppression, persecution, and exploitation. That section of mankind which was most completely enslaved to the machine, and whose lives were most heavily oppressed with material cares, was the proletariat, the workers of the world. Consequently, Marx found that his emotional sympathies and his intellectual interests tended to corroborate each other. Society was composed of a ruling class which, aided by the ecclesiastical hierarchy, held down the workers whose labour they ruthlessly exploited; but the basis of society was this very class of manual workers. In the same way, the universe of the philosophers was composed of a stratum of spiritual entities, more or less undefinable or (to use Kant's own term) unknowable, floating above a hard substratum of Matter: but whereas the philosophers had, with a few exceptions, assumed the greater reality of the spiritual entities, common sense dictated that Matter was the supreme reality. Hence materialism and socialism or proletarianism went hand in hand. The struggles of the working class throughout history were paralleled by the dialectical evolution of Matter: or, to speak more accurately, the historical manifestation of the dialectical evolution of Matter was the struggle of the working class towards freedom. 'All history,' the *Communist Manifesto* declares, 'is the history of class struggle.'

Historical or Dialectical Materialism was a 'deterministic' system: that is to say, it represented the dynamic forces of society as evolving by a process which nothing could arrest. Individual men may have thought themselves to be in possession of free-will; but such an illusion of freedom, like the kindred illusions regarding immortality and divine benevolence, were nothing but 'ideology', or the terms with which men have hitherto sought to disguise from themselves the naked truth of material interest. What matters is not so much the action of individuals (the cult of 'great men' is a bourgeois myth) as the action of classes; and the action of classes is dictated solely by class-interest. This is as true of the capitalist class as of the working class. The only difference is that the capitalist class, unaware that its historical mission is already discharged, seeks to maintain its position by even more intensive exploitation of the masses, hoping to divert their growing discontent by periodically mobilizing them for war. Here is the proletariat's opportunity. The workers should use the weapons placed in their hands not for fratricidal strife but for self-liberation from their exploiters. The expropriators must themselves be expropriated.

It should be observed at this point that Marx, if not always his disciples, has no quarrel with capitalist-bourgeois civilization as such. The *Communist Manifesto*, for all its violence and denunciation, goes out of its way to emphasize how great a contribution to knowledge and industry the bourgeois class has made. In the inevitable dialectic of history, the proletariat is poised, as it were, to assume the rôle of antithesis to the old bourgeois order. Nothing must be made to hinder the collision (the more delayed the more violent and bloody) out of which shall emerge the synthesis of a classless society. That is the crime of capitalism: not the crime of having taken the stage, but the crime of refusing to leave it.

Although Marx advanced a philosophy of life which appeared to deny all values as we understand them, he was himself a man of fastidious taste and high culture.

One of his favourite poets was Dante. Many a later disciple of the Marxist faith, preaching a cold materialism and denouncing the bourgeois intelligentsia as allies of the capitalist exploiters, would have suffered a shock to meet the actual Karl Marx, with his air of Victorian respectability, his addiction to cigars, and his refined tastes in art. Mistaken as it is to picture Marx as a raucous demagogue, however, it is still not altogether correct to represent him as a respectable Victorian gentleman. He was also a prophet, perhaps the last of the great Hebrew prophets, the castigator of his generation, the herald of approaching Judgment. For whereas Hegel had preached the eternal recurrence of his dialectical process, Marx, by inserting the process in time, represented history as soon about to come to an end. With the attainment of the classless society, the last contradiction and source of conflict in society would have been once and for all removed. Consequently the Marxist view of history is what may be called a messianic or Apocalyptic view. Its motive-force is not science but myth.

The development of the Marxist gospel supports this. The Chosen People becomes the Chosen Class. Faith becomes class-consciousness and solidarity. At the great Councils or Internationals, orthodoxy is proclaimed and heretics are excommunicated. The Marxist intellectuals exchange anathemas; and Lenin, in one of his politico-philosophical treatises, can accuse the philosopher Mach of 'betraying materialism with a kiss'. With the bourgeois spokesman beyond the pale, controversy becomes openly copro-logical; the protégés of the captialist era are nothing but 'a generation of vipers'.

In spite of the extravagances and distortions to which Marx's ideas have been subjected, his thought remains of profound significance in the history of modern philosophy. To insist that a philosophy is something to live by is particularly salutary at a time when philosophies are assumed to have neither practical application nor even passing utility. Secondly, to have developed the habit of considering problems from the historical point of view, instead of from a purely analytical scientific point of view, is to have increased our understanding of both the past and the present. Thirdly, to have endeavoured to appeal to the masses of mankind, across frontiers and through different tongues, by means of a myth calculated to spur them to a collective endeavour, was at least to demonstrate that, whatever gospel men of thought have to offer, it must be a common gospel, a universal truth, and not the creed of a sect or party. But two paradoxes remain unresolved in Marx's thought, and time has served only to accentuate them. The first is connected with his notion of a *dialectical* materialism. If Matter is in fact the hard, dead thing that the nineteenth century imagined, how can it suddenly burgeon forth in the dialectical phases which Marx, recalling the unfolding of the Hegelian Idea, regarded as the stuff of history? The second is connected with his notion of ideology. If material interests alone dictate human conduct, and if ideologies (*i.e.* systems of ethics and religion) are merely the 'reflection' of these interests, how do we account for the fact that the Marxist theory has exerted such enormous influence upon the course of history? The answers to these questions may become apparent in the sequel.

The full effects of the Marxist gospel did not become visible until many years after its author's death. But instead of the social revolution occurring in the most highly developed of capitalist countries, America, as Marx confidently believed that it would, it occurred in the country in which the capitalist system was least developed of all, namely, Russia. Thus the highly sophisticated philosophy of Dialectical Materialism, with its origins in the speculations of German professors, has become in our day the official creed of a population which, though hardly touched by academic philosophy, is gifted with precisely that religious insight to which the so-called apocalyptic element in Marx's thought might be expected to appeal. In his early days, Marx was in the habit of pouring scorn upon those social propagandists who, if nominally socialist, were in fact unpractical dreamers: Proudhon, Fourier, Owen, Saint-Simon, etc. These men, he argued, were not revolutionaries at all; they were skirmishers on the fringe of the great Liberal Movement that was in spirit and method bourgeois. A sentimental offspring of capitalism, Liberalism was an attempt to delude the masses into believing that *laissez-faire* economics, though causing them temporary ills, was ultimately to their advantage. What enriched their masters must finally enrich them; and the system was in any case grounded in the nature of things. Progress must therefore come about inevitably.

Against such sweetly reasonable philosophy, Marx preached the class-war, the Law of Increasing Misery, the Law of the Concentration of Capital, and the Theory of Surplus Value. Above all he preached anti-Liberalism. In this sense he takes his place among the great thinkers of the nineteenth century who attacked not merely the values of the day but the basis of that spiritual capital upon which Europe had been living since the Renaissance.

From Schopenhauer to Kierkegaard

No culture is all of a piece. Whereas it appears on the surface to be composed of homogeneous elements, it will always be found upon closer inspection to contain material of a totally different nature. As time goes on, these latter elements may work themselves to the surface and alter the whole structure. Thus beneath the apparently stable surface of nineteenth-century liberalism, deep cracks and fissures developed through which a lava of new and revolutionary thought began to well up. And this process developed at a time when, to the superficial eye, the European order had reached its highest level of material prosperity.

The success of the machine naturally brought about a change in accepted values. Indeed, the so-called triumph of mechanism was best observed not so much in the multiplication of mechanical apparatus as in the triumph of the materialistic philosophy that went with it. Against this philosophy, the so-called 'intellectual' elements in society, above all the Romantic poets at the beginning of the century and the Art for Art's sake writers at the end, protested. But they were all the while engaged in fighting a rearguard action. The Churches protested too; and such developments as the Oxford Movement (paralleled in the political domain by Disraeli's Young England Movement) were attempts to wean the Established Church from connivance in what Keble termed 'national apostasy'. Having lost the first round, which materialism won largely as the result of the arrival of a timely ally in Darwinism, the writers retired to their Ivory Tower, the philosophers to the shade of their 'dreaming spires', and the ecclesiastics to a *via media* that often became a *via mediocrita*. The field was left to the scientists, who proceeded forthwith to occupy, without much opposition, all the territories of thought not previously overrun by them.

The above statement, like all generalizations concerning matters of thought, requires due qualification. There were, among the professional thinkers at least, certain men to whom neither escape nor compromise was possible. These men refused to budge. They were determined not to accept the new order. If necessary, they were prepared to go down fighting. Of this small band of diehards, only three can be mentioned: Schopenhauer, Kierkegaard, and finally Nietzsche, to whom the next chapter is devoted.

Arthur Schopenhauer, born at Danzig in 1788, was the son of a merchant father and an author mother, both of whom claimed aristocratic descent. The boy was thus early surrounded with material blessings, which may account for his growing up a thoroughly spoiled and irritable youth. It was assumed that he would carry on the family business, and this for a time he did; but after his father's death, which put him in possession of a considerable fortune, he threw up everything with the object of devoting himself to the study of the subject most dear to him, which was philosophy. For a time he studied under Fichte at Berlin; but during the war of liberation he went into premature retirement, there to occupy himself with the composition of his first and most remarkable book, *The World as Will and Idea*, published before its author had reached the age of thirty.

Although Schopenhauer ought not to have resented the cold indifference with which this youthful work was received, he was extremely indignant. Thereafter, except at the end of his life when recognition came to him in full measure, he never ceased to rail at his fellow-practitioners of philosophy, whose elaborate systems he ridiculed with (it must be admitted) some effect. The philosophical ideas to which he gave expression in his book, however, were too novel to command immediate popularity, and indeed they have never been popular. Schopenhauer's views on any subject are not such as to command moderate approval: they either fascinate or disgust.

Temperamental hypochondria and a close study of both Buddhism and such German mystics as Boehme, combined to infuse into Schopenhauer's thought a strong strain of pessimism. The fundamental reality, he maintained, is not Being but Will; but the Will that drives everything in the universe, whether animate or inanimate, is a blind Will. Not merely is it ignorant of where it is going, but there is nowhere for it to go; it is therefore also an aimless Will. Now a blind and aimless force in the universe will be the cause not merely of more unhappiness than happiness, but of the most poignant variety of unhappiness, that for which there is no explanation. Existence is therefore nothing but an infinitely prolonged and infinitely recurring evil. Happiness, if such a state could be imagined, would be the opposite of existence: not death, for that is merely the termination of existence, but non-existence, the opposite of all that we mean by existence—Nirvana.

If this were the whole extent of Schopenhauer's thought, it would amount to very little, and to the Oriental it would be mere commonplace; but Schopenhauer has some very original observations to make about the manner in which the world as we know it has come into being. He declares it to be the direct product of Will. Take, for example, our bodies: 'Teeth, throat and bowels are objectified hunger; the organs of generation are objectified sexual desire; the grasping hand, the hurrying feet, correspond to the more indirect desires of the Will which they express.' In this way the whole of Nature has been created, and indeed the whole universe. Does this necessarily show an evil or irrational Will? Yes, answers Schopenhauer, for the Will, in creating our bodies, endows them with insatiable desires. Nothing satisfies us. The moment one desire seems to be appeased, another springs from its bosom clamouring for attention. The world is sustained by this continuous uprush of creative desire, just as a ball may be held aloft by a fountain-jet; but each drop, once having reached its limit, immediately descends and is replaced by others. That same Will which sustains existence renders existence intolerable.

Is there any way out for us? Can we either make existence at least supportable, or escape from it, not into death, but into some other existence? Schopenhauer believes that both solutions are possible, though for most people they are extraordinarily difficult. The first way out is through the experience of art. Art, of which the purest form is music, implies pure contemplation, pure detachment, and is therefore a calmer of the passions.

Without being a pain-killer in the literal sense, it is an anæsthetic. ('The world,' said Schopenhauer, 'is as much incarnate music as incarnate will': a theory to which Wagner, himself a philosophical influence in his day, subscribed.) Naturally we cannot live upon sedatives. At best they provide temporary relief, at worst they kill us, whereas we want something different from either distraction or extinction. The second way out provides the more satisfactory solution. Philosophical contemplation, if undertaken for its own sake, reveals to us the common plight of all beings, the universal bondage under which the whole of creation groans. This plight, this bondage, is simply the Will to Live. It must be eradicated from us. We must kill desire in our hearts, as the Oriental ascetic extinguishes his impetuous instincts. We must cease to desire happiness in order to arrive at a state of inviolability from which all agitation, whether of delight or care, has been removed. To commit suicide is neither prudent nor moral, because by so doing we have made no contribution to the eradication of the Will in others; we have merely shirked our task. Finally, we must realize that to help others to remove their burden of unhappiness is the best way of lightening our own. If the solution is to lose ourselves, let us do so in the service of our fellows.

Schopenhauer's philosophy is a mixture of querulous misanthropy (and misogyny: his views on women were almost pathological in their bitterness: perhaps his estrangement from his mother and his unfortunate love-affairs were responsible for this), acute perception, and sudden shows of wisdom, the whole being expressed in a literary style greatly superior to that of both Kant and Hegel and most of their contemporaries. As a personality, Schopenhauer was one of the few philosophers who may be called antipathetic. As a thinker, without being in the highest rank, he was original and disillusioned at a time when most thinkers were tending to drift with the tide. Like Marx, he was a bitter opponent of the idealism of the so-called Utopian thinkers (mostly Socialists); but, unlike Marx, he held out no vision of a New Jerusalem coming in the clouds and establishing the reign of justice upon earth. For him, such idealistic visions were merely part of the sustenance of that Will to Live which needed to be subdued. In the meantime —and in this respect he is a defender of the traditional values of Humanism—he bade his fellow-men cultivate the Stoic virtues and maintain their dignity in a world fast losing its standards in a general scurry for wealth and power.

More to be commended as a character but no less out of tune with the spirit of his age was the Danish philosopher and theologian Sören Kierkegaard (1813-55), whose thought has of recent years come to exert a profound influence throughout Europe. Like Schopenhauer, Kierkegaard exhibited the utmost contempt for all systems of thought, and in particular for such as represented the world as about to enter upon a new age of progress and enlightenment. He was equally opposed to Hegelianism, because although Hegel went to great lengths to show that the dialectical process involved perpetual struggle, pain, and even anguish, he ended with the anticlimax of assuming an immediate consummation of his scheme to have been reached in the Prussian State of his day. To this trite and chauvinistic attitude, Kierkegaard opposed a thorough-going pessimism of which the source was an intense but somewhat tortured religious faith. The remedy for our ills and above all our itch for system-making was to turn our thought inwards, to cultivate an interior life, and to realize our utter insignificance and helplessness in the sight of God. All that was universal, objective, and impersonal was merely a façade created by our intellect to give us the illusion of freedom and independence.

These sombre views, which brought Kierkegaard into collision with the church of his country and deprived his personal life of all normal enjoyment, were indeed contrary to everything that so-called enlightened persons had assumed to be obvious and desirable. He was like a man who, deliberately lying down on the track, allowed the express train of progress to run over and crush him. In his emphasis upon the interior life, the life of feeling, he is akin to Rousseau; but he is a Rousseau to whom Original Sin is the greatest of all realities, the highest of all mysteries, and yet the fact of which the world of his day remained most obstinately unaware.

Kierkegaard's refusal to live upon illusions, his contempt and disgust for life at the level at which it is lived today, and his mental toughness and stringency, has excited the respect and sympathy of a generation—our own—which, in consequence of the upheavals of war and post-war disorganization, experiences a similar revulsion from the traditional values of Western civilization. For this reason the apostles of the philosophy or quasi-philosophy of Existentialism claim Kierkegaard as one of their masters, though they do not always follow him all the way. For Kierkegaard, modern man, cut off from the natural world by his pursuit of technics and removed from God by his naïve humanism, is a 'displaced person': an individual with whom the world is having to reckon and whose psychology it does not yet wholly understand.

Friedrich Nietzsche

'Only he that altereth remains unalterably mine.'

The third enemy of decadence and degradation, and by far the greatest of the three, whose struggle to maintain his position proved fiercest, and who finally 'burnt himself out' (to employ his own phrase) in his own fire, was Friedrich Nietzsche. Of all the philosophers of the modern world he is the most tragic and in some ways the most terrifying figure. He is the one outstanding example in the whole history of thought of a man who, rebelling against the society of his time, took upon himself to do what society was too spineless to do, namely, to arrange his own martyrdom. In the fury of his contempt for the world of his day, his mental resistance gave way and he lost his reason. Nietzsche drove himself mad.

The family to which this extraordinary man belonged was that of the aristocratic Neitzkys, Protestant Poles who had settled in Germany in the eighteenth century. In spite of his admixture of German blood, Nietzsche never forgot his ancestry, and his features remained distinctly Polish. He could count among his forebears a large number of Christian ministers, a fact that is not without significance in view of his own mission as preacher of a gospel. As for mental and physical vigour, the Nietzsche family was particularly well-endowed; there is no record, however far back we go, of debility or mental oddity among them. Nietzsche's mother, also of a large and long-lived family, was eighteen years old when the most gifted of her three children was born. And she outlived his sanity by several years.

From his sister, who was later to write his Life and to assist in caring for him during his mental death, we learn that Friedrich was a good-looking, fair-haired boy, with exceptionally large dark eyes. At four years of age he could both read and write. He early showed signs of character; and although he was of quiet disposition, he would occasionally fly into a passion that startled everyone by its vehemence. But he was likewise capable of great feats of self-control: for instance, in order to demonstrate that the Roman Mucius Scaevola was not such a remarkable man after all, he several times held his hand in a flame without flinching.

After the death of his father (who fell down the steps of the parsonage one day and sustained injuries that finally killed him), the Nietzsche family went to live at Naumburg on the Saale. Here the boy Friedrich went to the town school, mixing with all types of boy; but he did not blossom out, even though he seems to have made a very great impression upon his teachers. We learn that he was nicknamed 'the little parson'; that he found Greek very difficult (though his understanding of the Greek spirit in later years was profound); and that about the age of ten he developed the habit of writing poetry and composing music. He was likewise renowned for a kind of precocious piety.

The next educational establishment which Nietzsche entered was a school at Pforta. Here, though the discipline was extremely strict, he began to reveal for the first time his many intellectual talents; and it became obvious to his instructors that an immense creative energy was stirring within him. He took up the study of philology more as a mental discipline than as a deep interest, but his chief discovery at this time was the music of Wagner. There was thus a mounting tension in his breast which brought about something in the nature of a breakdown in 1862. Although his health was still as robust as ever, he began to be afflicted with headaches and eyestrain, and for a time he was obliged to take a complete rest from all formal study.

It was in the next year, 1863, that he underwent what we gather to have been his first and only genuine experience of love. A fragile little girl, the sister of one of his schoolfriends, became for him the object of a romantic devotion. Nothing resembling this experience ever recurred in later life, though on two occasions he contemplated marriage; and we have no reason to disbelieve his sister's rather sententious statement that 'my brother remained all his life long completely apart from either great passion or vulgar pleasure; his whole passion lay in the realm of knowledge, only very temperate emotions remained over for anything else'. Psychologists have been inclined to explain his final breakdown in terms of an incapacity for ordinary sexual expression; but in the case of a man of intense mental activity, what may be a normal outlet in others need not obsess him to the same degree. Nietzsche neither shunned the society of women, nor exhibited for them that contempt which Schopenhauer, with his sordid *amours,* came to display. It is probable that he knew more of the meaning of passion than some others of more demonstrative nature; but he also knew how easily such an instinct can be exploited. Years after, in his *Zarathustra,* he declared: 'It is better to fall into the hands of a murderer than into the dreams of an ardent woman.' Men who are total strangers to passion do not usually talk in that strain.

After leaving Pforta in 1863, he entered the university of Bonn. The change of atmosphere exhilarated him. He could now express himself freely. That he should proceed to abandon the traditional beliefs of his youth was not surprising; he had reached the stage at which such abandonment is, for most youths, almost automatic. The only difference was with what thoroughness he did it. Beginning to criticize all the assumptions upon which his former ideas were based, he resolved to devote his life to the task of freeing men from illusions. To this end he put all his energies into unremitting study, leaving little time for the normal recreations of an undergraduate. He neither drank nor smoked ('there is too much beer in the German intellect', he later remarked); he even denied himself food in order to attend concerts and plays. Perhaps it was his admiration for the Greek ideals of balance and moderation that prompted his lifelong abhorrence of rowdiness and excess. At the same time he was distinguished at Bonn for his physical robustness; and it was observed, when he left for Leipzig, that he was precisely the same height as Goethe, whose humanist ideals up to this point he shared.

At Leipzig the problem that began to obsess him was that of finding a secure philosophical standpoint from which to launch his critical bombardment upon the world. So great was his perplexity that he frequently prolonged his meditations far into the night and occasionally until morning. One day, browsing in a bookshop, he came upon Schopenhauer's *World as Will and Idea*, a work of which he had not then heard. On the spur of the moment he bought it. The reading of this book marked a turning-point in his life, for it thrust his mind forward in a way that he could not have conceived possible. It assisted him over the brow of the hill. On the purely emotional side, too, he made more discoveries in music, above all Wagner's *Mastersingers*, which caused 'every nerve and fibre' in him to thrill. In 1868 came another momentous event in his life, namely, his meeting with Wagner himself. It was as if two explosive forces had come together; but the detonation was to occur later, when disillusion had followed upon rapture.

He still pursued his studies in theology and, without displaying any particular enthusiasm for the subject, made sufficient progress to attract the attention of experts. A lecture on Theognis, the Greek poet (sixth century B.C.), brought him particular commendation, and in 1867 he was offered the Chair of Philology at Basle, which he accepted. To everyone's surprise, however, his first real publication was not an academic treatise but a remarkable philosophical work entitled *The Birth of Tragedy,* which he dedicated to Wagner.

This essay, which appeared in 1871, excited considerable discussion. Its argument was as follows. In Greek thought, two themes are ever present and perpetually in conflict: that associated with Dionysus, with its ecstatic intoxication, its intuitive principle, its emphasis upon singing, dancing, music, and lyricism, and that associated with Apollo, with its dream-like serenity and classic equilibrium. In combination, these two principles produce folk-song and finally tragedy, the highest achievement of Greek art. The tragic art began to disintegrate, however, with the popularization of the teaching of Socrates. Socrates, as we have seen, maintained that viciousness and evil were a consequence of thoughtless ignorance. 'More knowledge, more virtue,' was the essence of his teaching; and virtue was the chief promoter of happiness. Such optimism was, in

Nietzsche's view, incompatible with the tragic view of life; and our continued acceptance of it, strengthened by the Christian teaching, has rendered our existence increasingly superficial. But now a new era is dawning. The art of Wagner is the beginning of a new Birth of Tragedy; for in Wagner's operas music is once more wedded to myth in the manner of the old tragedy. And this is the beginning of a resurgent German heathenism, which is to be the culture of the future.

Having so far departed in this work from strictly philological studies, Nietzsche was not surprised to find that his way to advancement was barred; but as his heart had never been in purely academic affairs, this hardly worried him. He knew he was making enemies. How could he expect otherwise? He was deliberately trying to overturn contemporary idols. Two of his 'heresies' in particular were the cause of public consternation and offence: first, his insistence that Socrates and Plato were perverters and diluters of the Greek tradition symbolized by Dionysus, and secondly, his assault upon Christianity. These two 'heresies' were of course interconnected. 'To ensure the eternal pleasure of creation,' he wrote, 'the eternal affirmation of the will to live, the eternity of birth-pangs is absolutely required. All this is signified by the word Dionysus. I know no higher symbolism than this Greek Dionysiac symbolism. In it the deepest instinct of life, of the future of life, the eternity of life, is experienced religiously: generation, the way to life, is regarded as a sacred way. Christianity alone, with its fundamental horror of life, has made sexuality an impure thing, casting filth on the beginning, the very condition, of our life.'

When in 1870 Germany defeated France, the event was regarded by many Germans (and some others) as the sign of the superiority and complete victory of German culture over that of France, so long reputed to be the highest in Europe and even the world. Nietzsche, it is interesting to note, did not share this view. Indeed, he poured more than his usual measure of scorn upon it. The Germans of his time were conspicuous, he said, for their lack of culture. Their thirst for information, their regimented efficiency, their coarse addiction to tobacco and beer was not so much culture as Philistinism. As yet they remained unworthy of the new ideals to which Wagner and his followers were giving expression; and the sabre-rattling of bragging soldiers was calculated to retard rather than to further their attainment of such sensitive life as true culture implied. In Nietzsche's view —and this is the central point of his book *Richard Wagner in Bayreuth*—art must go ahead to light the way; for art is a revolutionary force which, once accepted, will alter our whole conception of both education and morals. In a sense it simplifies life, is larger than life, and therefore serves as a guide to life: high enough to attract the most intellectual, yet broad enough to stir the most unpretentious. The secret of Wagner, as that of the Greek tragedians and of Shakespeare, was the secret of scope.

To a man of Nietzsche's sturdy individualism, a permanent attitude of hero-worship was not possible. Wagner was the hero so long as Wagner did what Nietzsche thought he ought to do. Their almost daily association at Basle had obscured the fact that each was developing upon different lines. To appreciate how much the other had changed, it was necessary for them to separate; and the separation came when Wagner left Switzerland. In 1876 there took place that momentous festival at Bayreuth at which the first performance of Wagner's *Ring of the Nibelungs* was held. Nietzsche was keyed up for what he assumed would be the climax of Wagner's creative life. He even wrote a prologue for the festival. It seemed to him, in fact, as if the whole gathering was to be in the nature of a 'sacred consecration on the morning of battle'.

When the *Ring* was enacted, with all its Teutonic splendour and oppressively barbaric mythology, Nietzsche realized with mounting distress that he had been horribly deceived. This, in the words of a modern poet, 'was not what he meant at all'. The very primitivism against which his heart and soul had been in rebellion was here displayed in gigantic, naked abandon. Wagner, who was to have been the prophet of a new life-giving cultural energy, had instead put the weight of his genius behind the movement towards Germanic barbarism, with Wotan as the symbol in place of Dionysus, and the Nordic blizzard as a substitute for the Hellenic calm. This was cultural apostasy of the most flagrant kind.

Nietzsche, whose personal friendship for Wagner had been sincere (though Wagner was many years his senior), felt betrayed and humiliated. He flung away from the whole concourse in a mood bordering upon hysteria. A doctor-friend who was with him at the time recorded his opinion that Nietzsche was suffering from advanced neurasthenia.

Whatever his immediate reaction, he managed in time to pull himself together. The effort was still possible. And, having rallied, he decided that he must now eradicate from his being all the poisonous growth that had been allowed to fester there: the philosophy of Schopenhauer, the false mysticism of Wagner, and indeed all the morbid mushroom-philosophies of his day. It was like applying the handbrake in the middle of a race downhill —almost like trying to regain one's balance after gathering for a parachute-leap. In his next book, *The Case of Wagner*, he explained what he had tried to do for himself and what he summoned his contemporaries to do after him. Possibly it would have been better if he had taken Wagner's advice (given half in jest and half in earnest), that he should seek out a rich widow, marry her, and travel on the proceeds. A little less self-absorption might have enabled him to keep his balance; but a genius, especially the lonely genius that he was, rarely solicits sound practical advice, nor was Nietzsche likely to listen to the suggestions, however realistic, of the man largely responsible for his condition. Naturally, the attempt to turn his back upon old enthusiasms was not easy to make: and it was not perhaps altogether salutary that, instead of listening to Wagner, he should have turned for consolation to Bizet. A mighty opiate could be made to lose its attractions only by recourse to one of equal potency. The French culture that he so much admired offered no antidote of sufficient strength.

It says something for German academic tolerance at this time that Nietzsche was permitted the maximum of freedom in the interpretation of his duties, the more orthodox of which he by no means neglected. He was a popular and painstaking teacher, never revealing in his manner, which was always courteous, the mental turmoil within him. Like the punctilious Kant, he was greeted by his fellows (or most of them) with an unaffected geniality that betrayed no suspicion of the explosive gospel he was engaged in harbouring.

His retirement from Basle, which took place in 1880, was due to the state of his health, and he received thereafter a generous pension. Being now as free as he had ever been in his life, he devoted his time to European travel, writing a series of learned books at his leisure. One of his favourite haunts of study was the Piazza in front of St. Mark's, Venice. It seemed on the whole that he was regaining the mental equilibrium which his break with Wagner had so rudely disturbed; and though appearances were deceptive, the publication in 1883 of his book *Thus Spake Zarathustra* suggested that he was then at the height of his powers, which was true. *Zarathustra*, undoubtedly Nietzsche's masterpiece, has very little to do with Zoroaster, the half-legendary prophet of Persia; but the symbolism of water and fire and the incantatory form in which the Master is supposed to speak were well adapted to Nietzsche's purpose, for he was able to use them to convey his own fragmentary ideas as if they possessed oracular significance. With *Zarathustra* Nietzsche ceases to be the apostle of Culture, a sort of German Matthew Arnold, and becomes a seer endowed with the capacity to see 'beyond Good and Evil' (the title of a later book). Nor is he any longer a mere critic, a satirist of petty vices and failings; he is the denouncer of morality itself (defined by him as 'the mob instinct working on the individual'), the castigator of man's stupidity in accepting the 'slave morality' of Christianity rather than the 'master morality' of which he claimed to be the prophet. The controlled passion of the earlier books, suddenly bursting its bonds, here (and still more later) pours out in torrential invective against modern ideas of right and wrong. Still clinging to the Dionysian symbolism, he rails at the trivial, comfortable doctrines of the bourgeois classes of his day, which betoken the 'plebeianization of Europe'. Never had such a terrific denunciation of human frailty been made in a style at once so majestic and so impassioned. And never had a modern writer indulged, apart from brief intervals of serenity, in such bouts of self-laceration and inward fury, as if he were working himself up to a kind of mental spontaneous combustion.

In writing *Zarathustra* and the books that followed, Nietzsche came increasingly to believe not merely that he had a mission but that his mission was the only one capable of saving mankind from spiritual anæsthesia. As his style became more didactic, and his opinions more dogmatic, so he developed a dangerous megalomania. Upon his literary works he placed a value which was, to say the least, extravagant: 'I have given men the deepest book they possess, my *Zarathustra*,' he remarked a little later. And there came a moment, just before—and no doubt heralding—the final collapse, when he seems to have regarded himself as embodying in his own person the genius of humanity. As his mind began to vibrate with even more tremendous throes of semi-prophetic fervour, he planned to write one last book—a super-Bible, a breviary of the Superman, the last will and testament of mankind's first human deliverer. It was never completed. It was never even begun.

The notion of insanity is not absent from Nietzsche's early works, but it is by no means obtrusive: his emphasis upon the Dionysiac symbolism reveals a preoccupation with an unfettered, uncontrolled individualism, but there have been as daring individualists before. The point at which he began to turn his back upon normality was the point at which he turned his back upon the whole complex of modern civilization—its art, its science, and above all its morality. In his first period, he denounces the 'slave morality' of his day as being a departure from the healthy robustness of Renaissance humanism; in his later work, he seems to be at issue with the whole of Western civilization, even including its pre-Christian founders, Plato and Aristotle. It is not enough for him to believe that by a process of natural selection and the survival of the fittest the Superman will automatically be born; he believes, like some other advocates of evolution, that the process must be given some assistance, that personal sacrifice is necessary, and that one man must die for the people, in order that the latter shall perceive its need of leadership and submission to authority. And he believes that he himself, to whom the 'joyful wisdom' has been given, must prepare for martyrdom—a martyrdom not so much of the body as of the mind. He will agree to 'take the strain' of that new morality or amorality to which man must in future learn to conform; and if the tension should prove unendurable, then he will accept the consequences, even if it should mean the ultimate collapse of his faculties.

And that is what in the end it did mean. Nietzsche had always been visited by strange dreams, and he likewise displayed a tendency to hallucination. One particular dream that he had as a boy was so vivid that he took the trouble to record it. He experienced the sensation, so he tells us, of being borne forward in company with others through the most beautiful country imaginable, with no sound save the sweet singing of birds. As he proceeded, it seemed that before him lay the whole of his life, a long vista of serenity and happiness. Then, to use his own words, 'suddenly a shrill cry reached our ears: it came from the neighbouring lunatic asylum'. This dream was merely the most outstanding of a number of others, but it was oddly prophetic. Not many years after the publication of *Zarathustra,* Nietzsche began to show signs of mental derangement. He became a prey to extravagant hallucinations. Writing to George Brandes, one of the first men in Europe to appreciate his genius, he signed himself 'The Crucified'. To the historian Burckhardt he wrote under the name of Ferdinand de Lesseps. At Turin, where he was staying, he went about declaring that he was God. A friend, Professor Overbeck, to whom Burckhardt had spoken, hurried to Turin to see Nietzsche, and found him in a terrible condition, obviously on the verge of mental collapse, uttering extravagant opinions and spending his money in the most careless manner. He still continued to write, but evidence of insanity was increasingly apparent. On 27th December, 1888, in a letter to Overbeck, Nietzsche declared that he was engaged in drawing up a Memorandum to be sent to all the courts of Europe inviting them to form an Anti-German League. Explaining himself, he stated coolly that he wanted to see Germany encircled so that she should be provoked into declaring war upon the world. The psychologist will see in this an expression of his own neurotic condition. By the following year his senses seemed to have quietly slipped their moorings.

He survived twelve years. For some time he remained

in a home in Basle and then at Jena. As he proved of gentle, almost child-like disposition, he was later taken to Naumburg to live with his mother, and after she died he was looked after at Weimar by his sister, whose account of him during that tragic period is the fullest record that we are likely to possess.[1] In spite of the general collapse of his intellectual powers, he could still enjoy music and literature, and he took pleasure in the conversation of friends. But it seemed that all recollection of his self-assumed mission—his war against the civilization of his day—had vanished beyond recall. On one occasion when a great author was mentioned in his presence, he observed mildly: 'I, too, have written some good books.' Nor did he seem to fret at the inactive, death-in-life existence that he was obliged to lead. Seeing his sister weeping one day, he said: 'Lisbeth, why do you cry? Are we not happy?' Perhaps he was for the first time in his life.

Nietzsche lost his reason out of loneliness and despair just at the moment when his name was becoming known all over Europe. 'A profound man,' he had remarked, 'needs friends, unless he has a God. And I have neither God nor friend.' Consequently, the solitude in his mind became unendurable. He departed from a world that had almost forgotten that he still inhabited it, on the 25th August, 1900, in the thirteenth year of his second childhood.

[1] Evidence has recently come to light that his sister later 'edited' his correspondence in order to suggest that she was his only confidante and to give the impression that he was much more addicted to chauvinistic and 'racial' ideas than he really was.

Scepticism and Faith in
Nineteenth-Century Philosophy

The lesson of Nietzsche may be summarized as follows: a philosophy is not something to be studied in a book—to be pondered in solitude and then, like any other book, shut up and put away—but something to be lived. Even if it exacts high or impossible standards, it must be tried and proved in action. The example of Nietzsche filled his contemporaries, as it has filled his successors, with something like awe and dread; but it is arguable that this revulsion was due as much to his insistence upon the importance of action and adventure ('A new world remains to be discovered—and more than one! Hoist sail, O Philosophers!'—the profession had rarely been addressed in such unorthodox terms), as to the perversity and paradox of his actual views. After Nietzsche, there was a scurry back to the study, the library, and even to that most sheltered of places, the laboratory, just as in literature and art there was concurrent flight to the Ivory Tower.

The contemporary thinkers upon whom Nietzsche vented his bitterest scorn were the English utilitarians, particularly John Stuart Mill (1806-73) and Herbert Spencer (1820-1903). The evil wrought by these thinkers was, according to Nietzsche, their *vulgarization* of the scientific spirit. They claimed to be apostles of Science; but all they did was to reduce Science to Technics, and to use technics to make their already demoralized life more easy, more comfortable, more smooth—as if that were the way to produce Supermen! 'The best and wholesomest thing in science, as in mountains, is the air that blows there.' In spite of his claim that religions were extinct because 'God is dead', Nietzsche had not the slightest intention of exalting a purely materialistic philosophy. To him, the scientific spirit, the spirit of disinterested enquiry, was an aspect of that unquenchable human thirst for experience which the ancient wis-

dom had endeavoured to cultivate. To declare oneself
a materialist, even an agnostic empiricist, was to betray
science, since it revealed a lack of faith in science. This
was the origin of Nietzsche's condemnation, along with
modern Christianity, of that school of philosophy according to which all ultimate problems were dismissed
as 'unknowable', the only 'realities' being sense-data,
money, steam-power, and cheap labour. 'The air that
blew' in that region was heavily polluted.

In spite of Nietzsche's admiration for France and
French thought, the nineteenth-century philosopher
who did most to make science an end in itself and therefore encouraged the growth of materialism was Auguste
Comte (1798-1857). But even Comte, who founded
what he called the Positive Philosophy (according to
which the scientific spirit evolved through three stages,
the theological or mythical, the metaphysical or abstract,
and the positive or concrete), failed to exclude altogether the mystical element: for at the conclusion of
the exposition of his system, he introduced, as if by the
back door, a brand new religion, the Religion of Humanity, which is the culmination and epitome of all
other faiths. A somewhat similar development occurred
in the thought of Herbert Spencer, an engineer by training, who was led to expound an evolutionary doctrine
before Darwin published *The Origin of Species* (1859),
but whose attempt to discern rigorous scientific laws
in the universe and the development of nature concludes
with the admission that behind the world of phenomena
there lies, as Kant himself had maintained, an Unknowable realm. John Stuart Mill, a disciple of Comte but a
less systematic thinker than Spencer, had likewise admitted to the existence of a 'final inexplicability' in all our
speculations about the universe. Thus the shadow of
Kant lay right across the thought of the nineteenth century, obscuring for many people the advances made by
Hegel. Even a realist such as T. H. Huxley (1825-
1895) was not immune from this influence: for Huxley
and a good many of his followers (George Eliot is an
example in the literary sphere), while believing that only
the phenomenal world is knowable by science, clung desperately, and for reasons not always fully appreciated by
themselves, to the moral ideas of the Christianity they

had repudiated, thereby adopting the argument of Kant that the 'unknowable' Thing-in-Itself may yet be contacted in moral experience. In fact, we might go so far as to say that the reputation earned by the nineteenth century (perhaps not altogether deservedly) as an era of moral effort, self-help, thrift, and respectability was due to the prolonged hang-over of the Kantian ethic. The first Victorian, with his regalia of top hat, frock-coat and umbrella, was the Sage of Königsberg.

In his Philosophy of History Hegel had emphasized the rôle of struggle, effort, and contradiction in the development of nations and communities. With an insight that few of his predecessors had possessed, he sought to prove that stability in a society is a symptom not of calm but of tension: the orderliness and dignity most apparent to the superficial eye is purchased only by ceaseless struggle against forces making for disintegration and chaos. The placid surface of the nineteenth century, observed at an oblique angle, is thus seen to be stirring with restless forces barely held in check. And the reality is in the tension, just as a man's character, as distinct from his personality, is in the measure of his self-control: a nation, like an individual, is said to 'come out strong' when its character, put to the test, survives the shock intact. At perpetual war with the materialistic complacency of the last century were, first, the poets and imaginative writers, who conducted a kind of rear-guard action as they retreated into their isolated coteries (the last stand being made by Oscar Wilde and Walter Pater), and secondly, the apostles of a somewhat out-of-date humanism such as Matthew Arnold, who fought the Philistines without any very clear notion of what he would have substituted for their philosophy, and third the theologians and philosophers, whose solidarity had been somewhat weakened by the confusion caused by the Darwinian hypothesis, dividing them into those who refused to have anything to do with it and those who, impressed by the concept of Evolution, endeavoured to remould their faith in conformity with its tenets. Fundamentalism and Modernism were the two extreme reactions within the Anglican Church, and a similar division appeared, though less violent, within the ranks of Catholicism. In philosophy, the crisis was somewhat delayed by reason of the obsession of academic thinkers with points of detail. In the universities there had arisen a school of 'minute philosophers' (on the model of Berkeley's *Alciphron*), neo-Kantians, neo-Hegelians, authors of text-books of Logic or monographs on some philosophical problem, polite sceptics, drawing-room agnostics, with bland 'scientific' arguments in their hands and dogmas up their sleeves. All this superficial pedantry seemed to have very little to do with ordinary life, and with the desires and aspirations of ordinary men and women. The Delphic maxim 'Know Thyself' meant little to an age in which the very possibility of Knowledge was held in doubt, and for which the Self, if it meant anything at all, was reduced to a fortuitous assemblage of instincts and impulses—a depersonalized ego, the wraith of Fichte's dynamic concept.

As long as Matter was regarded as being composed of hard 'billiard ball' atoms, invisible but assumed to be the ultimate constituents of Nature, over which were 'draped' all the qualities that the philosophers were accustomed to term 'secondary', materialism proved a reasonable and even a comfortable philosophy of life. Comfort and stability go together; materialism, if it did not permit men to sit down and dream, at least permitted them to stand secure. But just when it began to seem that all the traditional beliefs of mankind—their religion, their philosophy, their moral codes—were nothing but the products of imagination and fancy, survivals of tribal customs and taboos, maintained in large part merely by those (perhaps the capitalists or the churchmen) for whom their maintenance was a matter of self-interest, lo and behold! the solidity of Matter, its impenetrability and permanence, became the subject of doubt even among the materialists themselves. Before long the mechanical picture of the universe was being transformed, as through an X-ray, into a series of wave-like squiggles and curves, these being themselves the crude notation for forces inapprehensible by our senses and only inferred from the mysterious deflections of delicate instruments or from calculations beyond the capacity of all but mathematical experts. From being a comfortable faith, materialism was changed into something as incredible as the idealisms that it had claimed to supersede: indeed, it became a kind of idealism itself, for the more original of the scientists were daring to suggest that the only realities were the 'equations' whereby the universe (or what was left of it) was made intelligible, and that these existed only in the minds of mathematicians. They went further: if the only reality was a mathematical symbolism, the creator of that symbolism, God, must Himself be a mathematician, who 'thinks' the universe into being, and by thinking maintains it. And that was to return to the position of Bishop Berkeley.

It might have been expected that philosophy, observing the extremes to which science was being driven, would have exulted at the downfall or humiliation of a dangerous rival. But such celebrations were not at all appropriate. To speak of 'philosophy' and 'science' in this figurative manner is legitimate so long as we realize what we are doing: in fact it is not 'philosophy' that rivals 'science' but the human mind that seeks to reconcile two sides of its nature, the theoretical and the practical, the sensitive and the intellectual. At the period of which we are speaking (and we are not yet perhaps at the end of it), men came to realize that in relying upon the methods whereby physical science had been consistently pursued since the time of Descartes and Galileo, all that made life worth living—all the 'values' of existence— were being compressed into the ever-narrowing sphere of the irrational and the imaginary. The problem was no longer one of definition but one of salvage. The pursuit of knowledge, declared by Socrates to be the one road to happiness, had produced after all those centuries a state of mind that was incapable of serenity, since the knowledge most easily acquired had tended, like all scientific knowledge, to strip the world of its adornment. Sophia or Wisdom had demonstrated the folly of being wise. As a guide to truth, philosophy had done nothing (or so it seemed) but usher in illusion; as a guide to conduct, it had merely opened the way to a sterile utilitarianism. Perhaps the most complete revelation of the bankruptcy of thought, whether philosophical or scientific, was that contained in the work of the German philosopher Vaihinger entitled *The Philosophy of 'As If'*, according to which all human beliefs of a transcendental character were shown to be nothing but illusory wish-fulfilments, analogies without basis, or what Hume (himself a forerunner of this line of thought) had described as 'the playful whimsies of monkeys in human shape'.

In America a voice of protest was raised by William James (1842-1910), who bade his contemporaries forget the problem of abstract 'truth' and concentrate upon action; in 'pragmatism', or the identification of truth with what is efficacious in practice, lies the hope of wandering humanity. He was followed by John Dewey and George Santayana, to whom we devote a special chapter. In England, a philosopher of fine sensitivity and perceptions, F. H. Bradley (1846-1924), questioned a view which reduced the world to 'a ballet of bloodless categories'. Finally, in France, effecting one of those sudden and salutary renewals of thought which fill humanity with hope, the philosophy of Henri Bergson shot through the intellectual gloom with the brilliance of a meteor.

Henri Bergson

'In the Absolute we live and move and have our being.'

1

Bergson died in 1941, in a country under the shadow of foreign occupation, an old and ailing man, one of a persecuted race whose humiliations he elected to share. His death, which marks the end of an era in European thought, had about it something of the nobility and dignity of that of Socrates. Consequently, it is appropriate that his achievement and example, which presented so marked a contrast to the faint-hearted ideals of his time, should be the note upon which we conclude.

Like Nietzsche, Bergson was of mixed origin: his family can best be described as Irish-Jewish of Polish extraction.[1] This may account for his extraordinary versatility: his poetic instinct, his grasp of science and mathematics, his extreme curiosity, and above all his mysticism. For that reason alone, he became at the height of his powers a public figure, a social lion, and for some the preacher of a new gospel of comfort and exhilaration. His greatness lay in the fact that this universal adulation —and occasionally execration; it springs from the same source—failed in any way to turn his head. After holding his audiences spellbound by his eloquence, he retired into seclusion for a quarter of a century to rethink his whole position in the light of an intensive study of history, anthropology and theology. Then, in spite of increasing ill-health, he produced what some have described as his masterpiece, a study of Religion and Mo-

---

[1] Bergson, it is interesting to recall, was a British citizen until after he had obtained his Baccalauréat.

rality. Nor was this the end of his labours. At the time of his death he was engaged in what we have reason to believe were even more profound researches; but of these we possess nothing but the barest hints.

Born in the Rue Lamartine, Montmartre, Paris, Henri Bergson went to school at the age of nine at the Lycée Condorcet (then called the Lycée Fontanes), which was situated not far from his home. He immediately distinguished himself as a pupil of extraordinary ability. Science, mathematics, and literature were his best subjects; but he seems to have been good at everything, except apparently geography. His school career ended at eighteen with a notable achievement: namely the solution to a mathematical problem for which a competition had been set, his version being thought worthy of publication in the *Annales de Mathématique*. After such a display of virtuosity, it was natural that he should seriously consider taking up mathematics as a career; but, his Baccalauréat over, he decided that the choice must be between literature on the one hand and science on the other. In the end he decided upon a subject of study which partook of the nature of both. This, fortunately for the world, was philosophy.

Entering the École Normale Supérieure in 1878, one of the Grandes Écoles of France, he studied for the next few years under three of the most able French philosophers of his day, Ravaisson, Boutroux, and, perhaps most distinguished of all, Jules Lachélier. These thinkers were all idealists; but the young Bergson, while attracted to a form of thought that exposed the errors of materialism, gave much attention to the close study of texts, especially those of the ancient Greek philosophers, in which he succeeded in making some important emendations. This period of absorption in the thought of ancient Greece, with particular reference to such pre-Socratic philosophers as Zeno and Heraclitus, was crucial; for his own speculations took their origin from certain of the problems with which those pioneers of philosophical enquiry were concerned.

Like most other young students of philosophy, Bergson, having to decide upon a career, chose that which seemed most likely to afford him opportunity, if not necessarily leisure, for further study; namely teaching. He first joined the staff of the Lycée at Angers in Anjou, where he remained for the next two years; and then proceeded by promotion to the Lycée Blaise Pascal at Clermont Ferrand, where, under M. Bourget, father of the famous novelist, he spent one of the happiest periods of his life. It was at Clermont Ferrand that his maturing thought took definite shape. As a teacher, he began to display qualities not merely of lucidity but of passionate eloquence which transformed his subject, philosophy, from a dull academic study to a burning issue, a living topic, something that affected his pupils personally. Nor did he confine his attention to conventional academic themes; he was willing at all times to throw light, if possible, upon topics familiar to all. Thus it was a notable occasion in the intellectual life of Clermont Ferrand when M. Bergson delivered a public lecture on the subject of 'Why do we laugh?' Sixteen years later, in his book entitled *Laughter,* the ideas advanced in this lecture were developed in conformity with the now famous Bergsonian system. Another fruit of his stay at Clermont Ferrand was a scholarly edition of Lucretius, with an Introduction (still of great interest) on the relation between poetry and philosophy, which has served as a textbook for half a century.

Apart from an article on Hypnotism published in the *Revue Philosophique* (1886) and no doubt inspired by some experiments carried out by Dr. Montin in Clermont Ferrand, Bergson produced nothing of note until the two theses submitted in 1889 for his Doctorate. The first of these was in Latin; the second was entitled *Les Données Immédiates de la Conscience,* which was later worked up into a book and translated into English under the title of *Time and Freewill.* The latter, as we shall show, expounded a new and revolutionary theory of knowledge, which Bergson defended most ably in the oral part of his examination. He was accordingly made a Docteur-ès-lettres. Tiring of the provinces, he decided to move to Paris, where he obtained a post first at the College Rollin[1] and later at the famous Lycée Henri IV.

The articles that Bergson now began to write in philo-

---

[1] Now the Lycée Jacques Decour.

sophical magazines were attracting attention not merely in France but overseas. Apart from the fact that they were written in a style of pellucid charm, the subjects treated were fresh to most students of philosophy, and the conclusions to which they pointed, though only tentative, proved as exciting to the young and curious as they were alarming to the academically orthodox. That Bergson was no less able and charming a speaker than he was a writer became increasingly known. Moreover, his appointment in 1898 to the staff of the École Normale Supérieure suggested that he was already making a name for himself in the educational world. In the same year appeared the first comprehensive statement of his philosophical position in a book entitled *Matter and Memory*. The public was able at last to take some measure of him.

As to the new and revolutionary ideas that Bergson was putting forward, his own words speak for themselves. 'I set myself,' he later wrote, 'the following problem. What is it that modern psychology and pathology can teach regarding the time-honoured question of the relation between matter and mind? . . . When I began to study the subject I soon discovered that the problem could not be solved, even provisionally, unless it were narrowed down to that of memory.'

To explain how he arrived at this conclusion we must revert to the general assumptions upon which philosophers had relied since the time of Descartes. Not to repeat in detail what we have expounded elsewhere, it may be recalled that for the disciples of Descartes, and even in some degree for Kant himself, Mind and Nature were set over against each other in such a way that the problem for philosophical enquiry resolved itself into how there came to be any commerce between them. The conventional answer, as we showed, was that the mind made contact with nature by means of certain media called 'ideas'. Ideas, in fact, acted as a kind of currency whereby it became possible to effect transactions between the subjective and the objective spheres. The problem of knowledge, in short, was a problem of exchange.

One way of avoiding the complications arising from this theory of knowledge (and we have seen how Hume riddled it with criticism and then turned away with a shrug of his shoulders) was the way adopted by Hegel. Another was the way adopted by Bergson.

The point to which Bergson drew attention was that this whole 'picture' of the relation between Nature and Mind rested on a spatial metaphor. Naturally, if you place the Mind *here* and Nature *there,* leaving a gulf fixed between the two, the problem of how one establishes connection with the other becomes insoluble; you have automatically rendered it so. But surely, it may be said, we need to picture the problem to ourselves somehow, and this seems the most natural way of doing so. Certainly it is, replies Bergson; but it is natural only for our *intellect.* That, indeed, is how the intellect works. It spatializes. It folds things out flat. It goes round its objects and maps them from the outside, delineating one aspect after another and then, if necessary, building up a composite photograph to represent the whole. Hence the capacity of the intellect to perform the most accurate feats of analysis: for what it has built up from small counters it can as easily take to pieces.

Now the capacity of the intellect to reduce things to spatial units and to interpret everything in such terms, including the mechanism of knowledge itself, would fully suffice for our needs if the reality with which it has to deal were an inert, static reality, presenting sharply disposed contours and features susceptible to measurement. But it is not. Reality is not static but mobile. And the change in which it is engaged is not a mere shifting, a rearrangement of parts (which is no change at all), but a transformation producing real novelty. Consequently, if we rely purely upon our intellectual faculty, we shall never grasp what reality is like; we shall merely gain a distorted chess-board picture of it. Reality in its ceaseless flow and perpetual change must ever evade our intellectual categories. To seize reality, to apprehend it in its fullness, to *know* it in the fullest sense (and to know authentically is to know that we know, as if by a kind of inner conviction), we must and do have recourse to another faculty altogether.

This faculty, Bergson holds, is Intuition. By intuition we do not go round the object, taking individual observations; we enter into it. Intuition is the means whereby we plunge into the stream of flux or Becoming and apprehend it from inside. Whether we realize it or not, we are constantly doing this, or we should become so completely divorced from reality as to perish of a kind of inanition. In certain of our experiences—and these are often the most valuable—we become perfectly conscious of such interior illumination. To know another person in the complete sense is to penetrate his mind with our own, to 'enter into' his enthusiasms and aspirations, to identify ourself with his attitudes. Nor is this experience confined to what is called, in technical terms, the specious present; it involves past states of mind as well, both our own and those of our companion. In other words, to know in the sense here employed involves an interpenetration of past and present in memory, a taking up into the present of the sum of our past experience and that of others, and the carrying it forward as a unified whole, accumulating at each moment ever richer experiences, much as a snowball (the simile is Bergson's own) increases in size as it moves.

This description of knowledge may strike some people as nothing but an excuse for Bergson to indulge his lyrical gifts. That he constantly illuminates his argument by striking and original metaphors is true. But his argument is still an argument, and he supports it not merely by decorative imagery but by cogent reasons.

To return for a moment to the problem of memory: how, we may ask, is this interpenetration of present and past possible? Does it not presuppose what is clearly absurd, namely, a reversal, however slight, of the time-series? That depends, says Bergson, upon what we mean by time. This introduces us forthwith to one of the most original elements in Bergson's philosophy, namely, his distinction between scientific time and what he calls 'real time' or Duration.

Scientific time—or, as Bergson sometimes calls it, 'clock time'—bears no relation to change in the true sense at all. That may seem a bold statement. But, to take an example: if the planets travelled twice as fast as they do, they would follow precisely the same course. Now this is true of all natural processes: speed up the process—speed it up, if you like, to such an infinite degree that everything happened simultaneously—and you would in no way alter the relation between one stage or event and another. In other words, time (and here Bergson follows Kant) is not a characteristic of the world of natural things; it is something that our intellect, in effecting one of its typical distortions, projects into the world. Temporal succession, in fact, with its placing of one event before or after another, is merely an example of the way in which our intellect 'spatializes' the reality that it apprehends in the interests of practical action. We must live; and our intellect is the instrument that makes life on this planet a practical proposition.

If, however, the essence of reality is change—continuous and everlasting change without there being (as Bergson is careful to insist, in contrast this time to Kant) anything permanent that changes—it follows that such real change must depend upon a kind of time deeper, older, and more dynamic than that just described. This time or Duration, which is merely another word for Change, has been defined by Bergson as 'the continuous progress of the past which gnaws into the future'. Consequently, it is the vehicle of perpetual novelty. It is not something that passes us by: nor is it something that we make use of for practical purposes. It is something that pulsates through our very being: indeed, it *is* our very being, for we are ourselves the conscious expression of the life-flow from which the whole universe has ultimately been derived. Matter, then, is congealed, lifeless Spirit, the hardened lava thrown up by the volcanic discharge of the creative principle or *élan vital*. The ultimate reality is Duration. Everything, as Heraclitus said, flows.

In expounding this theory, Bergson adduced a wealth of examples from all the sciences. He is not content to make dogmatic statements, as thinkers like Schopenhauer and Nietzsche tend to do: he advances nothing for which he is not prepared to produce factual evidence. In attacking the materialists' account of consciousness, he goes very thoroughly into the question of how far the brain can be considered to be the seat of mental activity; and the conclusion at which he arrives is that, while the brain may be a link in the process of consciousness, it neither originates nor contains consciousness. A brain can be subjected to quite severe mutilation before mental activity shows any sign of being affected, still less stultified; nor, as we know, will the most careful dissection of the cerebral cortex and brain cells provide clues to the nature of what, for want of a better term, we call mental states. Moreover, the common types of psychological phenomena—split personality, aphasia (loss of memory for words), and all the so-called subconscious activities upon which so much theory has recently been based—have never been related satisfactorily to any given physical condition of the brain. The function of the brain, then, is not to originate mental activity, but, so far as we can see, to canalize it; for the brain is the point at which consciousness or Duration enters into matter. Acting rather like a transformer, it reduces the pressure of the life-stream, admitting just so much of consciousness as our physical make-up can stand. Without the brain, we should be flooded with a volume of vital experience calculated to render action impossible. The brain, then, is an instrument not for remembering but for forgetting. What we call the Mind overflows the brain, and is exempt from its limitations.

2

Two years after the publication of *Matter and Memory* Bergson was appointed Professor of Greek Philosophy at the Collège de France, and later, in succession to the philosopher and sociologist Tarde, Professor of Modern Philosophy. From now onwards he began to assume the rôle of a great intellectual force, a leader of thought, the preacher of a gospel—and a most eloquent preacher at that. His lectures, open to all, began to attract not merely the student working for his examinations but the men and women, as numerous then as now, who hungered and thirsted, if not for righteousness, then for certainty—the intellectual 'fringe' which, finding no solace in traditional religion and repelled by the cold materialism and relativism that claimed to have replaced it, clung at any straw of hope that might be borne by the latest wind of doctrine. In the philosophy of Bergson, no doubt partly because of the persuasiveness of its exposition, such people found comfort and inspiration, a new zest for life, an incentive to action, such as academic thought had in the past shown an incapacity to provide.

There are few descriptions more moving than that given by Raïssa Maritain, wife of the Catholic philosopher, of the effect upon her wayward generation of a single sentence of Bergson, delivered with an earnestness and conviction impossible to reproduce, and to some extent rendered lame in English translation: 'In *The Absolute* we live and move and have our being.' The impact of this statement acted, as she says, like a sudden draught of fresh air, a mental tonic: more than that—a reviver of the spirit itself, so long deprived of healthy nourishment. For what Bergson was in effect doing was not merely to put man back into the universe from which he had so long been alienated, but to give him a rich and living universe in which to be replaced. The Bergsonian philosophy, whatever its shortcomings, effected the repatriation of the human spirit.[1]

Like every other leader or pioneer, Bergson was often embarrassed and plagued by the attentions of admirers whose interest in his thought was frivolous and superficial. His audience contained its fair sprinkling of *demimondes* and society ladies to whom the *Elan Vital* and its spontaneous 'gushing forth of novelties' proved highly attractive, and who found it great fun trying to listen to the *ron-ron* of Duration pulsing through their delicate blue veins. As the new gospel was carried from *salon* to *salon,* so its author was bombarded with invitations, enquiries, personal disclosures, and requests for confidential advice; his mail, much of it carrying the scent of the boudoir, exceeded that of any living philosopher and also that of some film-stars. Importunate callers rendered his life so intolerable that, being obliged to make frequent changes of residence in Paris, he earned the title of 'The Wandering Jew'.

With the publication of his great work, *Creative Evolution*, in 1907, Bergson reached the height of his fame. In its pages, he seeks to show that 'reality is change, that change is indivisible, and that in an indivisible change the past is one with the present'; and his conclusion is

---

[1] The late Professor Floris Delattre once reproached me for suggesting in my book *The Approach to Metaphysics* that Bergson was responsible for purveying a variety of Couéistic propaganda. A great thinker is not, of course, answerable for the extravagances of disciples; and I wish to take this opportunity of correcting a misleading impression.

that 'philosophy is not only the return of the mind to it-self, the coincidence of the human consciousness within the living principle from which it emanates, an establishment of contact with the creative effort; philosophy is the deepening of becoming in general, the true evolutionism, and hence the true continuation of science'. In a word, it is 'seeing in time the progressive growth of the Absolute'.

His system apparently completed, Bergson spent the next fourteen years lecturing not merely in France but throughout Europe. At Bologna, at Oxford, at Birmingham, in London, in New York, the dapper figure in the cutaway coat, high collar and cravat poured forth a stream of silvery discourse, accumulating university degrees and honours and drawing huge audiences of enthusiasts. In 1914 he was elected to the French Academy. The war of 1914-18, exposer of so many reputations, left Bergson's prestige undimmed. Indeed, his philosophy received a kind of post-war boom which threatened to leave him without a moment's peace. In 1921, unable to endure the publicity in which he had become involved, he resigned his position at the Collège de France, retaining an honorary professorship there. In spite of ill-health, he had no intention of going into retirement, if retirement meant seclusion; he wished, as ever, to make himself useful. He therefore elected to serve on a number of committees for International Co-operation, and spent much time abroad. 'In recognition of his rich and life-giving ideas and the resplendent art with which they are presented', he became the recipient in 1927 of the Noble Prize.

That Bergson's public activities in no way exhausted his energies, his closest friends knew well. Every minute of his spare time was devoted to intensive study. He was not trying to buttress an old reputation (he had, needless to say, many critics, from Julien Benda, a fellow Jew, to Jacques Maritain himself, who soon moved on to Catholicism); he was busy, though without ambition, establishing a new one. The subjects to which he devoted particular attention were history, ethnology, anthropology, sociology, and theology, particularly the great mystical writers. To the philosopher Höffding he had written in 1912 that 'I have not touched on the problem (of

God) in my works; I believe it to be inseparable from moral problems, in the study of which I have been absorbed for some years'. Bergson went on being absorbed. Like the novelist Proust, whose cousin, Mlle. Neuberger, he had married, he remained silent for more than twenty years, during which time his health deteriorated considerably. The outside world assumed that his creative powers were extinct; and meanwhile a new generation had grown up to whom the apostle of the *Elan Vital* was a back-number, deserving of a passing respect in academic circles simply because *on porte partout le cadavre de son grandpère*.

Then, without any prior advertisement or announcement, there was published in 1932 a book entitled *The Two Sources of Religion and Morality*. Packed with closely reasoned thought, and written with even greater dignity and serenity than any of his previous works, it displayed a new insight and immense, if lightly worn, erudition. Surveying the course of history, Bergson traced the evolution of two kinds of human society: that in which morality is imposed through 'pressure' and that in which it is imposed through 'attraction'. In the former, or 'closed' society, the moral life is a matter of conformity, automatism, submission; in the latter, or 'open' society, it is a matter of creative spontaneity and freedom. Thus the religion of the 'closed society' is a static religion, characterized by taboo and totemism, whereas the religion of the 'open society' is a dynamic religion of which the finest flower is mysticism. As in his early work Bergson had maintained that there were two ways of knowing, the way of intellect and the way of intuition, so in his last book he traced the development of the two forms of society, the one from intelligence and the other from instinct, twin forces whereby life expresses itself. In reality, however, the human consciousness does not operate upon two different levels. It is one process, but a process which, in striving towards ever higher modes of expression, is weighted down by a constant crystallization, a 'falling away', a degeneration into habit, which is matter.

In discussing mysticism, Bergson examined the technique and experiences of the Greeks, the Orientals, the Hebrew Prophets, and finally the Christians; and it is

his considered opinion that in the latter alone we have
the most complete consummation of the spiritual process
which is called, at lower levels, life. From the evidence
of the mystics, the spiritual leaders of humanity, Bergson deduces the existence of God; for just as we must
take seriously the views of scientists about matter, so
we must take seriously the views of mystics about divinity. If, he writes, the 'philosopher attaches himself to
mystical experience, Creation will appear to him as God
undertaking to create creators, that he may have, besides Himself, beings worthy of His love'. And in the end
Bergson achieves a reconciliation between the dualism
which runs through his work—between Intellect and Intuition, Thought and Action, Time and Duration; for
as he says, 'man will rise above earthly things only if a
powerful equipment supplies him with the requisite ful-
crum. In other words, the mystical summons up the mechanical. . . . We must add that the body, now larger,
calls for a bigger soul, and that mechanism should mean
mysticism. . . . Machinery will find its true vocation
again; it will render services in proportion to its power
only if mankind, which it has bowed still lower to the
earth, can succeed, through it, in standing erect and looking heavenwards.'

3

In the years following the publication of *The Two
Sources*, Bergson, now almost a complete invalid through
arthritis, continued to pursue the line of thought which
he had opened up in that book; but just as he had formerly disclosed the purport of his meditations to none
but his intimate friends (and sometimes not even to
them), so now he worked on in silence, in seclusion, and
in pain. It was rumoured that he contemplated baptism
into the Catholic Church; but the growing wave of anti-
Semitism that swept Europe after 1933 moved him so
deeply that he felt he must stand by and with his own
people in the trails that lay ahead. From a passage in his
will that Mme. Bergson has since disclosed, we learn
that as early as 1937 he had quite made up his mind on
this issue. 'My reflections,' he there confessed, 'have led
me closer and closer to Catholicism, in which I see the

complete fulfilment of Judaism. I would have become a convert had I not seen in preparation for years the formidable wave of anti-Semitism which is to break upon the world. I wanted to remain among those who tomorrow will be persecuted. But I hope,' he added, 'that a Catholic priest will consent, if the Cardinal Archbishop of Paris authorizes it, to come to say prayers at my funeral.' This was done.

After the defeat of France in 1940, the Vichy Government ordered that all Jewish employees should resign from State positions. Bergson was offered exemption, but he refused it. Likewise, he was invited to retain his honorary Chair at the Collège de France in view of his 'artistic and religious services to the nation'; but he submitted his resignation on 9th December, thus breaking an association of forty years' standing. Finally, when the Government stipulated that all Jews must submit to public registration, Bergson was again offered the chance of exemption, but again refused. And so, at the age of eighty-one, the practically bed-ridden philosopher, fulfilling his resolve, rose for the last time, and waited his turn outside the Registration Office, supported by two servants.

That last silent protest in the inclement weather, unnoticed and almost anonymous in its humble dignity, hastened the end. On 4th January, 1941, Henri Bergson died of pulmonary congestion.

John Dewey and
George Santayana

It is a conventionally held belief that the United States of America is a new country. In one sense, this is obviously true; but in another sense it is far from being so. America is a country with a very ancient *ethos* or ideology. In that sense, it is unique among the nations of the world.

From the earliest times, man has dreamed of Utopias, or ideal societies in which people could dwell together in liberty and brotherhood; but not until the discovery of America—or rather its re-discovery in the late fifteenth century—did the possibility of actually establishing a Utopia on a grand scale arise. The Founding Fathers were practical idealists. Without idealism, they would never have been impelled to uproot themselves; without practical genius, they would never have succeeded in establishing a society on a far and untamed continent. The society which they set up was designed to be free, and if possible permanently insulated, from the corruption and tyranny of the old world. Even today, there is a feeling, especially in the Middle Western states, that the old world of Europe has an inveterate tendency to corruption and decadence. The Declaration of Independence of 1776 contains a clear statement of the principles on which the new society was to be based: life, liberty and the pursuit of happiness. Never before had Utopia been launched on the collective plane. Moreover, the land to which the pioneers came was potentially rich beyond imagination.

Until quite recently, perhaps until the beginning of the last war, American culture was regarded, even by Americans themselves, as an offshoot of the culture of England and of Europe. A book such as *The Education of Henry Adams*, published in 1905, is infused with this idea, and it is reflected in the career of Henry James. The American intelligentsia might be described as partly resident outside the United States: witness the thousands of Americans who took up permanent abode in such centres of culture as Paris, Rome, and Florence. Gertrude Stein, herself a pupil of William James, wrote: 'So I am an American, and I have lived half my life in Paris, not the half which made me but the half in which I made what I made.' Henry James, brother of the philosopher, and later on T. S. Eliot solved the dilemma by renouncing their American nationality and becoming British subjects, though James did so only on his death-bed. Another American, Stuart Merill, not merely became a French subject, but virtually turned himself into a Frenchman and wrote poetry in the language of his adopted country. There was some tendency on the part of American intellectuals to ridicule and belittle American society, and to regard Europe as the only true source of cultural values. H. L. Mencken is the figure most closely associated with this tendency. There was even a time when, especially in the South, the profession of literature was not considered a respectable one: it is only recently, but with great effulgence, that Southern writers have attained eminence. This set up a tension in American writers, since, in view of their upbringing, they simultaneously despised the Europe which, in another part of their minds, they worshipped.

All this has now changed. The tensions are there, but transmuted. Others have arisen. But the American intelligentsia is no longer a kind of government in exile. Americans living and writing abroad have ceased to represent what might be called, in Toynbee's phrase, an external proletariat. There is even a movement in the reverse direction. A genuine American literature, even when it is written by first-generation Americans, exists. Likewise, there is already a distinctively American tradition in philosophy.

If philosophy is the disinterested pursuit of truth, can the nationality of a philosopher affect his thinking? The answer is that it can and it does. The pursuit of any mental goal, not least the highest of all, must take as its point of departure the environment in which the thinker finds himself. And the further removed the goal, the more obviously will the thinker view it from his own standpoint, and with preconceived assumptions. We can detect a German, a French, a British, even an Indian approach to problems so apparently above or irrelevant to nationality as those of biology and psychology. The German will *tend* to adopt the *a priori* method; the British and American the empirical or mechanistic one. These particular slants will be no less present, if disguised, in subjects far more abstract in content. Metaphysics provides a good example. Perhaps the most elevated of enquiries, metaphysics is not so elevated as to have escaped bitter partisanship. On the contrary, metaphysics, its nature and its very legitimacy as an enquiry, has been subject to more controversy, especially in our time, than any other branch of thought. There are even thinkers who, far from discussing this subject in a non-partisan spirit, believe that metaphysics, especially in its more idealistic forms, is the result of an aberration of the German mind, a kind of Teutonic conspiracy against common sense. Not to confine such conspiracies to one nation, it might be argued that certain forms of extreme empiricism, such as Behaviorism, are conspiracies of the American mind.

One of the chief characteristics of American thought is that it presents a variety, a meeting of extremes, which results from the varied traditions which have gone to compose and to complicate the American character. In this chapter, we shall be discussing two thinkers who are as apparently different from each other as they are different from the thinkers of Europe, yet both of whom belong to a tradition distinctively American.

Born at Burlington, Vermont, in New England, on October 20th, 1859, John Dewey was descended from a pioneer family. His forebears probably came from Dorchester in the county of Dorset, England. The Dewey family sailed for America not many years after the *Mayflower* left Plymouth in 1620. The history of the English branch of the family has been subject to much research. It is possible that the family name was derived from the Flemish 'de Wei', meaning 'of the meadow', and that the Deweys were weavers from Flanders who, like many of their kind, took refuge in England from the persecution of their Spanish overlords. John Dewey's father, a farmer's son, owned a grocery business in Burlington. He was a man of some culture. We are told that he could quote Milton fluently, recite Burns in the Scottish dialect, and read Carlyle and the great Victorian novelists. His wife, from a well-to-do Vermont family and his junior by many years, was likewise both intelligent and resourceful. Their two sons, of whom John was the younger, were thus reared in a household where reading and study were encouraged. The boys developed an early interest in books. The Waverly Novels and Chambers Encyclopaedia were purchased from earnings from delivering papers and other odd jobs.

Dewey's schooldays were uneventful. He found school life boring, but he was not a bad scholar. He came under strong religious influence. The boys spent their holidays on the farm of their grandfather, and here they took their share of the heavy work. During the Civil War, the father joined a cavalry regiment in the Union Army. As the war dragged on, Mrs. Dewey finally decided to move the family to Virginia in order to be near him. This proved to be the last winter of the struggle, and life was hard.

At fifteen, John Dewey graduated from high school and entered the University of Vermont. The transition was negligible, since the family home was situated almost next door to the university buildings. The subjects prescribed for study were of wide range. Dewey took Greek, Latin, ancient history, mathematics, and the natural sciences. The textbook prescribed for physiology was that of the great T. H. Huxley. Apart from the interest which such a book aroused, Dewey's mental outlook was broadened by what he was able to assimilate from periodicals from overseas. In his senior year, he embarked on philosophy. A capable teacher, Professor H. A. P. Torry, took the students through Plato, Bishop Butler, Bain, and the Scottish school. Meanwhile, Dewey made acquaintance on his own with the English positivists through articles in the *Fortnightly Review*, and thus with the system of Auguste Comte. He finished his university career with high honours.

At this critical stage in his life, he lacked a clear idea

of what he wanted to do for a living. As we have often observed in the foregoing pages, the uncertain student usually drifts into education. Perhaps 'drift' is the wrong word. The profession with which he has been in closest contact is that of teaching. Once his student days are over, he finds little difficulty in exchanging the 'passive' rôle for the 'active'; for teaching and learning are parts of a single process, if the teacher is not an automaton and the student is more than a receptive mechanism. By accident rather than by design, Dewey found himself teaching at a school in South Oil City, Pennsylvania, of which a cousin, Clara Wilson, was principal. After two years of plodding routine, he moved to a village school in Charlotte, not far from his home town of Burlington. These years of apparent obscurity were not without influence upon the future educational theorist. He experienced at first hand the grandeur and the misery of teaching. Meanwhile, he did not neglect his higher studies. He continued to maintain close contact with his old teacher, Torry. In 1882, he wrote his first essay in philosophy, a study of materialism. This he offered to a review of ideas, the only one of its kind in the States, called *Speculative Philosophy*, and was gratified by its prompt acceptance. The editor, W. T. Harris, was much under the influence of German thought, particularly that of Schelling and Hegel. His journal was one of several sources from which German philosophy obtained so strong a hold over the American academic mind.

Dewey at last felt that he had discovered his *métier*. Borrowing a sum of money from a relative, he entered The Johns Hopkins University. This was in effect America's second university after Harvard; but at that time it was open only for graduate study. The new atmosphere proved exhilarating. In after life, Dewey confessed that he was heartily glad to leave Vermont. At Johns Hopkins, he met for the first time men of exceptional ability and originality. He had an opportunity for the free exchange of ideas not merely with his teachers but in such arenas of debate as the seminars. At that time the latter were almost unique to Johns Hopkins. In the realm of ideas, the greatest single influence upon his mind was that of Hegel. Against Hegelianism, he was later to react with a violence which carried him, together with many of his generation, to the opposite pole of thought; but he never underestimated the importance of the Hegelian 'moment' in his development. He described Hegelianism as an 'immense release or liberation'. In point of fact, he found in Hegel something more than a stimulus to profound and daring philosophical speculation. The philosophy of Hegel provided a kind of substitute religion. The rather narrow evangelical beliefs of his youth had shown no obvious point of contact with his broadening outlook; and their renunciation took place with less violence in the context of a system which seemed to embrace all experience. Another influence upon his religious opinions, though probably antedating that of Hegel, was Coleridge's *Aids to Reflection*. This book had enjoyed great popularity in free-thinking circles since its American edition was published in 1829. Dewey once told a friend that he had learnt from Coleridge all he ever was to believe on the subject of religion, but that he rarely referred to the fact because few people seemed interested.

It was at Johns Hopkins that, thanks to his teacher and later close friend George Morris, Dewey obtained some university teaching and later a fellowship. Soon after, he was offered an instructorship at the University of Michigan, where Morris held a professorship. Here, in Ann Arbor, Dewey met his future wife. Alice Chipman was taking the university course on money she had earned as a teacher. She was from a Vermont family likewise descended from pioneers. Of strong character and independent mind, she was at that stage a good deal more progressive in outlook than the man she married in 1886. Dewey's increasing preoccupation with social problems, his interest in formulating a practical philosophy, and his respect for the religious outlook which he formally repudiated, may be attributed largely to her influence. She bore him six children, was his constant helpmeet, and died in 1927.

An academic career, even one covering so long a period as that of Dewey, does not usually provide material for vivid biography. Dewey held a succession of appointments. He spent a year at Minnesota. He went back again to Michigan, where he made perhaps the greatest philosophical friendship of his life, that with the original

George H. Mead. He moved to Chicago in 1894, where he became Professor not merely of Philosophy and Psychology but of Pedagogy, and where he directed an experiment in education which came to be known as the Dewey School. The residence at Chicago was probably the most fruitful of all. Through his publications, he had already become well-known as a progressive thinker; he was now afforded an opportunity of gaining practical experience of educational and social problems. One of the institutions in which he took a close personal interest was Hull House, the famous Chicago social settlement directed by a remarkable woman, Jane Addams. This settlement was open to people of every belief and of any social position. Its purpose was to conduct an experiment in democratic living. Dewey felt that such ventures might point the way to a truly democratic society, first on a national and ultimately on an international scale. Years after he had left Chicago, and despite differences of viewpoint over America's entry into the Great War, Dewey remained a loyal champion of Jane Addams and her social ideals.

A dispute concerning the school associated with his name terminated his residence at Chicago in 1904. Before taking up a post offered him at Columbia, he paid a long-planned visit to Europe. This interval of relaxation was darkened by the death from typhoid of one of his sons. The Deweys later adopted an Indian boy whom they had met on their trip. The decision proved a happy one; the boy grew up to become an educationalist after his foster father's own heart. The period at Columbia which followed was no less crowded with activity. To his academic work Dewey now added political activity and, through his friendship with the scientist and collector Albert C. Barnes, art. He became chairman of many committees and organisations, among them the League for Independent Political Action. He also helped to establish new ones, including the American Association of University Professors.

Although he was by no means a brilliant lecturer, and despite a style of writing that was often plodding, sometimes musclebound, and clogged with qualifications, Dewey was by now an acknowledged leader of American thought. His pragmatism or instrumentalism, of which we shall speak, was the kind of philosophy which lent form and respectability to the dominant mood of his country. As much by her exertions as by her example, America was rapidly becoming the world's most powerful and dynamic nation. Moreover, she represented a people who believed, and who daily saw evidence for their belief, that they had a mission. This mission was to teach the world the lesson of democracy in action. In contrast with the imperialisms of both past and present, America stood for a kind of moral imperialism. At the end of the First World War, she combined unrivalled strength, immense prestige, and, in the view of many of her people and not a few foreigners, the practical idealism often lacking in countries placed at such eminence. Of this practical idealism, Dewey proved to be the natural mouthpiece.

Chiefly through the diffusion of his progressive educational theories, he was now also becoming known abroad. Countries engaged in the task of reconstruction, as well as those embarking on nationhood, were seeking ideas on social matters which were not merely practical but flexible enough to be applied to their own problems. Modern technical civilisation, a purely Western product, showed itself to be easily exportable. No other civilisation had ever shown such capacity for rapid expansion, nor so powerful an effect in breaking down long-established custom. Measured by the standards of the West and particularly by those of the United States, half the world appeared *underdeveloped*. People conscious of this discrepancy in standards felt the need not merely for machinery and technical knowledge, but for the philosophy that went with them. Consequently, a form of thought which laid primary emphasis on growth, on the type of knowledge which led to practical results, and on the repudiation of tradition, hierarchy, and absolute values, was a philosophy likely to exert widespread appeal. No doubt this philosophy, or its crude equivalent, had already been tacitly exported along with the technical processes and know-how; Dewey merely gave it articulation. The first country to extend an invitation to Dewey was that which had been opened up by Americans in the previous century, Japan. By contrast, the countries in which Dewey's ideas made least impact, both then and after the Second World War, were those which had succeeded in reconciling tradition and progress: Great Britain, for example.

Dewey's reception in Japan in 1918 was enthusiastic; but the enthusiasm was manifest largely among those already acquainted with his views, or at least ripe to receive them—that is, a minority. He was under no illusions as to the contrary influences at work, the enormous power still wielded by militarists and traditionalists. In the years 1918-1919, however, America's reputation in Japan was at its zenith; and most liberal-minded people, Dewey included, assumed that democracy would not merely triumph here and throughout the world, but that it must necessarily do so. Dewey's much longer and more rewarding visit to China was likewise the result of the enterprise of former students, among them the Chancellor of the National University of Peking. He travelled extensively, lecturing in most of the larger Chinese universities. He saw the growing power of the student, that substitute in new nations for a bourgeois intelligentsia; the beginnings of female emancipation (Mrs. Dewey was made Honorary Dean of Women at Nanking); and the awakening to modern ideas of a country gigantic in size and unparalleled in fertility. During the tour, one of his escorts was the Chinese Ambassador to the United States, Dr. Hu Shih, who had studied at Cornell and Columbia. At the time of writing he is in Formosa, and a change has come over Chinese affairs such as Dewey could not have foreseen.

Dewey also visited Turkey in 1924, the moment when Kemal Ataturk was consolidating his drastic, but beneficent, reforms. Two years later he went to Mexico. A visit to the U.S.S.R. took place in 1928. Here Dewey was able to observe a process of social regeneration inspired by ideas sufficiently in line with his own to rouse his enthusiasm: for Soviet education was at least a cooperative activity, and its aim was to build a new world on the ruins of an old. Despite some of his statements on return, which caused him to be denounced as a Bolshevik, he was not deceived by the political aspects of this experiment in 'unanimous' democracy. The tour was an exclusively educational one, and today we can hardly say that the Soviet experiment, at least in its technical aspects, has failed. When many years later Dewey agreed to sit on a commission of enquiry into the charges brought by Stalin's government against Trotsky, he arrived, by an impartial study of the facts, at a more critical view of Communist ideals and practice. And if the facts were responsible for bringing about the later change of attitude, their earlier disclosure would no doubt have modified his initial enthusiasm. The *Soviet Encyclopaedia* of 1952 later retaliated by dismissing him as a 'reactionary bourgeois philosopher and subjective idealist (sic) . . . serving the interests of aggressive American imperialism'.

Dewey may be said to have reached the height of his eminence, as well as the climax of his powers, when in 1929 he delivered the Gifford Lectures at Edinburgh. The invitation to join so distinguished a company proved him to be among the most vigorous minds of his day. The lectures were published in the same year under the title of *The Quest for Certainty*. Together with *Human Nature and Conduct* (1922), this book represents in both thought and style perhaps the highest level of his work, and his most enduring contribution to philosophy.

Many years were still to be allowed him; and though he published no major work, with the exception of *Art as Experience* (1934), this did not imply that he had said all he had to say. He was a man of immense energy, and he lived his philosophy as much as any modern thinker may be said to have done. He lectured frequently and always drew large audiences. He became Professor Emeritus at Columbia in 1930. In 1931, he delivered the William James Lectures at Harvard, and in 1934 the Terry Lectures at Yale. As each decade passed, he was accorded the honour to which age and achievement entitle a man. A massive tribute was the publication in 1939 of the volume *The Philosophy of John Dewey*, one of the distinguished compendia for which Professor Paul Schilpp has been responsible, and featuring essays by most of his distinguished colleagues, including Bertrand Russell and A. N. Whitehead. Another volume of essays in his honour was called *The Philosophy of the Common Man*, published in 1940 to mark his eightieth birthday. In 1946, he remarried. He died in 1952 at the age of ninety-three.

We have stated that Dewey's philosophy was above all a practical one; that it provided a liberation from much that philosophy currently stood for; and that it formed a fitting gospel for a new era. All this is true. What needs to be stressed, however, is its relation to the philosophy of the past, especially the immediate past. A thinker who seeks to break away from a tradition may at the same time be the last exponent of that tradition. That is the reason why a man who is hailed, or denounced, as an iconoclast in his day is often regarded by the next generation as already a back-number. The new generation, having absorbed from him all that was new, perceive retrospectively only the man who faces them, not the man whose back is turned to the past. A comparison with a figure of similar, if not much greater, stature may be illuminating. The generation in Britain which inherited the material advantages of the Welfare State tended to regard Bernard Shaw, who was perhaps its foremost ideological architect, as thoroughly *old hat*. In outlook and even in appearance, Shaw was indeed one of the last of the Victorians; and he achieved his impact by castigating Victorian standards. Dewey was in much the same position; and that is why the newest generation of Americans tends to find him pretentious and out-dated. Writing six years after his death, George Geiger remarks: 'This is a peculiar time to be writing about John Dewey. It is a time when almost every fundamental part of his philosophy seems to have been rejected.' [1]

The operation of this 'law of diminishing reputation' can be further illustrated with reference to Dewey's thought. After his initial addiction to Hegel, Dewey did not so much spurn the master as put his thought to a different use, exactly as Karl Marx did. Now, the foundation of Hegel's system is his Logic. Consequently, Dewey's early work, and that which may seem least remarkable to another generation, was concerned primarily with logical *reform*. Nevertheless, his approach and even his terminology remain those of Bradley and Bosanquet, the direct heirs of Hegel. The renewed interest at the time of writing in Bradley and Bosanquet, especially the former, is therefore part of a reaction against Dewey

---

[1] *John Dewey in Perspective* (1958), p. 3.

himself, who had endeavoured to push beyond these men.

Dewey published two major works in Logic, *Studies in Logical Theory* in 1903, and *Essays in Experimental Logic* in 1916, the original 'studies' being included in the later volume. The title of this second book, besides emphasising the current reaction against idealistic logic, revealed the philosophical direction in which he was moving. It represents something of a flourish, a challenge; for while logic itself is hardly to be called experimental, the uses to which it is put may be so.

In talking of judgment, Dewey wishes to move away from the idealist position according to which a *mind* comes to know and entertain an *idea*. This he regards as too abstract a view. Judgment for Dewey is first and foremost a practical activity, a man judging: a difference of emphasis not without novelty in its day. Furthermore, the person engaged in judgment is doing so always in a concrete situation. He acts upon this situation, and only thus does he arrive at knowledge. For the situation is not to be understood in a mere environmental sense. A man's actions are part of his situation, and the 'transactions' between the two comprise his total experience. Judgment is that which turns unreflective experience into reflective experience: for if judgment is the acquisition of knowledge, there must first be something concrete to know.

This is a crucial point. Dewey is as much an enemy of pure or naïve empiricism as Bradley. It is the contention, or the tacit assumption, of the empiricist that our experience consists of a series of sensations. What are sensations? If they are the 'feeling of this' or the 'apprehension of that', one distinct sensation following another, they are much more sophisticated than our ordinary experience would suggest. These sensations are *not* what our experience contains. A 'stream of consciousness', in William James's sense, is by definition the opposite of an articulated procession. In other words, pure empiricism, far from viewing experience as it really is, presents us with an artificial blueprint. We might say that empiricism, simply by being the 'philosophy' of experience, is the philosophy of 'experience'. And this is as much as to say that there can be no such thing as empiricism *tout court*.

When philosophers call themselves empiricists, they are employing a convenient and very general label. Consequently, the term, as used in philosophical argument, is almost always qualified. We have Hume's empiricism, or James's 'radical' empiricism, or the empiricism of the linguistic philosophers; and in each case we find that the view of experience so labelled is something different from what is called, perhaps with unintentional aptness, 'brute empiricism'.

If, however, unreflective experience takes the form of a stream, a continuum, how do we ever succeed in emerging from it in order to scrutinise or judge it? How does it become, in Dewey's phrase, 'an affair of history'? The answer is that the flux of experience, every now and then, is subject to disruption or arrest. A problem arises. We stop and think about it. The weight of our intelligence is brought to bear. We prescribe a remedy: that is to say, we consider what mode of *action* is best to adopt. Only when we have acted, when we have removed the barrier, can we be said truly to *know* what the situation is. The original plan of action is formulated partially in the dark: hence it is hypothetical. Knowledge, when we have it, is practical. The first is merely an instrument to knowledge; the second only is true judgment, and therefore knowledge itself.

This is the basis of Dewey's instrumentalism. As with all philosophical methods, a metaphysics lurks behind it. Dewey wishes, first of all, to dissociate his theory from those systems according to which knowledge 'makes no difference' to the thing known; but he is equally at pains to reject, or rather to reformulate, the standpoint which conceives of reality as being somehow moulded, even created, by the mind. Our intelligence, Dewey holds, does make a difference to what it knows, but only because it alters the *situation* which it has been called upon to judge. We pronounce judgment not in some abstract manner, but as responsible agents intent upon effecting changes for the better. Knowledge is not the passive contemplation of some higher object; 'philosophy will have to surrender all pretensions to be peculiarly concerned with ultimate reality'.[1] It is the active intervention in our

[1] 'A Recovery of Philosophy', from the symposium *Creative Intelligence: Essays in the Pragmatic Attitude* (New York, 1917), p. 12.

immediate situation. This intervention not merely clarifies our thoughts. It is not mere 'analysis'. It is diagnosis: and its diagnosis, like all diagnoses, is a prelude to remedy.

The whole of Dewey's conception of ethics, education, and even æsthetics, is the logical consequence of his instrumentalist theory of knowledge. Ethics, or the science of conduct, is more than the analysis of concepts such as good, duty, interest, etc.; it is the act of passing from diagnosis to cure. It is practical reason at work. Education, in turn, is practical training, controlled growth. Art, finally, is the *élan*, the spirit of exultation, the sense of equilibrium, which accompanies all positive, fruitful activity; it 'celebrates with peculiar intensity the moments in which the past reinforces the present and in which the future is a quickening of what now is.' [1]

A crucial question next arises. How do we know that our knowledge, practical though it may be, is *true?* Such a question is one which gave Dewey a certain amount of trouble. He deals with it by making another plea for reformation. If 'true' means the conformity of the mind to reality, in some abstract fashion, the word is misleading. Dewey substitutes the phrase 'warranted assertibility'. It occurs for the first time in his *Logic, The Theory of Enquiry*, published in 1938, and owes its formulation to drastic criticism by Russell. But by what criterion is any statement warranted? By the warrant of the discipline most practical in method, namely science, with which philosophy must at all times 'take its stand'. Does this mean that science is infallible? Indeed not: the history of science is the history of error as well as of truth. In every assertion, we need to make allowance for an element of distortion and one-sidedness, just as we need to allow, in every warrant, for an element of inaccuracy, of faulty drafting. Then can we never arrive at truth? This again is a problem which Dewey associates with the traditional and superannuated philosophies of knowledge. To 'arrive' is to presuppose a settled and definite destination. It presupposes a reality at the foot of which the seeker after knowledge, having finished his course, bows down in reverence. To

[1] *Art as Experience* (1934), p. 18.

Dewey, reality is not of this nature. If we have the power to control our lives and our destiny, as is now the case, we can also control what used to be called Reality. The sciences of man, far from having completed their task, are every day making further progress. We 'live forward'. The future is 'implicated in the present', rather than the present being implicated in the past. And this is the best guarantee against error and illusion. Science goes on making mistakes, but it also goes on correcting them. Its 'going on' is the guarantee against mental sloth on the one hand, and rash claims to infallibility on the other.

In *The Quest for Certainty*, Dewey puts forward perhaps the most comprehensive and plausible case that has been made, at least in modern times, for a view of life which lauds risk, adventure, and experiment. Although the traditional philosophies were not deliberate attempts to evade the responsibilities of experiment, they tended inevitably towards a contemplative view of life. This was because, prior to the great discoveries of the sixteenth and seventeenth centuries, the notion of human control over nature did not arise. Man was passive by necessity. Apart from clockwork, windmills and waterwheels, he had no machinery for subduing nature. By contrast, we are the heirs of a great and continuing scientific revolution. We are risk-takers, instrumentalists, by adoption. Our quest for certainty is not a search for some haven of security. Having started out on our voyage, our only security lies in the seaworthiness of the craft in which we sail.

The great merit of Dewey's thought, and perhaps the reason for its influence on his time, lies in his conception of philosophy as *diagnosis* and *cure*. Philosophy has something to do. Logic is a weapon in our hands. The cultivation of these disciplines exclusively in some theoretical or academic 'reservation' is not the best way to preserve their efficacy; it is rather to encourage their deterioration. Granted, the books in a library must be well cared-for and accurately classified; but they must be also taken out and read. So it is with all the sciences. They require sedulous cultivation, if necessary in the laboratory and the study, but only for the sake of being applied and tested in the rough and tumble of life. This is true even of the most abstract sciences. We become convinced that certain mathematical equations are true not merely because they are coherent in themselves, but because they are compatible with the measures needed to put them into practice. For example, it was by no means certain, before the achievement of atomic fission, that a general destructive chain-reaction would not occur. Thus, before the crucial experiments undertaken in Germany, France, in Cambridge, England, and later in Chicago, no atomic physicist could be said genuinely to *know* what his theoretical formulae meant.

Exhilarated by a pragmatic philosophy which really worked, some followers of Dewey pushed his ideas to a point which he regarded as extremist. Pragmatism, it was realised, might be abused. If truth was that which worked—if the only legitimate ideas were those which promoted success in practice—the irresponsible pragmatist, or even the genuine but thoughtless one, might encourage conduct of an anti-social kind. What constituted success? Was it material gain? Was it the acquisition of power? Many comfortable philosophies were put forward within the shadow of pragmatism which defined success in the crudest terms. The test to which such philosophies appealed was frankly materialistic: a well-known book on the technique of winning friends and influencing people frequently quoted the impressive incomes of men who, according to the author, had practised his pragmatic ideas. William James would have been horrified, as were his followers, at Mussolini's claim that Fascism was based on the pragmatic philosophy of the American thinker. Even though the error was pointed out,[1] it cannot be denied that some such inference was, on the face of it, excusable. Like every theory which defined truth in a utilitarian manner, pragmatism was a doctrine depending at heart upon a system of values; and these values were necessarily non-utilitarian ones. The most persuasive exponent of utilitarianism,

[1] I.e. in an interview that Mussolini gave in Rome to Professor Horace Kallen, a pupil of William James, now Professor Emeritus in the Graduate Faculty at Harvard University and successor to Dewey as president of the Conference on Methods in Philosophy.

John Stuart Mill, was also the man who provided the most cogent of all its refutations. This was his declaration that it was 'better to be Socrates dissatisfied than a pig satisfied'. He even unconsciously added more force and universality to the refutation by later substituting 'a man' for 'Socrates'. Why was it better? How could dissatisfaction be valuable, unless satisfaction were measured by non-material standards?

Dewey was aware of this dilemma, and he discussed it at length in the chapter on values in *The Quest for Certainty*. It is doubtful whether he escaped from it. He speaks of the replacement of 'the older theory regarding the authority of the immutable and transcendent values by conceptions more congruous with the practices of daily life'.[1] We might ask whose daily life he had in mind. The practices of the daily life of Nero or Ivan the Terrible, or even of the ordinary man who pursues success and is entertained by portrayals of men and women in recurrent states of sexual excitement, depend on standards which every philosopher, save perhaps the hedonist Chinese sage Hsun Tze, would reject. Dewey's answer is that we should 'change from forming ideas and judgments of value on the basis of conforming to antecedent objects, to construing enjoyable objects by knowledge of consequences'; and he adds rightly enough that this represents a 'change from looking to the past to looking to the future', even though we must take into account past experiences as tools or 'intellectual instrumentalities'. One difficulty of this argument is that 'knowledge of the consequences' depends upon the 'construction of enjoyable objects' being itself past, in order that we may perceive what their consequences have been. Past experiences earn the title of 'instrumentalities' precisely because their consequences have been judged to be enjoyable: and that is why we are able to distinguish one set of instrumentalities from another, and to decide to what form of value or even enjoyment they have been instrumental. (One feels that Dewey does not always distinguish the enjoyable and the desirable.) In other words, instrumentalism as a 'philosophy of the future' depends upon instrumentalism as a 'philosophy of

[1] *Op. cit.*, p. 257.

the past'; for the future must become past in order that
we may know what it is. We 'look to the future', if we
look at all, only to justify or judge the past, not to render
it superfluous. We must, as Dewey admits, 'form the
best judgment possible about what led us to like this sort
of thing, and what has issued from the fact that we liked
it'. Agreed: and this is to form 'the best judgment possible' of 'ideas and judgments . . . conforming to antecedent objects'. Any method of thought 'congruous
with the practice of daily life' which does not conform
to this method would make daily life a precarious business. Moreover, Dewey's own philosophy, which we
have sought to relate to its antecedents, must be judged
by the same criterion.

The kind of philosophy preached by Dewey can be
of value only if it is practised by men similar in integrity
to its founder. Dewey was a man of firm character. He
had all the solid virtues. He had common sense. Much
of what he says on the subject of social life in *Human
Nature and Conduct* is sound; but we sometimes feel
that this wisdom springs from sources deeper than his
philosophy. In quality though not in content, his thought
is similar to that of Walter Pater. It is safe reposing in
his hands, but it might prove corrupting in others. Just
as certain forms of decadence resulted from the view
that life should be, in Pater's words, 'a series of beautiful moments', so certain forms of vulgarisation and
materialism resulted from the view that life should be a
repudiation of all 'immutable and transcendent values'.
Indeed, the decadence consequent upon the latter, since
it affects the practices of the daily life of the many, is
potentially more dangerous than that of the former, since
it affects only the practices of a few. Dewey saw the possibility that 'the force of new conditions will produce
disruption externally and mechanically'; but this is
hardly the kind of disturbance to constitute what he elsewhere called 'genuine danger'.

A danger to which he did not seem alive, possibly because of an intrinsic optimism of temperament, was that
his new gospel might result in the kind of 'new
decadence' which existentialist philosophy has sometimes encouraged; and this danger is the more likely in
that his own belief, taken in its metaphysical aspect, has

much in common with existentialism. The latter philosophy is equally a repudiation of 'immutable and transcendental values'; and there is some parallel between its view of man as being 'thrown into the world' and creating his own values, and Dewey's call to his fellows to 'throw themselves into the future' and work out their salvation experimentally. Existentialism admittedly has several varieties, and what is true of Sartre is not true of Marcel; but in his hostility to religion, Dewey is at one with the former rather than with the latter. Moreover, the chief difference between his own metaphysics (a word he was quite willing to employ, much to Santayana's disapproval) and that of Sartre is that the French philosopher, with a more powerful imagination and a mind wholly averse to the Protestant ethic, pushes his belief to a logical conclusion. Dewey, with his addiction to qualification, obscured the conclusion to which his thought pointed. He was probably too old to grasp the post-war versions of existentialism, even if he was sufficiently aware of them; but we may hazard the guess that had he studied them, he would have disliked them as much as he disliked logical positivism. Yet the latter, with its liquidation of traditional philosophy, might be held to stem from his own particular brand of pragmatism. To declare a man responsible for the abuses or exaggerations of his beliefs would be unjust; but some measure of responsibility must be laid at his door if, in expounding them, he betrays no awareness of dangers other than the most superficial.

Even allowing for the resemblance 'on paper' between the instrumentalist and the existentialist philosophy, the defenders of Dewey might well draw attention to the complete dissimilarity between the robust patriarch of pragmatism, a figure more venerable even than William James, the preacher of manly virtues, the apostle of a muscular non-Christianity, and the morbid, febrile, almost haunted apostle of existentialism. Difference there is; and yet the comparison is not all to the advantage of Dewey. As Morris Cohen has stressed,[1] Dewey seems to have had little or no sense of what is called, in traditional thought, the problem of evil. He

---

[1] *American Thought* (1954), pp. 296-297, and *Studies in Philosophy and Science* (1949), pp. 139-163.

looked at life broadly, but not deeply. Evil existed; but it was identified with something which could be repudiated. To Dewey, as to most apostles of militant secularism, evil was 'the past', man's superstitious heritage. That is why we must turn our backs upon it. Now Sartre, who has himself no liking for the past, is a thinker morbidly aware of evil, even though he may not conceive it in conventional terms. Existentialist man, because he has been thrown into existence, has plumbed its depths. Even in his repudiation of values, the existentialist philosopher lives at the level at which the *sense* of values has become acute. Of Nietzsche we can say the same. To be 'beyond good and evil' is to live in a moral void, Sartre's *néant;* and to live in such a void, as Nietzsche knew, was to suffer a particular sort of agony, that of having 'neither God nor friend'. The agony was precisely to be aware of loss, as thirst becomes most acute in the desert. The more negative the philosophy, the more positive becomes its indirect message. Dewey's thought is lacking in this dimension. Indeed, he expressly repudiated it. He affirmed that the fate of the cosmos had nothing to do with the problems of education, politics, and morals. But, other matters apart, does not the fate of the cosmos have something to do with evolution? If evolution has no connection with education and morals, then what becomes of our trust in democracy, progress, and the future?

In the year of Dewey's decease, there died in seclusion in Rome a philosopher, seven years Dewey's junior, who, Spanish by birth, is regarded nevertheless as one of America's foremost thinkers, even though he had left the United States as far back as 1912. On December 16th, 1863, George Santayana was born in Madrid, Spain. His family moved soon after to Avila, the birthplace of St. Teresa, and a town possessing to this day the atmosphere and much of the fabric of the sixteenth century. We know a good deal about Santayana's life, both as a child and as a man, from the lengthy autobiographical writings to which he devoted his later years. Yet he remains the kind of figure which it is conventional to call enigmatic. If a man spends so much time upon himself, it is likely that he is endeavouring either to discover who he is, or to put into circulation a view of his character which he feels may otherwise elude the biographer. This is especially the case if, as with Santayana, he likewise experiments with autobiography in the form of fiction. If *The Last Puritan* is 'A Memoir in the form of a Novel', his three-volume autobiography is, in great tracts, a novel in the form of a memoir. Such an approach does not necessarily imply insincerity, still less an attempt to conceal or manipulate facts. A man who has deliberately changed his cultural background, and who has all but changed his nationality, may need to write his autobiography, if he is to write one at all, in his own special manner. More than once in this book we have stressed how, by necessity, the most important part of the life of a philosopher is his thought; and since a man's thought includes his conception of who he is, his self-revelation may take a form totally different from that which the biographer, viewing the man from the outside, will present.

Before the marriage of which Santayana was the sole issue, his mother, who came from a Catalonian family, had married an American, George Sturgis. Sturgis was a Protestant merchant from Boston who had settled in Manila in the Philippines. He died in 1857 at an early age; and in accordance with his wish that his children should receive an education in the United States, where he owned property, his widow forthwith moved to Boston. In 1862, she revisited Spain on holiday. The stay became protracted, and in the course of it she renewed acquaintance with an old friend and finally married him. Her husband, Don Augustin Ruiz de Santayana, who had known Sturgis well, approved of her educating the children of her first marriage in America; and although Jorge, as he was called, was born the following year, he was left behind with his father when she returned to Boston six years later. The arrangement proved increasingly unsatisfactory. When George was nine years old, his father took him across the Atlantic, possibly with a view to settling permanently on American soil; but one severe winter in Boston was sufficient to induce him to return home. George remained with his mother.

At this time the boy knew no English. He tells us that he learnt the language wholly by ear. This he did in a

kindergarten on Chestnut Street where, perhaps fortunately, no books were used, and the children were
mostly younger than himself. This may have been responsible both for his perfect accent, and for his having
assimilated the natural rhythms of a language of which
he became a spoken and written master. He proceeded
in due course to the Brimmer School, the Latin School,
and finally to Harvard.

Despite his American education, Santayana always
claimed that his spiritual roots remained Spanish, Latin,
and Catholic. This is probably true, and the fact that he
thought it so explains much of his outlook. His half-sister,
Susana, to whom he remained devoted, instructed him
in Catholic doctrine, and he attended mass from an early
age. In the Unitarian atmosphere of the Sturgis family,
however, he felt a stranger. He revisited Spain after his
first year at the university. With his father's encouragement, he even considered entering the Spanish diplomatic service; but he found that he had become too
American by training, if not in spirit, to do so, and also
that his proficiency in Spanish had declined. If he deliberately assumed the cultural guise of his adopted country, it was, he claimed, for a special reason: he was
enabled thereby to 'say plausibly in English as many un-
English things as possible'. Certainly he remained a critic
of America all his life, as he was a critic of England; but
in another sense his foreign roots, which he shared with
many others in the United States, enabled him to say a
good many 'English' things, especially those which may
be labelled American.

At Harvard, Santayana's teachers were Josiah Royce
and William James. In his *Character and Opinion in the
United States* (1920), he criticised both, but the former
more devastatingly than the latter. He was at first much
attracted by James, and it was to James that he owed his
appointment in 1889 to a post in the Department of
Philosophy. In 1907, on Royce's death, he succeeded
to the Chair of Philosophy. Santayana proved to be an
admirable teacher and lecturer. Like Bergson, whom in
this respect he resembled, he talked as gracefully as he
wrote. There was no hesitation, no correction; his manuscripts are calligraphic models. He was aloof, but kind

to students, finding their company more congenial than that of the faculty. Among his colleagues he was not especially popular. He declared later that he disliked academic teaching. He never showed it, except in so far as he chose to sever all university connections when, on his mother's death in 1912, he was able to travel freely overseas. He visited Germany in 1886 and France in 1905, but perhaps his most remunerative visit was that which took him to England for a year, on sabbatical leave, in 1896. He spent most of the time reading Greek with the English scholar, Henry Jackson, at Trinity College, Cambridge. This was a crucial stage of his life: for the study and meditation which he undertook in England, especially on Plato and Aristotle, provided much of the basis of his first great—some say his greatest—work, *The Life of Reason* (1905-1906).

Santayana's philosophical career, following the publication of this *magnum opus,* amounted to a series of commentaries on it, though as the years passed he slowly modified and even transformed his views. This applies as much to his novel, *The Last Puritan,* written in 1936, as to such works as *Winds of Doctrine* (1913), *Scepticism and Animal Faith* (1923), and *Platonism and the Spiritual Life* (1927). He wrote copiously. By way of compensating for his isolation, his literary meditations also served to deepen it. In a late essay, he spoke of 'the silly home poetry in which I talk to myself about everything'. He also produced much journalism, if the word can still be used to denote intelligent commentary on affairs and people: the *Soliloquies in England* (1922) is a masterpiece in its *genre.* He also wrote poetry, of which few have disputed his own modest estimate. At the age of eighty-eight, he published a book on politics and society entitled *Dominions and Powers* (1951). This study received a somewhat patronising press. It was as if the critics were surprised not so much at its contents as at its having come from his pen at all; but it is not without value, and contains some original and constructive ideas. He was a prolific letter-writer; the collection published in 1956 under the editorship of his faithful disciple, Daniel Cory, is highly readable. His *Three Philosophical Poets* (Lucretius, Dante, Goethe), published in 1910, has exerted much influence on literary criticism. Of his autobiographical writings we have spoken.

To expound the main principles of Santayana's thought is no easy task. One obstacle is the seductive style in which they are written. His philosophy is borne in on the reader on wave after wave of limpid prose. Thought and style are commingled. If some have been inclined to dismiss the whole as a lyrical or (to use Santayana's own word) rhetorical *tour de force*, their reaction is understandable; but we feel that a man could not have launched so grandiose a display of fireworks unless he meant seriously to show us something, and to show us something more than a show. Santayana is on record as saying that he is a naturalist, a materialist, a Catholic, a behaviourist, a dreamer, a believer in happiness, a disillusioned man, and withal an apostle of reason. Furthermore, he is apt, as his argument proceeds, to give to each of these terms an individual twist: we have to read him as a whole to discover the meaning of the parts. The consistency, if he ever prided himself on such a quality, lies in the unflagging exposition. We become accustomed to a voice, persuading, sometimes cajoling, beating down opposition almost with the luminous wings of a Shelley, before we can reconcile ourselves to what is said. Or his style may be compared to a turning wheel. At first the spokes are visible and articulate. Then, as the revolutions speed up, it composes a pattern, vibrating finally on a thin note of ecstasy. The more naturalistic his theme, the more elevated becomes the style, and the more frequent the intrusions of the vocabulary of the transcendental—spirit, soul, eternity. On one brief page of his last autobiographical volume, *My Host the World,* he employs in a purely naturalistic context the words 'holy ghost', 'divine essence' and 'spirit', the latter several times. Never did the vocabulary of the spirit come so easily to the lips of this avowed materialist. Yet we have the uneasy feeling that, slowed down, the impression of exultation, which is so subtly communicated, will vanish; and so we shall find. Once we close the book, the intrusion of more human voices causes us to lose the thread.

The clue to Santayana's outlook is his attitude to religion. Whereas to Dewey religion was outmoded, a survival of a time when men looked to heaven for their salvation because they could not look anywhere else, Santayana regards religion, all religion, as a permanently valid human impulse, 'the head and fount of everything'. But here comes the paradox. The validity of religion lies not in its truth, still less in its falsity, but in its imaginative import. Religion is all symbol; and being all symbol, the source of every other symbolism, including that of science, it is universal, catholic. The human imagination alone is real, because it is the highest form of faith of which man is capable. Therefore we cannot accept any religion, any faith; we can accept only that which, by its elevation and inner consistency, can be trusted. Such trust is the product of much seeking, much pursuit, much disillusionment; for—and this is the final paradox —only when we have perceived that no religion, even the Catholic, is literally true, do we arrive at that *total* disillusionment or 'disintoxication' which is wisdom. We have to surrender conventional faith in order to arrive at that higher faith which, having created religion, transcends it. And this faith is imagination itself.

Once we have grasped this argument, upon which Santayana played variations all his life, the inner workings of his philosophy become clearer. That they become wholly clear is too much to claim. He bewilders us by proceeding, on the basis of this attitude, to employ all the terms with which philosophy has made us familiar. Of the traditional systems of thought, he observes: 'The philosopher . . . must still ask whether any of these successive views were true, or whether the later ones were necessarily truer than the earlier: he cannot, unless he is a shameless sophist, rest content with truth *pro tem*.[1] What does 'true' mean here? And what is the force of the word 'still'? He acknowledges that we must hold, as a matter of 'animal faith', that 'the conventional belief in the natural world' is valid; but this conventional view has itself been challenged by philosophers, and is therefore merely one of the 'successive'

[1] 'A General Confession', *The Philosophy of George Santayana*, edited by Paul Arthur Schilpp (New York, 1951), p. 9. Further references to this volume are labelled Schilpp.

views which have been put forward *pro tem*. Is our time to be the criterion? But that would be a parochialism from which Santayana would naturally recoil.

Santayana's standpoint is in one sense rendered difficult to criticise by his adoption of a position similar to that defined by a French thinker as 'the freedom of doubt'. He feels free to question everything; therefore he is free to assume anything. In one place he refers to truth as a 'mental fiction'.[1] We soon learn that when he speaks of truth, and more particularly eternal truth, he understands these words only within the context of imagination. 'My subject being the imagination,' he writes,[2] 'I was never called on to step beyond the subjective sphere. I set out to describe, not nature or God, but the ideas of nature and God bred in the human mind'. Yet there is a basis, objective enough, for these symbols and images, and this is revealed in the succeeding sentence. 'I assumed throughout that the whole life of reason was generated and controlled by the animal life of man in the bosom of nature'. In other words, he has what he calls a 'vital philosophy'; and a man may 'perfectly well cultivate more than one *Weltanschauung* if he has a vital philosophy of his own to qualify his adoption of each, so as to render them complementary and not contradictory'. Hence his apparent eclecticism. 'The movement of my mind among various systems of belief has tended merely to discover how far my vital philosophy could be expressed in each of them.' Thus Santayana has no system in the orthodox sense, the sense in which Plato, Aquinas, Hegel, even Royce, had a system; his is the truth of every system in so far as it promotes vital harmony.[3] And if we ask, what is harmony? he would answer, the Life of Reason, which is something we must cultivate.

With its evident circularity, this argument may seem to come dangerously near to solipsism. For a man who never steps out of subjectivity is nothing but a solipsist. If he does, and lives to tell the tale, he is no solipsist. Santayana recognises this. He even says that the natural rhythm of the human mind is to oscillate between solip-

[1] *Apologia Pro Mente Sua* (Schilpp, p. 581).
[2] 'A General Confession' (Schilpp, p. 14).
[3] *Scepticism and Animal Faith*, p. vi.

sism and pure scepticism, which he describes as 'the chastity of the intellect'.[1] To our protestations at this point, we can imagine him uttering the words of André Gide: *'Ne me comprenez pas trop vite!'* ('Don't be too quick to understand me!') To be able to talk about solipsism, and to credit the mind with the ability to oscillate between it and scepticism, is to be outside both: Santayana is merely obeying his own edict to sample all systems, and to accept the dictates of animal faith. Again and again he falls back upon the inescapable fact that we are organic emergents of nature. Psyche and spirit are still further emergents, but how they emerge we do not know. Their origin is 'unintelligible only in the sense that all existence, change, or genesis is unintelligible'.[2] This, then, is the meaning at once of his scepticism and of his naturalism, his vital philosophy. We are a mystery. 'To execute the simplest action we must rely on fate: our own acts are mysteries to us.[3] Scepticism, the natural propensity of the human mind to doubt, cannot touch mystery; it can only enhance it. The 'drawing-room' scepticism of the academic philosopher is a more superficial attitude; for it first asserts a concept—that of the external world, for instance—and then proceeds to deny or doubt it. This is a game that can be played *ad infinitum,* while the human animal goes about its business. Santayana underpins the *Cogito ergo sum* of Descartes with another *Cogito,* which is the affirmation of life. Before the human spirit can say 'I think, therefore I am', which is the culmination of a process of doubt, the animal has said its 'yes' to life. 'Animal faith . . . requires no special philosophical evidence for its validity. All experience, all knowledge, all art, are applications of it, and reason has no competence to defend this faith because it is based on it.' [4]

The culmination of Santayana's first philosophical phase is best mirrored in *Scepticism and Animal Faith,* perhaps his best known and most readable work. It forms likewise the introduction to his next and more rarefied

---

[1] *Scepticism and Animal Faith,* p. 69.
[2] The process itself is outlined in the glossary of terms appended to Chapter I of *The Realm of Spirit.*
[3] *Reason in Common Sense,* p. 214.
[4] *Apologia* (Schilpp, p. 381).

phase. The volumes on the Realms of Being are highly metaphysical in character, though he would have repudiated the term. Dealing with Essence, Matter, Truth, Spirit, they form the 'Life of Reason' of his maturity, which has become the 'Life of Spirit'. It is Santayana who insists that he is a materialist; he even declares himself to be 'the only living one'.[1] But by suggesting that he alone of a fairly large company is in step, he renders his claim suspect. To be a complete materialist would be to admit only one realm, the material, and not, as Santayana in principle does, a vast number. What Santayana would seem to mean, however, is that he rejects any view which conceives of spirit as descending upon matter like a logos, and *fertilising* it. 'Spirit is incarnate by nature, not by accident'.[2] He has no use for the idealist or vitalist insertion of an occult principle, an entelechy, into matter. The Realms of Being are those which imagination generates from itself.

Thus when Santayana speaks of *essences,* which he does increasingly as his thought matures, he refers not to P'atonic ideas or forms subsisting in a supernatural world, but to those qualities which imagination at its highest level, that of spirit, isolates for its own delectation and contemplation. In theory, there can be any number of essences. Every predicate, everything said of anything, is an essence. Santayana does not preach essential segregation: essences are not limited to what is refined or disinfected. Admittedly, spirit will by nature choose for contemplation certain essences rather than others; but this itself implies a vast field from which to select, for 'the potentialities of spiritual life are infinite'.[3] Nor are essences capable of action or influence upon everyday existence; they are merely pointers by which we may be guided, or, to use Peirce's term, 'indices'. The sign-post does not usher us on our way; we merely take a cue from it.

A philosopher's importance cannot necessarily be measured by his influence. Indeed, it is difficult to speak of the influence of a philosopher who has been dead only

---

[1] *Scepticism and Animal Faith,* Preface.
[2] *The Realm of Spirit,* p. 43.
[3] *The Realm of Spirit,* p. 51.

a few years. It may take some decades, even generations, for him to acquire importance, or to lose such as he possesses. His contemporary impact is another matter. Santayana has had little influence in England, and almost none in France. The indifference may be due to his having little to contribute to immediate preoccupations in those countries. In empirical circles in Britain, 'literary' philosophies are unpopular; the charm of the style is considered to distract from, or to conceal, the argument. Santayana contended that he was by nature a scholastic, but that he abhorred disputation. 'Argument', he says in one of his letters, 'has never been, in my opinion, a good weapon in philosophy, because I feel that real understanding or difference in sentiment usually rests on hidden presuppositions and limitations that are irreconcilable'.[1] In only one essay, that entitled *Some Meanings of the Word 'Is'*,[2] does he engage in analysis in the accepted sense; but even in that argument, the poetry is there, straining to be unleashed. In America, his thought received enthusiastic and prolonged attention. This is understandable, apart from the fact that he was in his way a great interpreter of Americanism. Both in thought and character, he provided an antithesis to Dewey. And that is a good reason for considering them together.

Dewey, obsessed with the need to reform society, eschewed cosmological speculations. Although Santayana devoted little or no attention to cosmology, he deplored Dewey's limited attitude, and argued that such indifference was incompatible with naturalism. Dewey, who was unable to follow Santayana into the realm of spirit, maintained that Santayana's naturalism was little more than a pose. Yet Santayana was surely right in his insistence that whatever ideals man may hold, however exalted his speculations may be, he remains an organic product of nature. If you ignore cosmology, you ignore not merely super-nature but sub-nature; the cosmos is below as well as above. Where Santayana may appear to err is in his implied assertion that because man is pure nature, therefore he is in no sense transcendent.

[1] to Professor Yolton, dated 2nd May, 1952.
[2] *Obiter Scripta* (1936).

Why cannot the natural, with all its potentialities, transcend *itself*? Indeed, when a man lays down his life for his friend or for a cause, is not this what he is doing?

When we try to determine Santayana's exact view of the aim of philosophy, we encounter first of all an olympian contempt for the preoccupations of other philosophers (with obvious exceptions like Spinoza), and secondly we discover to our surprise that philosophy is not the search for enlightenment at all. We begin to wonder what philosophy is supposed to be about. In his essay on Royce,[1] Santayana holds his teacher up to ridicule for seeking *possession* of the truth. 'He longed', writes Santayana, 'to believe that all his troubles and questions, some day and somewhere, must find their solution and quietus: if not in his own mind, in some kindred spirit that he could, to that extent, identify himself with. There must not only be cold truth, not even cold truth personified, but victorious knowledge of the truth, breaking like a sun-burst through the clouds of terror'. It is not only Royce who has entertained this view; he has had some distinguished predecessors. Without the common pursuit of truth, where would be the history of philosophy? Santayana, and not only Santayana but men wholly at variance with him, might well say: Look at it! Granted, what we see is not always edifying; but the impulse behind the delusions, the fallacies, even the verbiage, is more edifying to contemplate than the spectacle of men, some professedly philosophers, pursuing any lesser aim. A few pages later, Santayana concedes that 'this faith and this struggle' may be the 'supreme good'; but they can be good only if the goal is worth pursuing. Mere pursuit, mere activity for activity's sake, is futile and ludicrous. What, we may ask, is Santayana's 'life of spirit' which he claimed to be following, if not a faith and a struggle to uphold values in a world not prone to honour them? Why pursue philosophy if philosophy itself pursues a will-o'-the-wisp? In his 'General Confession', Santayana protests his recognition of 'the spiritual truth in the Neo-Platonist and Indian systems'; but these two systems have no end but the 'enlightenment' upon which he pours scorn. Finally, if, as

[1] *Character and Opinion in the United States.*

he repeatedly says, spirit needs to be 'saved' or 'delivered', there must be a road to salvation, and philosophy, if it is to be of any use, must point us on our way.

There is another respect in which Santayana tries to eat his cake and have it. His attitude to Catholicism is ambivalent, to some exasperatingly so. While calling himself a Catholic for all official purposes, he makes it clear that he is a total unbeliever. He holds implicitly that all religious action, aspiration and sacrifice have been made not for a reality but for a symbol. Indeed, we suspect that one of the conditions for a form of thought to be worth while, so far as he is concerned, is that it can be shown not to be true. Yet he insisted on exactness in others: 'I always disliked mystics who were not definite in their logic and orthodox in their religion'.[1] Despite his rejection of dogma, he feels entitled to regard as his own, more freely than most believers, the entire emotional capital of the Catholic faith. His work reeks of the Liturgy. He writes 'General Confessions' and 'Apologias'. Although his last autobiographical volume is called *My Host the World,* it was the Church, not the World, at whose board he sat. In middle age, finding himself able to retire to any part of the world which took his fancy, he chose to settle not in the country which had nurtured him, America, nor in that for which he had so deep an affection, England, nor even in the country of which he remained a citizen, Spain, but in Rome itself. Moreover, when in old age the time came for him to withdraw still further into solitude, he took refuge in a Catholic hospital, to be cared for by nuns, the Sisters of the Little Company of Mary. Now this was an Order which, had Santayana's views prevailed, could never have come into being, nor Rome become the spiritual centre—*omnis urbis et orbis ecclesiam mater et caput* —to which Santayana, the unbeliever, gave so much devotion.[2] And he seemed symbolically to emphasise still further his allegiance by living as close as possible to the spiritual centre of Rome itself, namely the Vatican.

[1] 'A General Confession' (Schilpp, p. 27).
[2] The volume in *The Life of Reason* entitled *Reason in Religion* is nothing but a sustained assault on Protestantism, though he regards scholasticism as the beginning of Catholic decadence.

Finally, at his own wish, he was buried in a Catholic cemetery, though in an unconsecrated plot.

The primary criticism of a view such as Santayana's, as of all those which venerate tradition purely for its symbolic value, is that it implies living on emotional or spiritual credit. Now credit has a way of running out. To say that everything has symbolic value is much like saying that everything has exchange value; but this must depend ultimately upon a standard or principle which is valuable in itself. The symbols must ultimately be redeemable or 'cashed'. Difficulties will not arise so long as the symbols retain a measure of potency; but this cannot go on forever. If the symbols are not periodically re-charged, the faith in spiritual 'values' must inevitably decline. The life of the spirit, symbolically conceived, cannot be lived for more than one or two generations from orthodoxy. Moreover, there is little difference at bottom between a symbolic view of reality and a utilitarian or instrumentalist one: for what is a philosophy of symbolism but a kind of higher utilitarianism, a pragmatism for purists? When their thought is probed deeply enough, Dewey and Santayana do not seem so far apart as they or their disciples have supposed; and that is perhaps why each contended for the same title of naturalist. It is as if they were fellow passengers on the same ship, bound for the same destination, but in different classes. Nor is it necessary to specify which class each would have chosen.

Santayana's mysterious character, his love of solitude, his repudiation of conventional allegiances both spiritual and social, have been the source of much speculation. Bertrand Russell found him a trifle old-womanish; others found him a snob. He possessed a kind of genius for friendship; but what man or woman could have established an enduring relationship with a man who could write of his friends that 'it was only the *numen* in them that I loved, who, as I passed by abstracted, whispered some immortal word in my ear'? One could wish that occasionally this abstracted being could have been startled by the whisper of some mortal word. Yet he was not perhaps quite so aloof a man as he makes out. He had a taste in food and wine; he was a great traveller and observer of mankind; and of his personal kindness there is much evidence. His isolation was perhaps inevitable. He was a displaced person. Displacement has become associated with misery, destitution, and persecution; Santayana was a displaced person of means. Having repudiated his native country and her traditional religion, he was thrown back upon his inward resources. The truth was henceforth to be found within; there was no outward criterion. This perhaps accounts for the disproportionate amount of sheer personal writing for so impersonal a thinker. He is as self-exploratory as Nietzsche. Indeed, all his philosophy is a kind of interior dialogue, which we are privileged to overhear. Towards the end, his form of higher complacency seems for a moment to have been disturbed. He told reporters on his eighty-eighth and last birthday that 'I find things are not so simple to explain as I had imagined, and so I am not reconciled'. It is perhaps the only public utterance in which he reveals a lapse in self-assurance.

It is difficult to compare Santayana with any of his contemporaries. Among his Spanish compatriots, Unamuno perhaps resembles him most; Santayana had 'the Tragic Sense of Life'. Among Anglo-Saxon thinkers, he shows some kinship with an equally aloof figure, Havelock Ellis. Here was another gentle, spiritual mind that venerated, while repudiating, Catholicism, and who was incidentally a devotee of Spain. There is likewise some resemblance in the literary style of the two men. Allowing for obvious exceptions, we can imagine each to have written the other's books. Santayana could not have written the *Studies in the Psychology of Sex,* though he might have benefited from some of the experience with which it deals; but neither can we imagine Ellis writing *The Last Puritan*, though there is in Ellis something of the thwarted novelist. Being unconceptual but intuitional, the thought of the two men lends itself to the essay form, and to liberal quotation: we have Ellis's *Little Essays on Love and Virtue,* and we have the selection by Logan Pearsall Smith entitled *Little Essays Drawn from the Works of George Santayana.* Long after his contemporaries have been forgotten, the anthologies of English prose may serve to perpetuate Santayana's memory; and the style which his fellow thinkers dismissed as a mere ornament may turn out to be the means whereby his ideas, and not least the spirit which animated them, are handed on. The world of John Dewey, practical and democratic, has already come into being. Dewey himself witnessed its birth; for he lived into the future for which he had struggled. The world of George Santayana, ideal and aristocratic, will never fully come into being, and thus it may continue to haunt generation after generation with its elusive appeal.

The Modern Outlook

It is tempting, in concluding a work such as the present, to embark upon a series of generalizations upon what it is that makes a great philosopher. Some readers will already have remarked upon the fact that our list contains the name of no woman; and the cynic may perhaps be tempted to say that this is not surprising, since the female character is that about which man philosophizes. In the words of a modern poet:

> 'You, madam, are the eternal humorist,
> The eternal enemy of the Absolute.'[1]

But to turn away from fanciful speculations. Let us suppose, for the sake of argument, that all the works of all the philosophers were suddenly to be destroyed (as indeed many of them have already been): would the loss to mankind be very great, or would we carry on much as before?

The answer, to put it bluntly, is that we should not be able to carry on at all. For 'philosophy' is not simply the collective works of great philosophers. Philosophy is an attitude of mind; at bottom it is nothing but that irrepressible impulse towards enquiry, that itch to probe at the meaning of things, which is the spur behind science itself. There are only Great Philosophers because there are little philosophers, and only little philosophers because there are little ironies and frustrations that need daily to be circumvented or overcome; and in the end the great philosopher will flourish only if there is general agreement among ordinary people that what he is doing is both legitimate and worth while. If the philosopher loses touch with society, then, like Nietzsche, he will end by losing touch with reason; and if society loses touch with those who engage in the disinterested pursuit of knowledge, then the people will perish for lack of vision. Today, as never before, we

[1] T. S. Eliot.

realize that the traditional view of the scientist as pursuing truth for its own sake, without fear or favour, is not something obvious or self-evident and therefore incorruptible, but a view which, in the last resort, is based upon a philosophical assumption, namely, that there are such things as absolute values. As a modern historian, Christopher Dawson, has observed: 'We cannot be sure that the world which science has made will be as favourable to the production of scientific genius as the world that made science'; for, to continue with the words of R. G. Collingwood: 'Science is a plant of slow growth. It will not grow (and for a plant the end of growth is the end of life) except where the scientist as the priest of truth is not only supported but revered as a priest-king by a people that shares his faith. When scientists are no longer kings, there will be (to adapt a famous saying of Plato's) no end to the evils undergone by the society that has dethroned them until it perishes physically for sheer lack of sustenance.'[1]

There are signs that both philosophers and non-philosophers—that is, both professional thinkers and those who are obliged to think without reflecting upon their thinking (or at least without reflecting systematically) —are alive to the serious issues which confront us today. Nothing less than civilization is at stake: not material civilization, but the attitude of mind which makes for that complete enjoyment, relish and worthwhileness of life without which material possessions are a mill-stone around the neck. First there is a coarsening of thought, an indifference to the finer values, and then, almost imperceptibly, a corruption, and finally a kind of *rigor mortis*—and some centuries afterwards a flock of visitors with guide-books contemplating the ruins. Today, however, in spite of every portent of decline, collapse, and even annihilation, there are reasons for hope that mankind will weather this, the most terrible storm that has broken over it. The demand for art, music, and poetry is greater and more insatiable than ever before; and the immense popularity of such institutions as the Brains Trust in England, and the television forums in the

[1] It will be observed that we are using the word science here to signify 'ordered knowledge' (Scientia): in other contexts we usually refer to 'natural science' or physico-mathematical science.

United States, testified to what C. E. M. Joad well described as a vast 'unsatisfied seriousness' in the general public. There may be some people who fear that such popular manifestations of enthusiasm will serve merely to vulgarize the high art of philosophical enquiry. That which is so easily vulgarized is neither high nor an art, and might as well be exposed, here and now, for the sophistry that it is. Philosophy began, as far as Socrates was concerned, in the open air; let it continue in the air, on the air, and by the fireside. Let it continue in plain language rather than jargon or recondite symbolism. Let it confound the dogmatic, expose the hypocrite, encourage the curious, and enlighten the bewildered.

The collection of thinkers of whom we have written includes no living philosopher. This was intentional. For it seemed better to conclude with a man universally pronounced to be great than to select one from among a number of living men whose claim to distinction is neither established nor assessible. At the same time there is some justification for casting our eye over the present scene, and for mentioning a few of our leading modern philosophers, and in particular some who have recently died. Naturally we cannot mention by name all who have produced work of importance.

For some years the philosophical world has been disturbed by a conflict which even today is by no means settled. This is a conflict between two conceptions of the function of philosophical enquiry. On the one hand, there is the school which, following Hume, distrusts everything in the nature of *metaphysical* speculation; and on the other hand there are a number of thinkers who, adopting a much wider and freer viewpoint, are seeking to recall philosophy to its traditional function, which is to reflect upon the nature of reality as a whole. During the unsettled period between the two world wars, the former group achieved much notoriety; and it was a common experience for students of philosophy at that time to be instructed and harangued by teachers who, in spite of their official status as lecturers in philosophy, spent the major part of their time denouncing the whole subject as a fraud—the result, as one of them put it, of a disease of language. For such iconoclasts there was but one justification for philosophy, namely, that it should be reduced to logic, which in turn should confine itself to the 'analysis' of the meaning of ordinary propositions about matters of fact. In order to effect such delicate analysis a special technique was evolved, often introducing mathematical symbolism intelligible only to the expert; and it was tacitly, if not openly, assumed that all propositions about the world, or about anything whatever, which failed to yield to this specialized technique of dissection were nonsensical. So much for theology, metaphysics, poetry, and so forth.

What we are here being invited to accept, and thus to condone, is nothing less than a 'closed shop' in philosophical speculation. Accept my language, my terminology, my assumption—in the one case, a purely 'rational' language; in the second case, a purely scientific terminology; in the third case, the assumption that only sensuous experience is genuine—or stop calling yourself a philosopher. Come in, or keep out: that, in sum, was the attitude of the apostles of 'analysis' and 'positivism', the contemporary enemies of metaphysics.

It was a mischievous attitude. For once you begin to introduce a distinction between two kinds of language— a specialist, esoteric, private language on the one hand, and ordinary common, everyday language on the other hand, and announce that the first is the language of philosophers and the second the language of everyday life, then you are simultaneously dividing men into two kinds, the initiates and the outsiders, those who know the philosophical password and those who do not: in which case your final criterion is no longer truth or principle (as it has hitherto been) but something quite different, namely, class-distinction or 'snobisme'. Nor would this division prove so harmful to the cause of thought if the members of the specialist clique were not all the while engaged, as we have shown, in making an end among themselves of that which distinguished traditional philosophy; in showing that even if philosophy meant anything at all, it was frankly useless; and in suggesting that as it is nonsense anyway, the proper course for enlightened persons is to issue, from the recesses of their academies, brief communiqués to the effect that everything associated with philosophy in the past— above all, the Socratic belief that knowledge promotes virtue, that truth, goodness and beauty are absolute values, that reflection is superior to passion, and so on, down to the ordinary notions of what is right and decent —are purely matters of whim and expediency, subject to neither rules nor principles, or, to employ a more popular if more barbarous term, a mere floating 'ideology', concealing the brute facts of economic or material pressure. The situation is rather like that which would come about if, for example, the highest conclave of a Church, having met in secret session, had forthwith announced to its devotees that, for reasons which they could not be expected to comprehend, orthodox theology had been found to be based upon a misunderstanding, and that in consequence all the naïve piety upon which generations of devout persons were nourished had no foundation other than arbitrary sentiment; and that whereas people were at liberty to go on believing if they wished, they were in fact under no obligation to do so, though there were admittedly certain 'psychological' benefits to be derived from the disposition to believe, which might recommend that attitude to pedagogues, sociologists, youth leaders, probation officers, statesmen, and indeed all who were charged with the responsibility of keeping other people in order. Thus, to turn once more to our philosophers, one well-known enemy of metaphysics went so far as to say that while metaphysics, theology, poetry and so on are undeniably nonsensical, they represent, as compared with mere gibberish, a 'special kind of nonsense', to which even the enlightened person may be excused for giving some attention, since they exercise a therapeutic effect upon the nervous system and thereby provide some relief from the cold, dry universe that physical science offers for our acceptance.

We have dwelt at length upon this line of thought, because it is one with which almost everybody—certainly everyone who has had the patience to read this book— has at some time come into contact. We hear much talk about the 'decay of standards'. We are aware of a definite lowering of the canons of behaviour, not necessarily or exclusively moral behaviour but the ordinary behaviour

of people with one another. We may infer a certain de-
basement of the idea of education not so much from the
condition of modern schools and colleges as from the
kind of press that people supposed to be educated choose
to read. Is it absurd to suggest that this observable decline in values is the result of treachery in high places;
that those whose business it is to sustain our belief in the
highest good are either shirking their job or mistaking it
for something else; and that among these guardians (as
Plato called them) our teachers of philosophy or metaphysics are not without their share of blame? Not that we
should attribute our present wayward state of mind solely
to the propagation, by those who should know better, of
a neutral materialism. It is not so simple as that: for, as
the American humanist Irving Babbitt aptly remarked,
'what is disquieting about the time is not so much
its open and avowed materialism as what it takes to be
its spirituality'. We are faced not so much with the denial
of the spirit as with its repeated counterfeit.

In the foregoing pages we have several times indicated
that where an age appears to exhibit a particular trend
of thought, we can be fairly sure that this trend is all the
time being dogged and shadowed by another movement, which, though recessive for the time being, may
at any moment assume a dominant position. So it is today. Against the view of philosophy as a specialist technique, accessible only to the initiated, and of little more
value than a parlour-game, there is a growing conviction
that, of all the sciences, philosophy, the traditional
science of sciences, should be open to everybody; that
the attempt to demarcate its limits, to prescribe its rules,
and to limit or 'screen' its devotees is precisely to indulge in the kind of dogmatism from which philosophy,
in order to remain reasonable, must at all costs preserve
itself; and that far from being a parlour-game—a
superior amusement for superior people—it must reas-
sume its former function as a guide to life, an incentive
to right action, a light to wisdom. In order to discharge
these responsibilities, however, it must cease to busy
itself solely with abstruse definitions and minute feats of
analysis, and broaden its outlook to include all human
experience. It must fight itself back to favour by re-
occupying its former estates, now heavily mortgaged to

mathematical science. For if philosophy fails to act as a guide to wisdom, there are a hundred other substitutes decked out to look like philosophy that will hasten to steal its custom.

Among modern philosophers, a man who did much to recall philosophy to a sense of its true vocation was Alfred North Whitehead (1861-1948). A mathematician by training and a man of immense learning and wisdom, Whitehead endeavoured to heal the wound opened first by Descartes with his unbridgeable distinction between mind and body,[1] and his consequent division of the world into two halves, a 'subjective half' (including the mind and the 'secondary qualities' which it originates) and an 'objective' half (including a substratum of matter characterized by the 'primary qualities' which are measurable by mathematics). This 'bifurcation of Nature' is, as Whitehead shows in his *Science and the Modern World,* the most vicious error that runs through modern thought. For consider what it implies. If your colours, and sounds, and scents are purely 'subjective', then what of such values as beauty? If beauty lies solely 'in the eyes of the beholder', then what of all the other values of life? They, too, must be 'subjective'. But if, as Galileo had maintained and as his successors believed, only that which is measurable is truly real, then it follows that every 'subjective' quality, being outside the scope of measurement, is unreal; and in consequence the whole of what we call culture or civilization (*i.e.* the values which we have been traditionally accustomed to uphold and venerate) has been lumped together with the intractable, unstable element in our minds, *i.e.* the emotions, passions, instincts, and impulses, with which no science claimed to have anything to do except psychology, the so-called science of the irrational. This was indeed a paradoxical situation: the human intellect, having painfully built up a conception of the good, the true, the beautiful, and having devised an elaborate system of education to inculcate a respect for these values, proceeds forthwith to propound a philosophy according to which such values,

---

[1] 'Unbridgeable' because it is doubtful whether much traffic can be got across the pineal gland, which Descartes declared to be the link between soul and body.

however admirable, enjoy no objective existence at all. If there is such a thing as the Modern Dilemma, this surely is it. It is the dilemma of a split-man.

Whitehead refutes the subjective-objective distinction by pointing out that in the elementary case of a man looking at a rose, there are not two spheres—the mind of the man (or subjective sphere) and the primary qualities of the rose (objective sphere)—but a unity: namely, the man-seeing-a-rose. This single sphere Whitehead calls a 'society', and the whole of his philosophy as outlined in his most important book, *Process and Reality,* is an attempt to show that the universe is a hierarchy of such societies: the society of electrons that go to form an atom, the society of atoms that go to form a molecule, and so on up to human society and the even higher society of minds. In this hierarchical conception of the universe he was closely followed by the philosopher S. W. Alexander (1859-1942) in his great work *Space, Time and Deity,* and, with certain modifications, by Field-Marshal Smuts (1870-1950), the philosopher-statesman, in his book *Holism and Evolution.* These three philosophers are therefore concerned with the branch of philosophy known as Cosmology, in which the human mind is given back the autonomy and freedom denied to it by the 'minute' philosophers. Moreover, in their work the conflict between Science and Religion, which so perplexed the nineteenth century but which is really Pascal's old problem of head and heart, is resolved in a conception which reveals the dialectical relation between the two.

A thinker of remarkable gifts who sought to analyse the above-mentioned relation from an original point of view was Robin George Collingwood (1889-1943), philosopher and historian, as well as artist and musician. Profiting from a study of the philosopher Benedetto Croce (1866-1952), the greatest of modern Italian thinkers and a vigorous defender of liberty under the Fascist régime (he was rescued by British parachutists when the Allied armies were advancing upon Naples), Collingwood outlined in his book, *Speculum Mentis,* what he called 'the map of knowledge'. The development of the human mind from imaginative gropings to complete self-consciousness may be conceived, he contended, as the dialectical development of art, or imagination, into successively religion, science, history, and philosophy: where by 'dialectical' he meant what Plato and Hegel meant, namely, the pitting of a thesis against its antithesis out of which developed a synthesis, which in turn provided the thesis for further development. Largely as a result of his archaeological investigations, Collingwood became more and more absorbed in the problems of historical knowledge, thereby pursuing the line of speculation begun by Giambattista Vico and continued by Hegel. In his *Essay on Metaphysics* and his posthumous *Idea of History,* he outlined a philosophy of history according to which metaphysics itself was shown to be a historical science, since 'all history is the history of thought'. The importance of Collingwood's work has yet to be appreciated, for it represents one of the most far-reaching attempts of modern times to demonstrate how philosophy can become of immediate use to men of action: this being possible, in Collingwood's view, by abandoning its three-hundred-year subservience to the method of natural science, which has led to increasing chaos in practical affairs as a result of the assumption that 'science is power', and its adoption of a method of understanding human affairs from the only point of view likely to shed light upon them, namely, by submitting them to the scrutiny of the historical imagination.

It would be an error to suppose that the movement of hostility to metaphysics has taken full possession of the Anglo-Saxon mind, or that it represents more than one current in the philosophy of the West. There are many such currents, and the deeper ones have not yet perhaps come to exert their full pressure. On the other hand, we must not underestimate the 'hygienic' value of the movement: it has swept away obscurantism and verbiage, and it has pricked the bubble of the conventional 'idealism' which for some people had come to be identified with 'philosophy'. Writing in the review *Mind* in 1952, Sir Isaiah Berlin spoke of 'the great logico-philosophical revolution of the last half-century initiated by Frege and Russell', and he went on to describe this as 'perhaps the most complete transformation of thought in this field since the seventeenth century'. Berlin might have added the name of another innovator: Ludwig

Wittgenstein (1889-1951), who came to Cambridge from Berlin in 1912. With Bertrand Russell's help, Wittgenstein's *Tractatus Logico-Philosophicus* was published in 1922. This book exerted an enormous influence over modern philosophy, yet in his posthumous *Philosophical Investigations* (1953) Wittgenstein appeared to move away from his early radical position and to adopt a point of view almost mystical in character. Knowledge of ultimate reality, he affirmed, is incapable of conceptual expression. As the Taoist sage Lao Tze observed, our duty at the limits of thought is to remain silent. Latterly, too, British philosophers have begun to show wider sympathies and maturer judgment than some of the iconoclasts of the Thirties. There is a serene quality about some of A. J. Ayer's later writings, just as there is a markedly traditional quality about their subject matter. Although Gilbert Ryle's famous book *The Concept of Mind* (1949) appears to be a reversion to Behaviourism (the Italian translation is significantly entitled *Lo Spirito come Comportamento*), the author is aware that he is cultivating merely a plot in a vast field awaiting investigation. 'The time is not ripe,' he has said, 'for global syntheses'; but he added that 'A philosopher cannot invent conceptual stresses and strains; he has to feel them if he is to be irked into dealing with them.' One may hazard the opinion that life will prove sufficiently irksome during the next decade or so to impel philosophers to embark once more on the path of metaphysical speculation.[1]

Meanwhile, it is a paradox that the influence of Anglo-Saxon empiricism should have made itself felt in Europe and beyond at a moment when it had lost some of its impetus at home. Thus, in a book of considerable insight and interest we are told that 'philosophy . . . is simultaneously a name both for the conceptual confusions that arise in thinking about any subject and the attempt at the clarification of these confusions. . . . It is time that philosophers dispel the general impression that they are on intimate terms with Reality with a capital R, and on hobnobbing terms with the Absolute and God Al-

---

[1] The quotations are from the symposium *The Nature of Metaphysics*, edited by D. F. Pears (London, 1957), pp. 156, 160.

mighty'.[1] It is not easy to see how philosophy can be merely a name for its own confusions and their clarification, unless we are to assume that philosophical thinking, inherently prone to obscurantism, is also inherently endowed with the capacity to dispel it; for this would raise the question why, given this saving capacity, so many errors should have been committed. Nor is it evident that the greatest of thinkers (by whose standards the matter should be judged) were on such familiar terms with God and the Absolute as is here suggested. Most of them were distinguished for their humility. It is more often the sceptic, dismissing all traditional thought as 'nonsense', who assumes this arrogant pose. Happily, there is observable today a decline in what G. J. Warnock has called 'restrictive iconoclasm' among Anglo-Saxon thinkers. Meanwhile, philosophers like Radhakrishnan, Vice-President of the Republic of India, continue to expound the Vedanta tradition, and in Europe the influence of Oriental thought has made itself felt not merely in the brilliant writings of René Guénon, but in works not strictly classifiable as philosophical: we may cite the concluding volumes of Arnold Toynbee's *A Study of History* and his even more illuminating work *An Historian's Approach to Religion*. What seems to be needed is the fruitful exchange of ideas between Occident and Orient: for with the polished technique of argument perfected in the West and the grasp of profundities characteristic of the East, a philosophy might emerge not unworthy of the standards set by the great masters with whose thought we began.[2]

This chapter has provided merely the briefest sketch of the present state of philosophical enquiry, and it will be open to the criticism of being incomplete. The comment is just, but it is not strictly a criticism. No philosopher has so demonstrably reached the end of his tether as to maintain that his system of thought is a complete and closed one: that is why the 'closed shop' attitude of which we have spoken is the product not of

[1] Daya Krishna, *The Nature of Philosophy*, Calcutta, 1955, p. 233.
[2] This point is taken up in the companion volume *The Oriental Philosophers*.

philosophy but of sophistry. All the greatest philosophers have been conspicious for an openness of mind, an honest candour, which has prevented them from becoming engrossed in such petty squabbles as make up the lives of the sophistical thinkers. That, incidentally, is the reason why all the great philosophers, with a few exceptions that must themselves be excepted at their highest moments, have been masters of their own language— artists in words as well as artists in ideas. The reputations of our poets and novelists undergo change with each generation. As long as our civilization lasts, the names of Socrates, Plato, Aristotle, Augustine, Aquinas, and indeed all the major figures of whom we have written in this book, will be remembered with undiminished and perhaps increasing veneration. However lacking in formal instruction, the reader who turns his attention to the lives and works of the great philosophers comes forthwith into possession of that which will last him all his life: faith in the ability of the human mind to grasp, in however fragmentary and fugitive a way, the essence and infinite variety of reality, and inspiration from the struggles of those who, in Whitehead's words, were 'individually powerless but ultimately rulers of the world'.

Suggestions for Further Reading

SOCRATES
  Francis M. Cornford, *Before and After Socrates* (1932)
  Benjamin Farrington, *Greek Science*, Vol. I, Thales to
    Aristotle (1944)

PLATO
  R. C. Lodge, *Plato's Theory of Ethics* (1936)
  David Ross, *Plato's Theory of Ideas* (1951)
  A. E. Taylor, *Plato* (1927)

ARISTOTLE
  Werner Jaeger, *Aristotle* (1934)
  A. E. Taylor, *Aristotle* (1943)

From Stoicism to Neo-Platonism
  E. R. Beven, *Stoics and Sceptics* (1913)
  Philip Merlan, *From Platonism to Neo-Platonism* (1953)
  Paul Elmer More, *Hellenistic Philosophies* (1923)

ST. AUGUSTINE
  A. Papini, *St. Augustine* (1930)
  H. Pope, *St. Augustine* (1937)
    A Monument to St. Augustine, Symposium (1930)

PETER ABELARD
  J. Huizinger, *The Waning of the Middle Ages* (1955)
  J. G. Sikes, *Peter Abelard* (1932)

Moslem and Jewish Philosophers and the Revival of
Aristotelianism
  T. W. Arnold and A. Guillaume, *The Legacy of Islam*
    (1931)
  E. R. Bevan and Charles Singer, *The Legacy of Israel*
    (1928)

ST. THOMAS AQUINAS
  F. Copleston, *Mediaeval Philosophy* (1952)
  M. C. D'Arcy, *St. Thomas Aquinas* (1930)
  E. Gilson, *The Spirit of Mediaeval Philosophy* (1936)

Scholastic Decline and Scientific Advance
  F. H. Anderson, *The Philosophy of Francis Bacon* (1948)
  S. C. Easton, *Roger Bacon and His Search for a Universal Science* (1952)
  E. A. Moody, *The Logic of William of Ockham* (1936)

RENÉ DESCARTES
  A. Boyce Gibson, *The Philosophy of Descartes* (1932)
  S. V. Keeling, *Descartes* (1934)
  J. Maritain, *The Dream of Descartes* (1944)
  H. F. Stewart, *The Secret of Pascal* (1941)

BENEDICT SPINOZA
  S. Hampshire, *Spinoza* (1951)
  R. McKeon, *The Philosophy of Spinoza* (1928)
  R. Roth, *Spinoza* (1929)

GOTTFRIED LEIBNITZ
  B. Russell, *The Philosophy of Leibnitz* (1937)
  R. L. Saw, *Leibnitz* (1957)

Religious Conflict and the Rise of Rationalism
  Paul Hazard, *The European Mind* (1953)
  J. Laird, *Hobbes* (1934)
  A. E. Taylor, *Hobbes* (1908)

GEORGE BERKELEY
  G. Dawes Hicks, *Berkeley* (1932)
  G. J. Warnock, *Berkeley* (1953)
  John D. Wild, *Berkeley* (1936)

The Precursors of Hume
  E. Cassirer, *The Philosophy of the Enlightenment* (1951)
  B. Croce (translated by Collingwood), *The Philosophy of Giambattista Vico* (1923)

DAVID HUME
  A. Basson, *David Hume* (1958)
  H. H. Price, *Hume's Theory of the External World* (1940)
  N. Kemp Smith, *The Philosophy of Hume* (1941)

Encyclopaedists and Romantics
  E. Cassirer, *Rousseau, Kant, and Goethe* (1945)
  Paul Hazard, *European Thought in the 18th Century* (1954)

IMMANUEL KANT
  A. C. Ewing, *A Short Commentary on Kant's Critique of Pure Reason* (1938)

A. D. Lindsay, *Kant* (1934)

T. D. Weldon, *Introduction to Kant's Critique of Pure Reason* (1945)

German Romantic Philosophy from Fichte to Hegel
A. D. Pringle-Pattison, *From Kant to Hegel* (1924)
E. B. Talbot, *Fundamental Principles of Fichte's Philosophy* (1906)

JOHN LOCKE
R. I. Aaron, *Locke* (1937)
D. J. O'Connor, *Locke* (1952)
A. N. Whitehead, *Science and the Modern World* (1926)

GEORG WILHELM HEGEL
B. Croce, *What Is Living and What is Dead in the Philosophy of Hegel* (in the translation by Ainslie, 1915)
G. R. G. Mure, *An Introduction to Hegel* (1940)
W. T. Stace, *The Philosophy of Hegel* (1924)

The Marxist Philosophy
H. P. Adams, *Karl Marx and His Early Writings* (1940)
I. Berlin, *Karl Marx, His Life and Environment* (1948)
S. Hook, *From Hegel to Marx* (1935)

From Schopenhauer to Kierkegaard
F. Copleston, *Schopenhauer* (1953)
W. Lowrie, *Kierkegaard* (1938)
R. Thomte, *Kierkegaard's Philosophy of Religion* (1948)
H. Zimmern, *Schopenhauer, His Life and Philosophy* (1932)

FRIEDRICH NIETZSCHE
Crane Brinton, *Nietzsche* (1941)
F. Copleston, *Nietzsche, Philosopher of Culture* (1942)

Scepticism and Faith in Nineteenth-Century Philosophy
M. H. Carré, *Phases of Thought in England* (1949)
R. W. Church, *Bradley's Dialectic* (1942)
G. S. Carter, *A Hundred Years of Evolution* (1957)
F. R. Leavis, *Mill on Bentham and Coleridge* (1950)
E. Neff, *Carlyle and Mill* (1924)
R. B. Perry, *The Thought and Character of William James* (1936)
H. Peterson, *Huxley, The Prophet of Science* (1932)

HENRI BERGSON
  I. W. Alexander, *Bergson* (1957)
  A. D. Lindsay, *The Philosophy of Bergson* (1911)

JOHN DEWEY and GEORGE SANTAYANA
  M. G. White, *The Origin of Dewey's Instrumentalism* (1943)
  R. Butler, *The Mind of Santayana* (1955)
  M. Cohen, *American Thought* (1954)
  S. Hook, *John Dewey* (1939)
  G. H. Mead, *The Philosophy of the Present* (1932)
  A. Schilpp (Editor), *The Philosophy of George Santayana* (1940)
  A. Schilpp, *The Philosophy of John Dewey* (1939)

The Modern Outlook
  A. J. Ayer, *The Problem of Knowledge* (1956)
    The Revolution in Philosophy (1956)
  Ivor Leclerc (Editor), *The Relevance of Whitehead* (1961)
  M. Macdonald (Editor), *Philosophy and Analysis* (1954)
  D. Pole, *The Later Philosophy of Wittgenstein* (1958)
  Radhakrishnan, *East and West* (1955)
  G. Ryle, *The Concept of Mind* (1949)
  C. L. Stevenson, *Ethics and Language* (1944)
  E. W. F. Tomlin, *R. G. Collingwood* (1960)
  A. J. Toynbee, *An Historian's Approach to Religion* (1956)
  G. J. Warnock, *Modern Philosophy* (1956)

Index

345

About the Author

E. W. F. Tomlin is the author of a number of provocative books that have enjoyed a growing public in his own country Great Britain as well as in Europe. He has been described as "one of the most interesting and original philosophers writing in England, a writer in real contact with the intellectual conflict of the age."

Mr. Tomlin has spent most of his career in the service of the British government, working for many years in the Middle East and in the Far East. In 1960, having been awarded a Bollingen Foundation Fellowship, he visited several universities in the United States. He is at present the cultural attaché to the British Embassy to Japan.